武井宏之

I switched to contact lenses.

—*Hiroyuki Takei*

Unconventional author/artist Hiroyuki Takei began his career by winning the coveted Hop Step Award (for new manga a........................rd (named after the fam.......................... working as an assistant............................., Takei debuted in **Weekl**......................**u Zone**, an action series ba.................................multicultural adventu.................................buted in 1998, became a hit and was adapted into an anime TV series. Takei lists Osamu Tezuka, American comics and robot anime among his many influences.

SHAMAN KING VOL. 27
SHONEN JUMP Manga Edition

STORY AND ART BY
HIROYUKI TAKEI

English Adaptation/Lance Caselman
Translation/Lillian Olsen
Touch-up Art & Lettering/John Hunt
Design/Nozomi Akashi
Editor/Eric Searleman

VP, Production/Alvin Lu
VP, Sales & Product Marketing/Gonzalo Ferreyra
VP, Creative/Linda Espinosa
Publisher/Hyoe Narita

Printed in the U.S.A.

Published by VIZ Media, LLC
P.O. Box 77010
San Francisco, CA 94107

10 9 8 7 6 5 4 3 2 1
First printing, March 2010

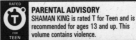

viz media
www.viz.com

RATED T FOR TEEN
PARENTAL ADVISORY
SHAMAN KING is rated T for Teen and is recommended for ages 13 and up. This volume contains violence.
ratings.viz.com

SHONEN JUMP MANGA

Shaman King

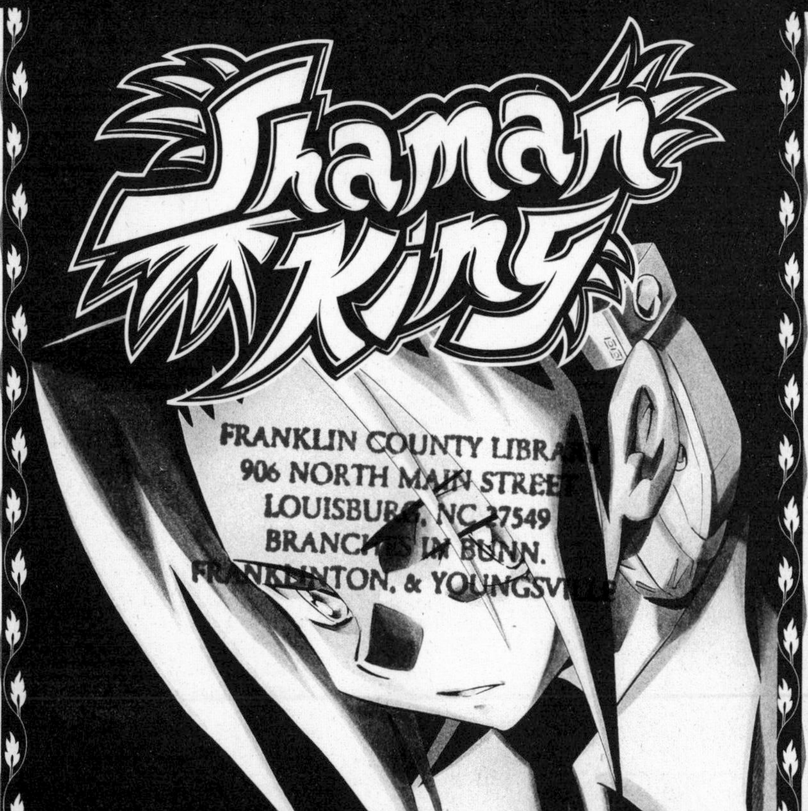

VOL. 27
EXOTICA

STORY AND ART BY
HIROYUKI TAKEI

CHARACTERS

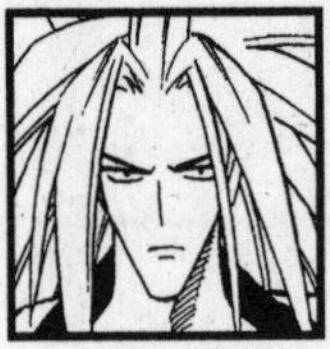

Amidamaru
"The Fiend" Amidamaru was, in life, a samurai of such skill and ferocity that he was a veritable one-man army. Now he is Yoh's loyal, and formidable, spirit ally.

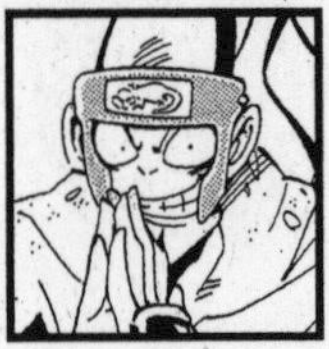

Tokagero
The ghost of a bandit slain by Amidamaru. He is now Ryu's spirit ally.

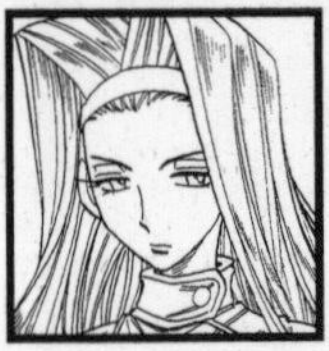

Eliza
Faust's late wife.

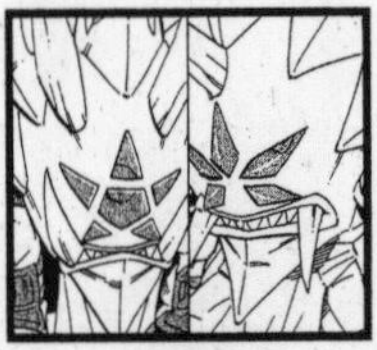

Zenki & Goki
Spirits who formerly served Hao but now serve Anna.

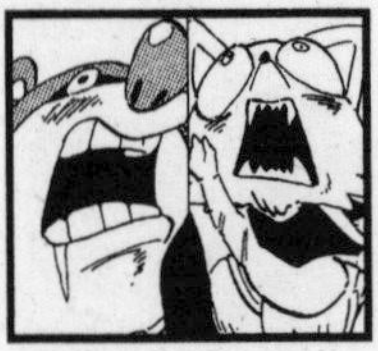

Ponchi & Konchi
Tamao's spirit allies. Not known for their genteel ways.

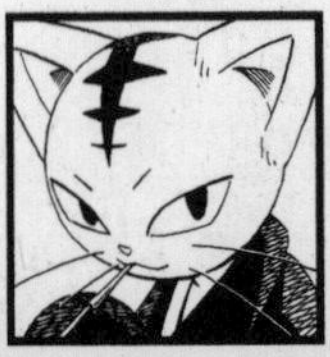

Matamune
A split-tailed cat who helped Yoh save Anna from her own powers.

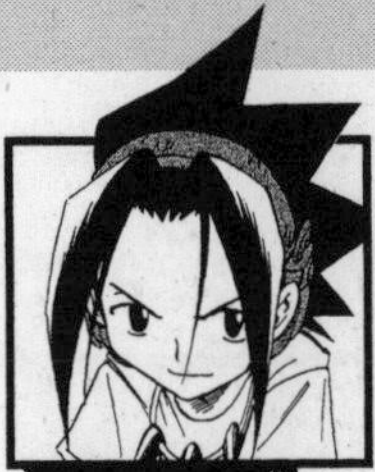

Yoh Asakura
Outwardly carefree and easygoing, Yoh bears a great responsibility as heir to a long line of Japanese shamans.

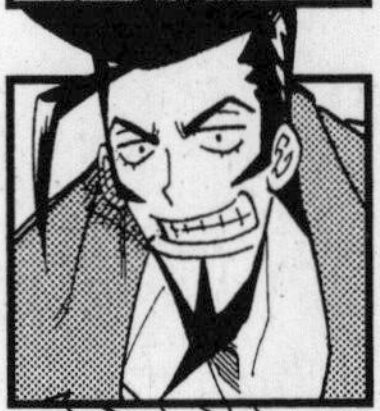

"Wooden Sword" Ryu
On a quest to find his Happy Place. Along the way, he became a shaman.

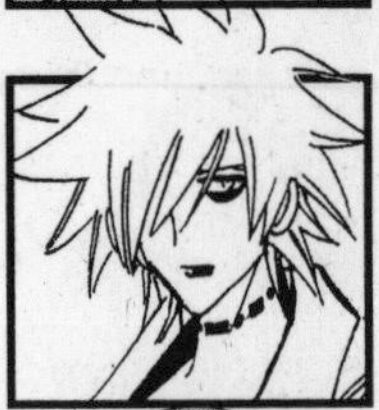

Faust VIII
A creepy German doctor and necromancer who is now Yoh's ally.

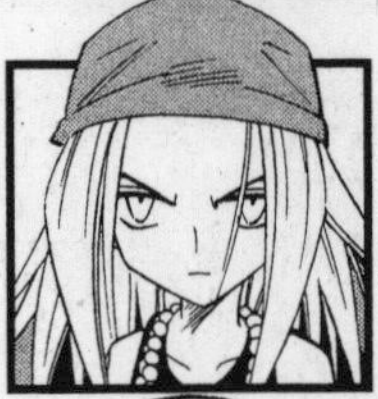

Anna Kyoyama
Yoh's butt-kicking fiancée. Anna is an itako, a traditional Japanese village shaman.

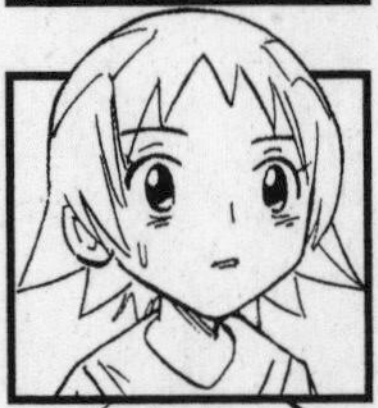

Tamao Tamamura
A shaman in training who uses a kokkuri board. She's in love with Yoh.

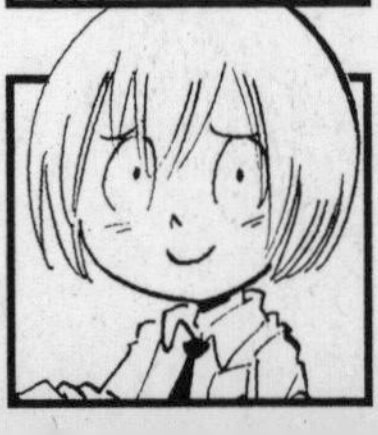

Manta Oyamada
A high-strung boy with a huge dictionary. He has enough sixth sense to see ghosts, but not enough to control them.

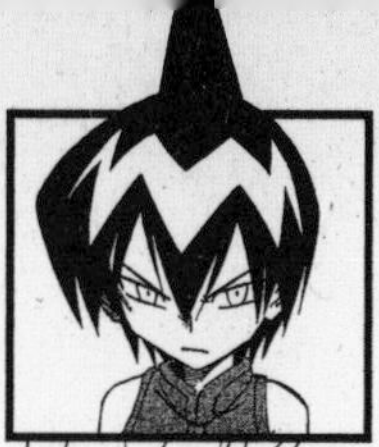

Tao Ren
A powerful shaman and the scion of the ruthless Tao Family.

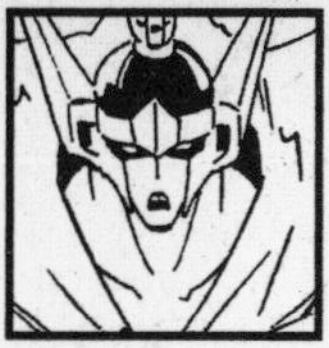

Bason
Ren's spirit ally is the ghost of a fearsome warlord from ancient China.

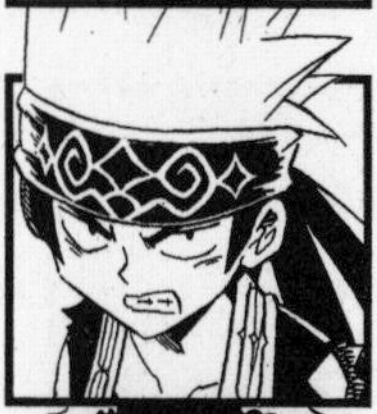

Horohoro
An Ainu shaman whose Over Soul looks like a snowboard.

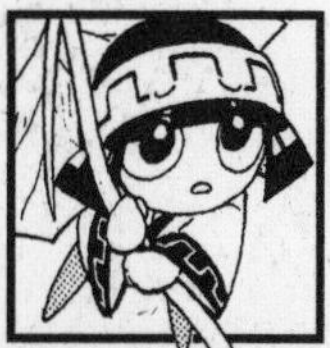

Kororo
Horohoro's spirit ally is one of the little nature spirits that the Ainu call Koropokkur.

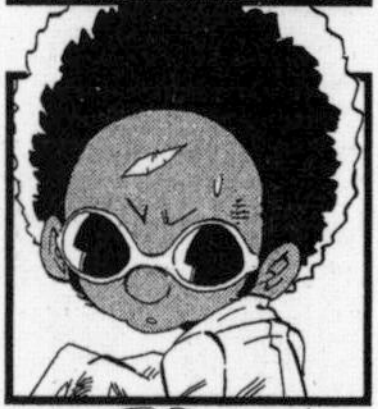

Joco
A shaman who uses humor as a weapon. Or tries to.

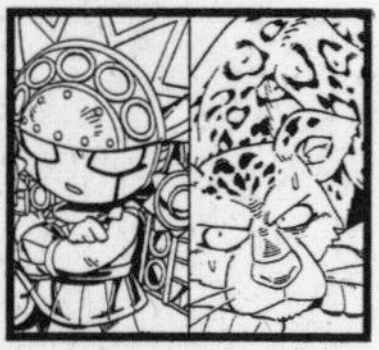

Mic & Pascual Abaj
Joco's jaguar spirit ally and the ghost of an Indio shaman.

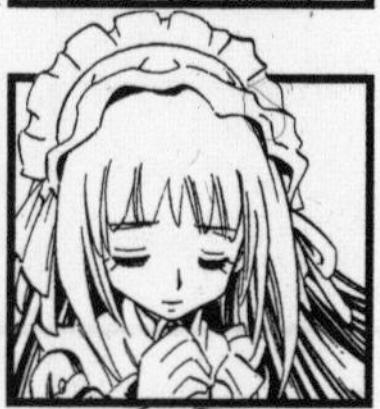

Jeanne, the Iron Maiden
The nominal leader of the X-LAWS. Spends most of her time in a medieval torture cabinet.

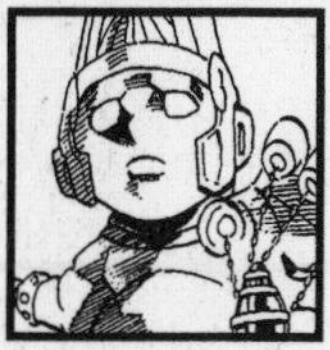

Shamash
Jeanne's spirit ally, a Babylonian god.

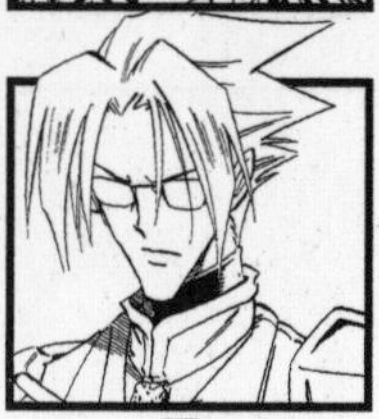

Marco
The true leader of the X-LAWS.

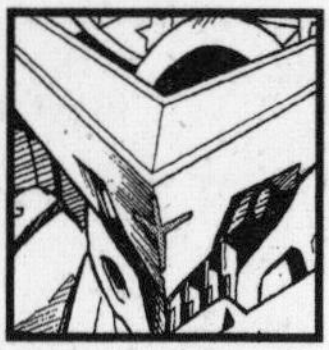

Michael
Marco's Archangel.

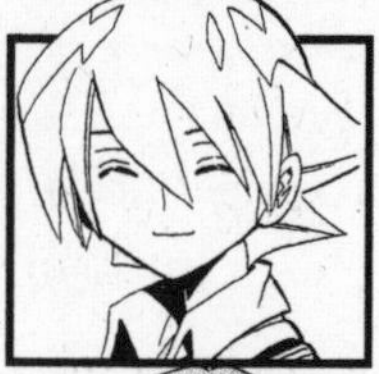

Lyserg
A young shaman with a vendetta against Hao.

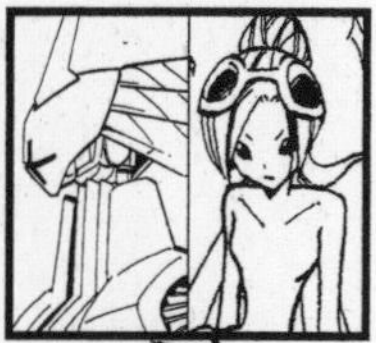

Morphea & Zeruel
Lyserg's poppy fairy and his new Angel.

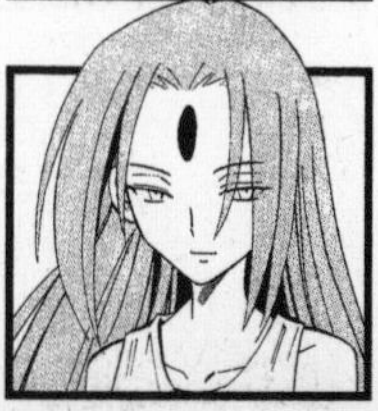

Sati
The leader of Gandala. She brought Ryu and Joco back from the dead.

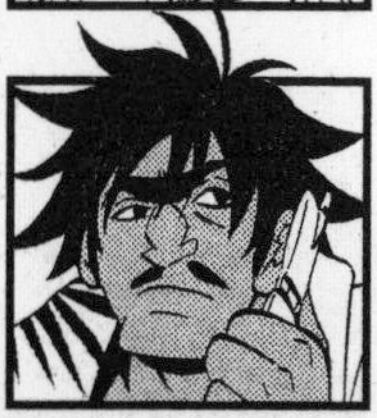

Kadu
A member of Gandala with Ragaraja.

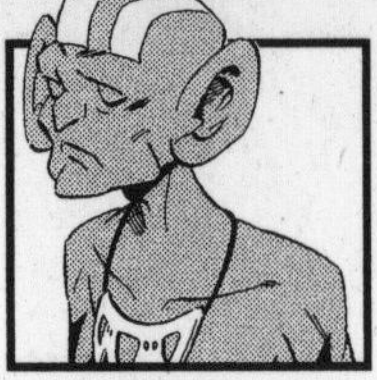

Yainage
A member of Gandala with Kundali.

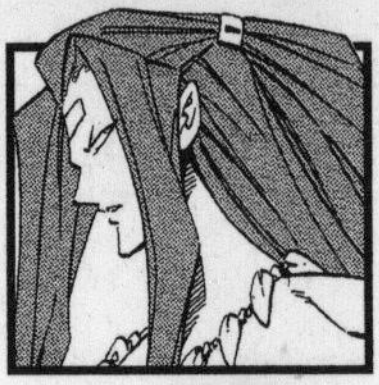

Jackson
A member of Gandala with Acala.

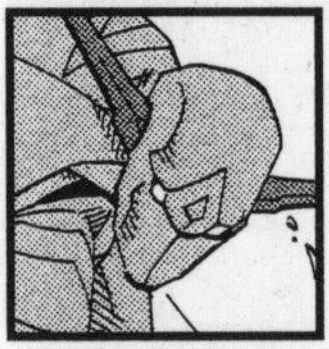

Spirit of Fire
One of the five High Spirits that belonged to the Patch.

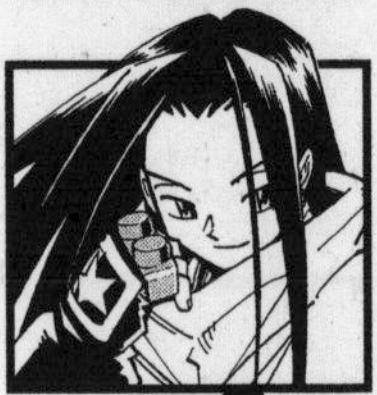

Hao
An enigmatic figure who calls himself the "Future King."

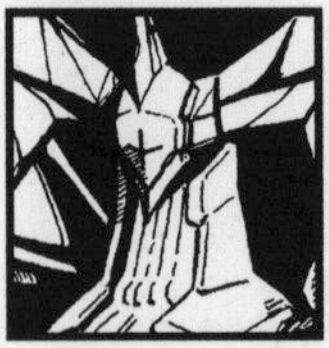

Lucifer
The first Angel, controlled by Luchist.

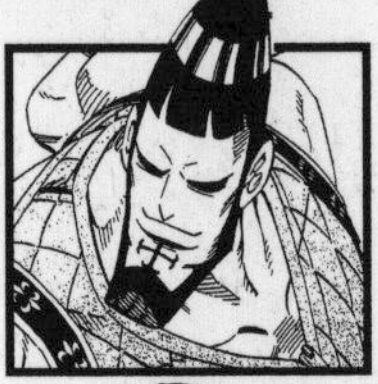

Luchist
The founder of the X-LAWS who now wants to destroy them for his master, Hao.

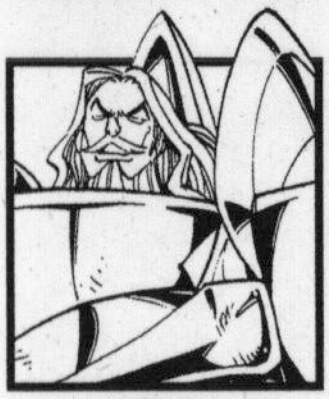

Ashcroft
Canna's spirit, an aged knight who seems chivalrous but actually has a foul mouth and a worse temper.

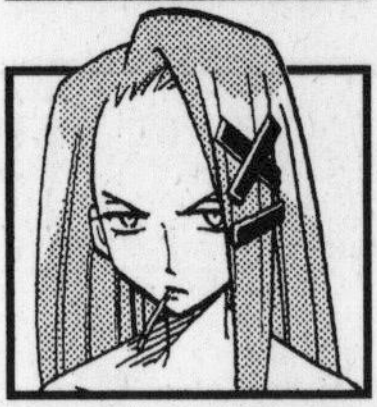

Canna Bismarck
A member of Hana-gumi, one of Hao's teams.

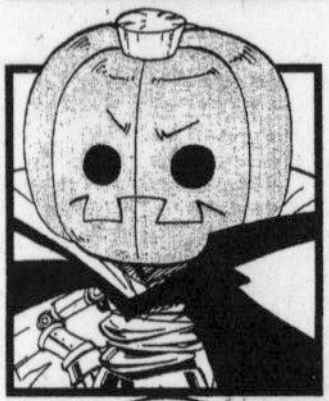

Jack
Mattie's pumpkin doll, which uses knives as weapons.

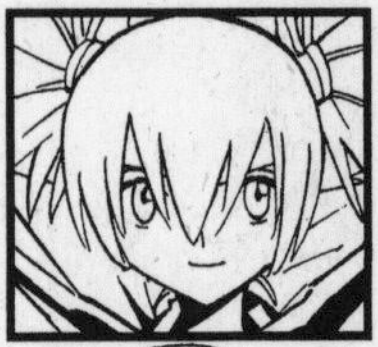

Mathilda
Nicknamed "Mattie," she's a druid with Hana-gumi.

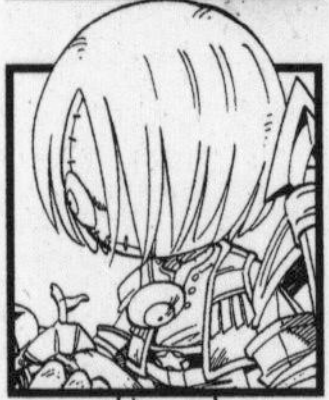

Chuck
Marie's cowboy gunslinger doll.

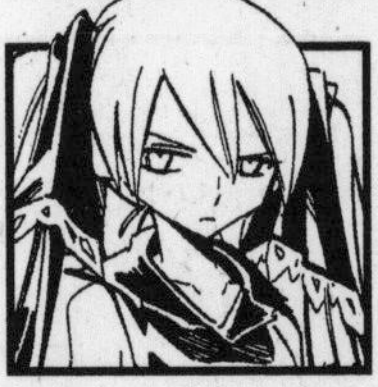

Marion Fauna
Nicknamed "Marie," she's a quiet doll-master with Hana-gumi.

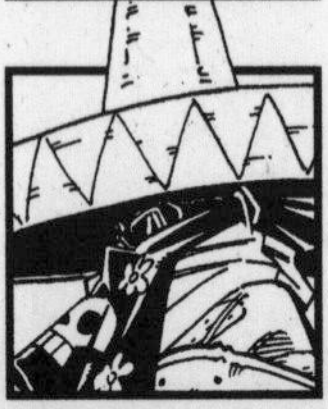

Peyote
Formerly with Tsuchi-gumi. He was defeated by Team Ren but continues to work for Hao.

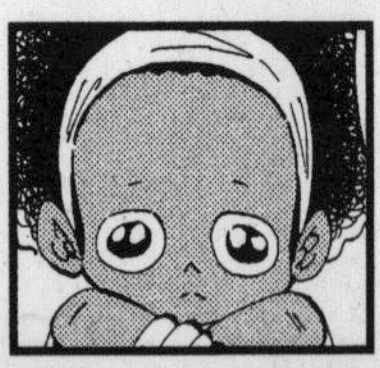

Opacho
Hao's devoted minion who has the power to see the future.

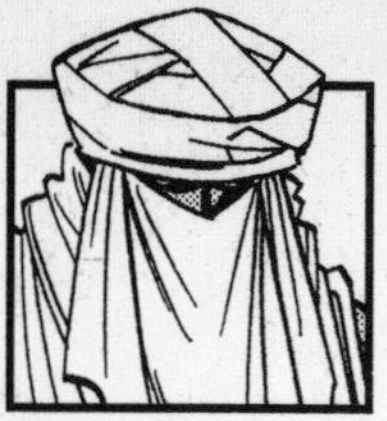

Turbine
A minion of Hao's who hides his face behind a turban and a veil.

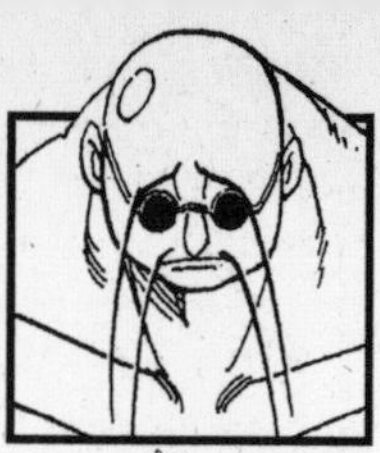

Zang Ching
A minion of Hao's whose spirit ally is a panda ghost called Xiong Xiong.

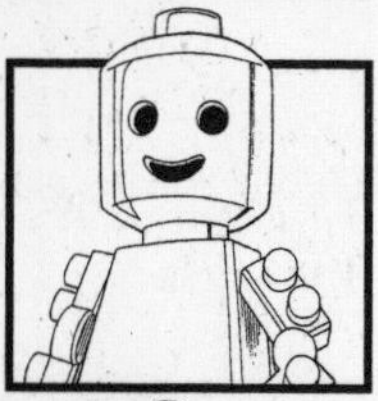

Blocken
A minion of Hao's whose body is made of toy building blocks.

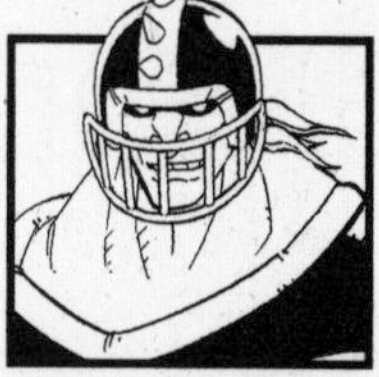

Big Guy Bill
Hao's minion, a football player whose spirit allies are his 21 former teammates.

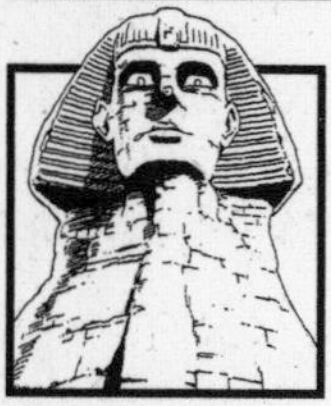

Sphinx
Anahol's flying spirit ally.

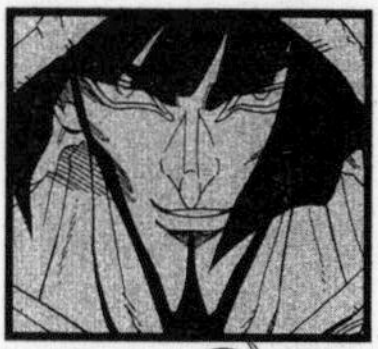

Anahol
A minion of Hao's whose brother, Anatel, was killed by the X-LAWS.

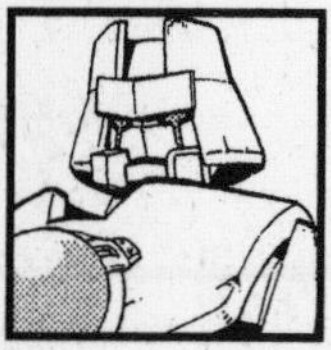

Golem
A robotic creature constructed by Dr. Munzer, Salerm and Ludsev's father.

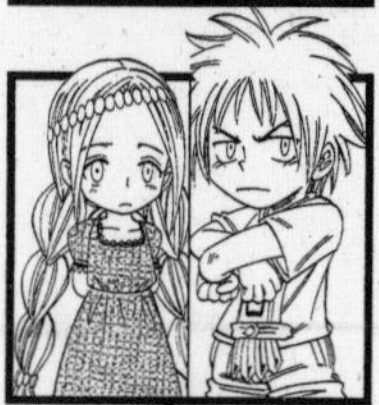

Salerm & Ludsev
A brother and sister who own the Golem.

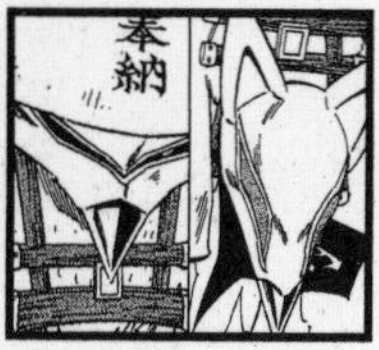
奉納

Shigaraki & Imari
Mickey's shape-shifting mountain spirit allies whom he also used for transportation.

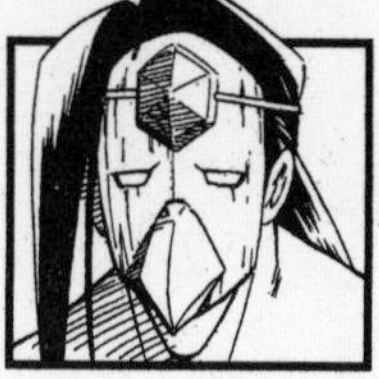

Mickey Asakura
Yoh's father. He wears a tengu mask.

THE STORY THUS FAR

Yoh Asakura not only sees dead people, he talks and fights with them too. That's because Yoh is a shaman, a traditional holy man able to interact with the spirit world. Yoh is now a competitor in the Shaman Fight, a tournament held every 500 years to decide who will become the Shaman King and shape humanity's future.

The twists and turns mount as Yoh leaves and then reenters the Shaman Fight, and Hao and his minions attack the other competitors both in and out of the arena. Meanwhile, an unauthorized attack on Hao ends in disaster for some X-LAWS, and Sati, the leader of Gandala, sends Yoh to Hell!

SHAMAN KING 27
「エキゾチカ」
目次

VOL. 27
EXOTICA

CONTENTS

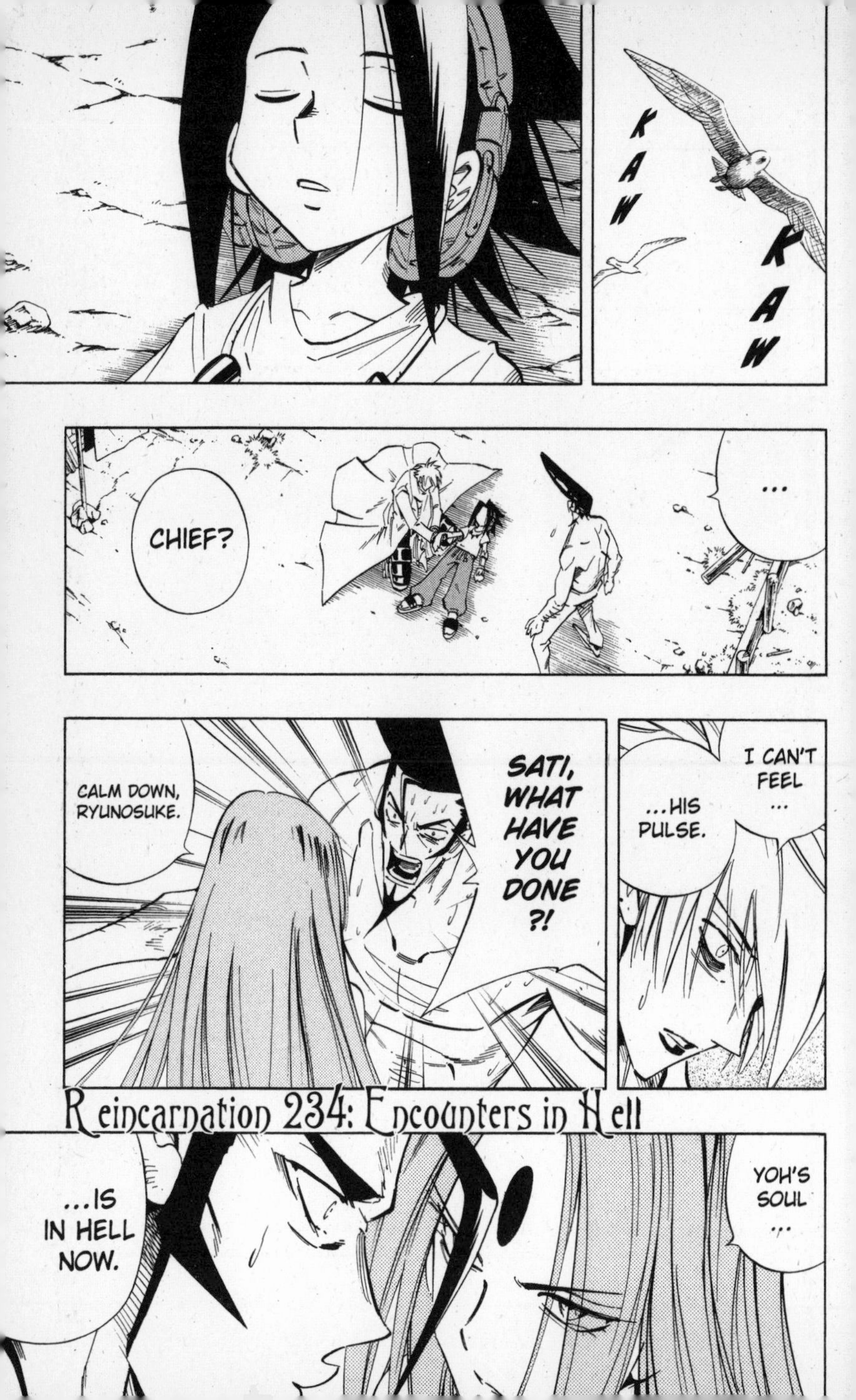
KAW KAW
KAW KAW
...
CHIEF?
I CAN'T FEEL ...
...HIS PULSE.
SATI, WHAT HAVE YOU DONE?!
CALM DOWN, RYUNOSUKE.
Reincarnation 234: Encounters in Hell
YOH'S SOUL ...
...IS IN HELL NOW.

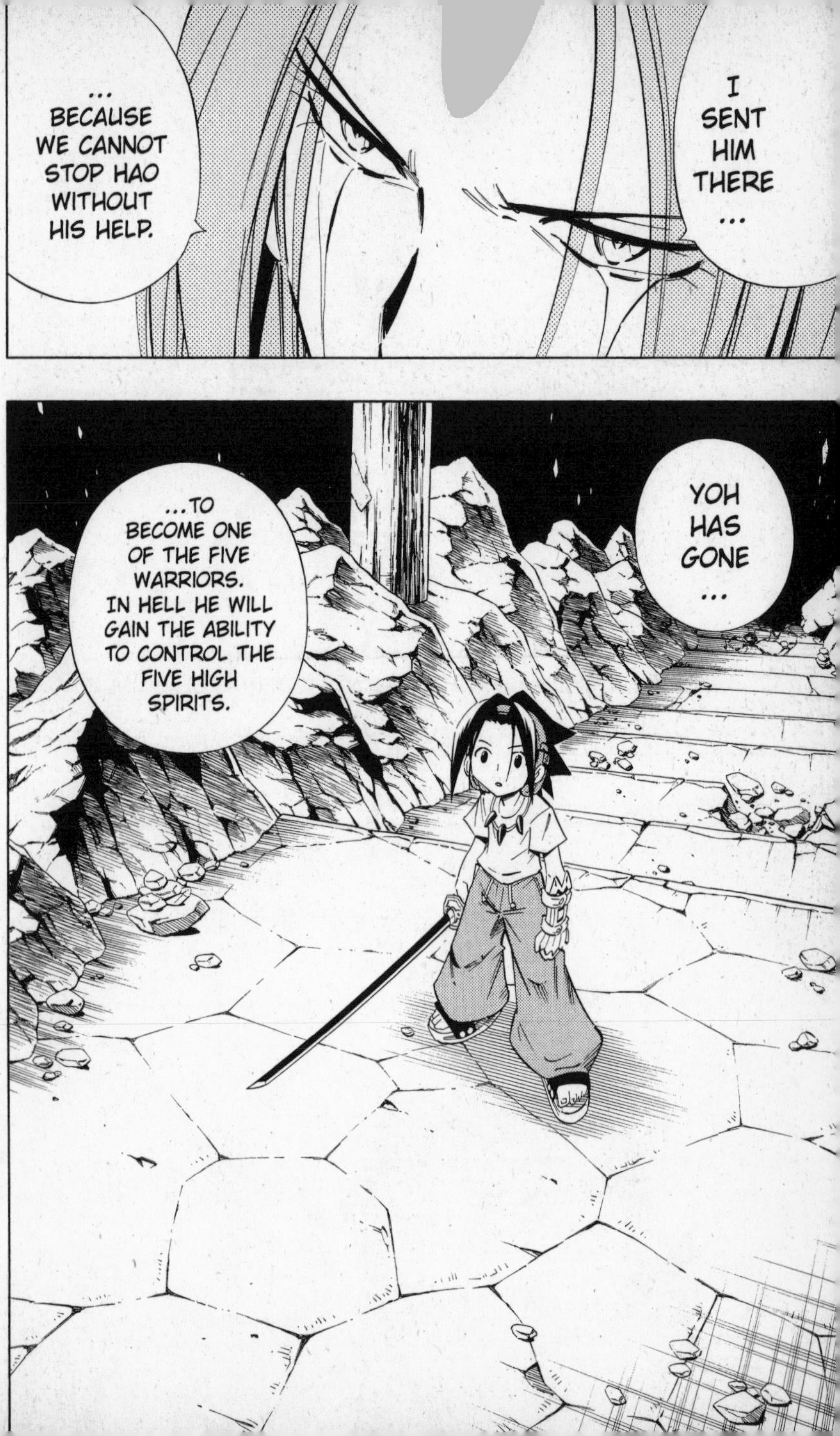
I SENT HIM THERE...
...BECAUSE WE CANNOT STOP HAO WITHOUT HIS HELP.
YOH HAS GONE...
...TO BECOME ONE OF THE FIVE WARRIORS. IN HELL HE WILL GAIN THE ABILITY TO CONTROL THE FIVE HIGH SPIRITS.

Reincarnation 234: Encounters in Hell

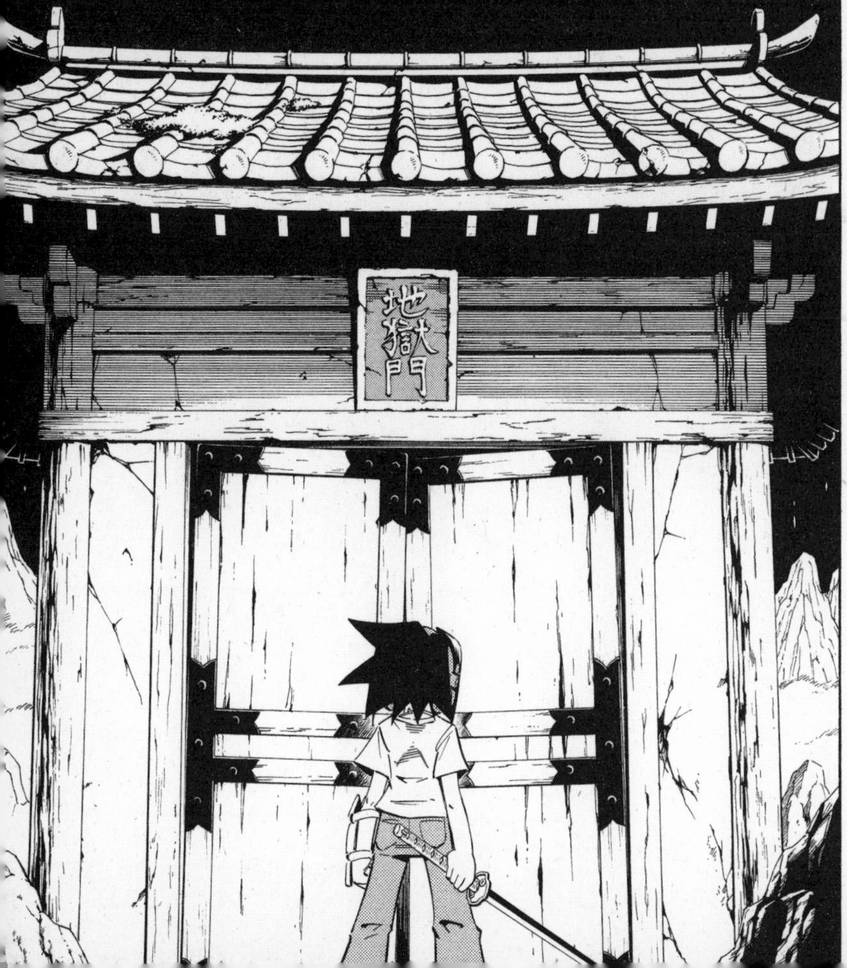
地獄門

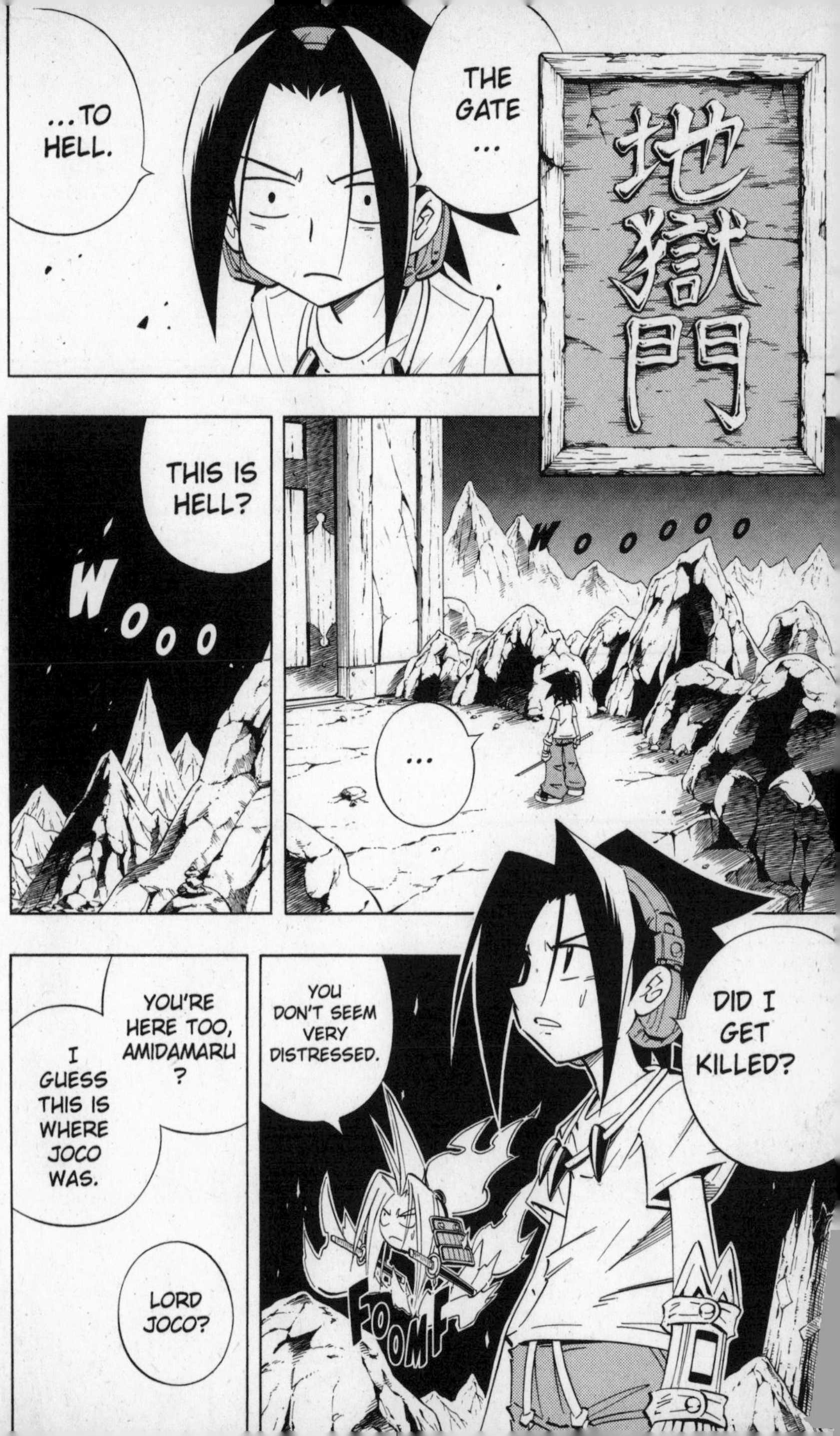
地獄門
THE GATE ...
...TO HELL.
WOOOOOO
...
THIS IS HELL?
WOOO
DID I GET KILLED?
YOU DON'T SEEM VERY DISTRESSED.
FOOMF
YOU'RE HERE TOO, AMIDAMARU?
I GUESS THIS IS WHERE JOCO WAS.
LORD JOCO?

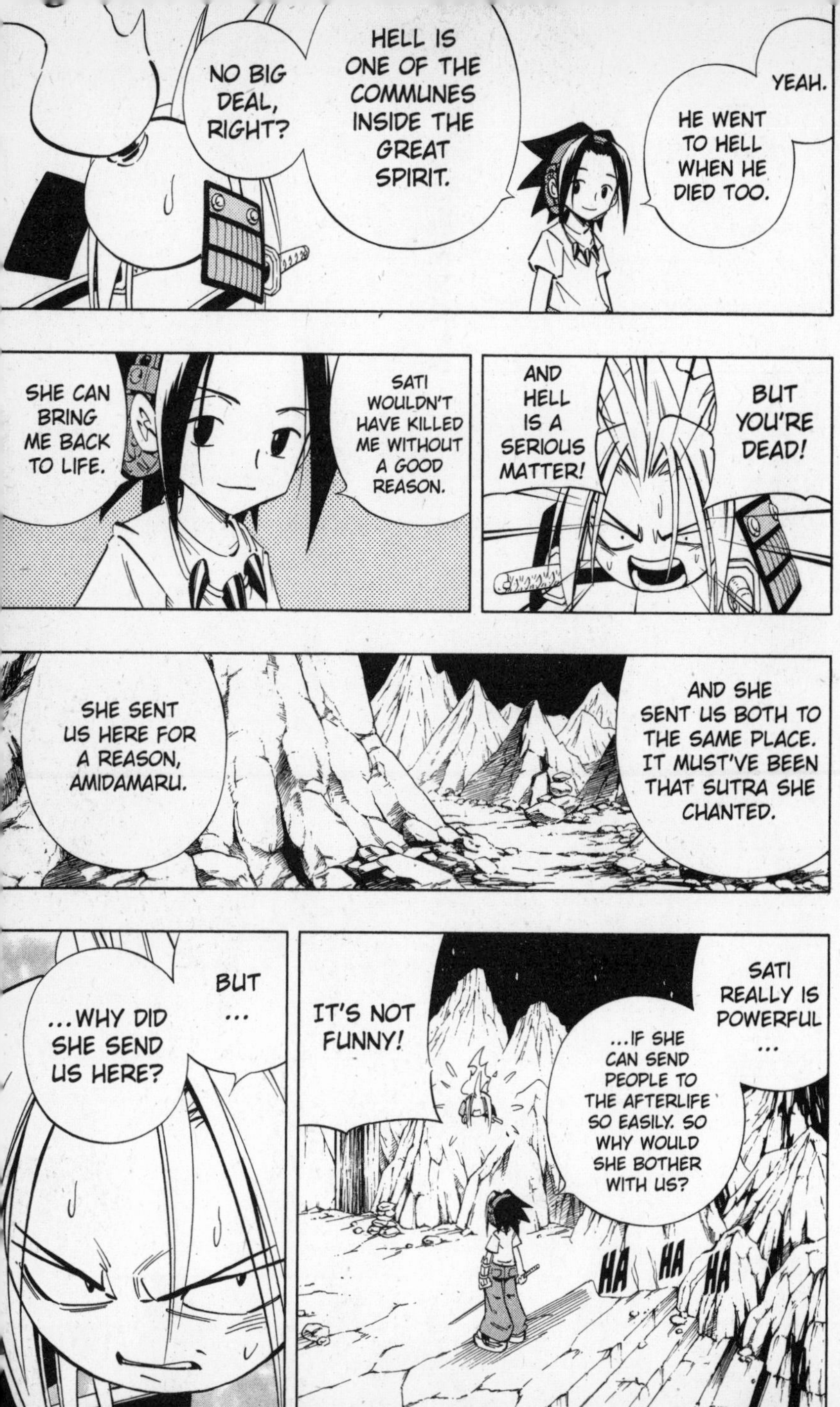
YEAH.
HE WENT TO HELL WHEN HE DIED TOO.
HELL IS ONE OF THE COMMUNES INSIDE THE GREAT SPIRIT.
NO BIG DEAL, RIGHT?
BUT YOU'RE DEAD!
AND HELL IS A SERIOUS MATTER!
SATI WOULDN'T HAVE KILLED ME WITHOUT A GOOD REASON.
SHE CAN BRING ME BACK TO LIFE.
AND SHE SENT US BOTH TO THE SAME PLACE. IT MUST'VE BEEN THAT SUTRA SHE CHANTED.
SHE SENT US HERE FOR A REASON, AMIDAMARU.
SATI REALLY IS POWERFUL ...
...IF SHE CAN SEND PEOPLE TO THE AFTERLIFE SO EASILY. SO WHY WOULD SHE BOTHER WITH US?
HA HA HA
IT'S NOT FUNNY!
BUT ...
...WHY DID SHE SEND US HERE?

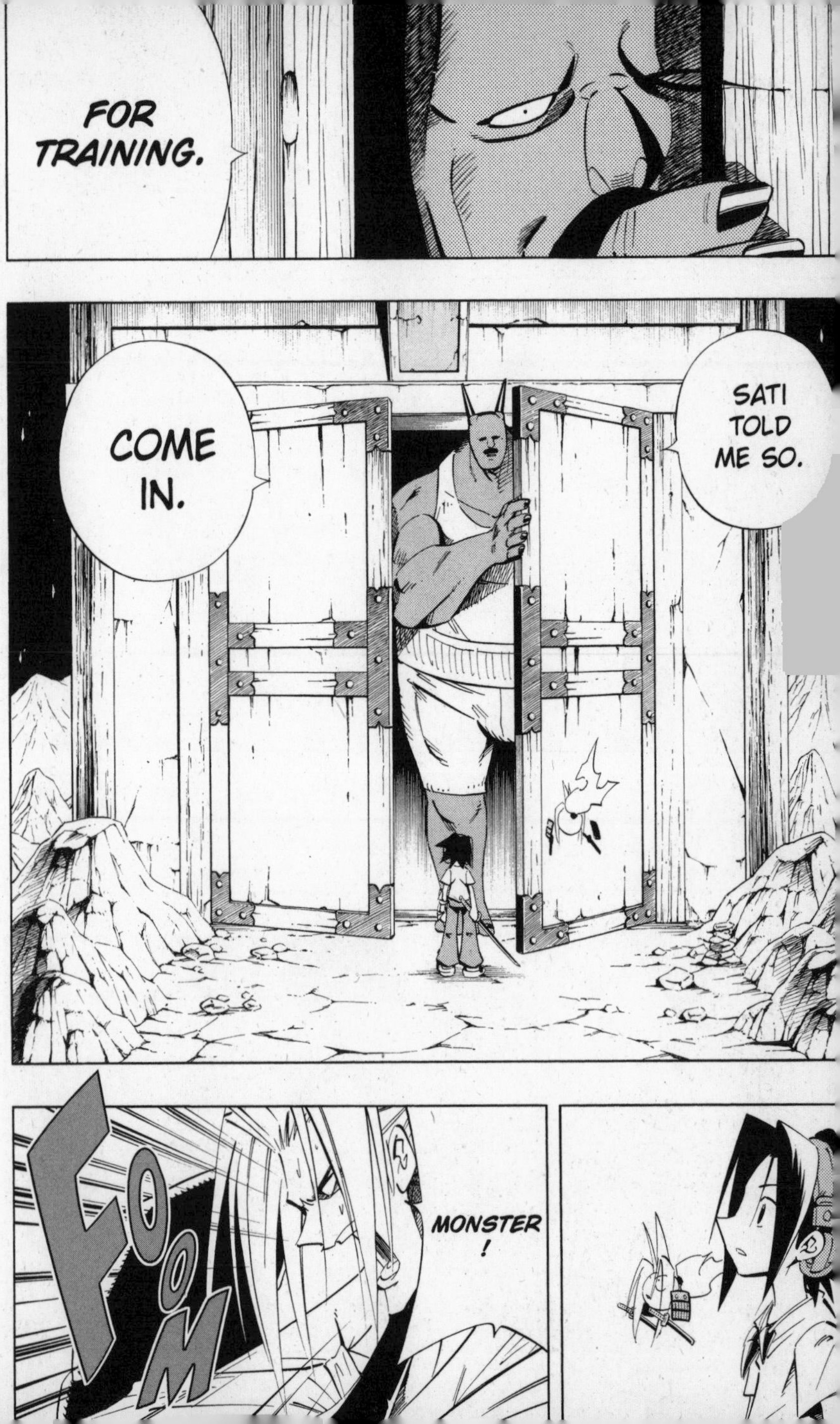
FOR TRAINING.
SATI TOLD ME SO.
COME IN.
FOOM
MONSTER!

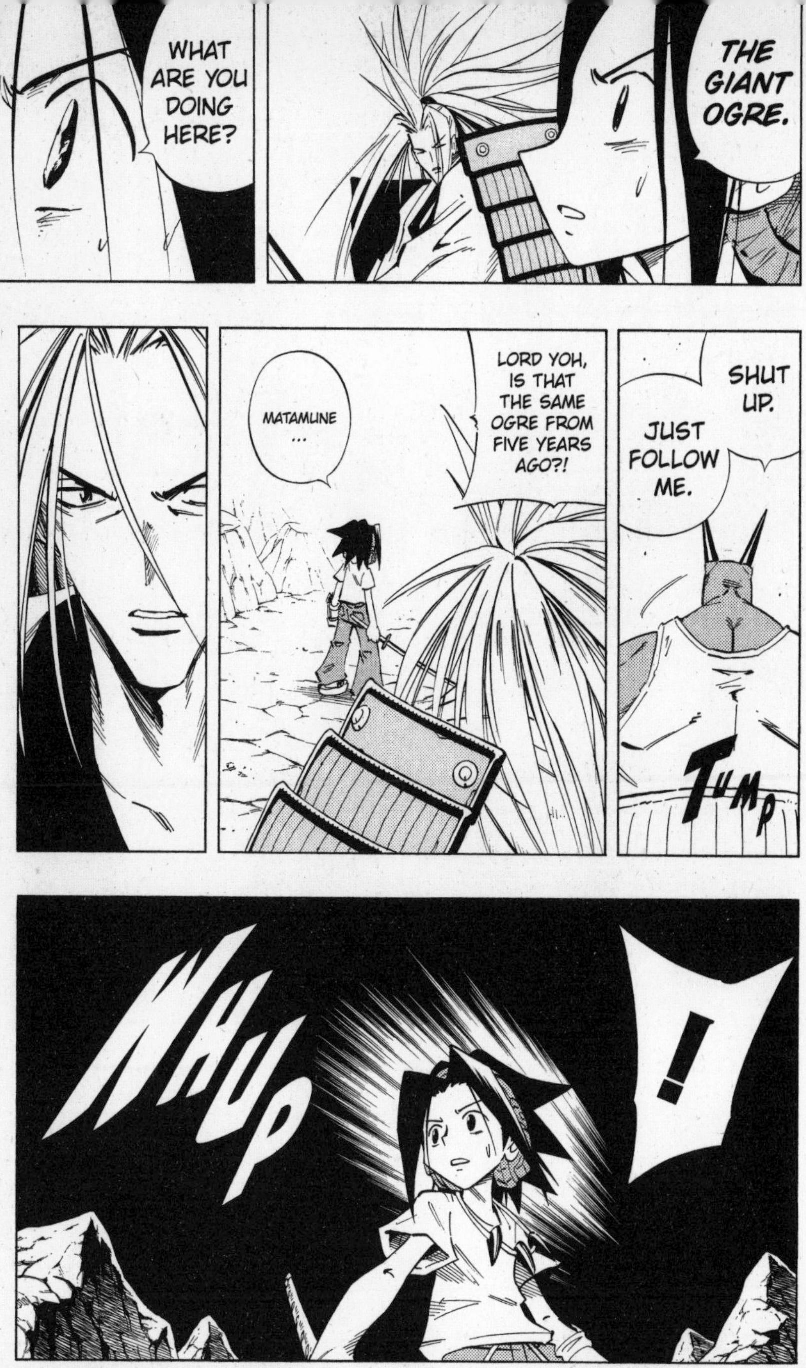
THE GIANT OGRE.
WHAT ARE YOU DOING HERE?
SHUT UP.
JUST FOLLOW ME.
TUMP
LORD YOH, IS THAT THE SAME OGRE FROM FIVE YEARS AGO?!
MATAMUNE ...
!
WHUP

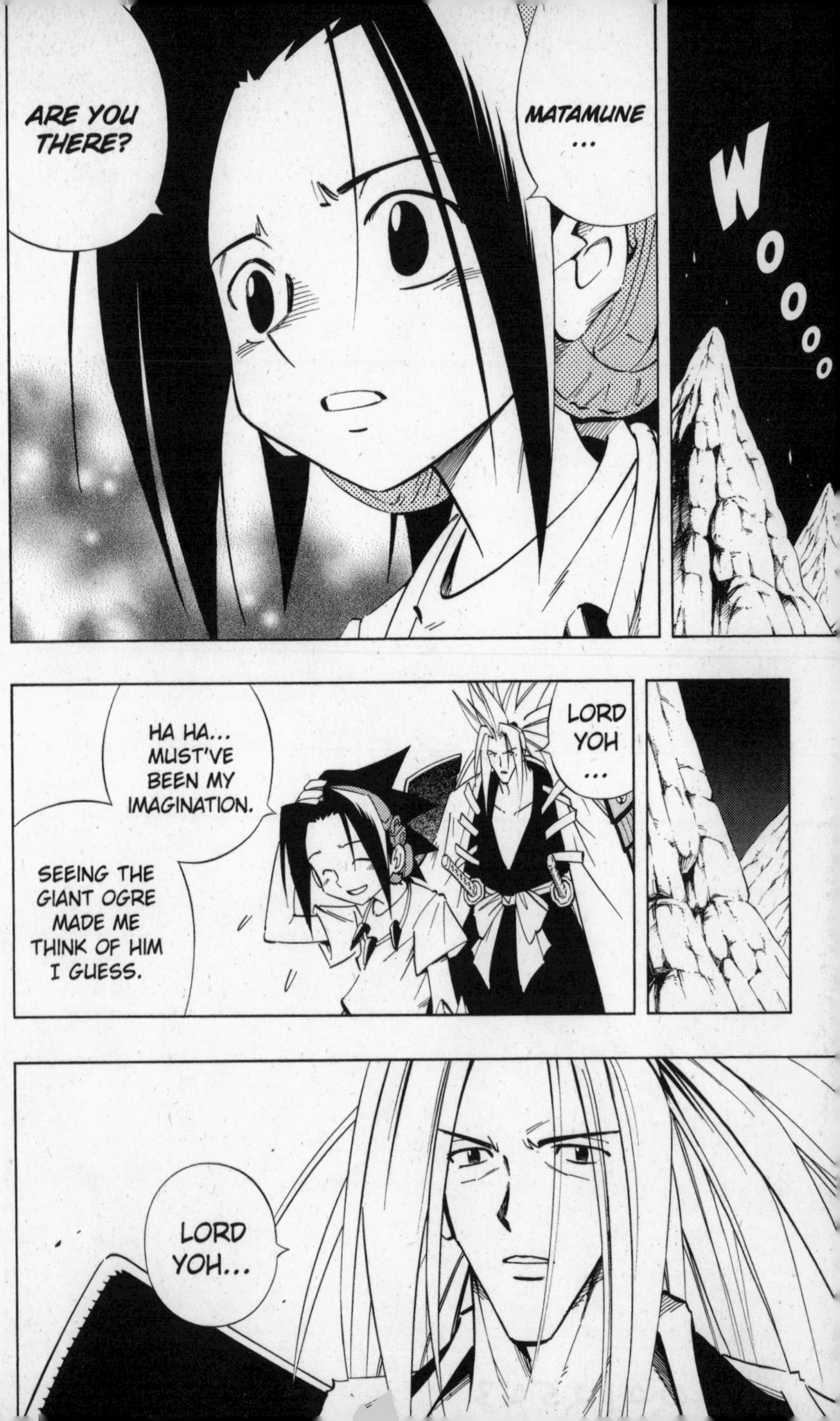
WOOOOO
MATAMUNE ...
ARE YOU THERE?
LORD YOH ...
HA HA... MUST'VE BEEN MY IMAGINATION.
SEEING THE GIANT OGRE MADE ME THINK OF HIM I GUESS.
LORD YOH...

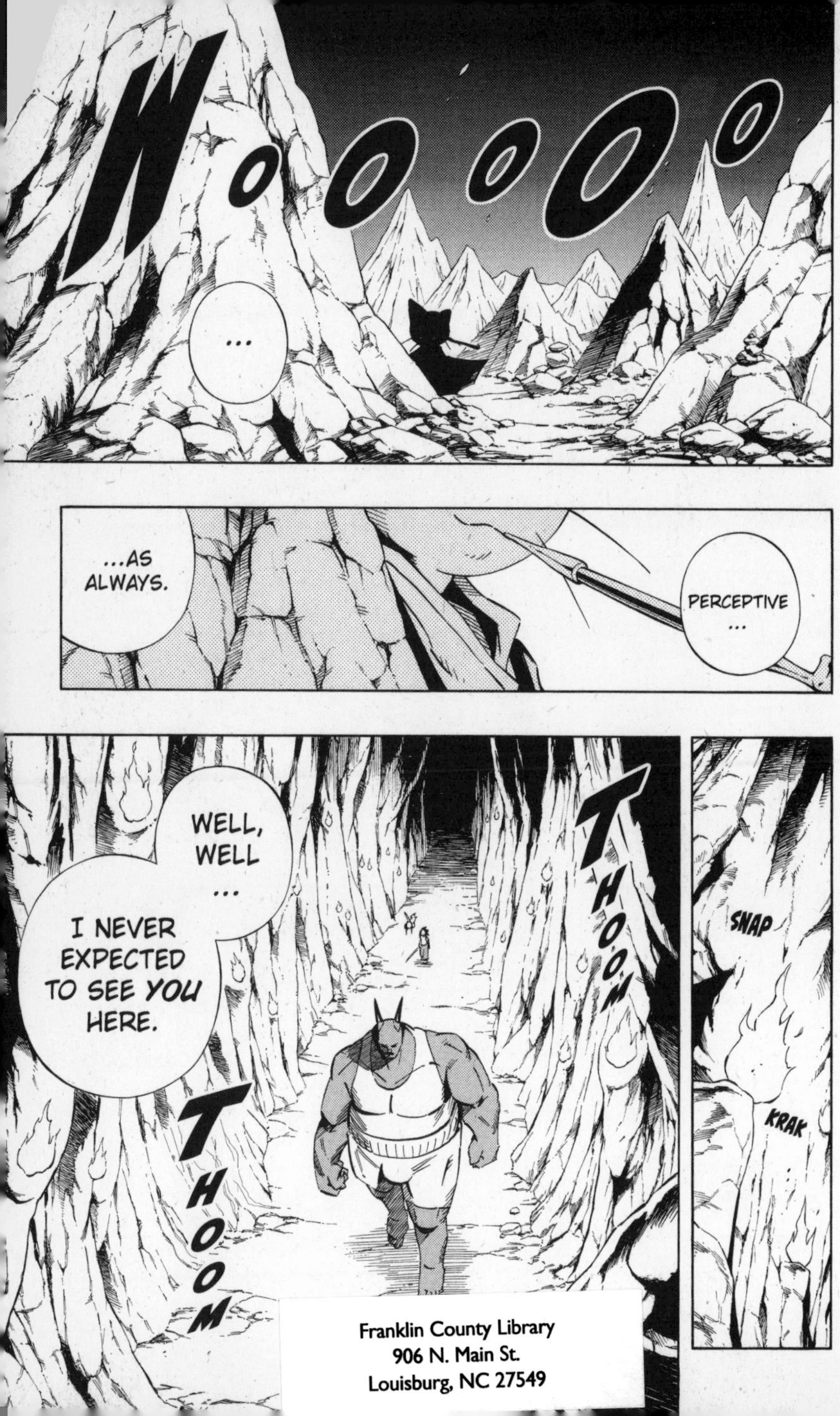
WOOOOOO
...
PERCEPTIVE ...
...AS ALWAYS.
SNAP
KRAK
THOOM
WELL, WELL ...
I NEVER EXPECTED TO SEE *YOU* HERE.
THOOM

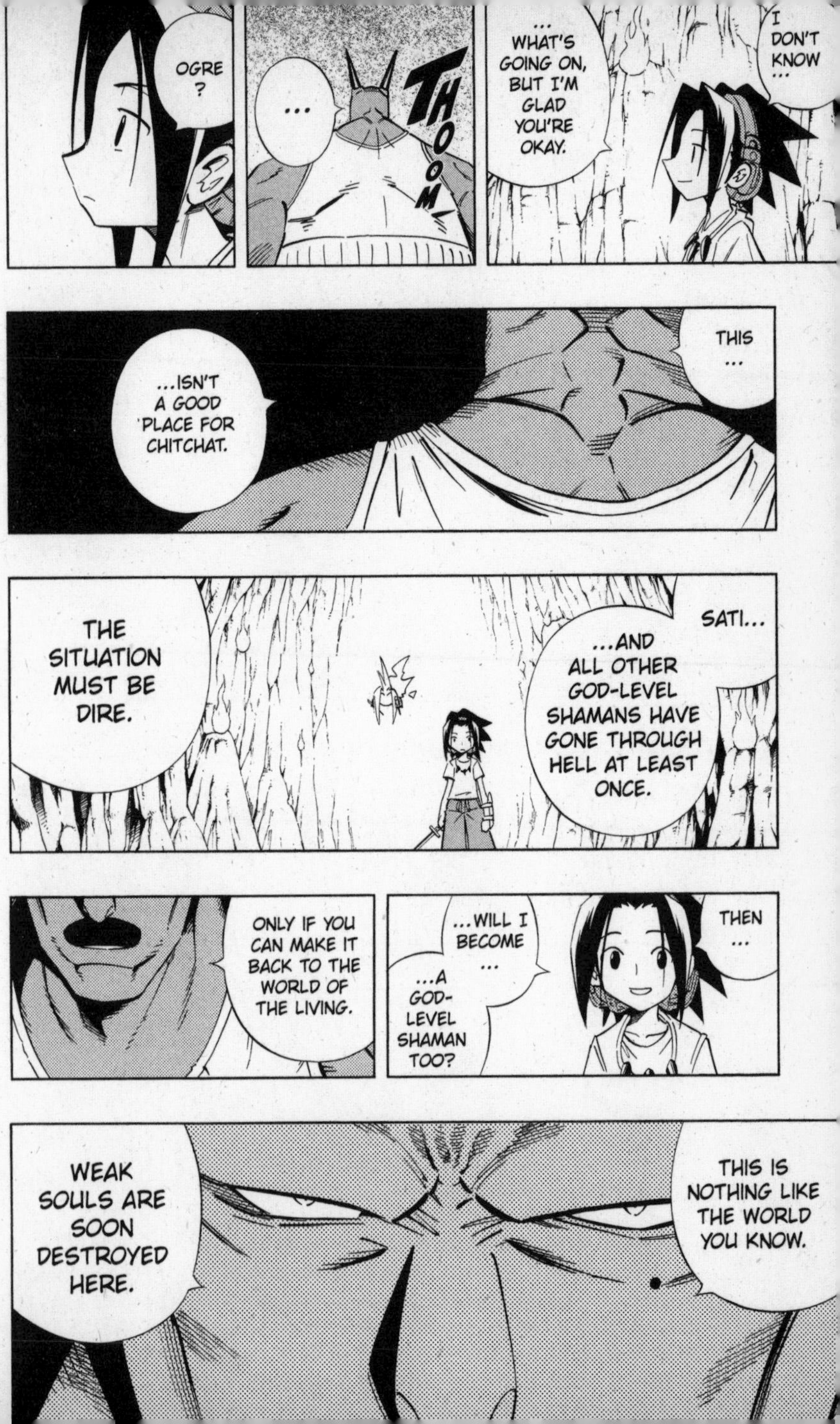
I DON'T KNOW...
...WHAT'S GOING ON, BUT I'M GLAD YOU'RE OKAY.
...
THOOOM
OGRE?
THIS...
...ISN'T A GOOD PLACE FOR CHITCHAT.
SATI...
...AND ALL OTHER GOD-LEVEL SHAMANS HAVE GONE THROUGH HELL AT LEAST ONCE.
THE SITUATION MUST BE DIRE.
THEN...
...WILL I BECOME...
...A GOD-LEVEL SHAMAN TOO?
ONLY IF YOU CAN MAKE IT BACK TO THE WORLD OF THE LIVING.
THIS IS NOTHING LIKE THE WORLD YOU KNOW.
WEAK SOULS ARE SOON DESTROYED HERE.

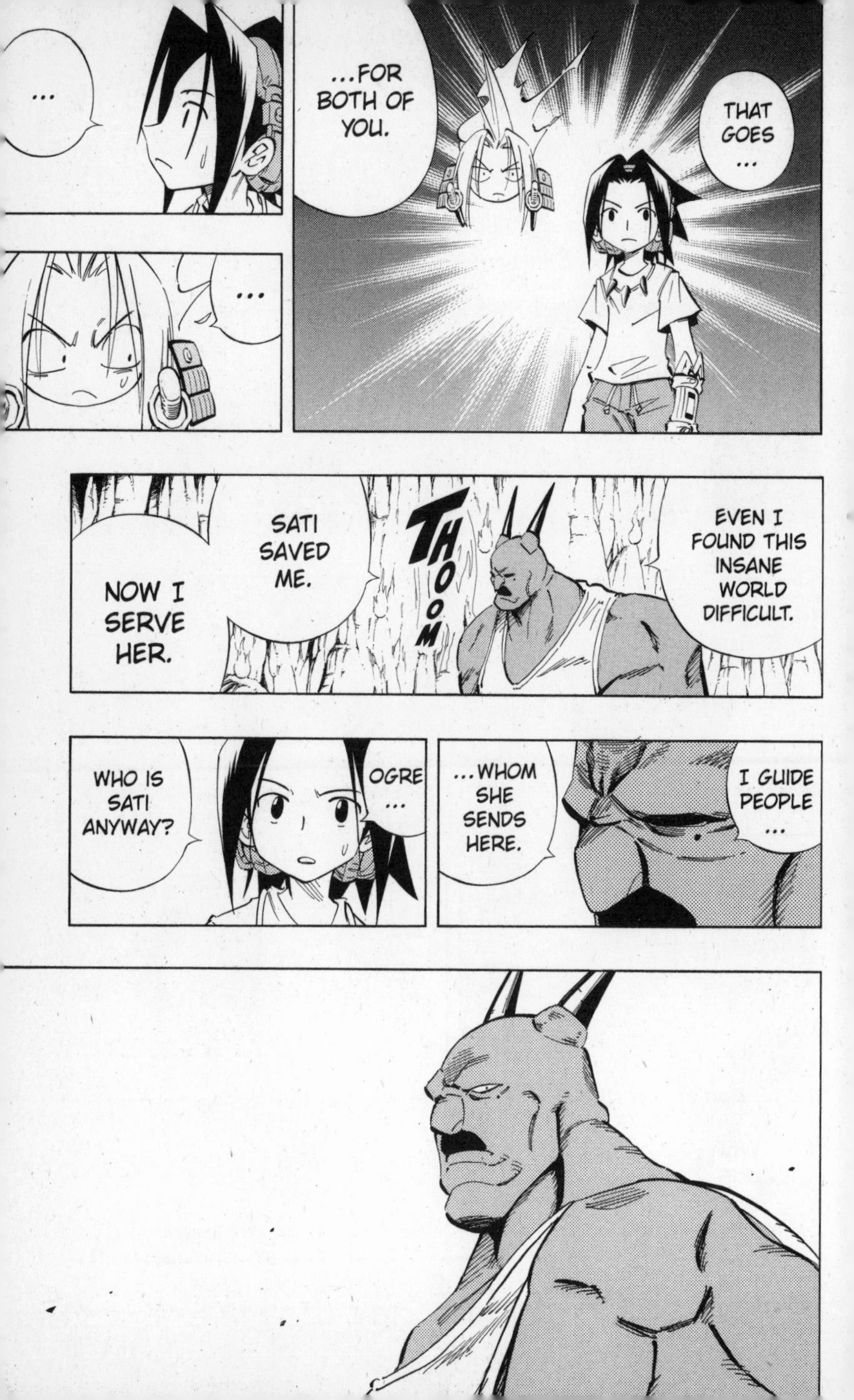
THAT GOES ...
...FOR BOTH OF YOU.
...
...
EVEN I FOUND THIS INSANE WORLD DIFFICULT.
THOOM
SATI SAVED ME.
NOW I SERVE HER.
I GUIDE PEOPLE ...
...WHOM SHE SENDS HERE.
OGRE ...
WHO IS SATI ANYWAY?

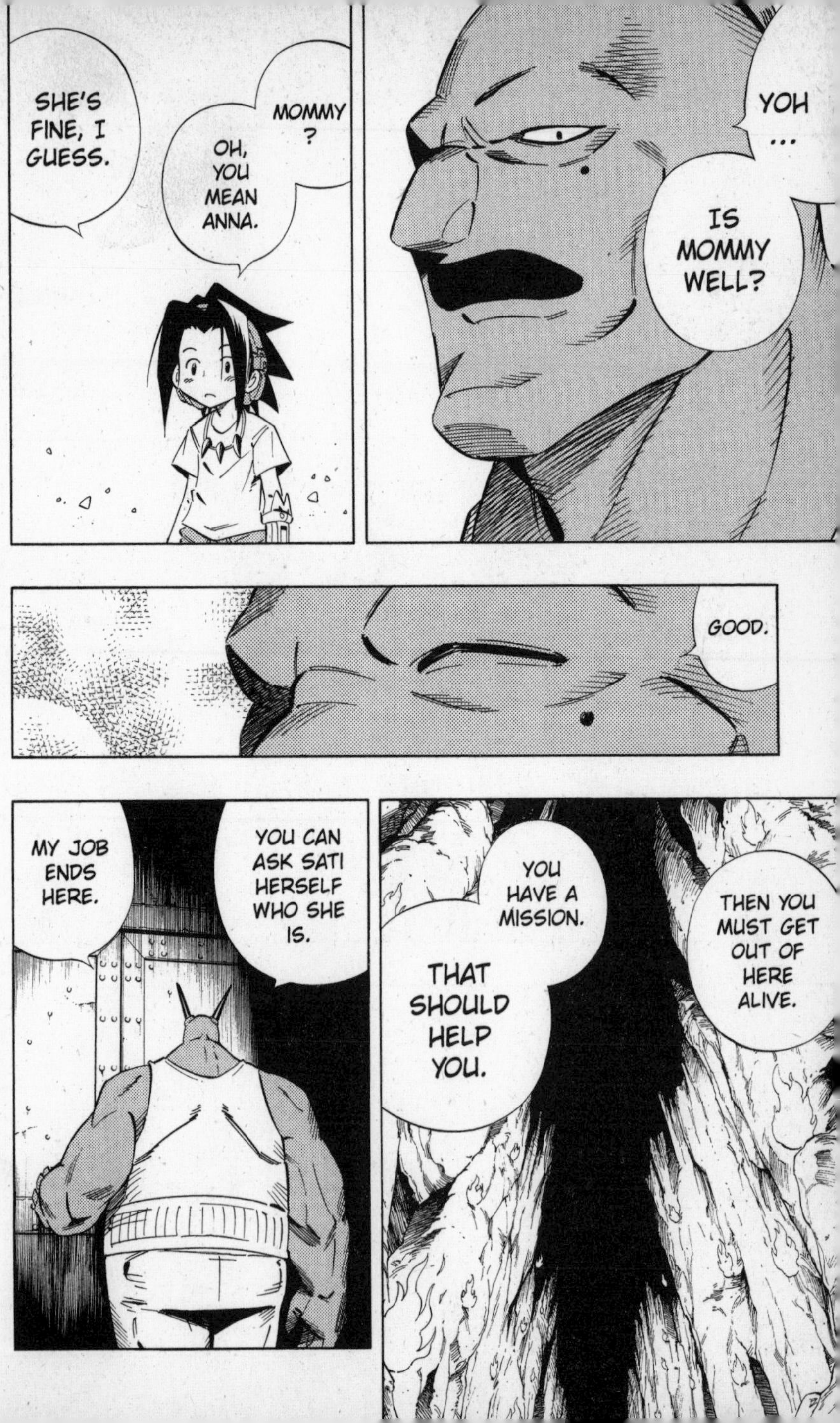
YOH ...
IS MOMMY WELL?
MOMMY ?
OH, YOU MEAN ANNA.
SHE'S FINE, I GUESS.
GOOD.
THEN YOU MUST GET OUT OF HERE ALIVE.
YOU HAVE A MISSION.
THAT SHOULD HELP YOU.
YOU CAN ASK SATI HERSELF WHO SHE IS.
MY JOB ENDS HERE.

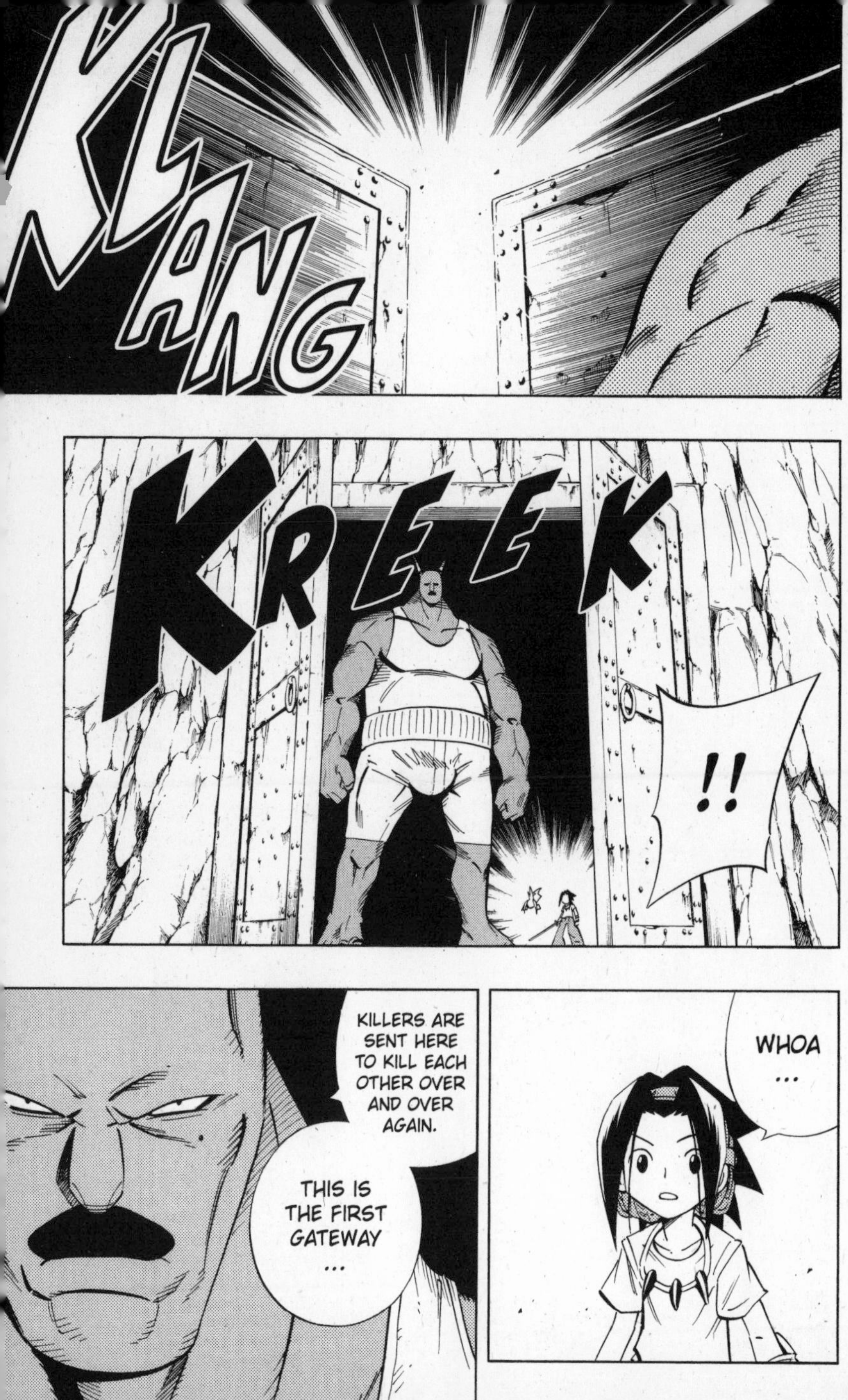
KLANG
KREEK
!!
WHOA ...
KILLERS ARE SENT HERE TO KILL EACH OTHER OVER AND OVER AGAIN.
THIS IS THE FIRST GATEWAY ...

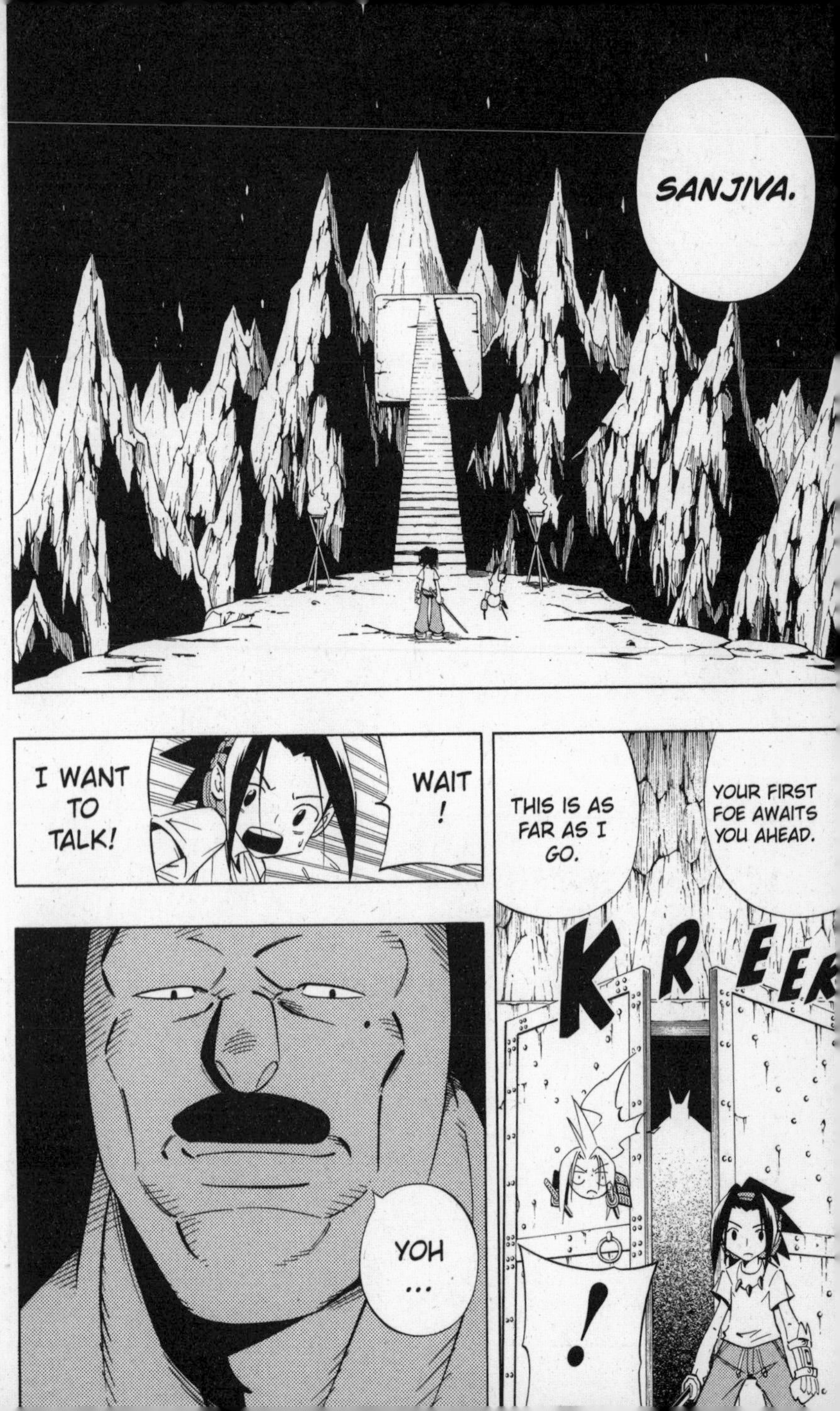
SANJIVA.
YOUR FIRST FOE AWAITS YOU AHEAD.
THIS IS AS FAR AS I GO.
KREE
!
WAIT!
I WANT TO TALK!
YOH ...

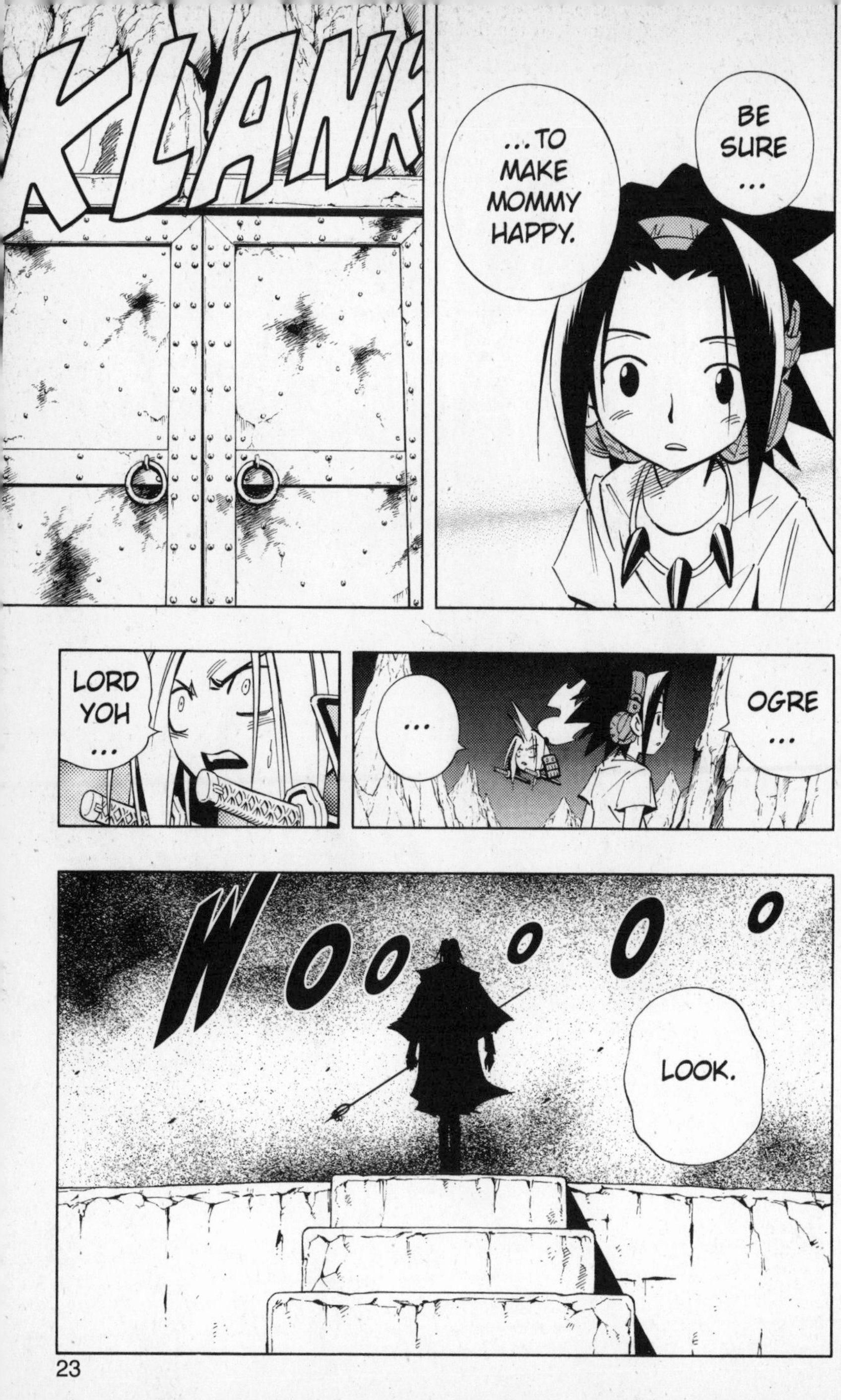
BE SURE ...
...TO MAKE MOMMY HAPPY.
KLANK
OGRE ...
...
LORD YOH ...
WOOOOO
LOOK.

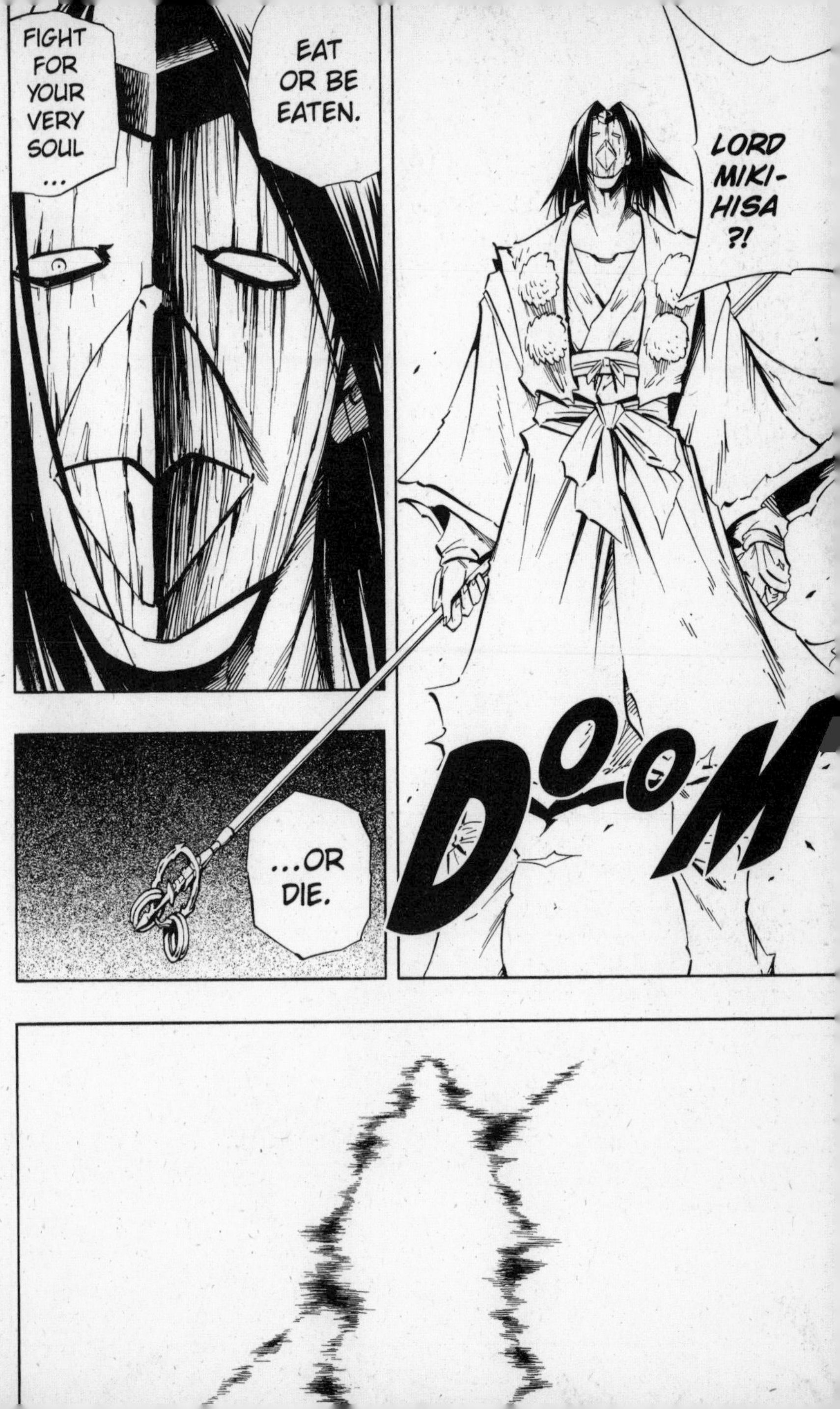
LORD MIKI-HISA ?!
DOOM
EAT OR BE EATEN.
FIGHT FOR YOUR VERY SOUL ...
...OR DIE.

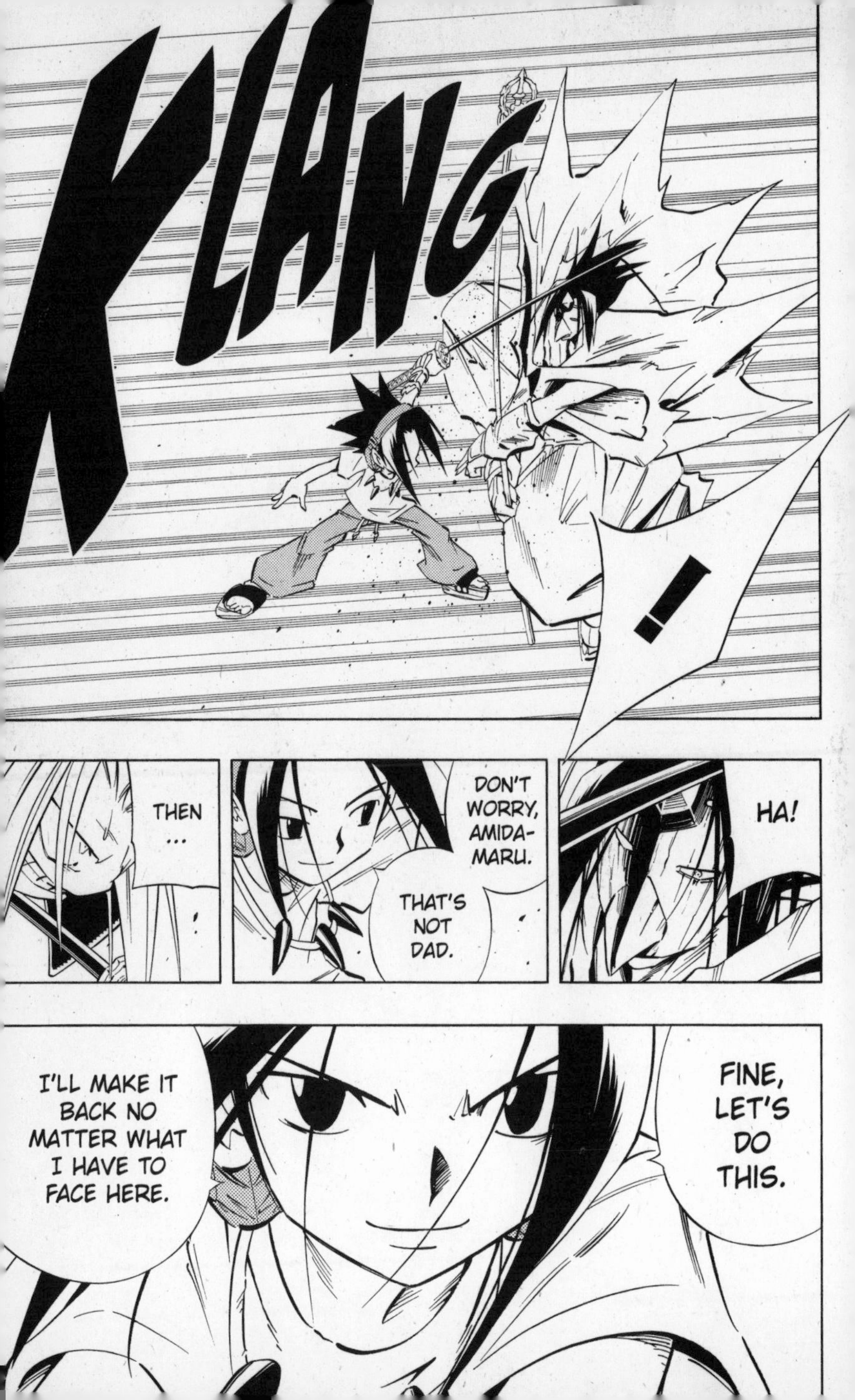
KLANG
!
HA!
DON'T WORRY, AMIDA-MARU.
THAT'S NOT DAD.
THEN...
FINE, LET'S DO THIS.
I'LL MAKE IT BACK NO MATTER WHAT I HAVE TO FACE HERE.

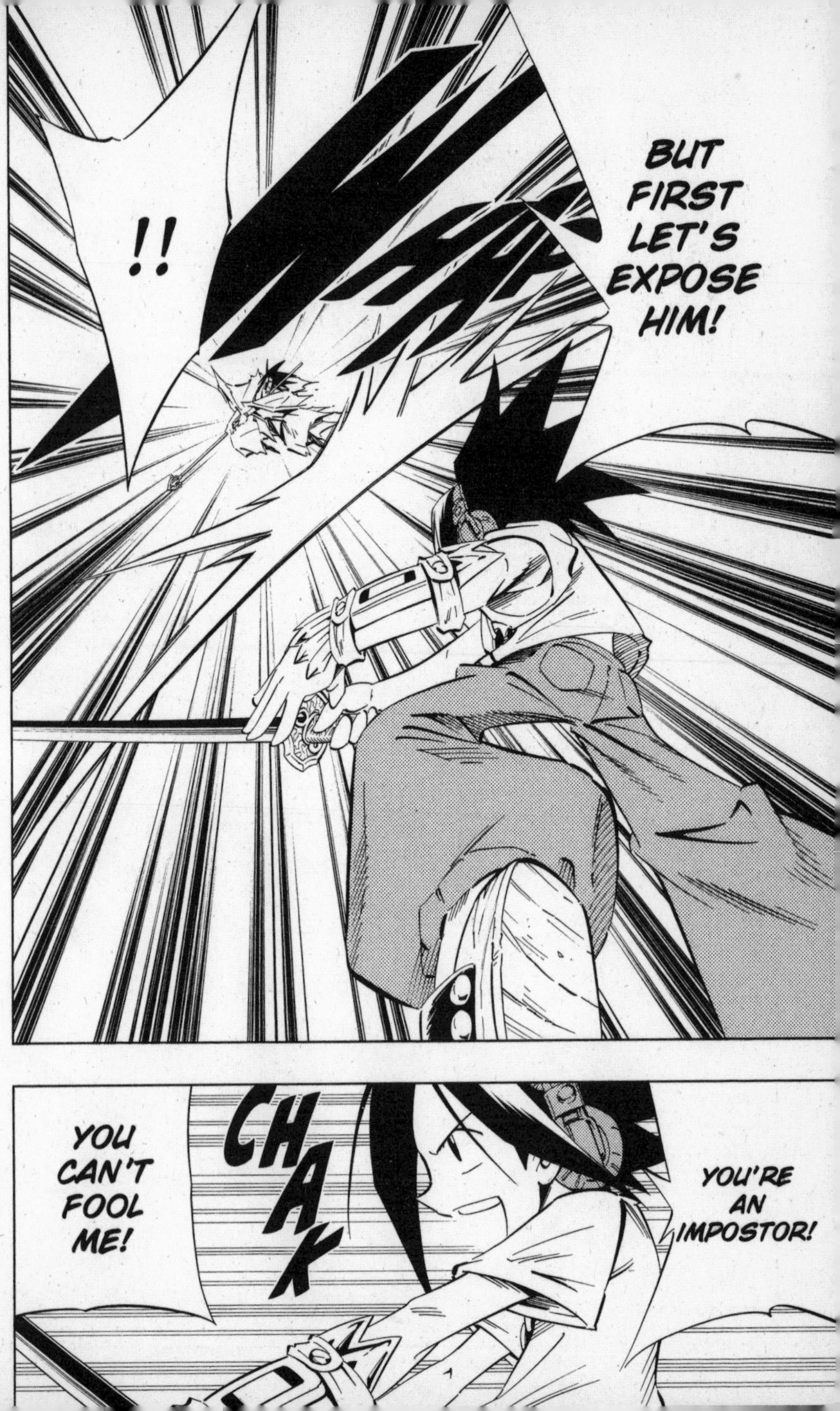
BUT FIRST LET'S EXPOSE HIM!
!!
YOU'RE AN IMPOSTOR!
CHAK
YOU CAN'T FOOL ME!

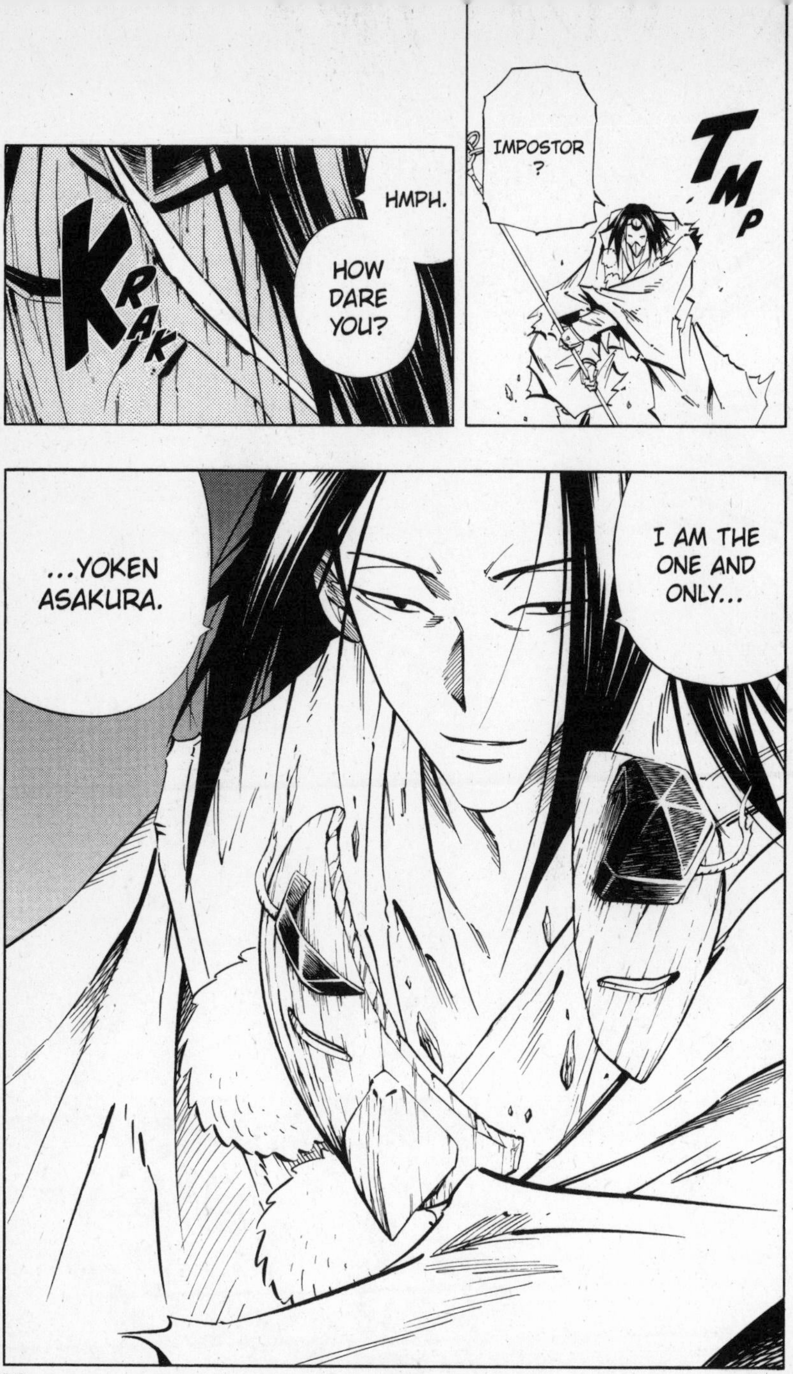
IMPOSTOR ?
TMP
HMPH.
HOW DARE YOU?
KRAK
I AM THE ONE AND ONLY...
...YOKEN ASAKURA.

Shaman King

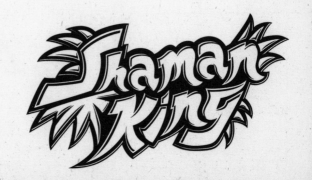

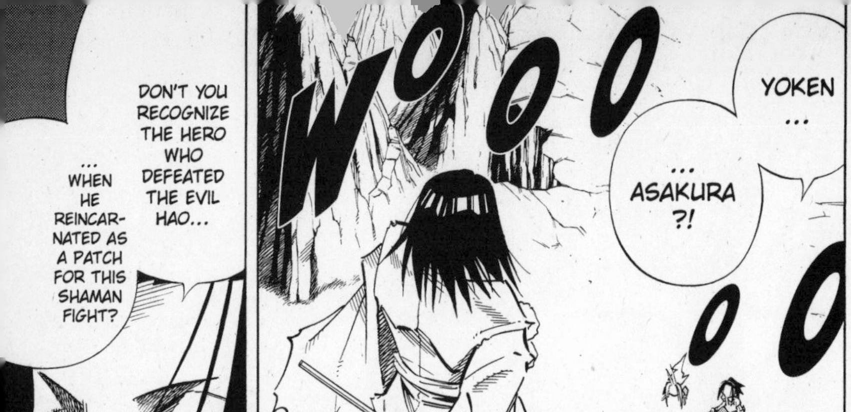
YOKEN ...
... ASAKURA ?!
WOOOO
OOO
WHAT?
DON'T YOU RECOGNIZE THE HERO WHO DEFEATED THE EVIL HAO...
... WHEN HE REINCARNATED AS A PATCH FOR THIS SHAMAN FIGHT?

Reincarnation 235: Ancestor

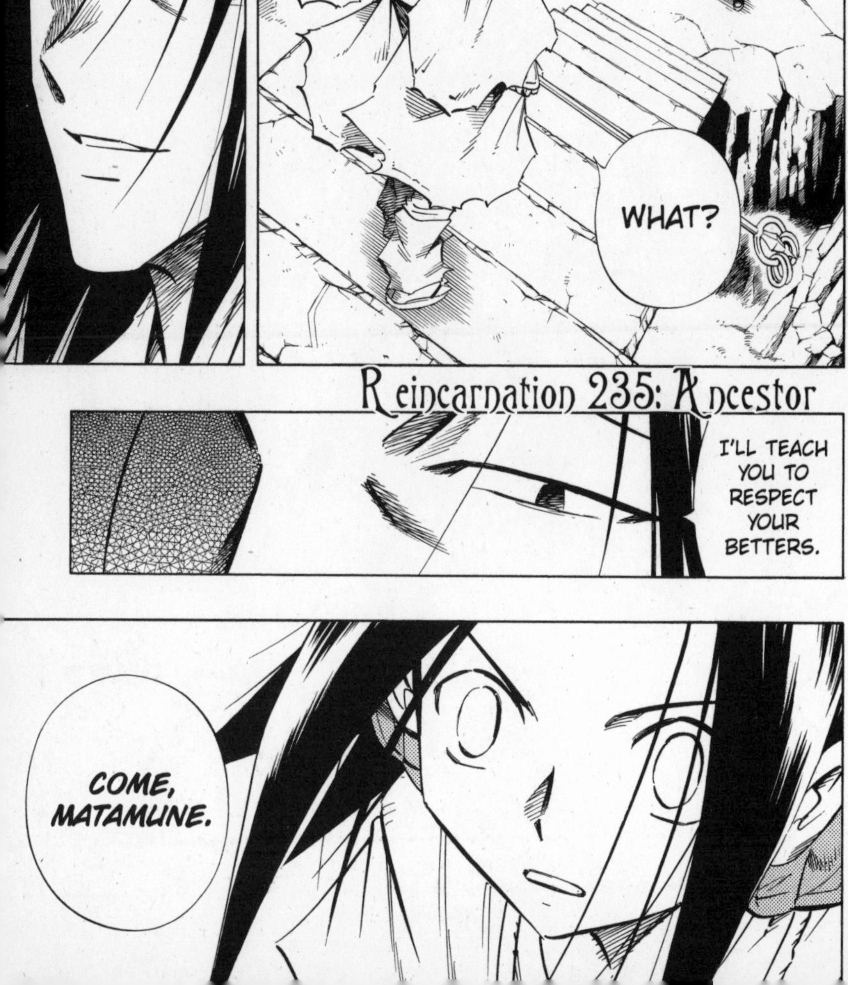
I'LL TEACH YOU TO RESPECT YOUR BETTERS.
COME, MATAMUNE.

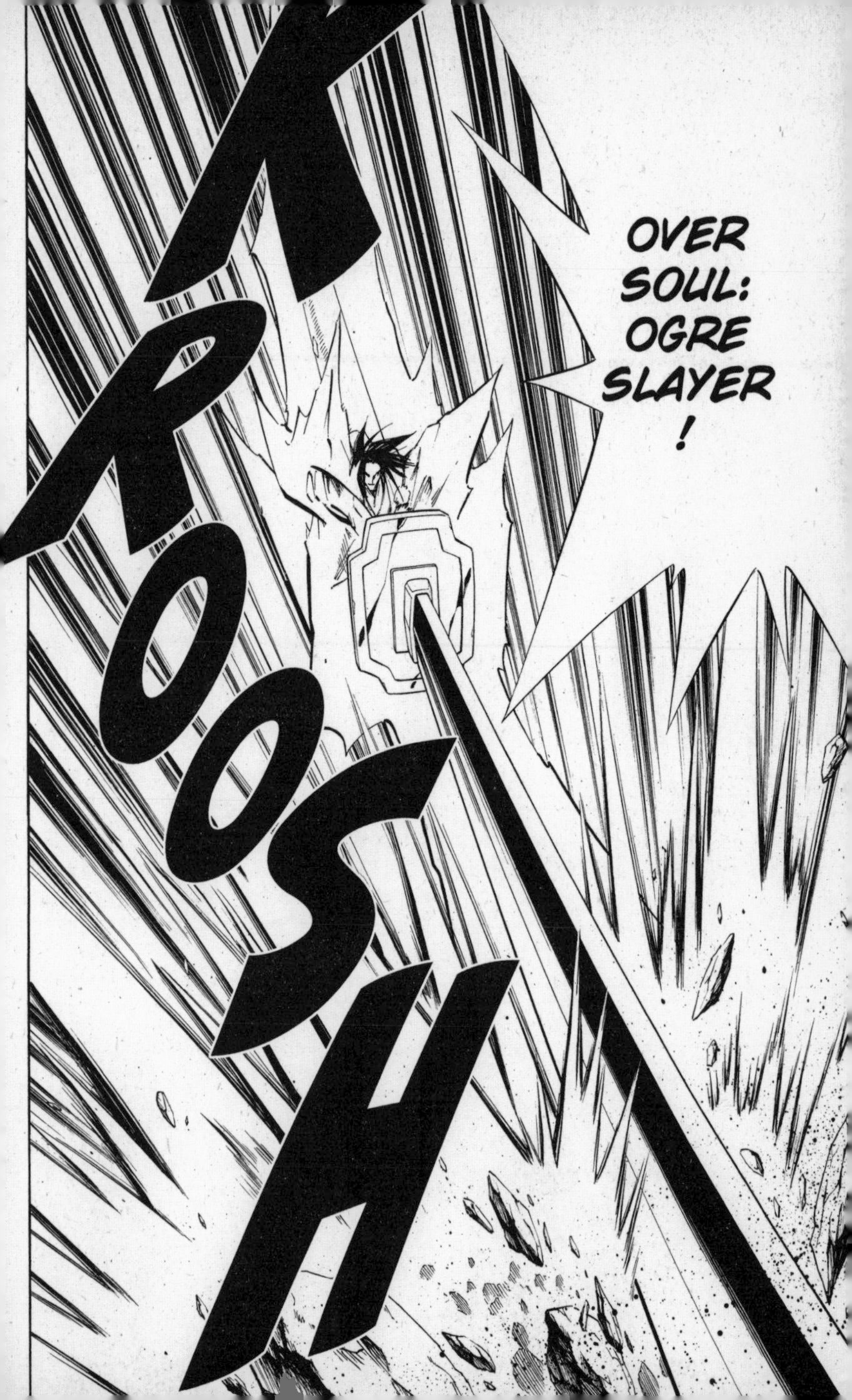
OVER SOUL: OGRE SLAYER!
KROOSH

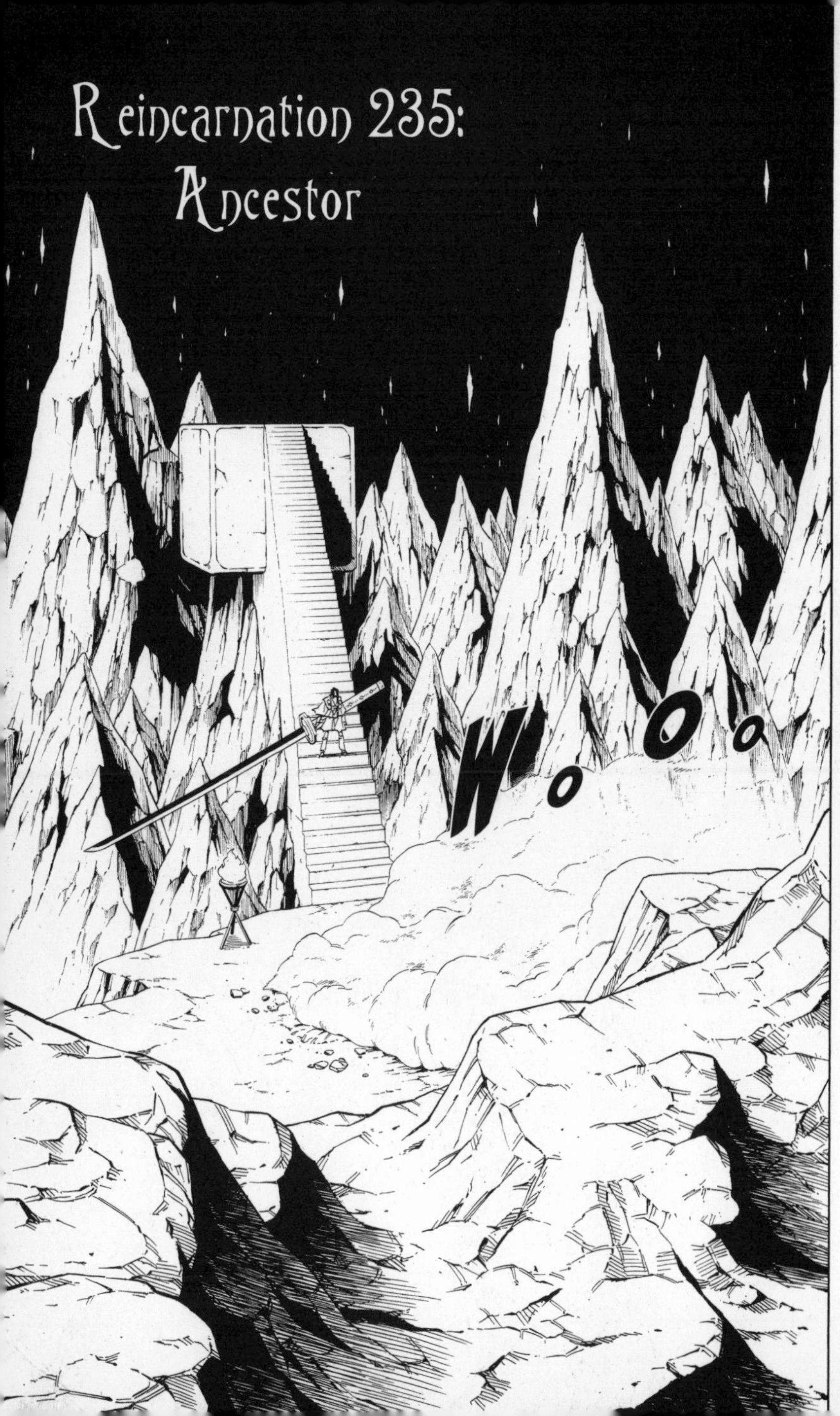
Reincarnation 235:
Ancestor
WoOOo

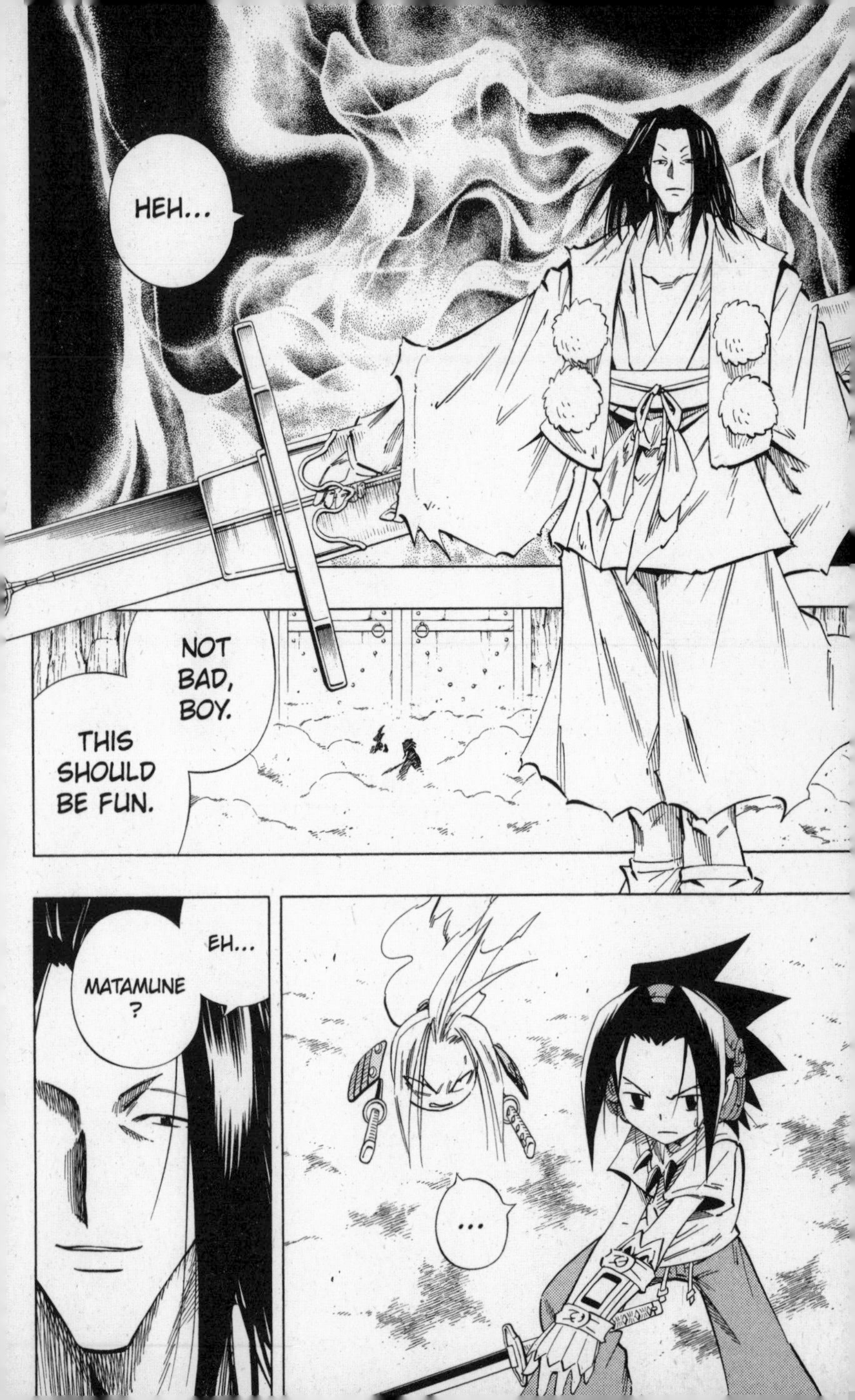
HEH...
NOT BAD, BOY.
THIS SHOULD BE FUN.
...
EH... MATAMUNE?

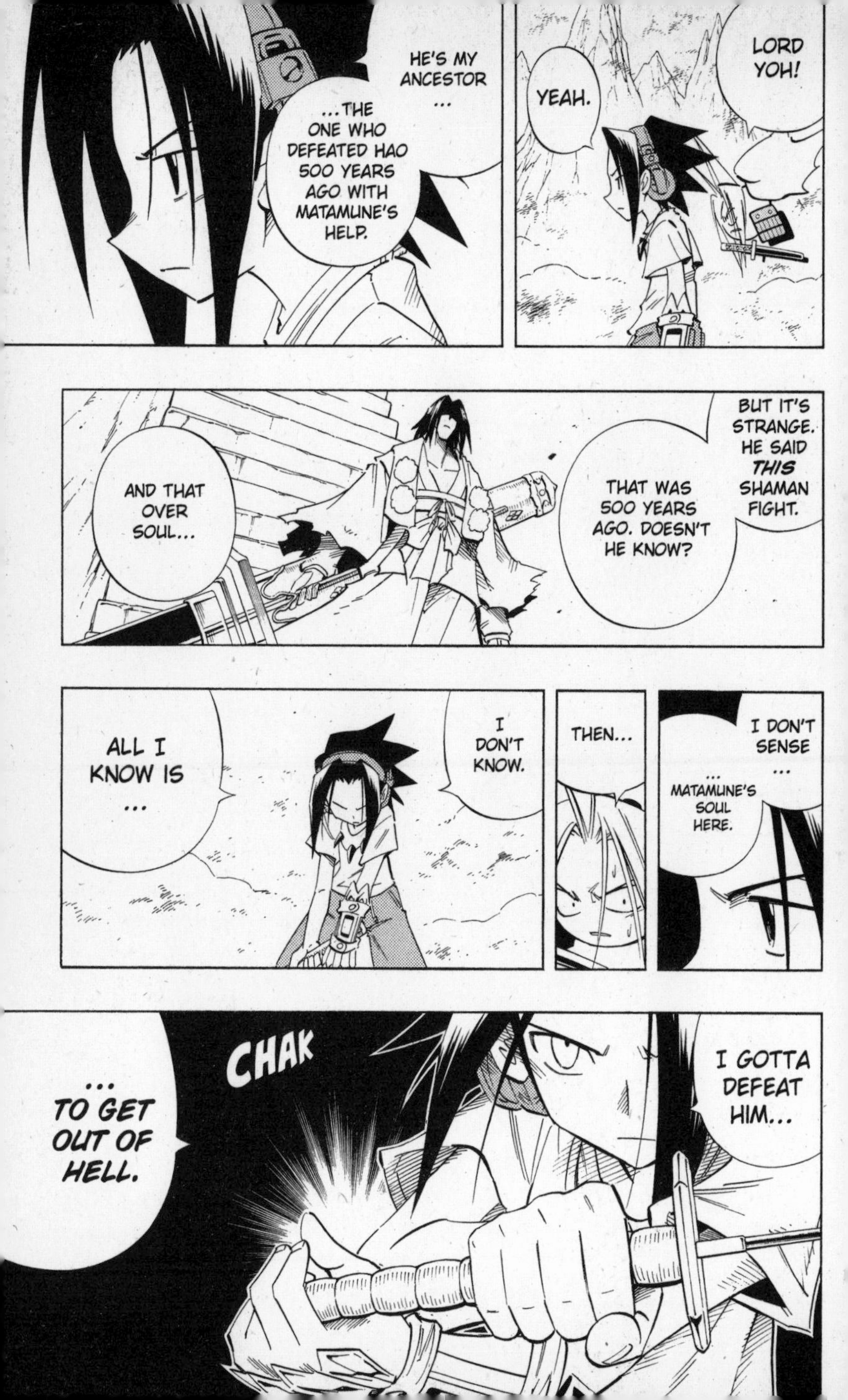
LORD YOH!
YEAH.
HE'S MY ANCESTOR ...
...THE ONE WHO DEFEATED HAO 500 YEARS AGO WITH MATAMUNE'S HELP.
BUT IT'S STRANGE. HE SAID *THIS* SHAMAN FIGHT.
THAT WAS 500 YEARS AGO. DOESN'T HE KNOW?
AND THAT OVER SOUL...
I DON'T SENSE ...
... MATAMUNE'S SOUL HERE.
THEN...
I DON'T KNOW.
ALL I KNOW IS ...
I GOTTA DEFEAT HIM...
CHAK
... TO GET OUT OF HELL.

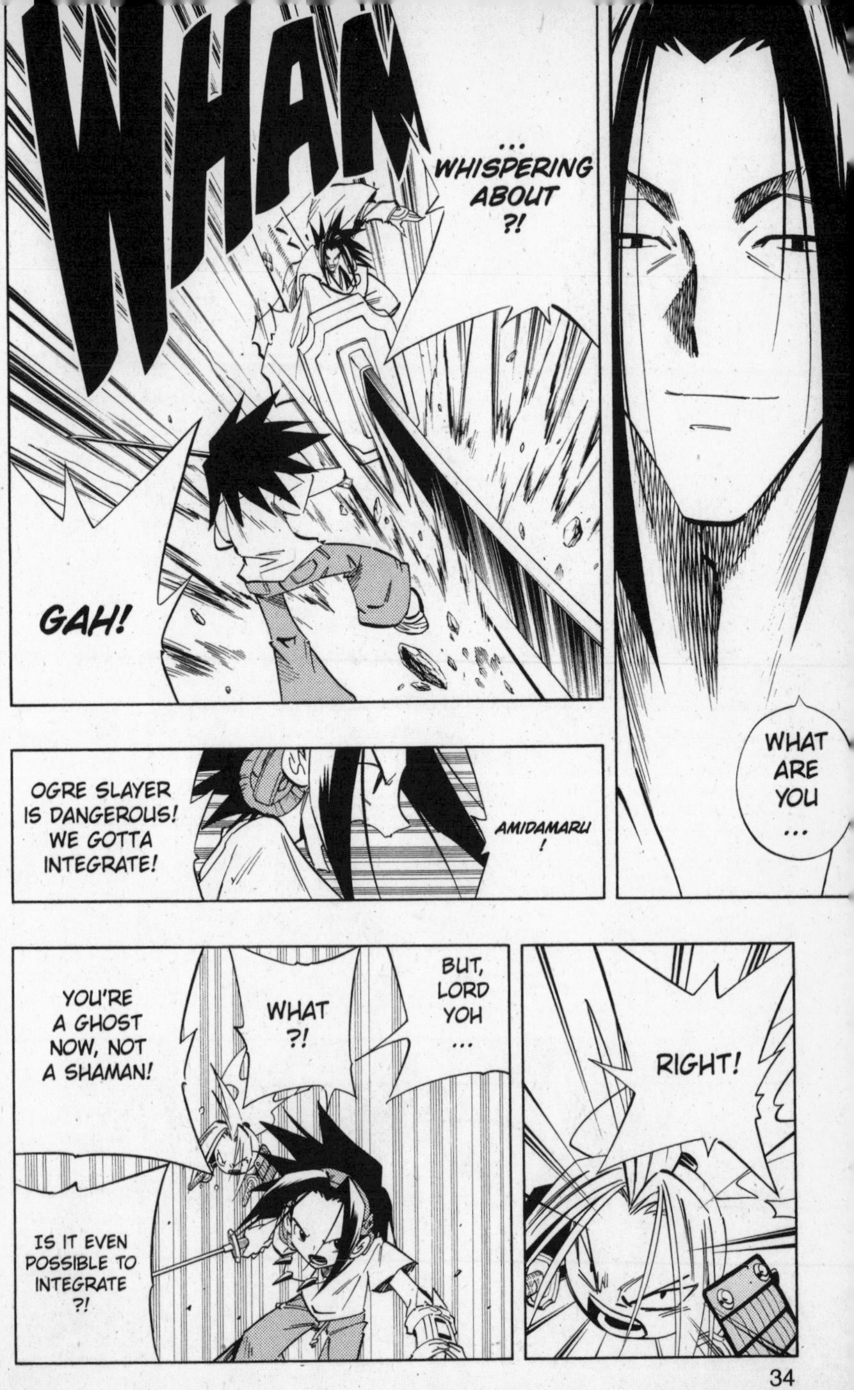
WHAT ARE YOU ...
... WHISPERING ABOUT ?!
WHAM
GAH!
AMIDAMARU!
OGRE SLAYER IS DANGEROUS! WE GOTTA INTEGRATE!
RIGHT!
BUT, LORD YOH ...
WHAT ?!
YOU'RE A GHOST NOW, NOT A SHAMAN!
IS IT EVEN POSSIBLE TO INTEGRATE ?!

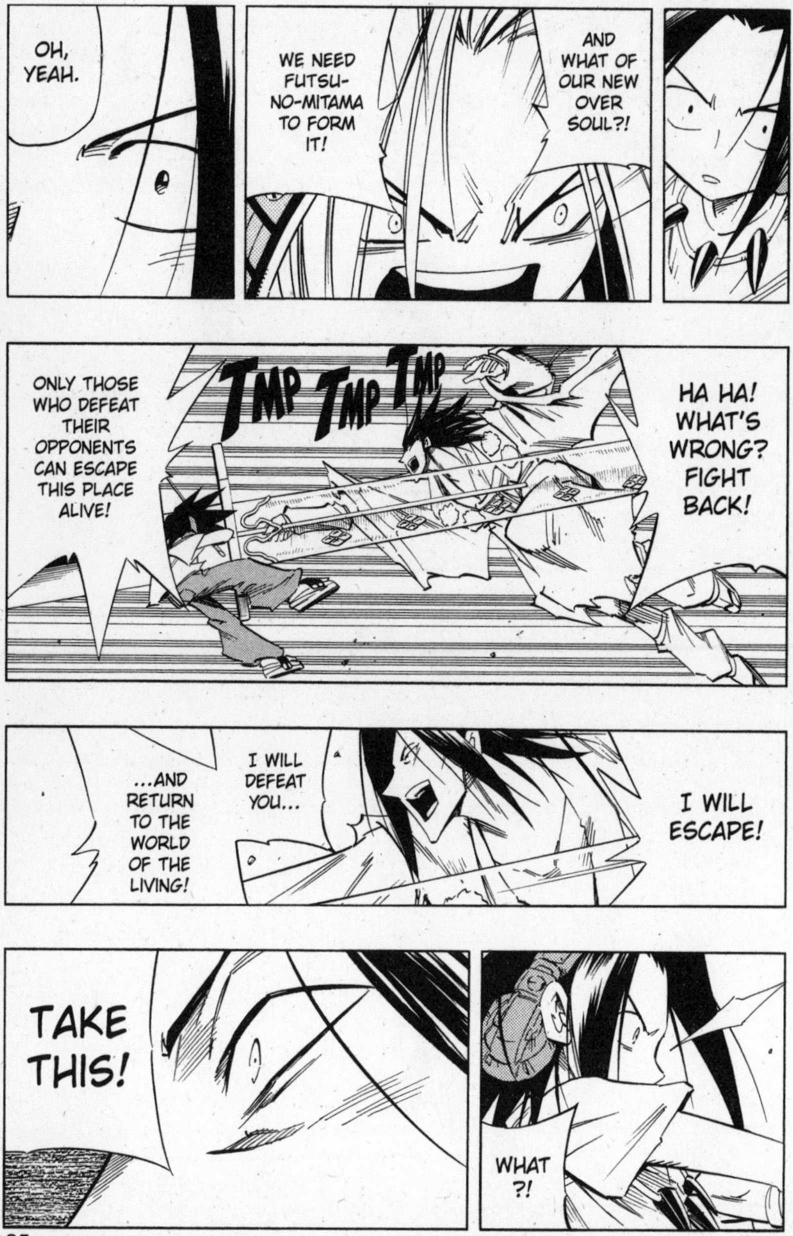
AND WHAT OF OUR NEW OVER SOUL?!
WE NEED FUTSU-NO-MITAMA TO FORM IT!
OH, YEAH.
HA HA! WHAT'S WRONG? FIGHT BACK!
TMP TMP TMP
ONLY THOSE WHO DEFEAT THEIR OPPONENTS CAN ESCAPE THIS PLACE ALIVE!
I WILL ESCAPE!
I WILL DEFEAT YOU...
...AND RETURN TO THE WORLD OF THE LIVING!
WHAT ?!
TAKE THIS!

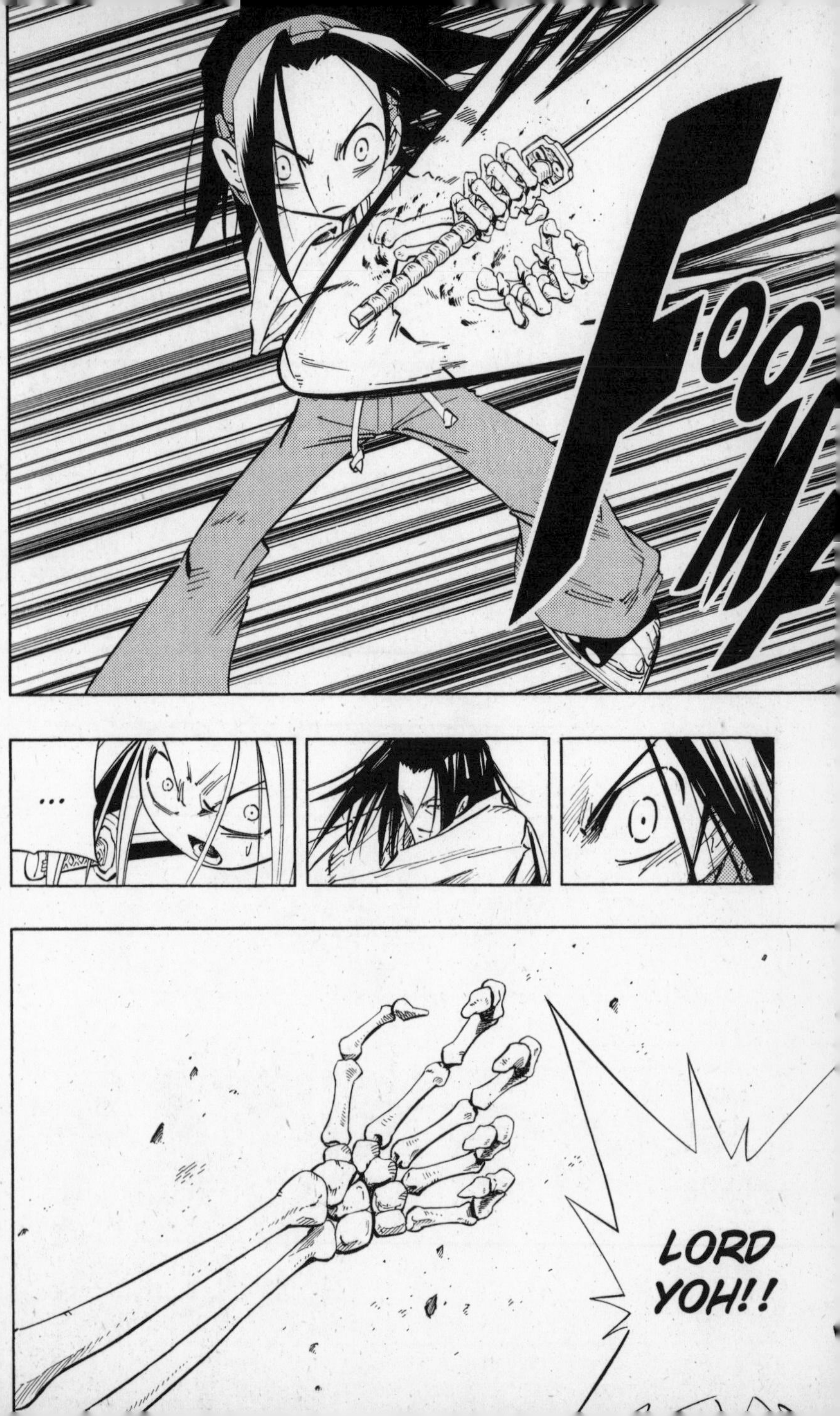
FOOM
...
LORD YOH!!

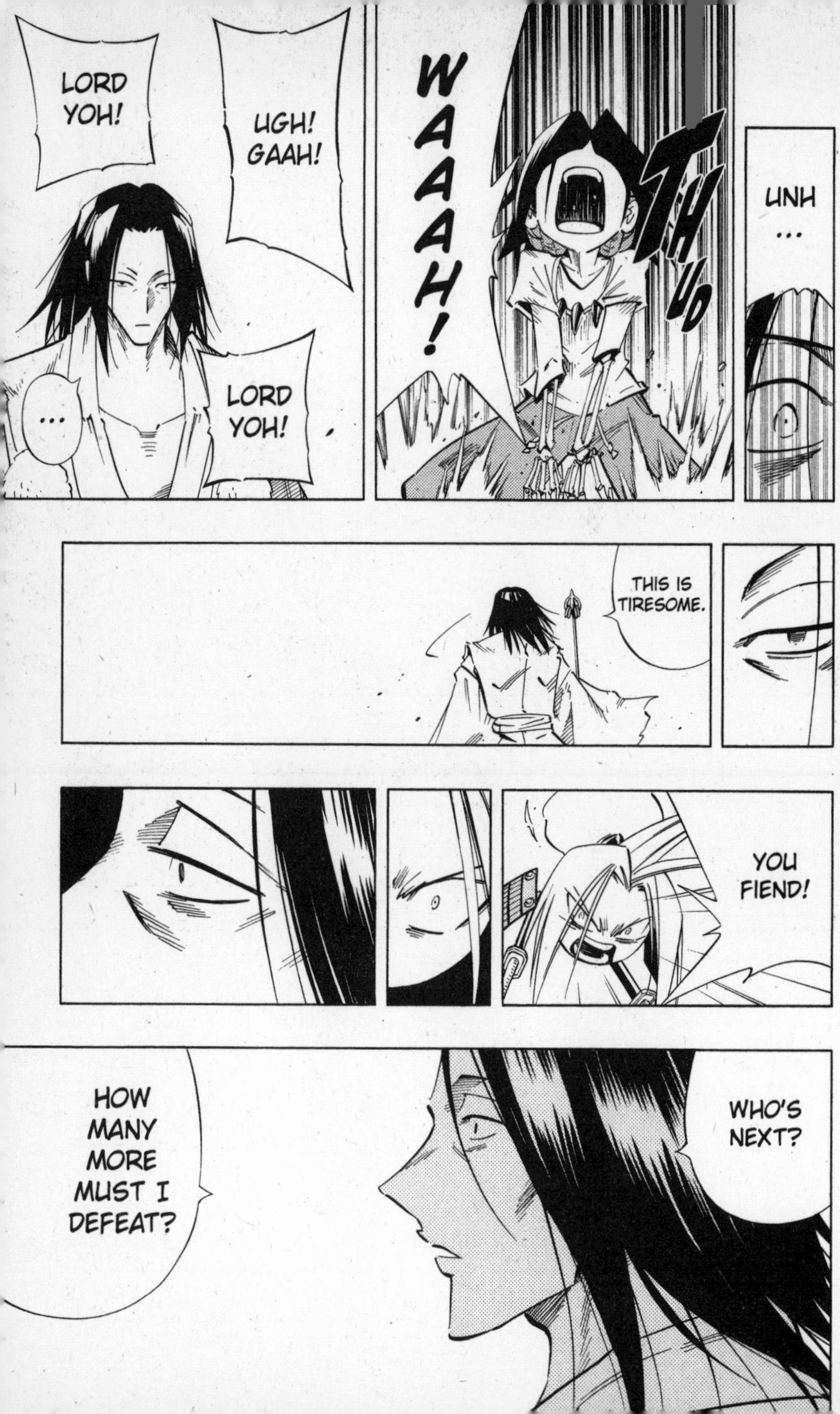
UNH ...
WAAAAH!
THUD
UGH! GAAH!
LORD YOH!
LORD YOH!
...
THIS IS TIRESOME.
YOU FIEND!
WHO'S NEXT?
HOW MANY MORE MUST I DEFEAT?

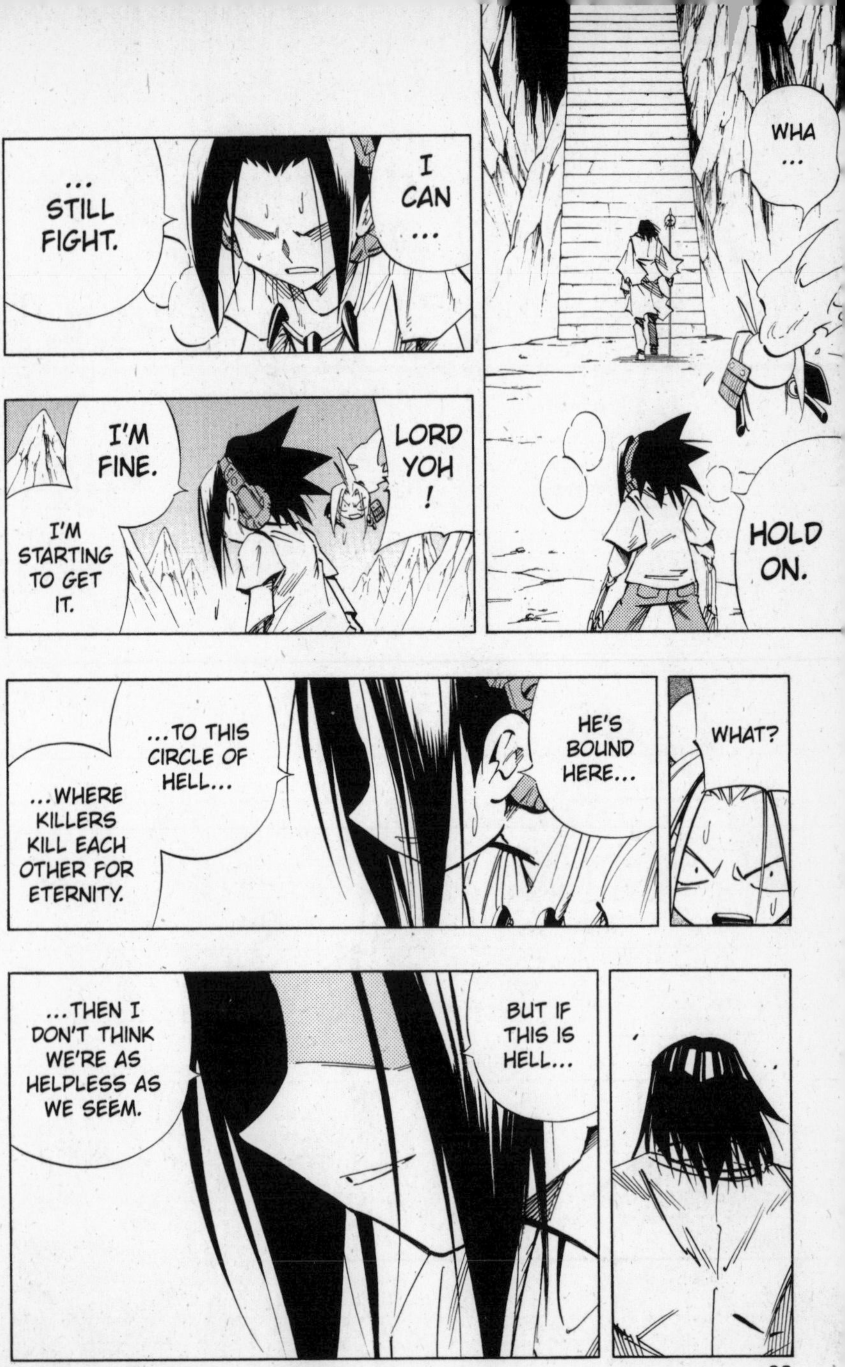
WHA ...
HOLD ON.
I CAN ...
... STILL FIGHT.
LORD YOH !
I'M FINE.
I'M STARTING TO GET IT.
WHAT?
HE'S BOUND HERE...
...TO THIS CIRCLE OF HELL...
...WHERE KILLERS KILL EACH OTHER FOR ETERNITY.
BUT IF THIS IS HELL...
...THEN I DON'T THINK WE'RE AS HELPLESS AS WE SEEM.

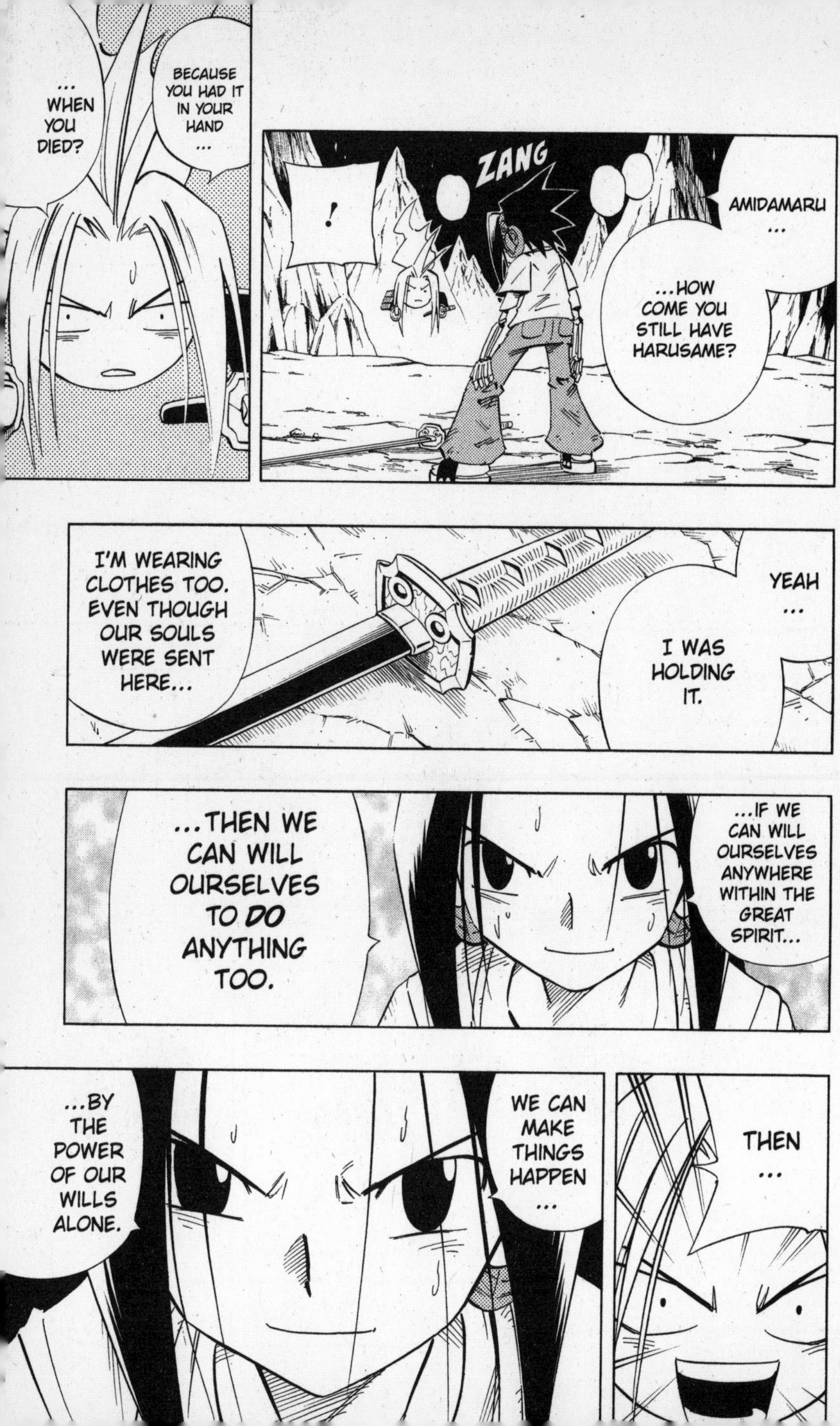
AMIDAMARU ...
...HOW COME YOU STILL HAVE HARUSAME?
ZANG
!
BECAUSE YOU HAD IT IN YOUR HAND ...
... WHEN YOU DIED?
YEAH ...
I WAS HOLDING IT.
I'M WEARING CLOTHES TOO. EVEN THOUGH OUR SOULS WERE SENT HERE...
...IF WE CAN WILL OURSELVES ANYWHERE WITHIN THE GREAT SPIRIT...
...THEN WE CAN WILL OURSELVES TO DO ANYTHING TOO.
THEN ...
WE CAN MAKE THINGS HAPPEN ...
...BY THE POWER OF OUR WILLS ALONE.

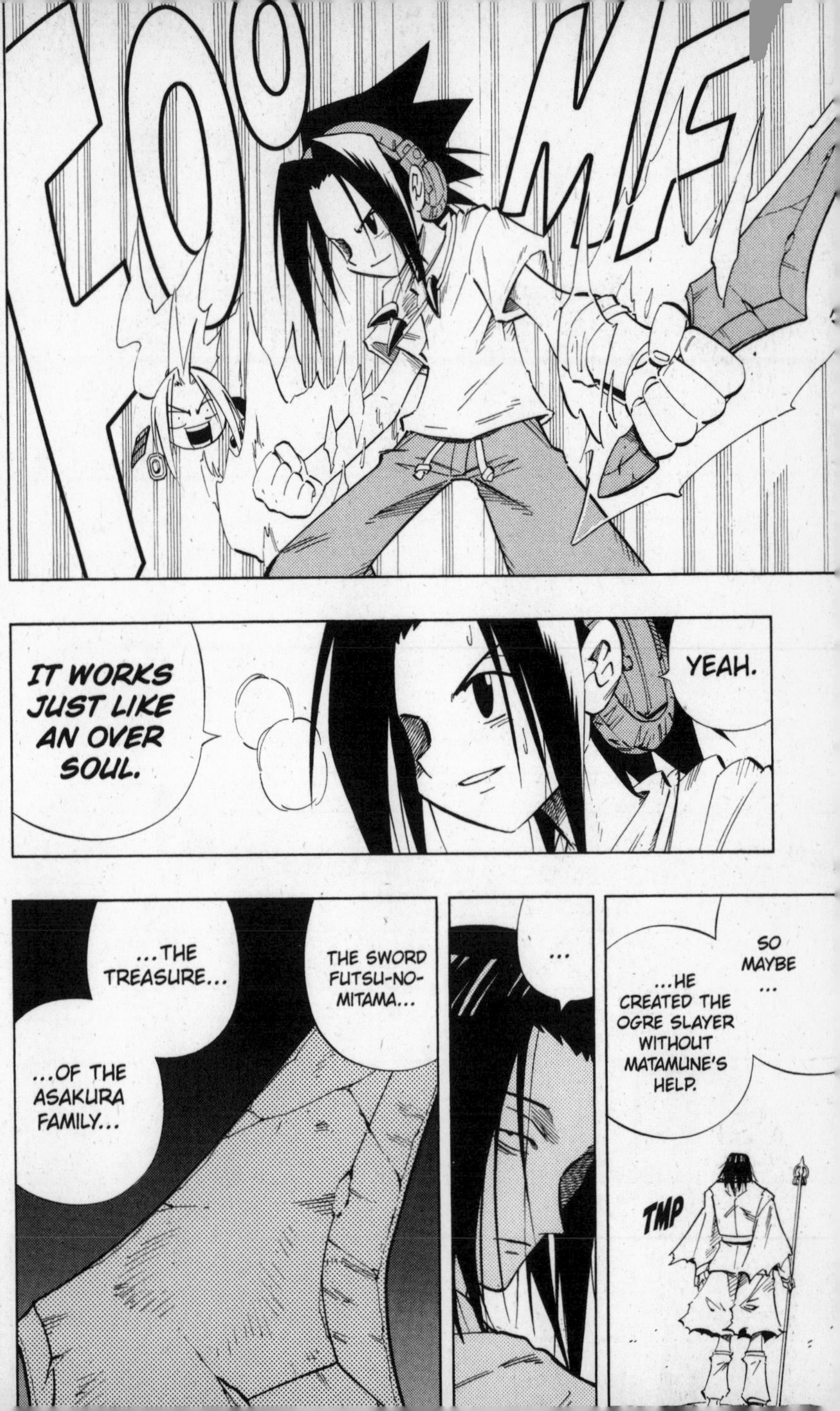
ZOOMF
YEAH.
IT WORKS JUST LIKE AN OVER SOUL.
SO MAYBE ...
...HE CREATED THE OGRE SLAYER WITHOUT MATAMUNE'S HELP.
TMP
...
THE SWORD FUTSU-NO-MITAMA...
...THE TREASURE...
...OF THE ASAKURA FAMILY...

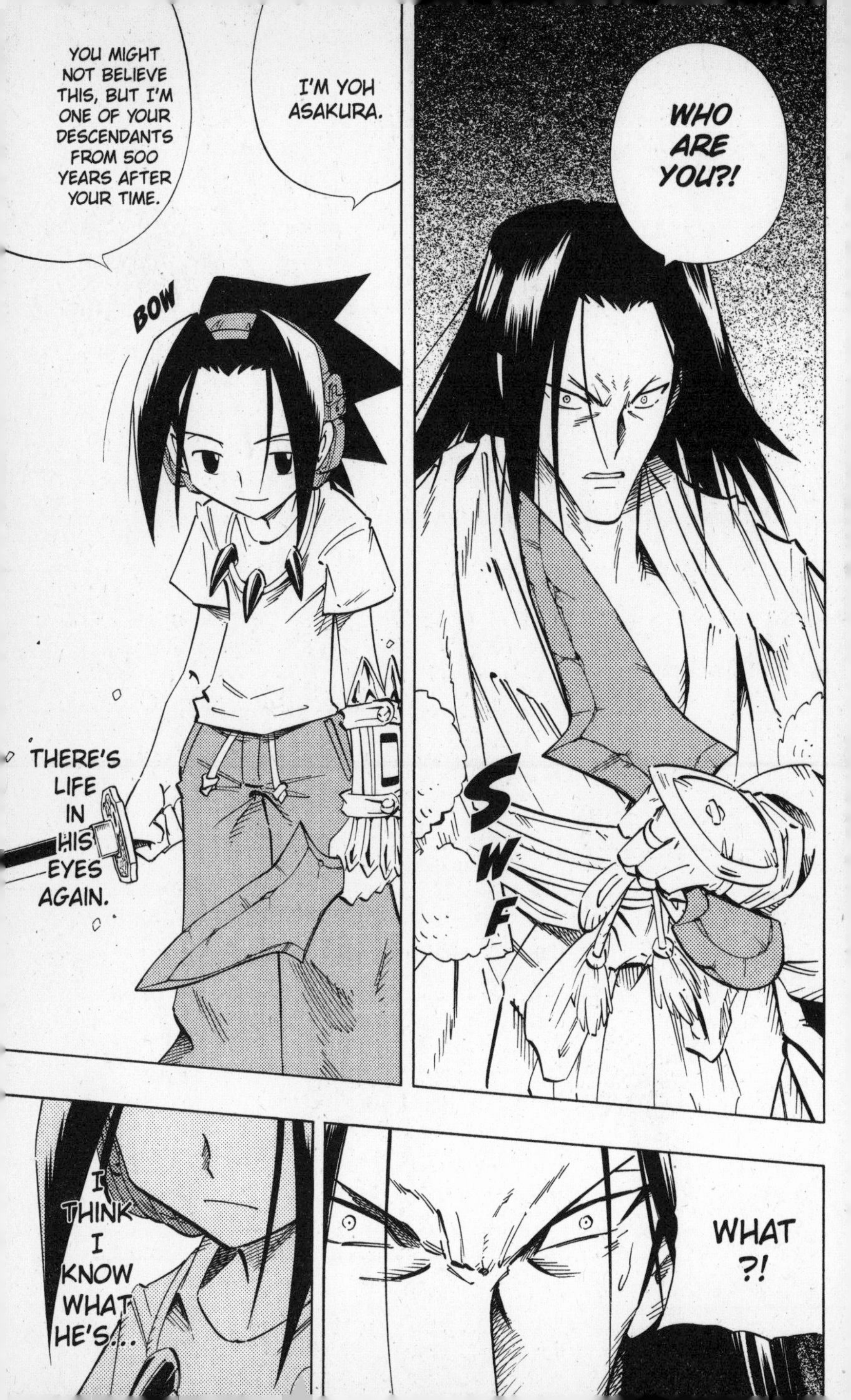
WHO ARE YOU?!
SWF
I'M YOH ASAKURA.
YOU MIGHT NOT BELIEVE THIS, BUT I'M ONE OF YOUR DESCENDANTS FROM 500 YEARS AFTER YOUR TIME.
BOW
THERE'S LIFE IN HIS EYES AGAIN.
WHAT?!
I THINK I KNOW WHAT HE'S...

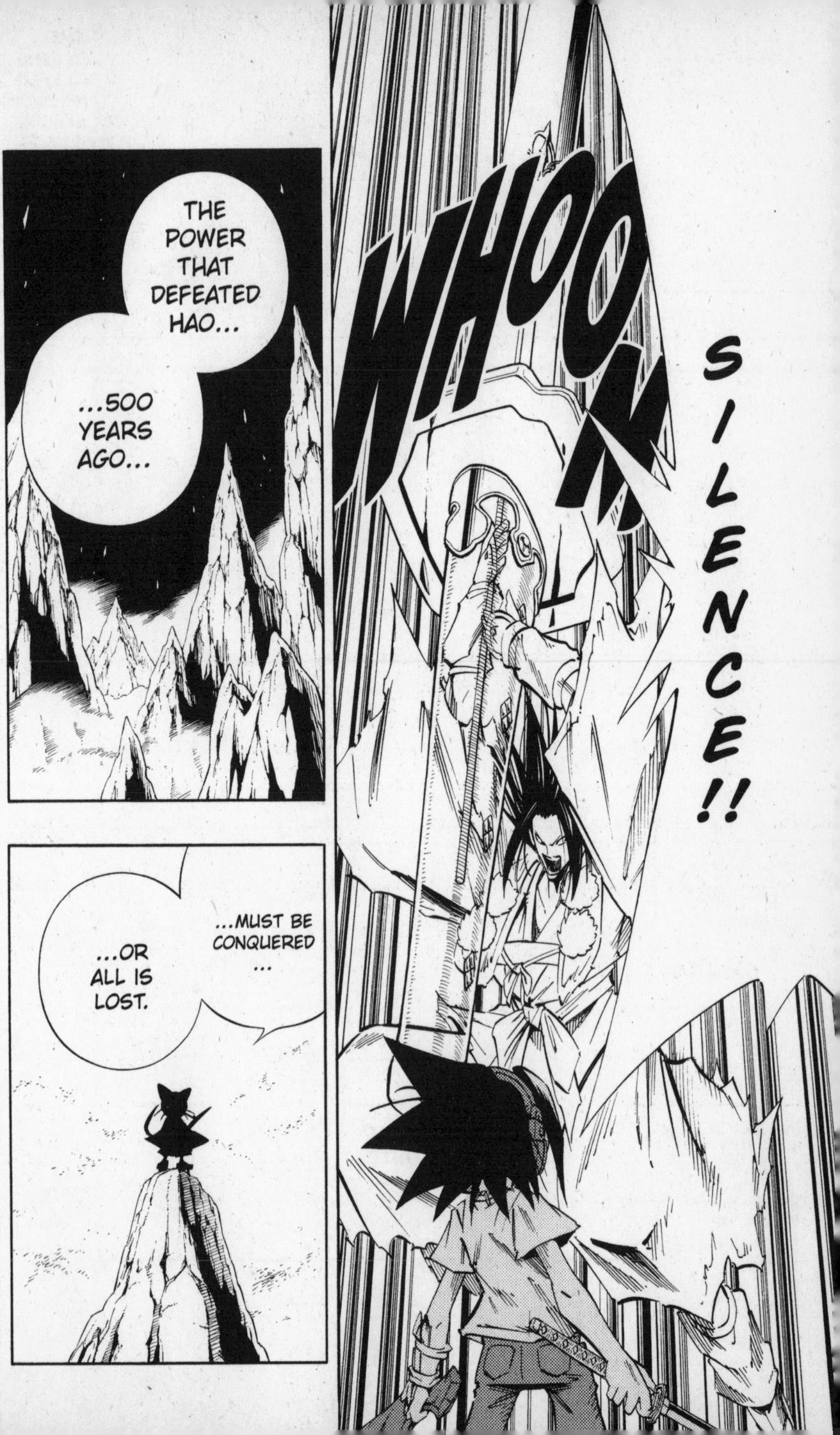
WHOOM
SILENCE!!
THE POWER THAT DEFEATED HAO...
...500 YEARS AGO...
...MUST BE CONQUERED ...
...OR ALL IS LOST.

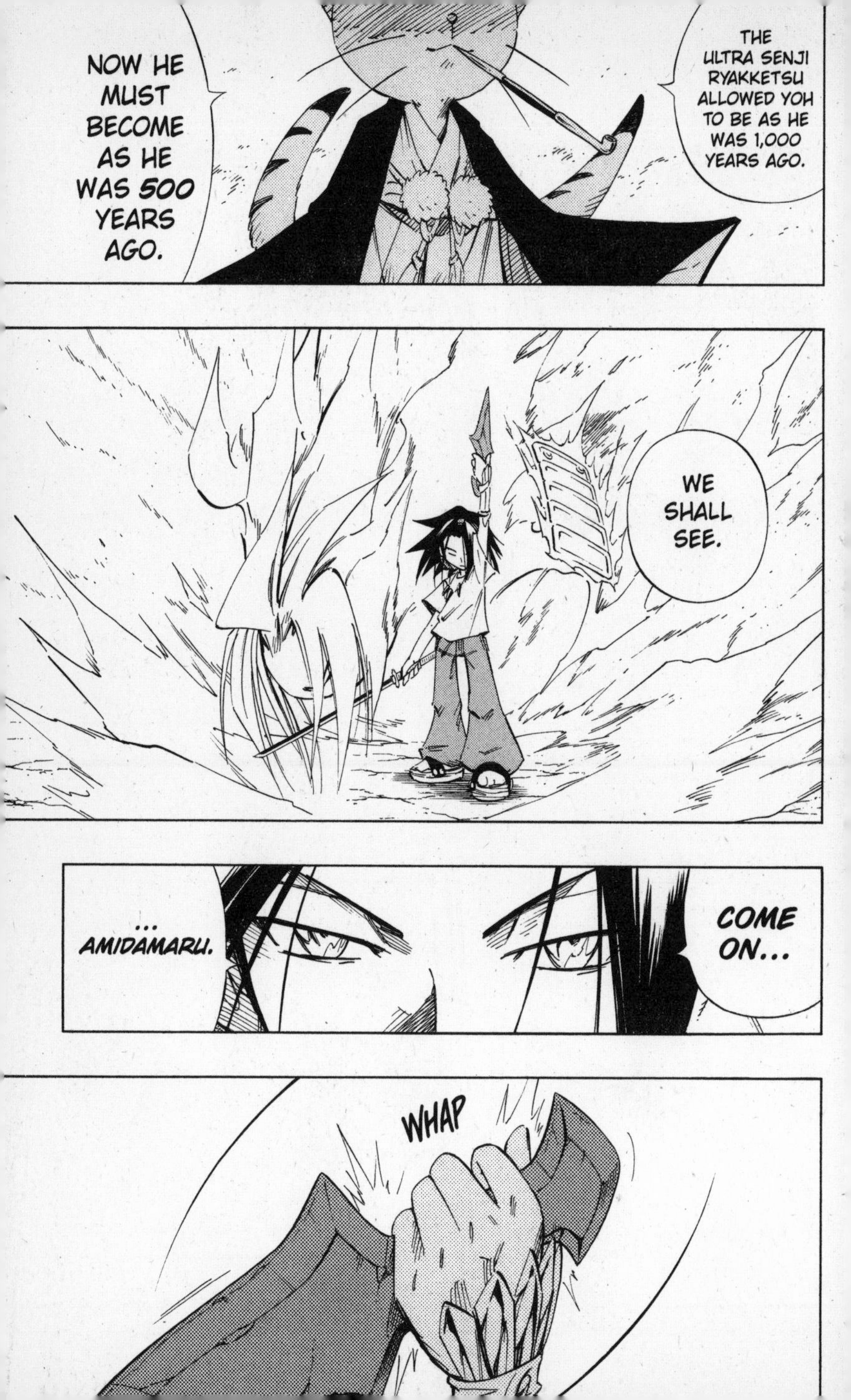
THE ULTRA SENJI RYAKKETSU ALLOWED YOH TO BE AS HE WAS 1,000 YEARS AGO.
NOW HE MUST BECOME AS HE WAS 500 YEARS AGO.
WE SHALL SEE.
COME ON...
... AMIDAMARU.
WHAP

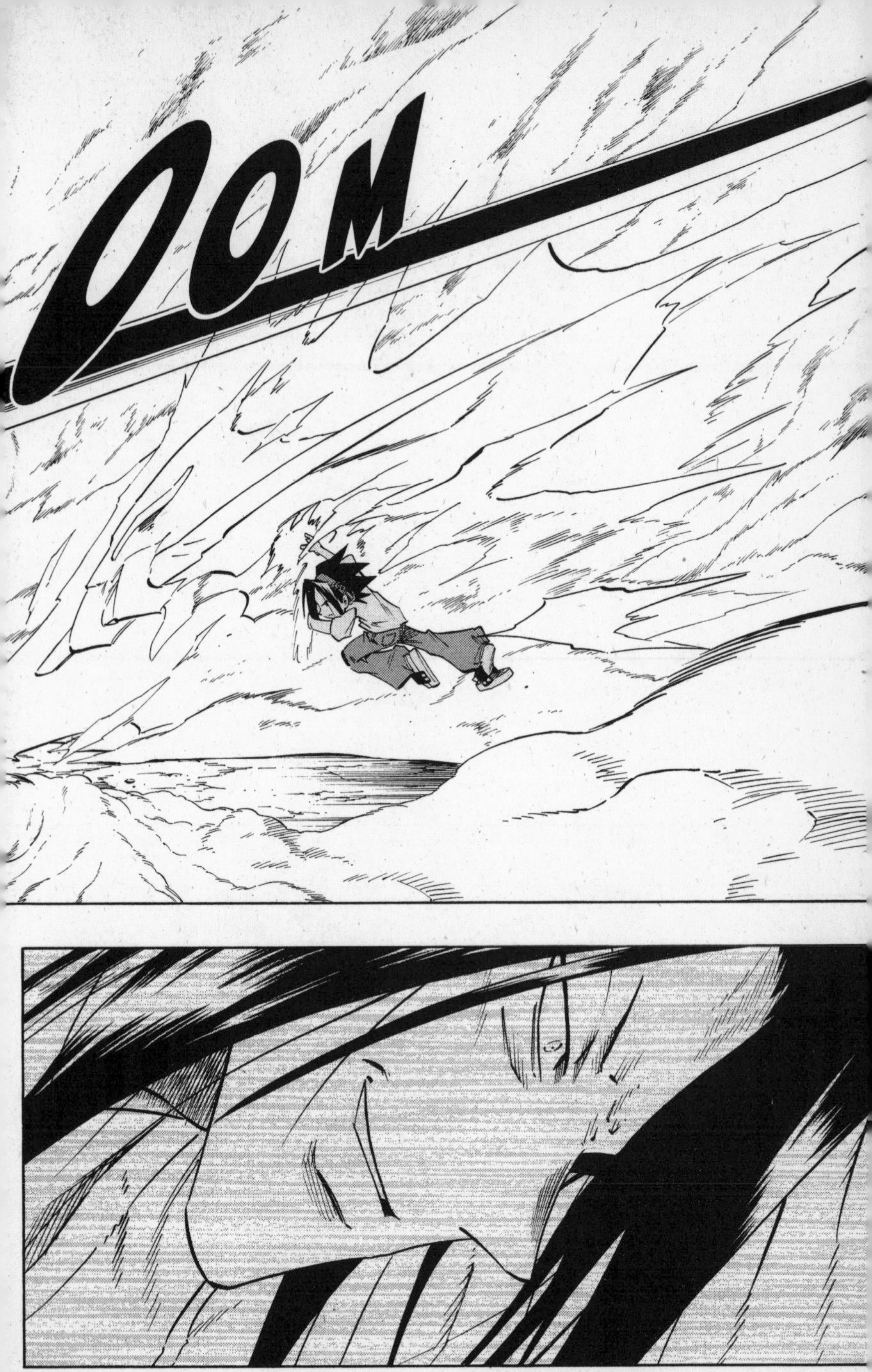
OOM

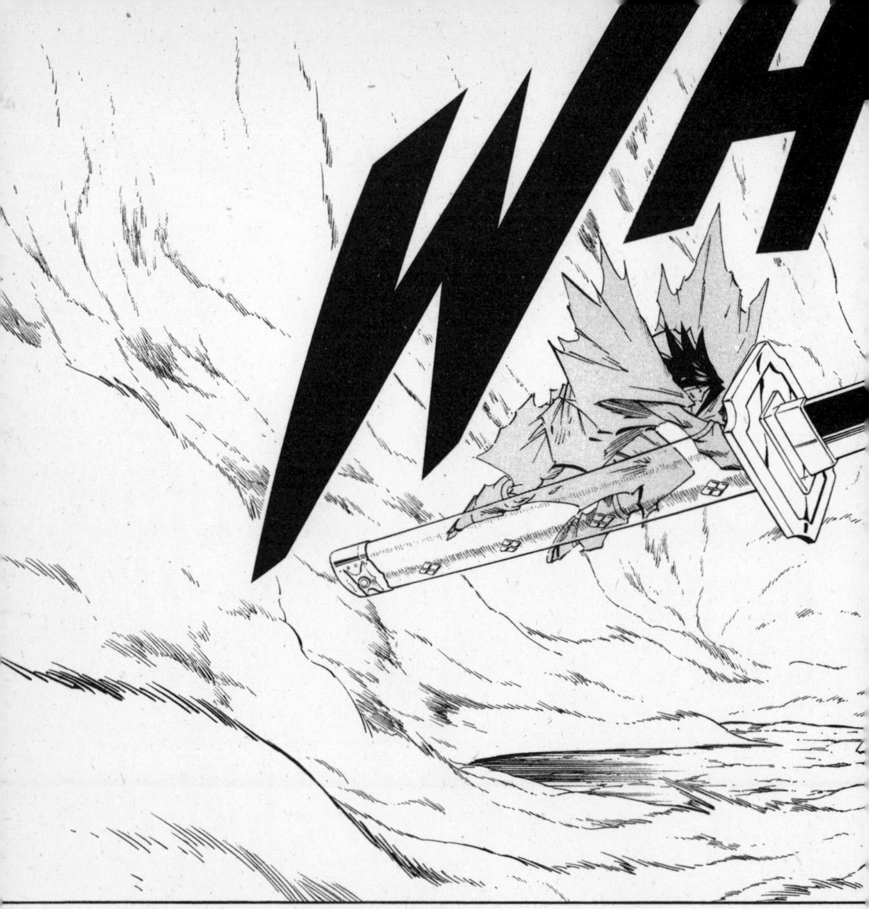
WH
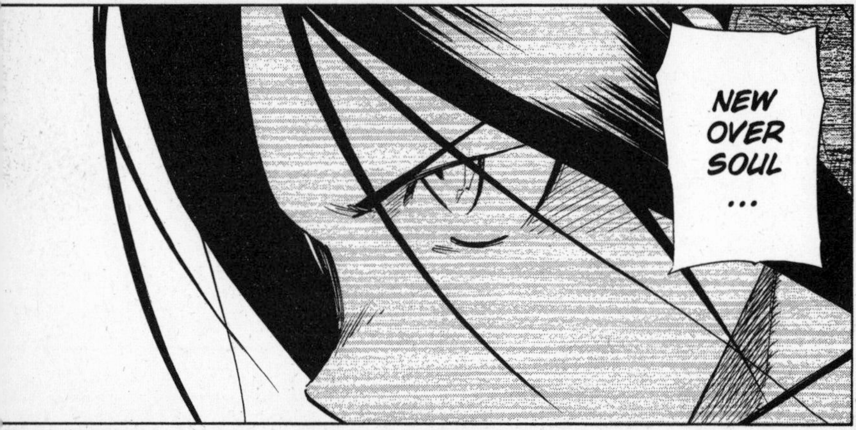
NEW OVER SOUL ...

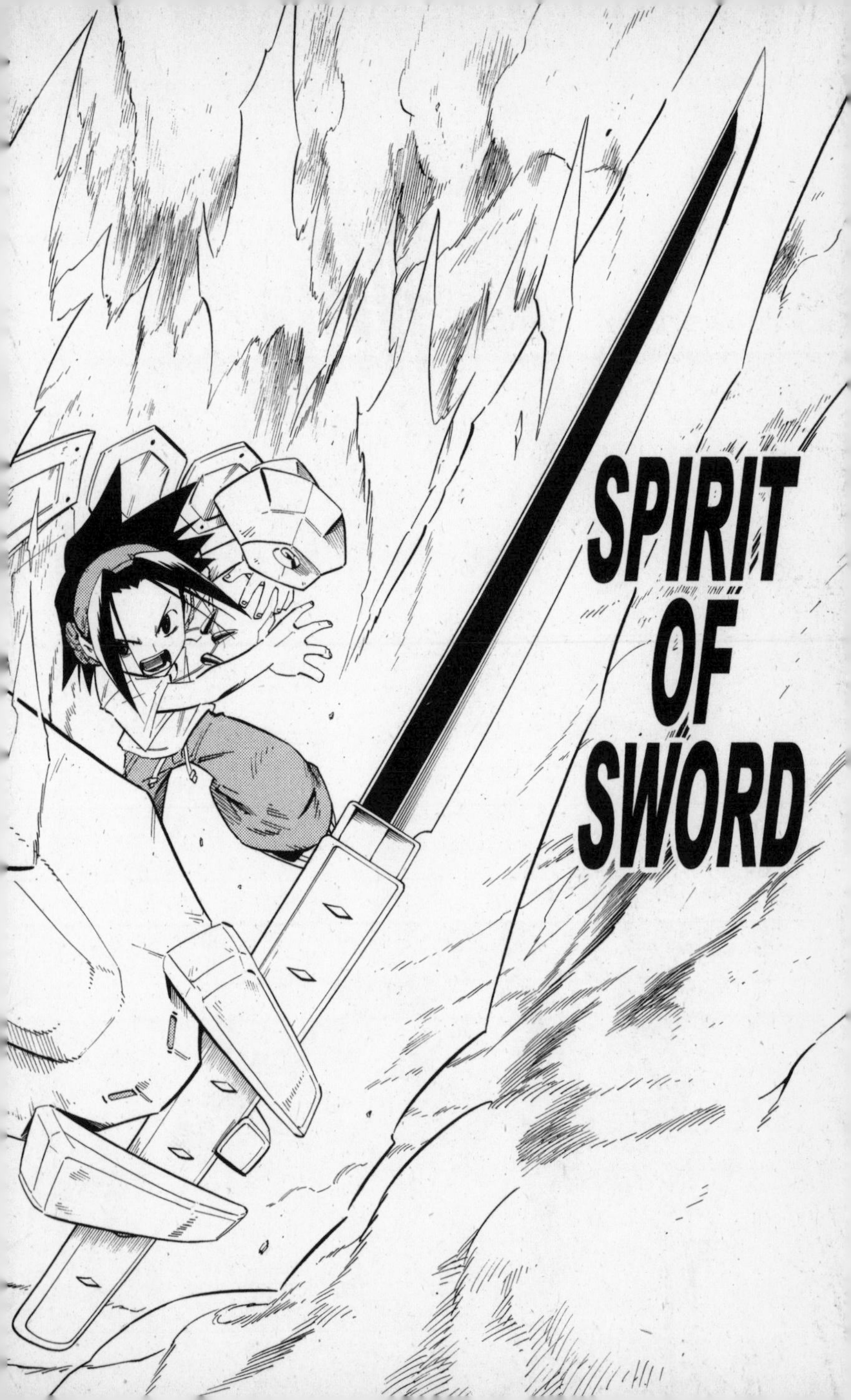
SPIRIT OF SWORD

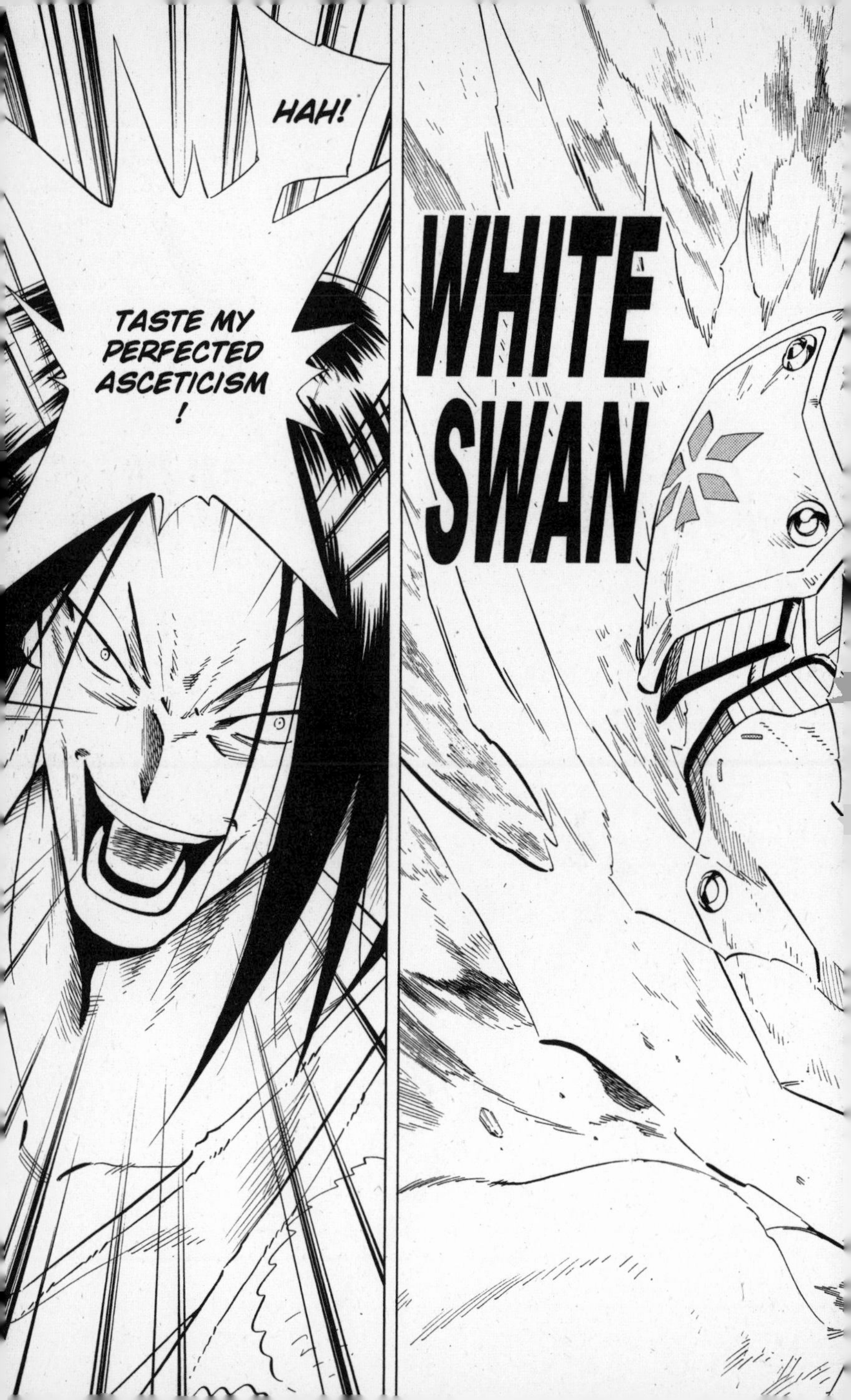
WHITE SWAN
HAH!
TASTE MY PERFECTED ASCETICISM!

SHAMAN KING CHARACTER FILE No.140

2001
(JAN)

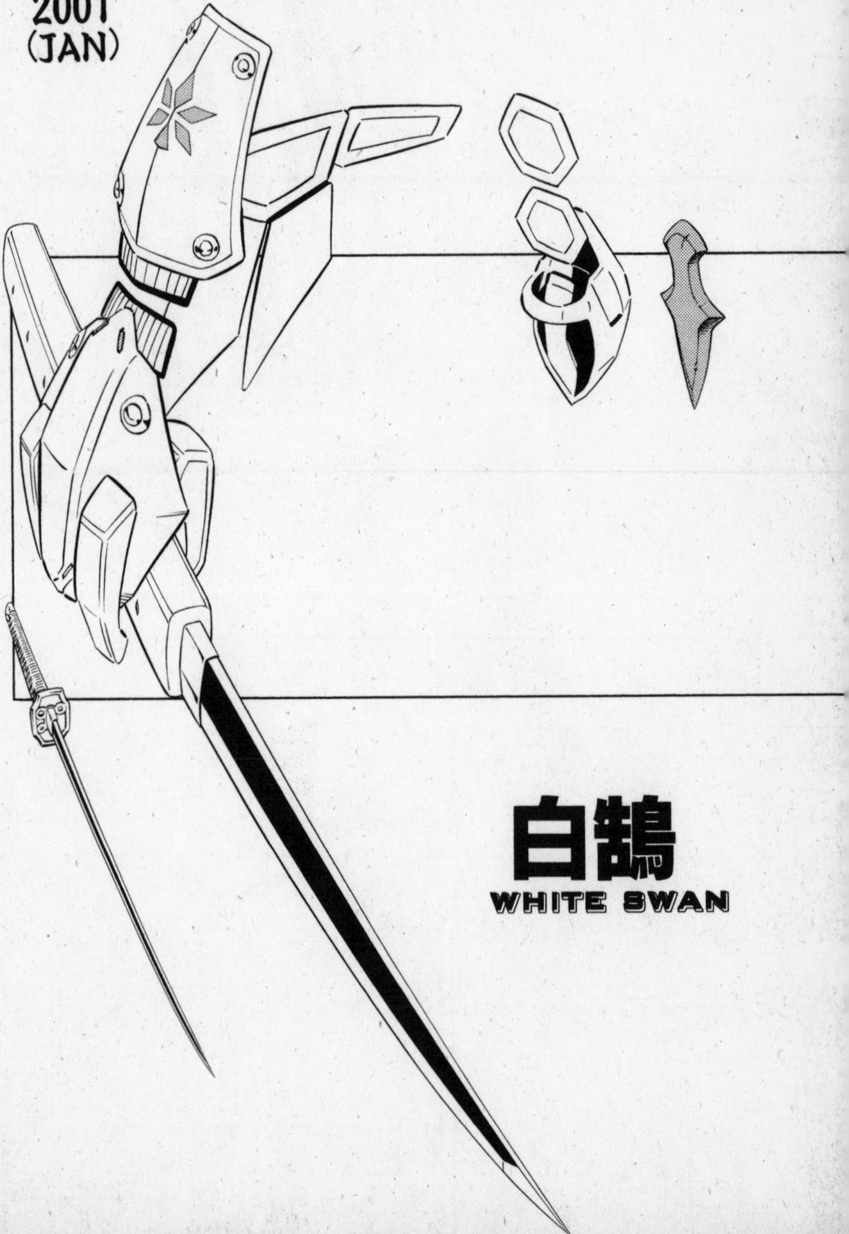

白鵠
WHITE SWAN

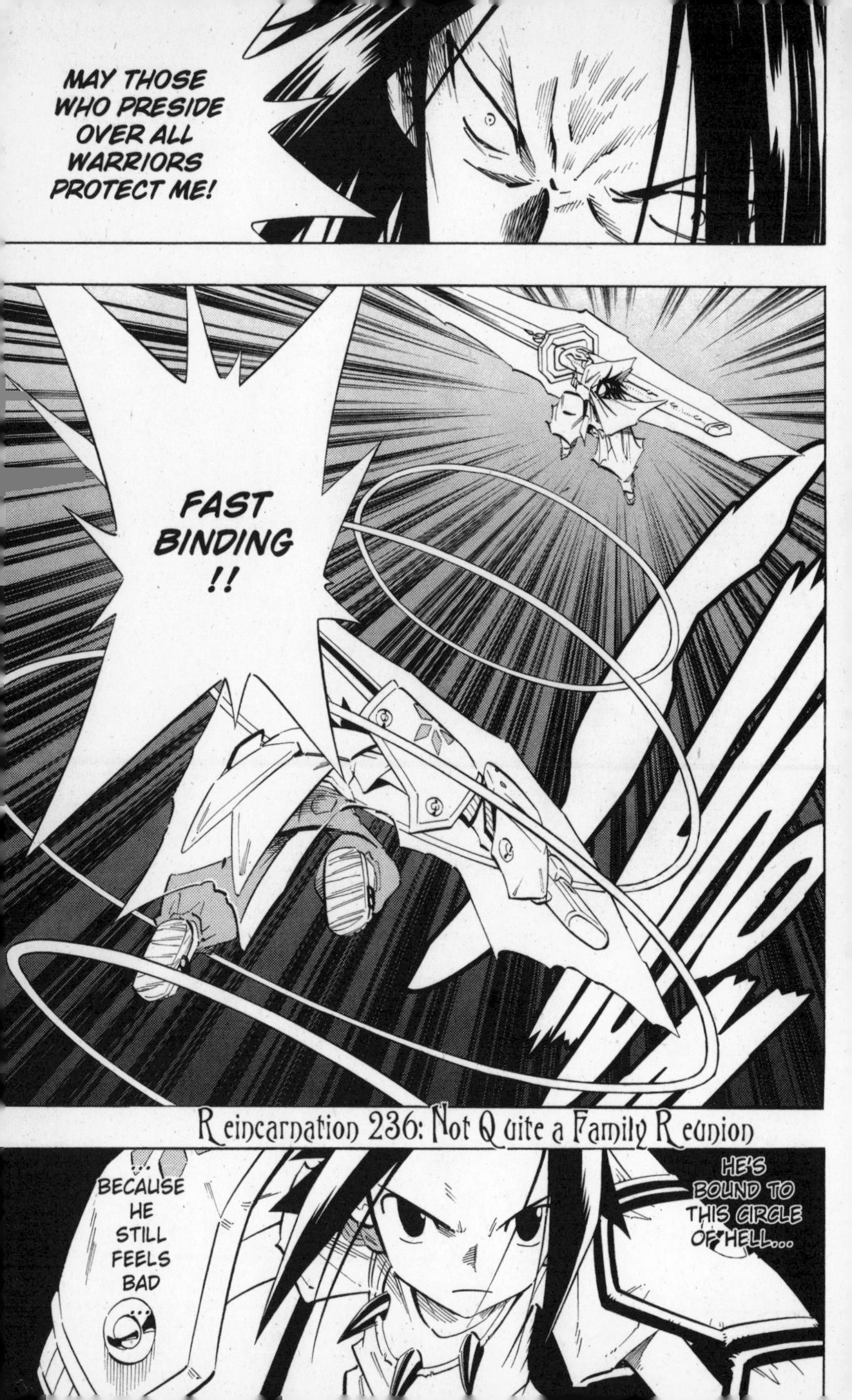
MAY THOSE WHO PRESIDE OVER ALL WARRIORS PROTECT ME!
FAST BINDING !!
HE'S BOUND TO THIS CIRCLE OF HELL...
...BECAUSE HE STILL FEELS BAD

Reincarnation 236: Not Quite a Family Reunion

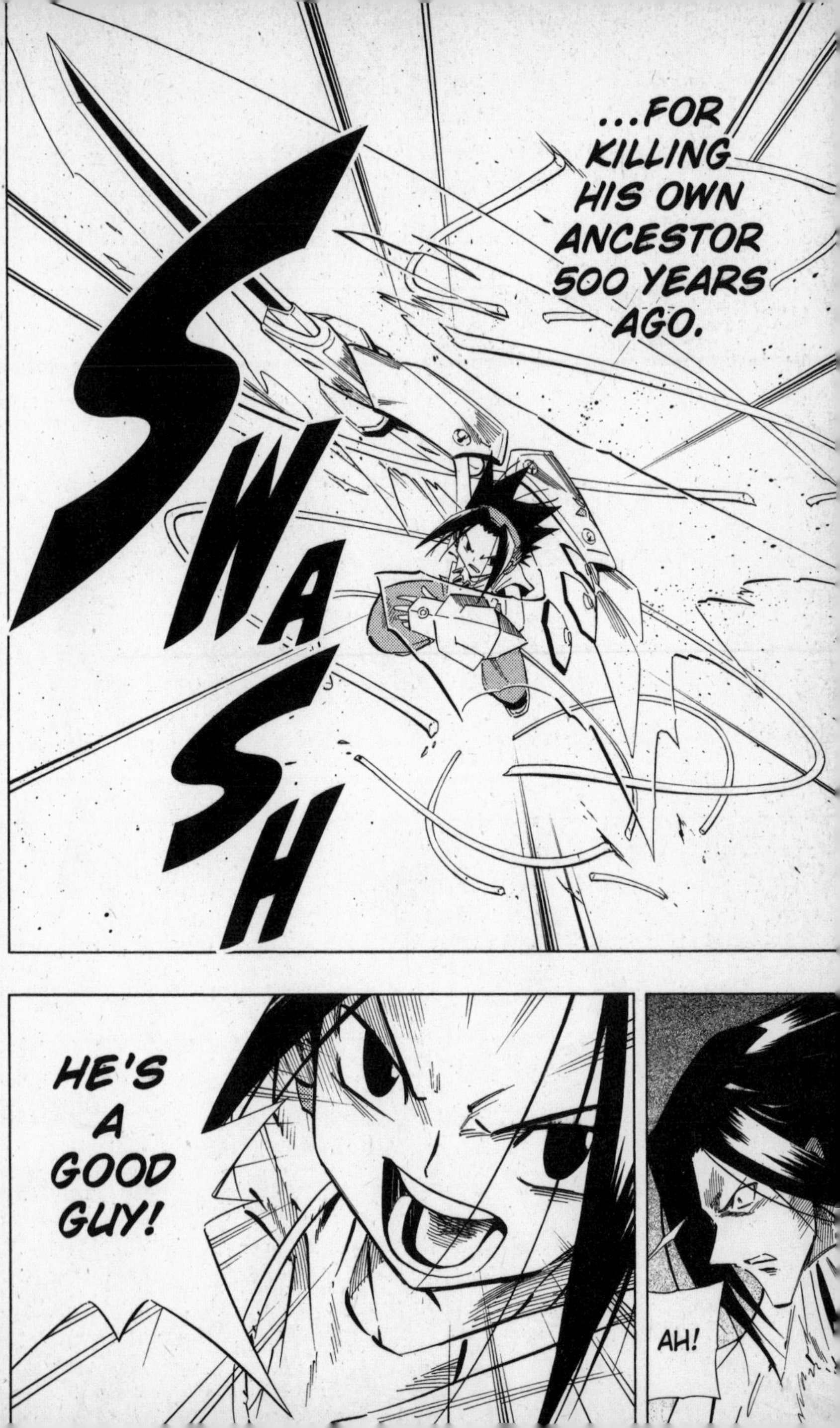
...FOR KILLING HIS OWN ANCESTOR 500 YEARS AGO.
SWASH
AH!
HE'S A GOOD GUY!

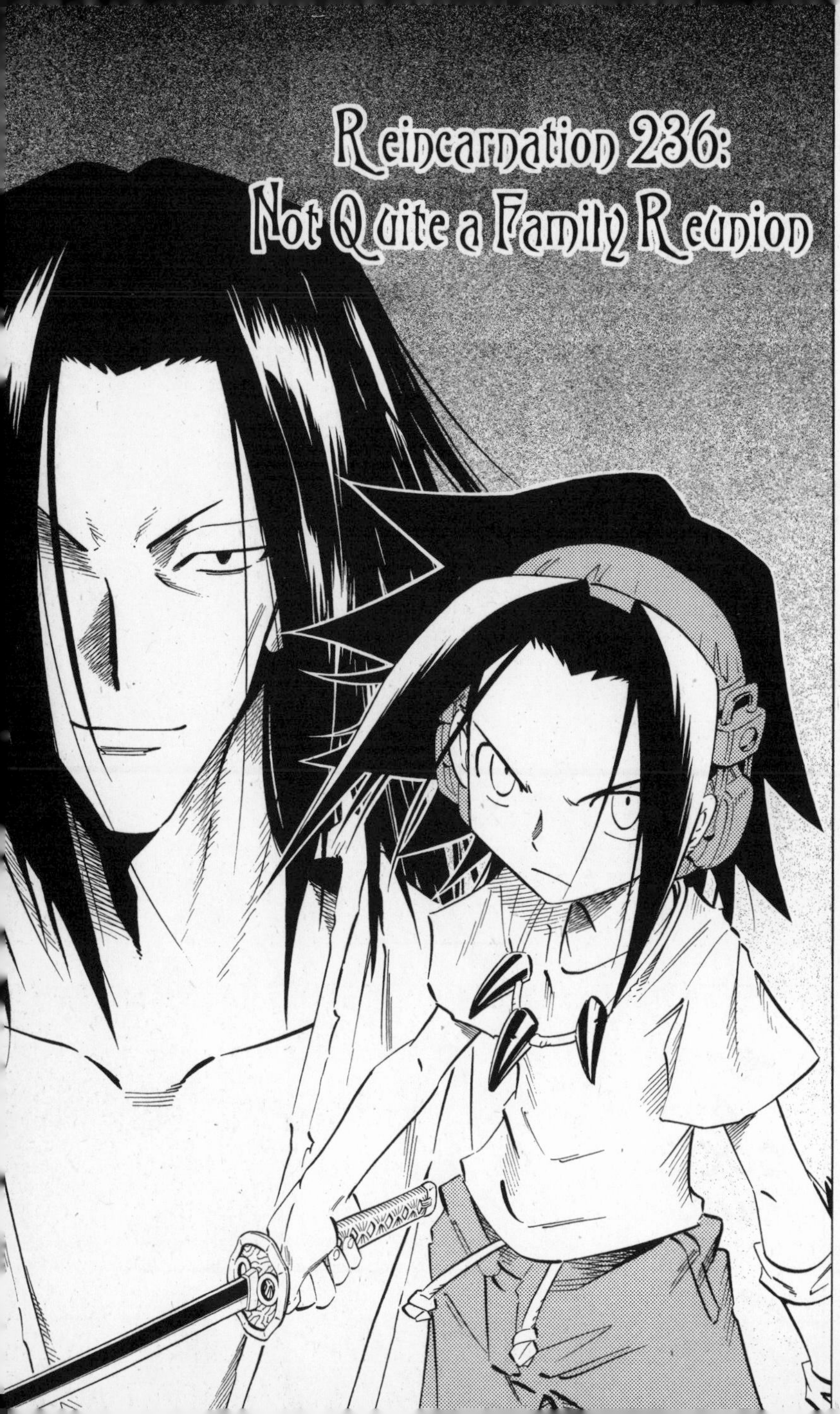
Reincarnation 236:
Not Quite a Family Reunion

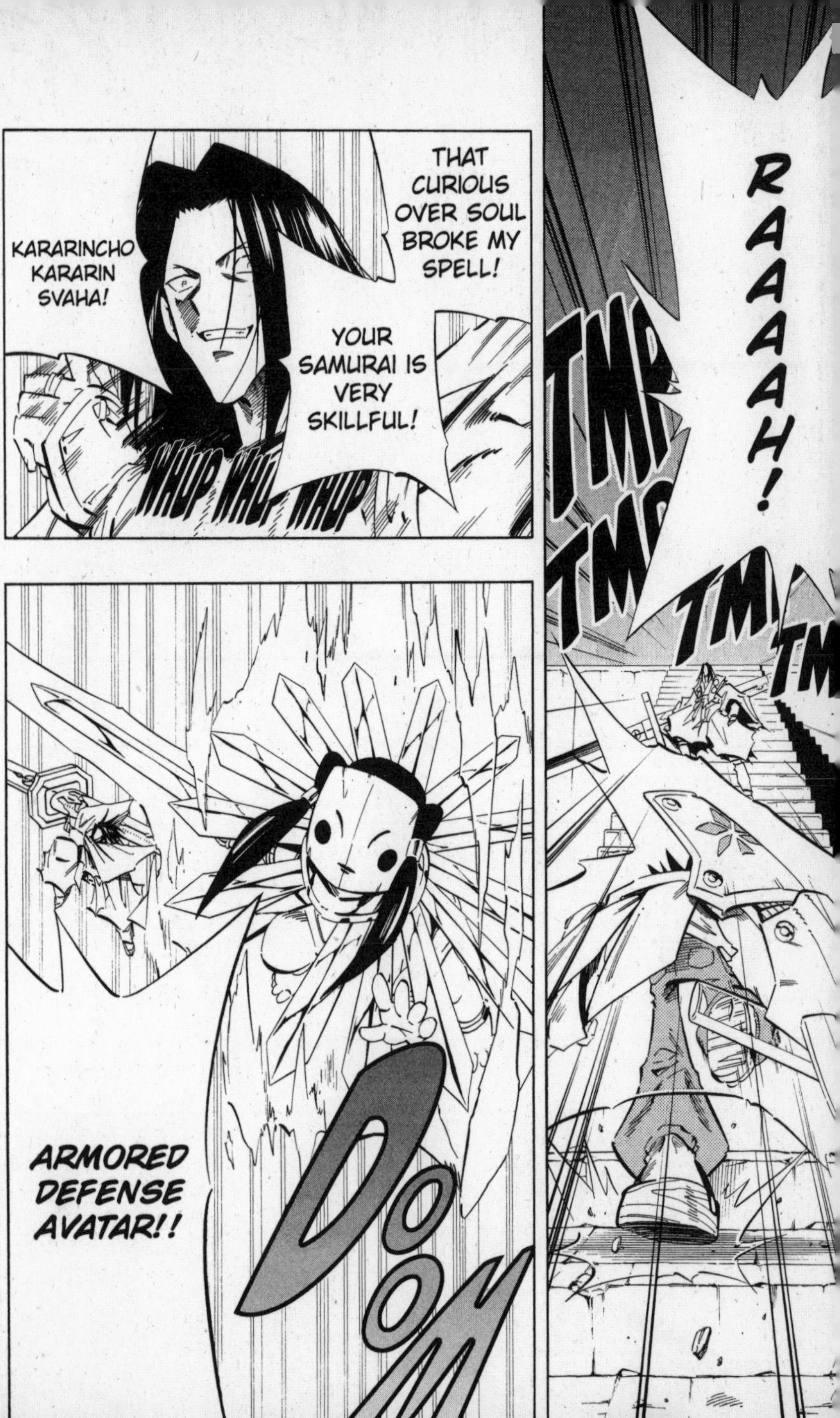
RAAAAAH!
TMP TMP
TM TM
THAT CURIOUS OVER SOUL BROKE MY SPELL!
KARARINCHO KARARIN SVAHA!
YOUR SAMURAI IS VERY SKILLFUL!
WHUP WHUP WHUP
DOOOM
ARMORED DEFENSE AVATAR!!

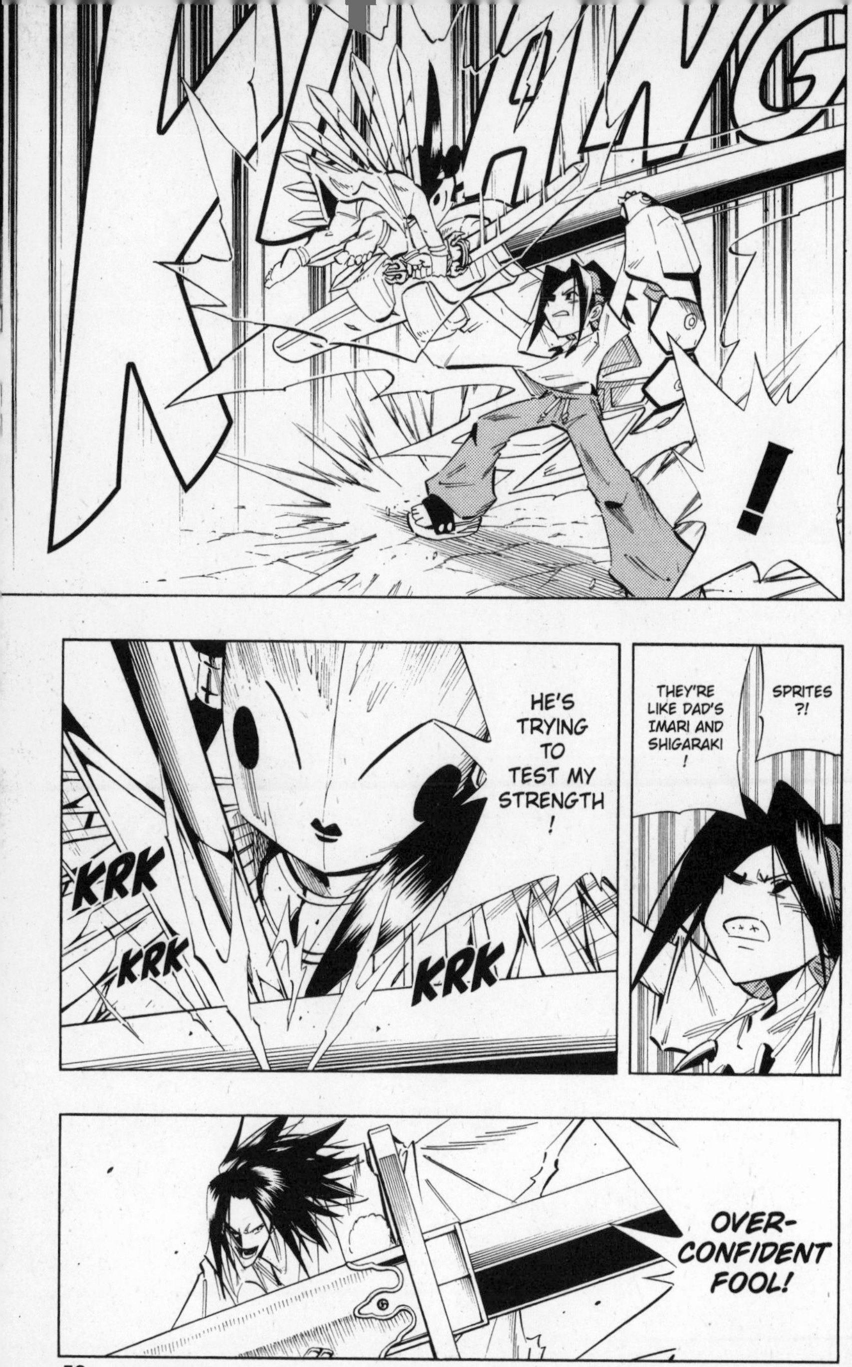
!
SPRITES ?!
THEY'RE LIKE DAD'S IMARI AND SHIGARAKI !
HE'S TRYING TO TEST MY STRENGTH !
KRK
KRK
KRK
OVER-CONFIDENT FOOL!

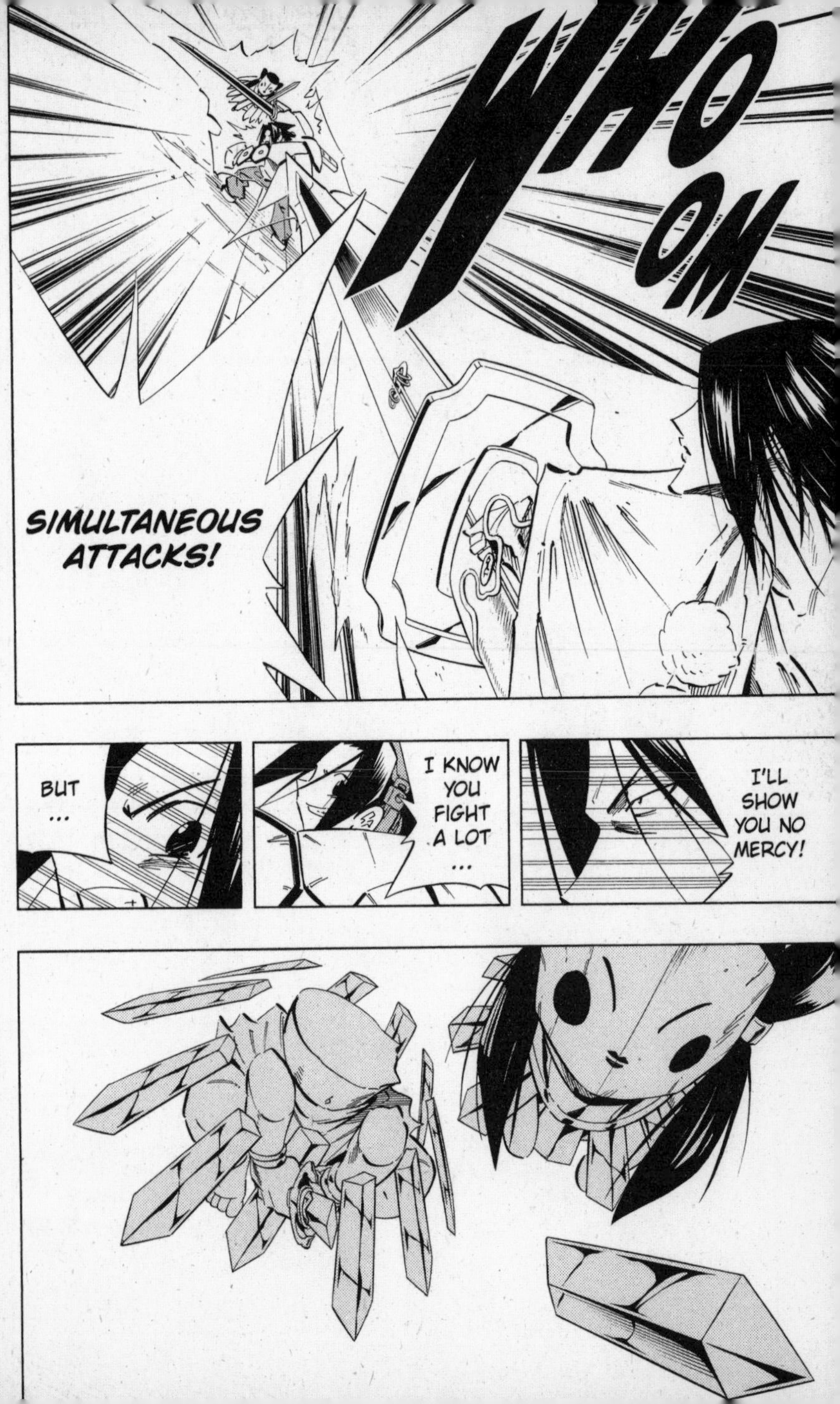
WHOOOM
SIMULTANEOUS ATTACKS!
I'LL SHOW YOU NO MERCY!
I KNOW YOU FIGHT A LOT ...
BUT ...

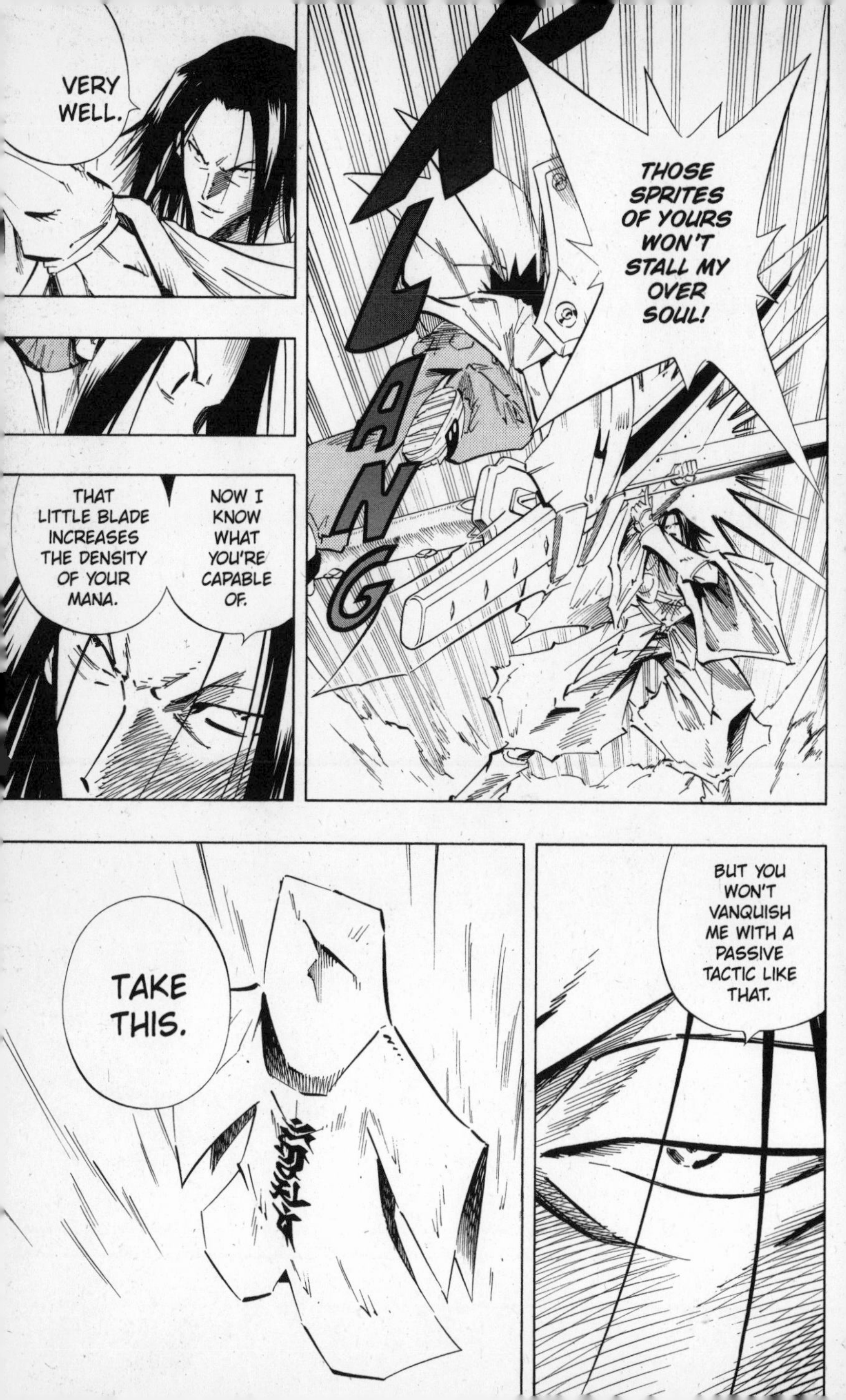
CLANG
THOSE SPRITES OF YOURS WON'T STALL MY OVER SOUL!
VERY WELL.
NOW I KNOW WHAT YOU'RE CAPABLE OF.
THAT LITTLE BLADE INCREASES THE DENSITY OF YOUR MANA.
BUT YOU WON'T VANQUISH ME WITH A PASSIVE TACTIC LIKE THAT.
TAKE THIS.

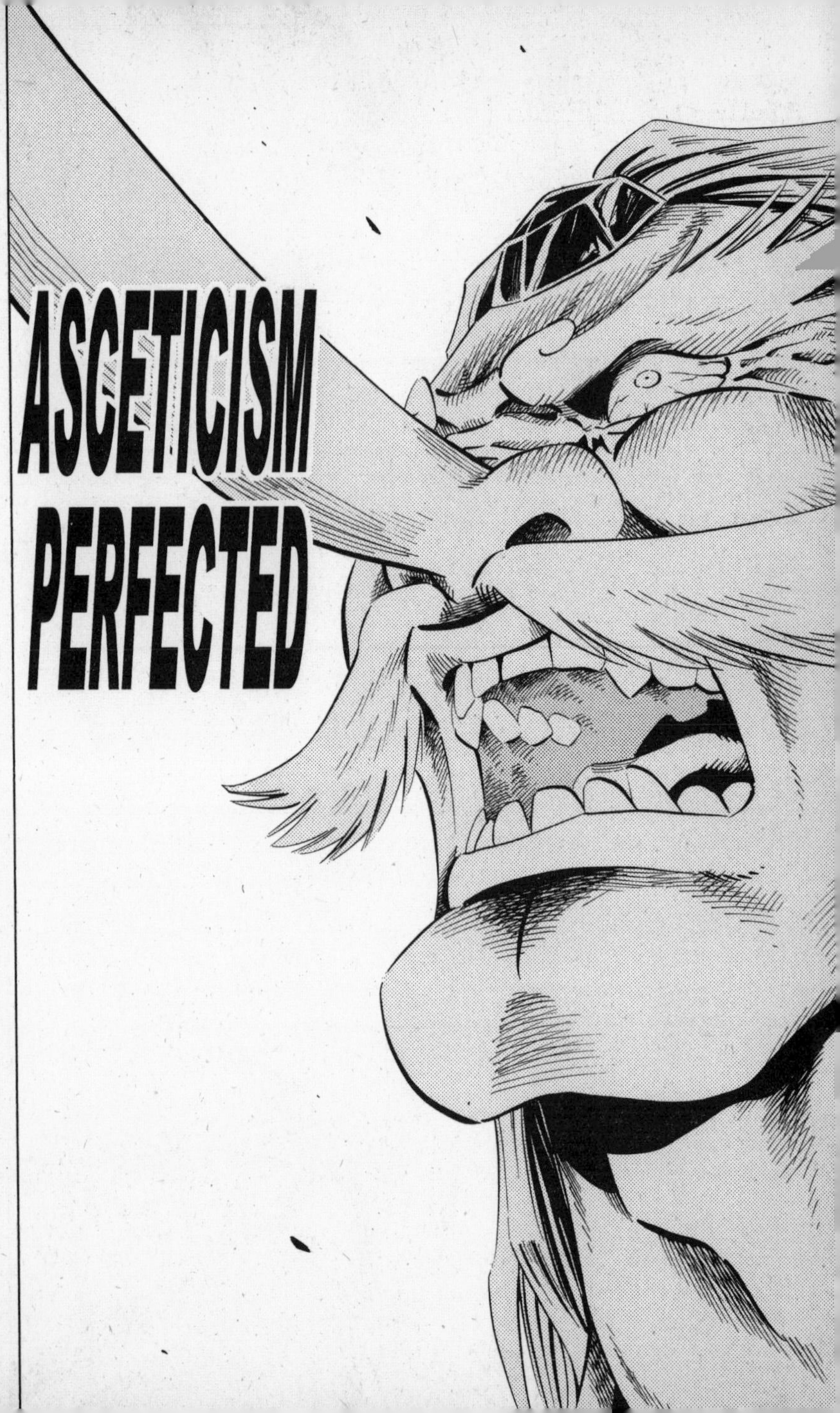
ASCETICISM
PERFECTED

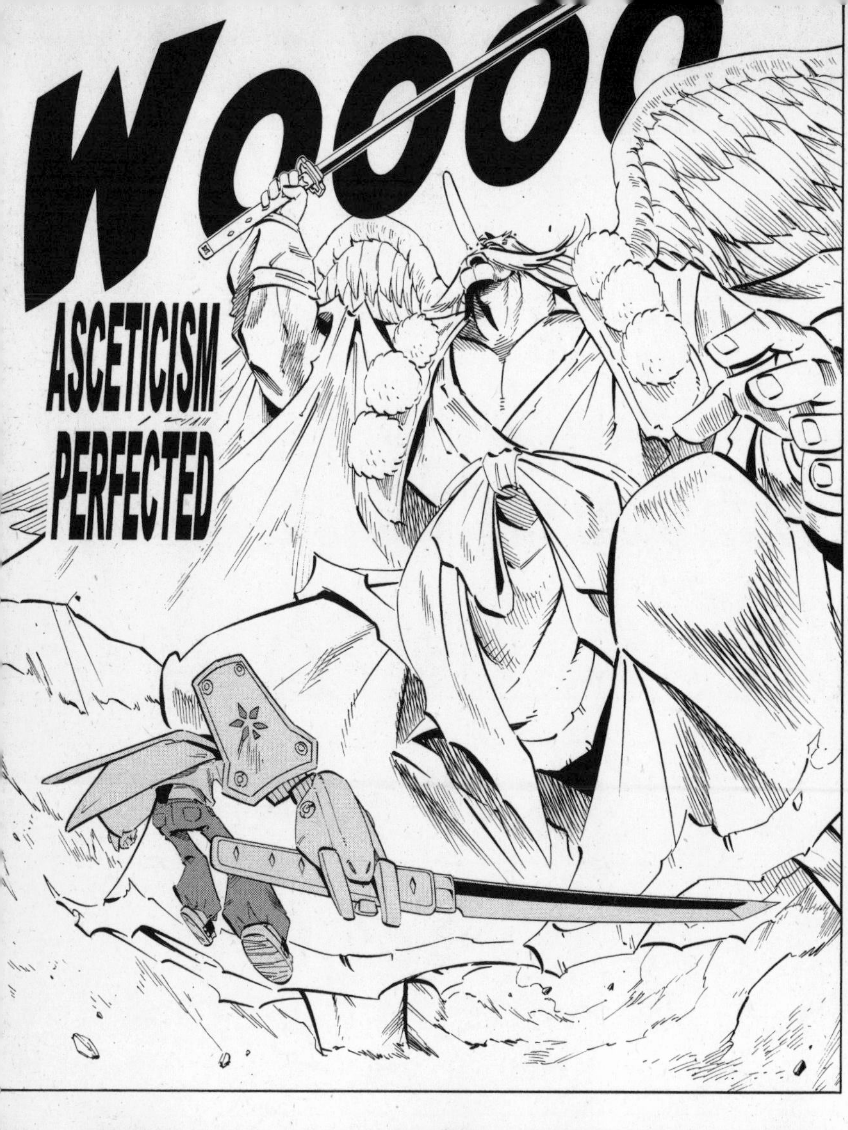
WOOOO
ASCETICISM PERFECTED
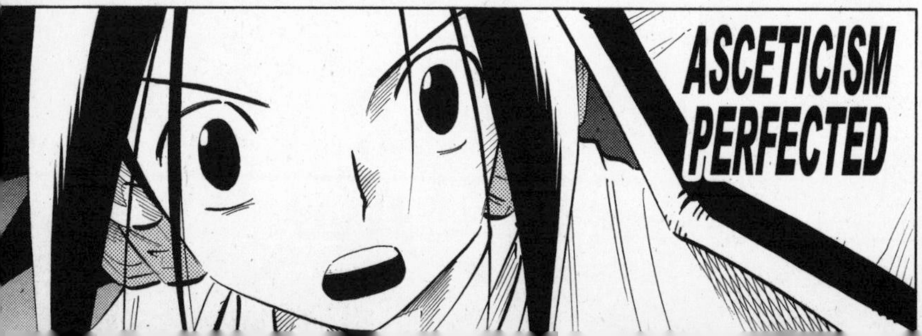
ASCETICISM PERFECTED

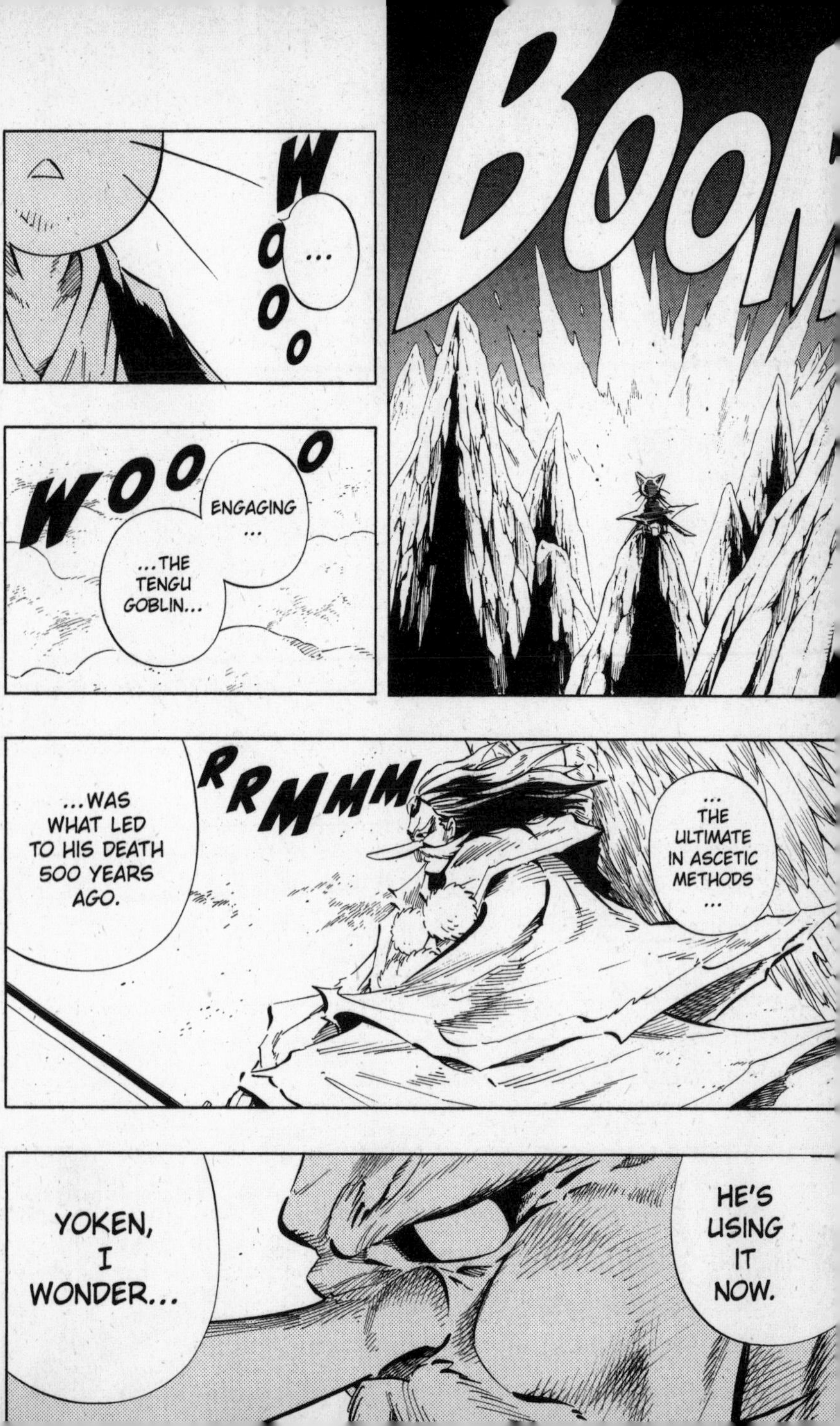

BOOM
WOOOO
...
WOOO
ENGAGING...
...THE TENGU GOBLIN...
... THE ULTIMATE IN ASCETIC METHODS ...
RRMMM
...WAS WHAT LED TO HIS DEATH 500 YEARS AGO.
HE'S USING IT NOW.
YOKEN, I WONDER...

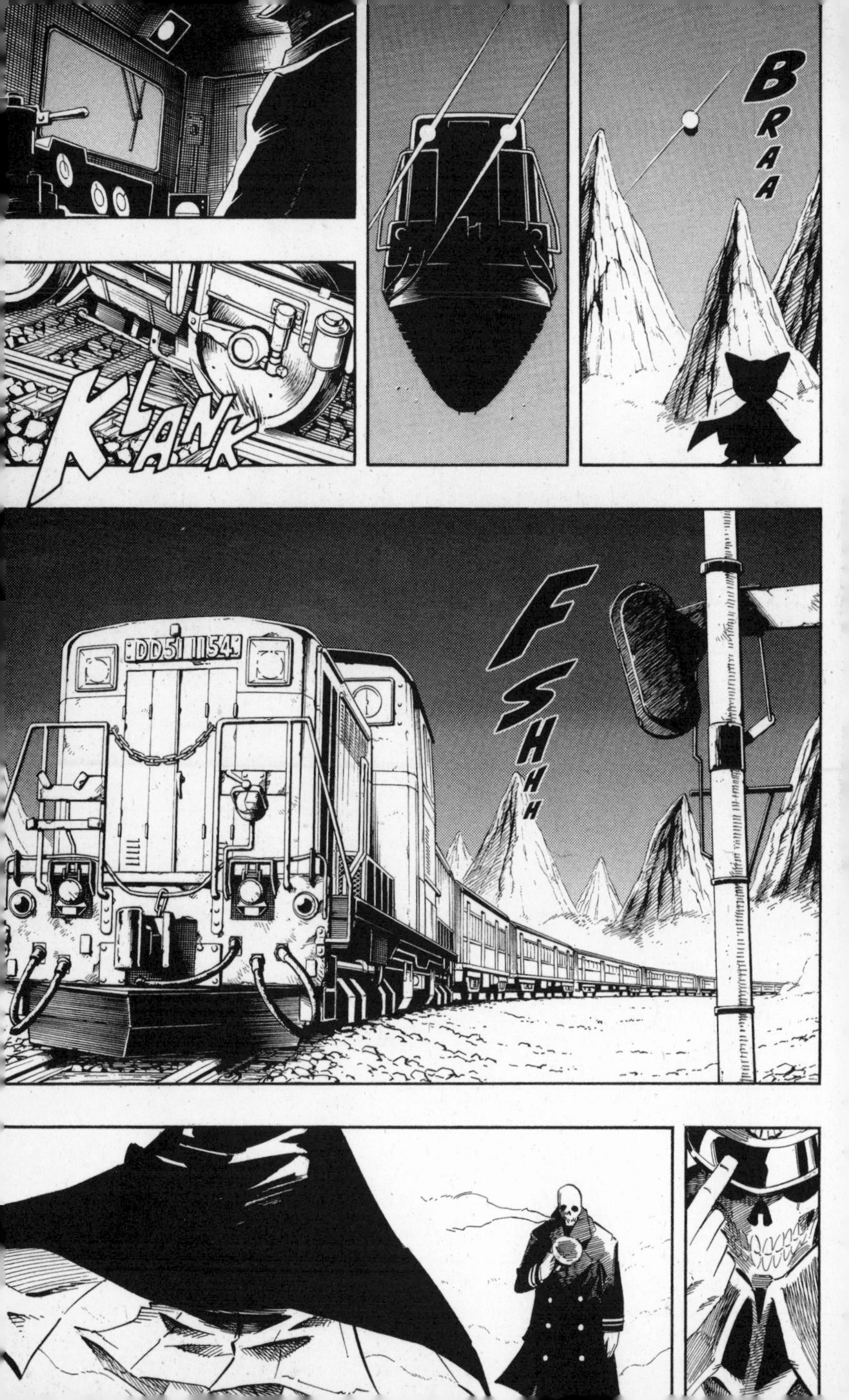
BRAA
KLANK
DD51 1154
FSHHH

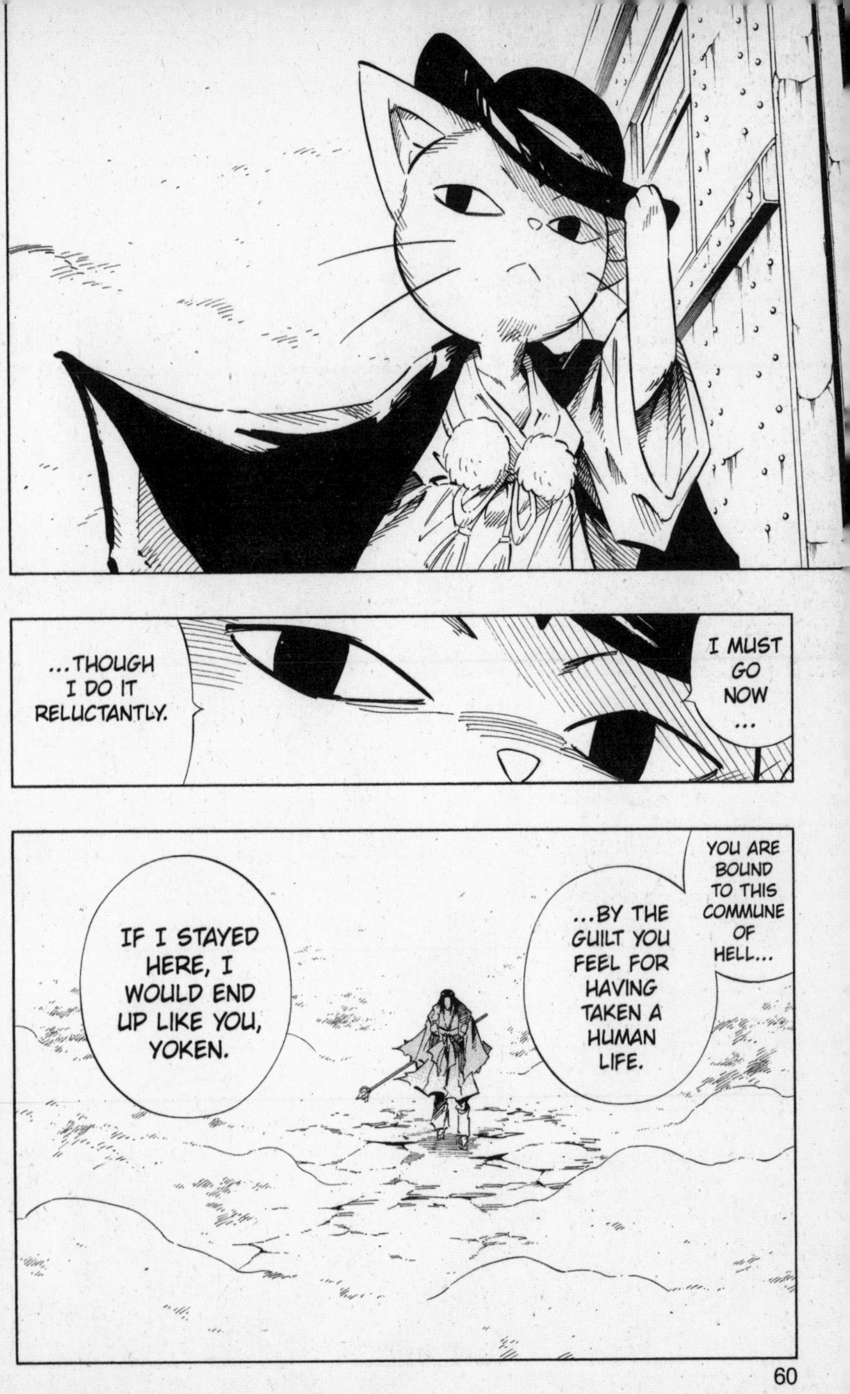
I MUST GO NOW...
...THOUGH I DO IT RELUCTANTLY.
YOU ARE BOUND TO THIS COMMUNE OF HELL...
...BY THE GUILT YOU FEEL FOR HAVING TAKEN A HUMAN LIFE.
IF I STAYED HERE, I WOULD END UP LIKE YOU, YOKEN.

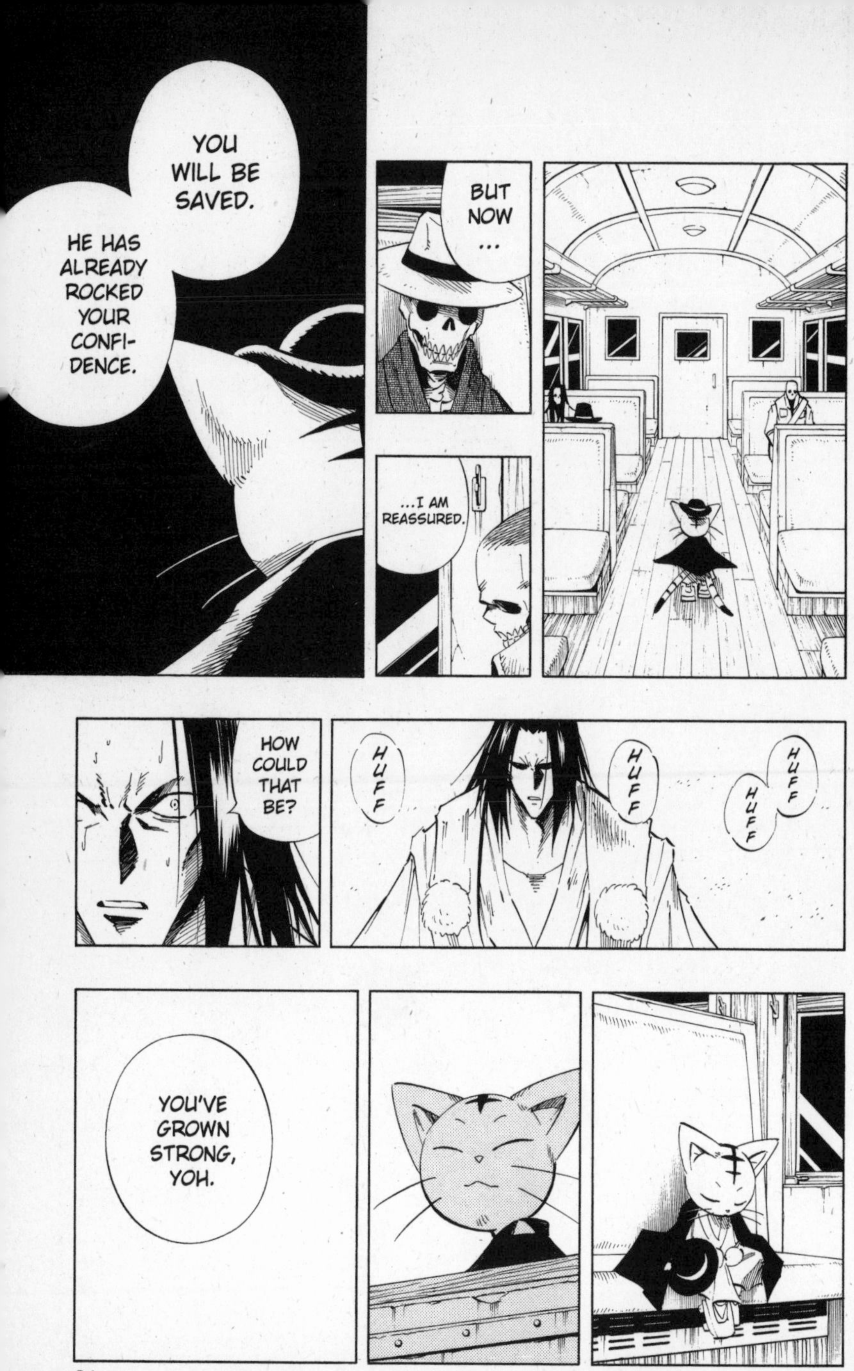
BUT NOW ...
...I AM REASSURED.
YOU WILL BE SAVED.
HE HAS ALREADY ROCKED YOUR CONFIDENCE.
HUFF
HUFF
HUFF
HUFF
HOW COULD THAT BE?
YOU'VE GROWN STRONG, YOH.

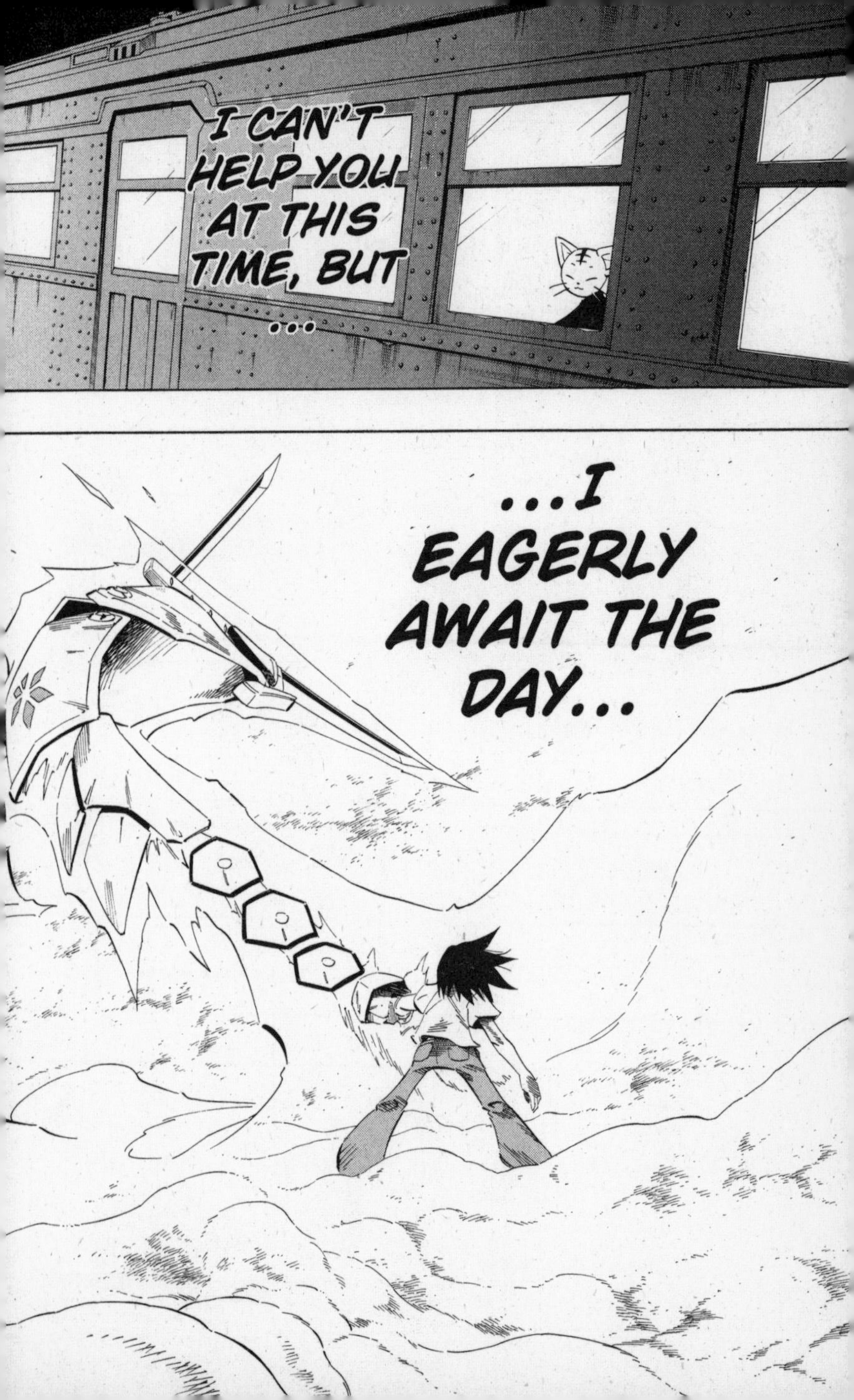
I CAN'T HELP YOU AT THIS TIME, BUT ...
...I EAGERLY AWAIT THE DAY...

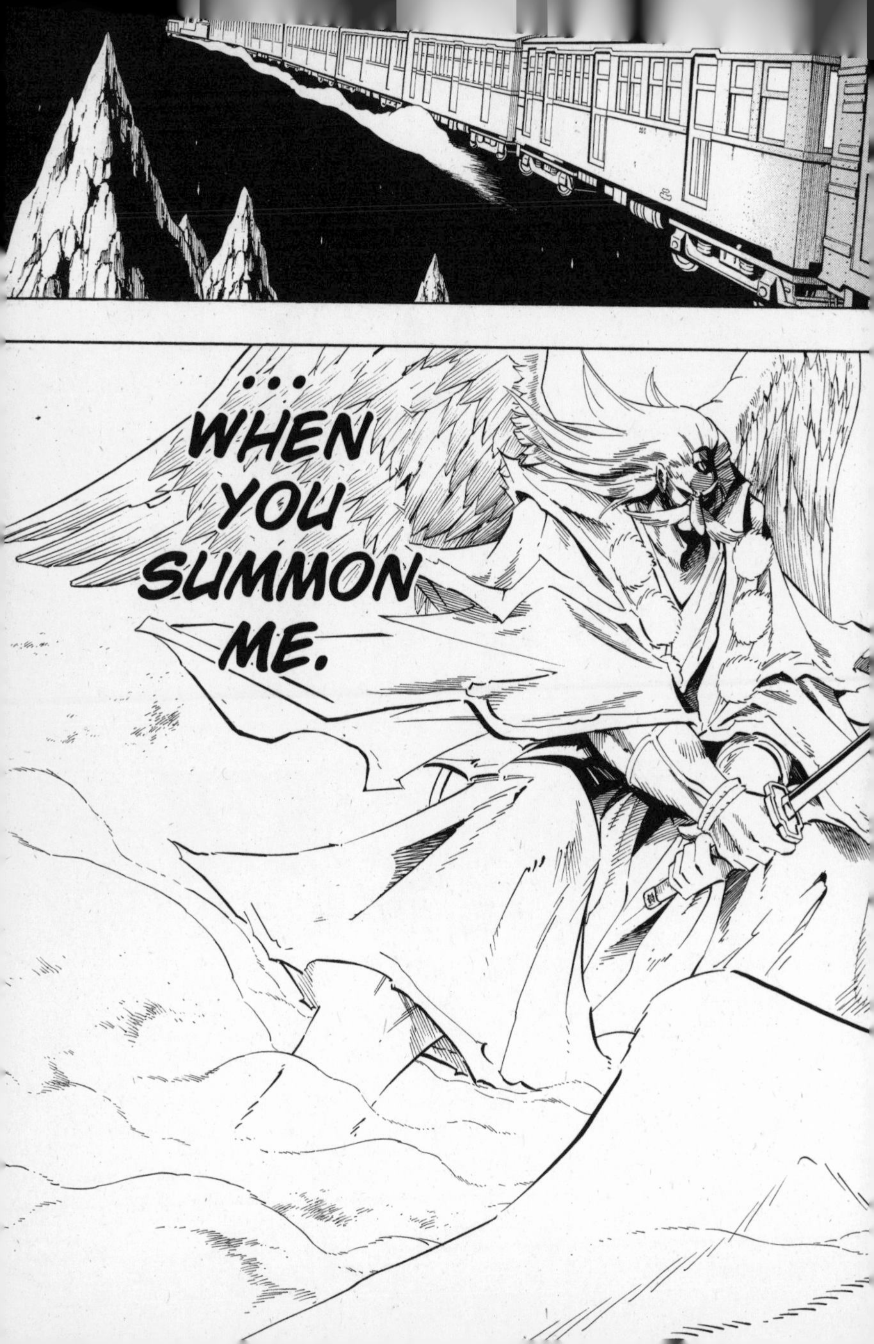
...WHEN YOU SUMMON ME.

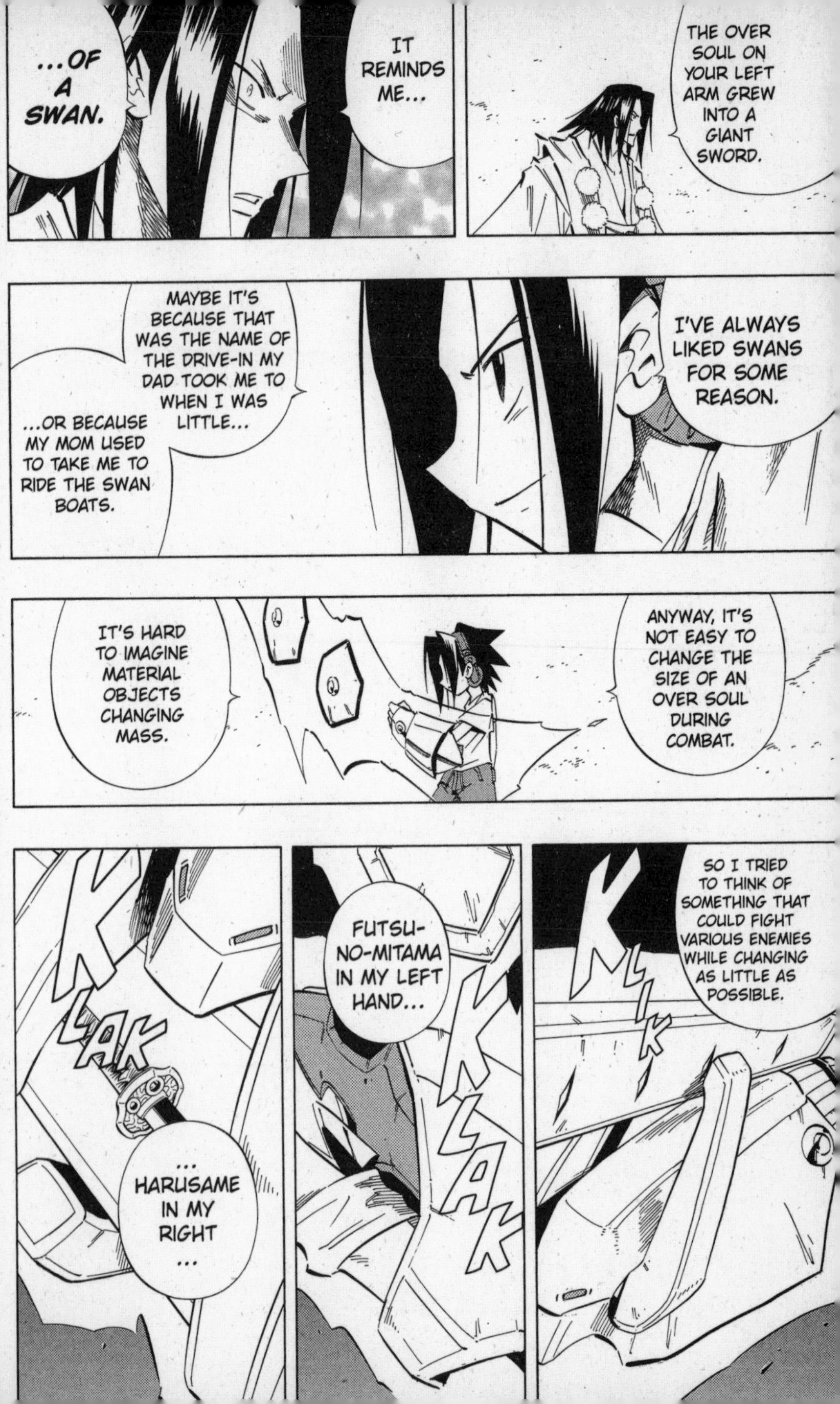
THE OVER SOUL ON YOUR LEFT ARM GREW INTO A GIANT SWORD.
IT REMINDS ME...
...OF A SWAN.
I'VE ALWAYS LIKED SWANS FOR SOME REASON.
MAYBE IT'S BECAUSE THAT WAS THE NAME OF THE DRIVE-IN MY DAD TOOK ME TO WHEN I WAS LITTLE...
...OR BECAUSE MY MOM USED TO TAKE ME TO RIDE THE SWAN BOATS.
ANYWAY, IT'S NOT EASY TO CHANGE THE SIZE OF AN OVER SOUL DURING COMBAT.
IT'S HARD TO IMAGINE MATERIAL OBJECTS CHANGING MASS.
SO I TRIED TO THINK OF SOMETHING THAT COULD FIGHT VARIOUS ENEMIES WHILE CHANGING AS LITTLE AS POSSIBLE.
KLIK
FUTSU-NO-MITAMA IN MY LEFT HAND...
KLAK
KLAK
...HARUSAME IN MY RIGHT...

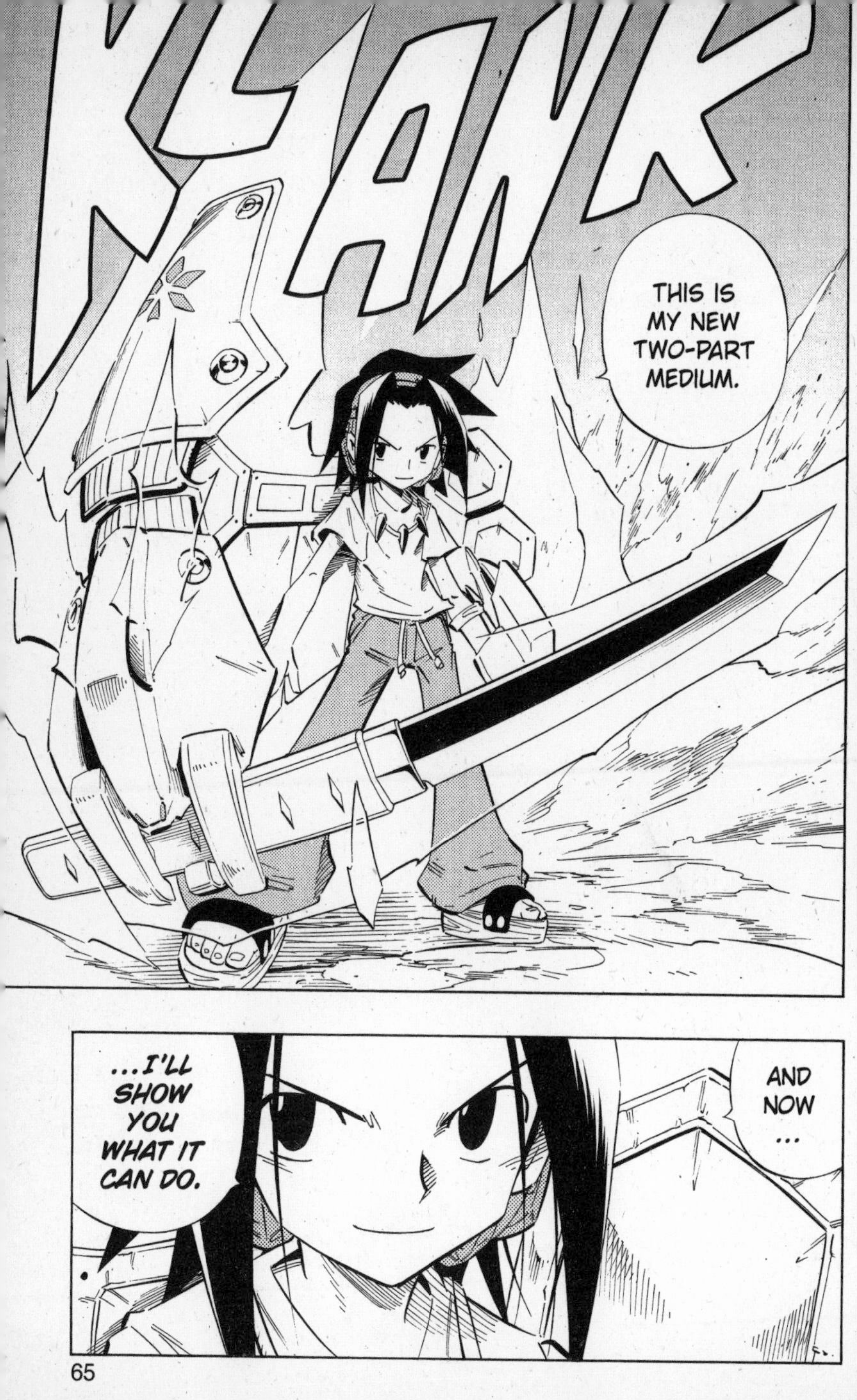
KLANK
THIS IS MY NEW TWO-PART MEDIUM.
AND NOW ...
...I'LL SHOW YOU WHAT IT CAN DO.

Shaman King

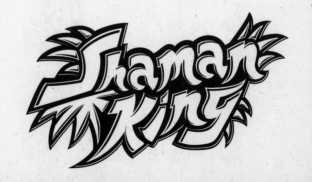

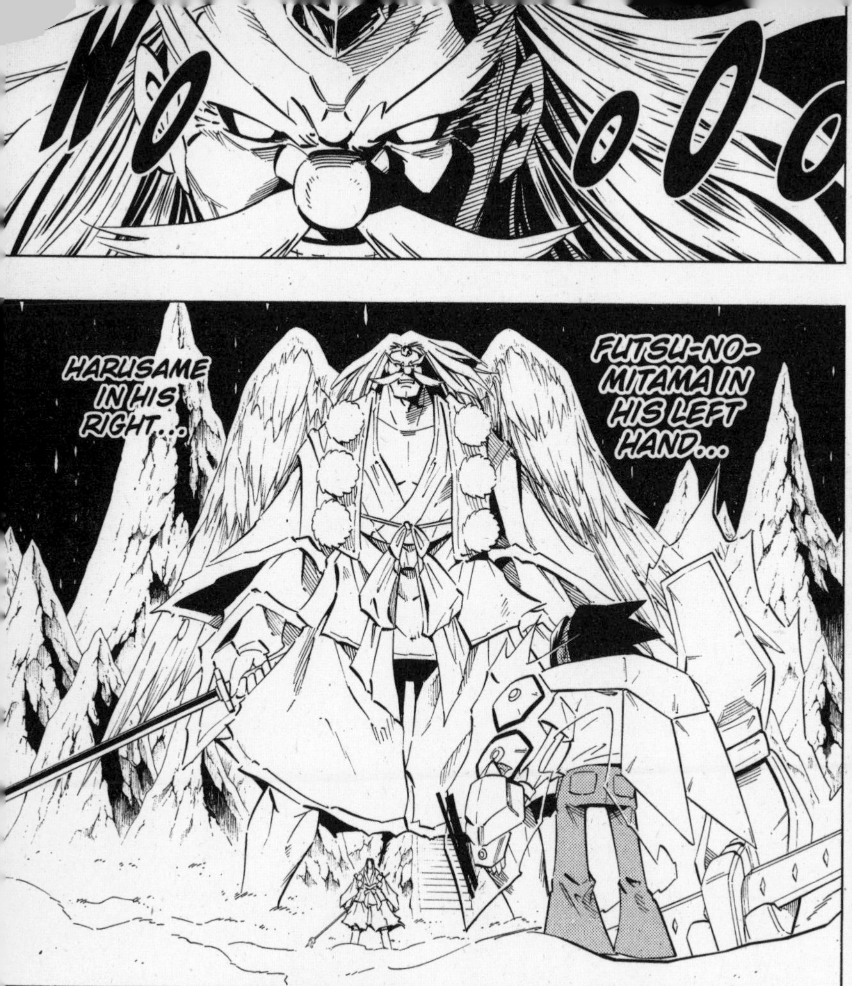
WOOOO
FUTSU-NO-MITAMA IN HIS LEFT HAND...
HARUSAME IN HIS RIGHT...

Reincarnation 237: What's Wrong with a Memorial?

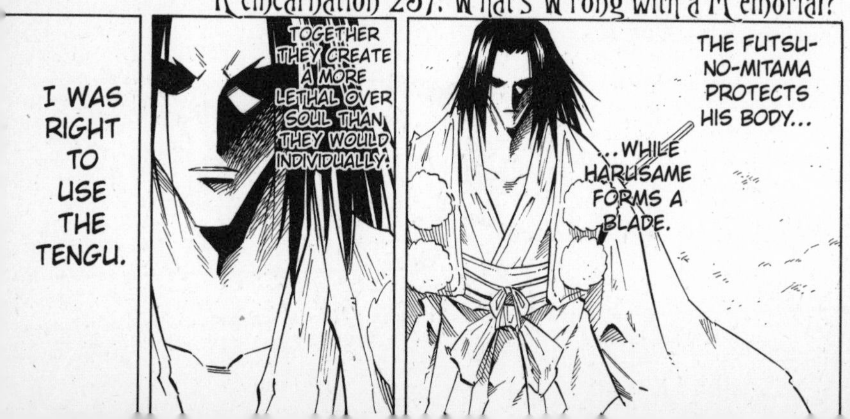
THE FUTSU-NO-MITAMA PROTECTS HIS BODY...
...WHILE HARUSAME FORMS A BLADE.
TOGETHER THEY CREATE A MORE LETHAL OVER SOUL THAN THEY WOULD INDIVIDUALLY.
I WAS RIGHT TO USE THE TENGU.

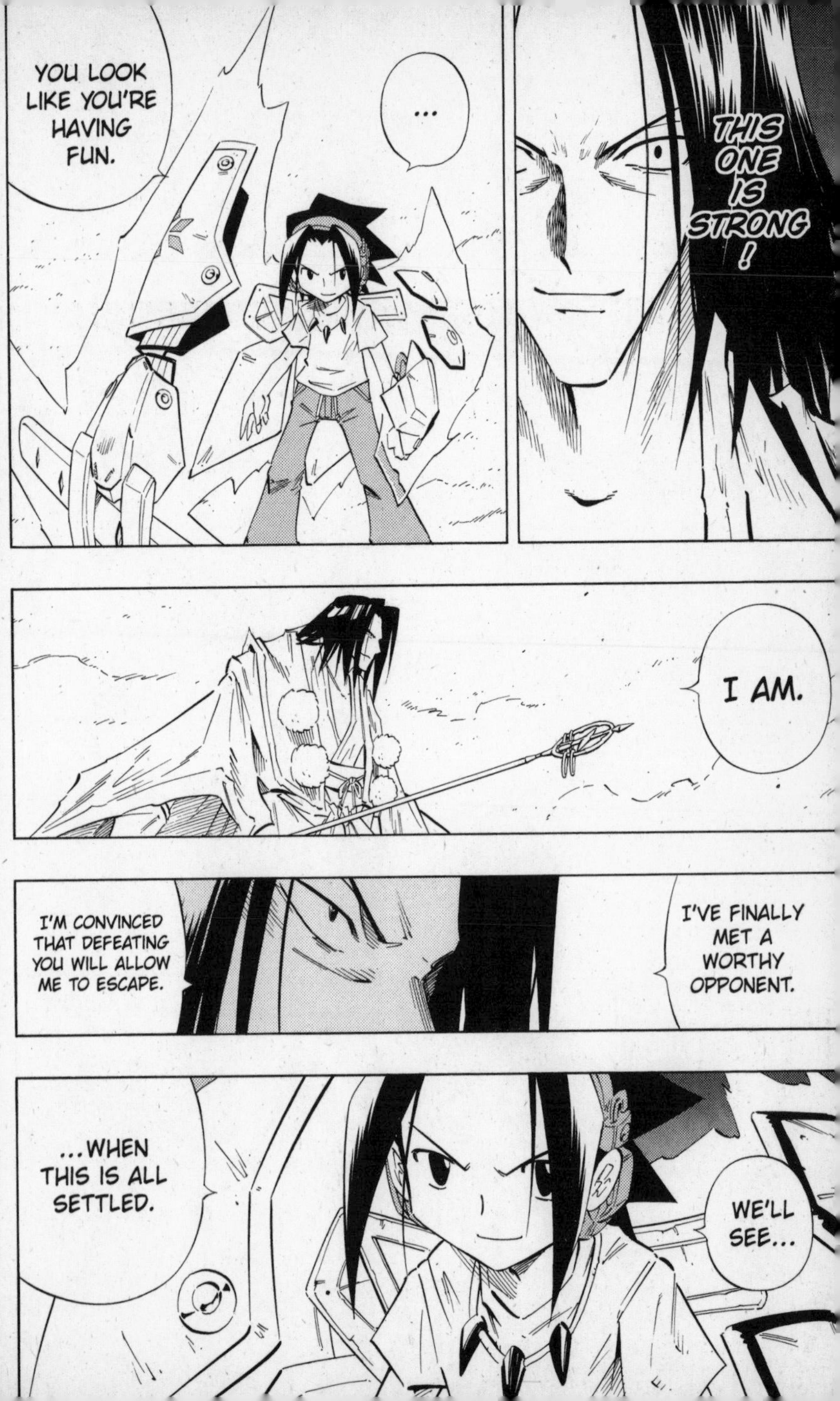
THIS ONE IS STRONG!
...
YOU LOOK LIKE YOU'RE HAVING FUN.
I AM.
I'VE FINALLY MET A WORTHY OPPONENT.
I'M CONVINCED THAT DEFEATING YOU WILL ALLOW ME TO ESCAPE.
WE'LL SEE...
...WHEN THIS IS ALL SETTLED.

Reincarnation 237: What's Wrong with a Memorial?

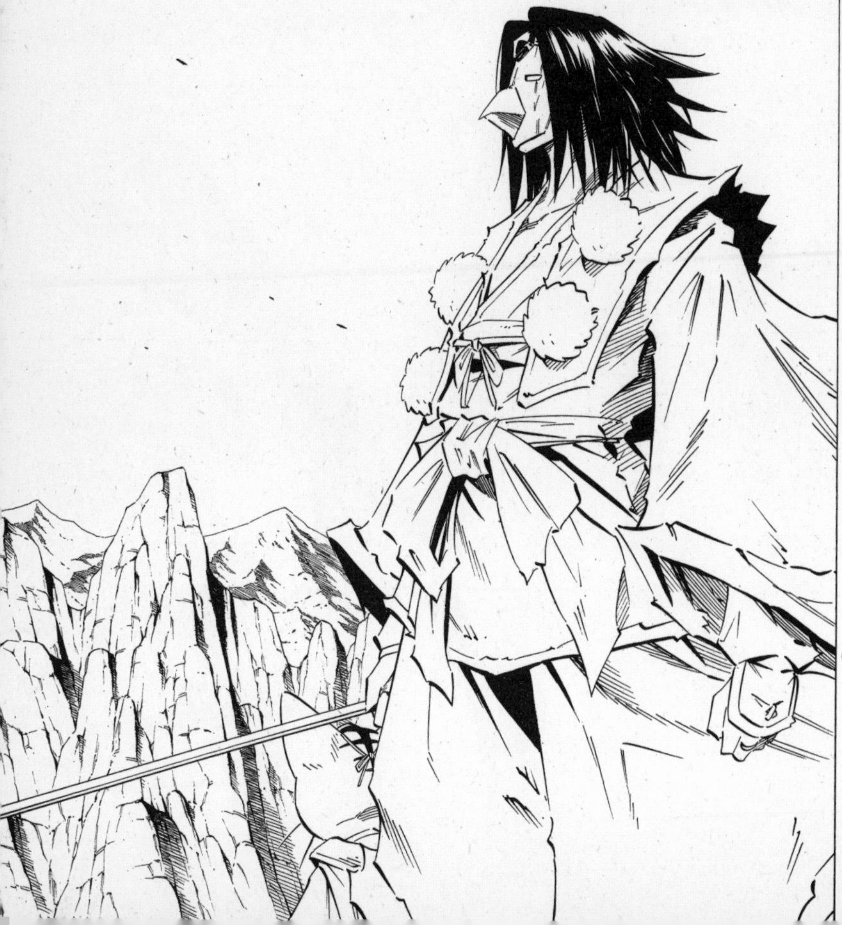

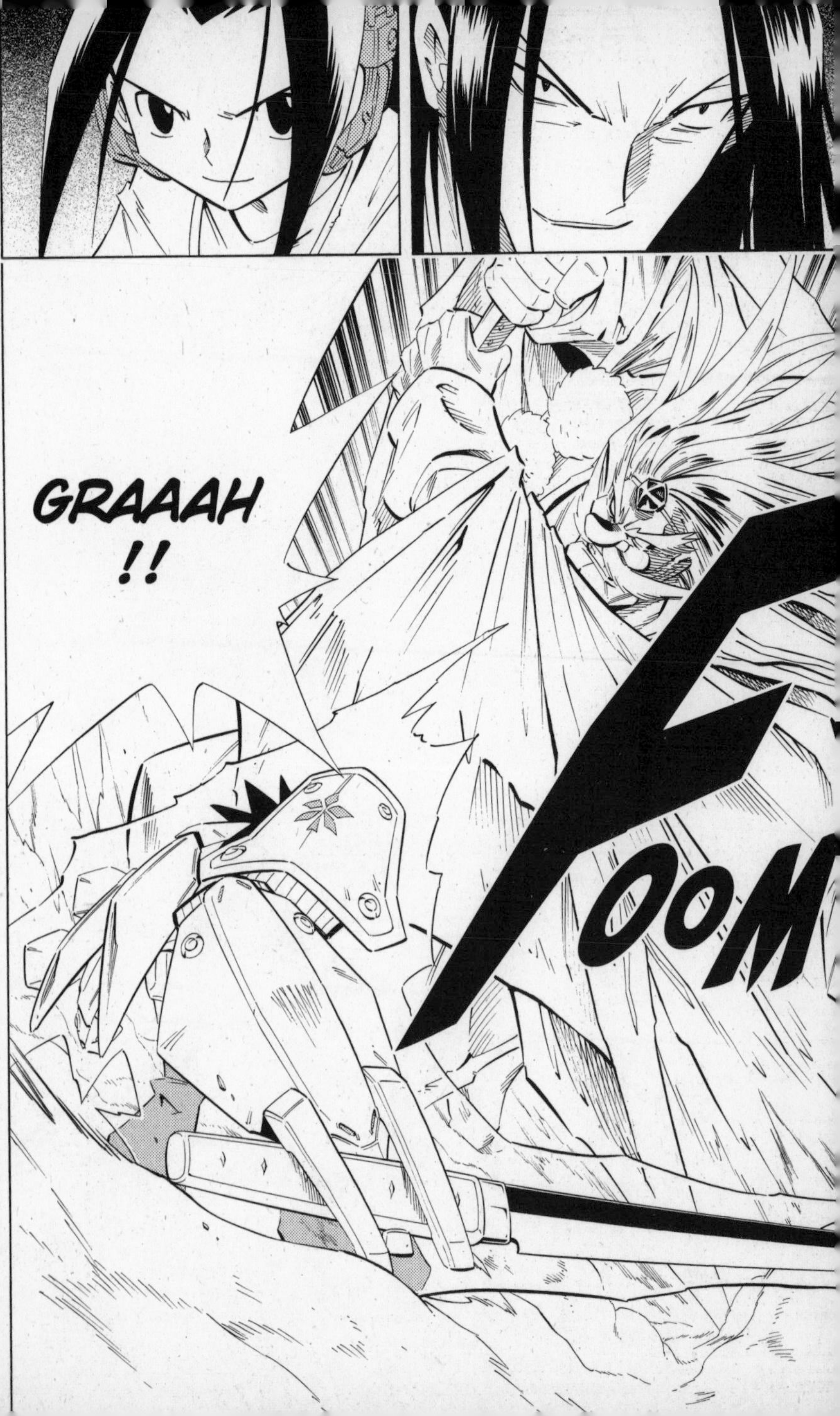

GRAAAH !!
OOM

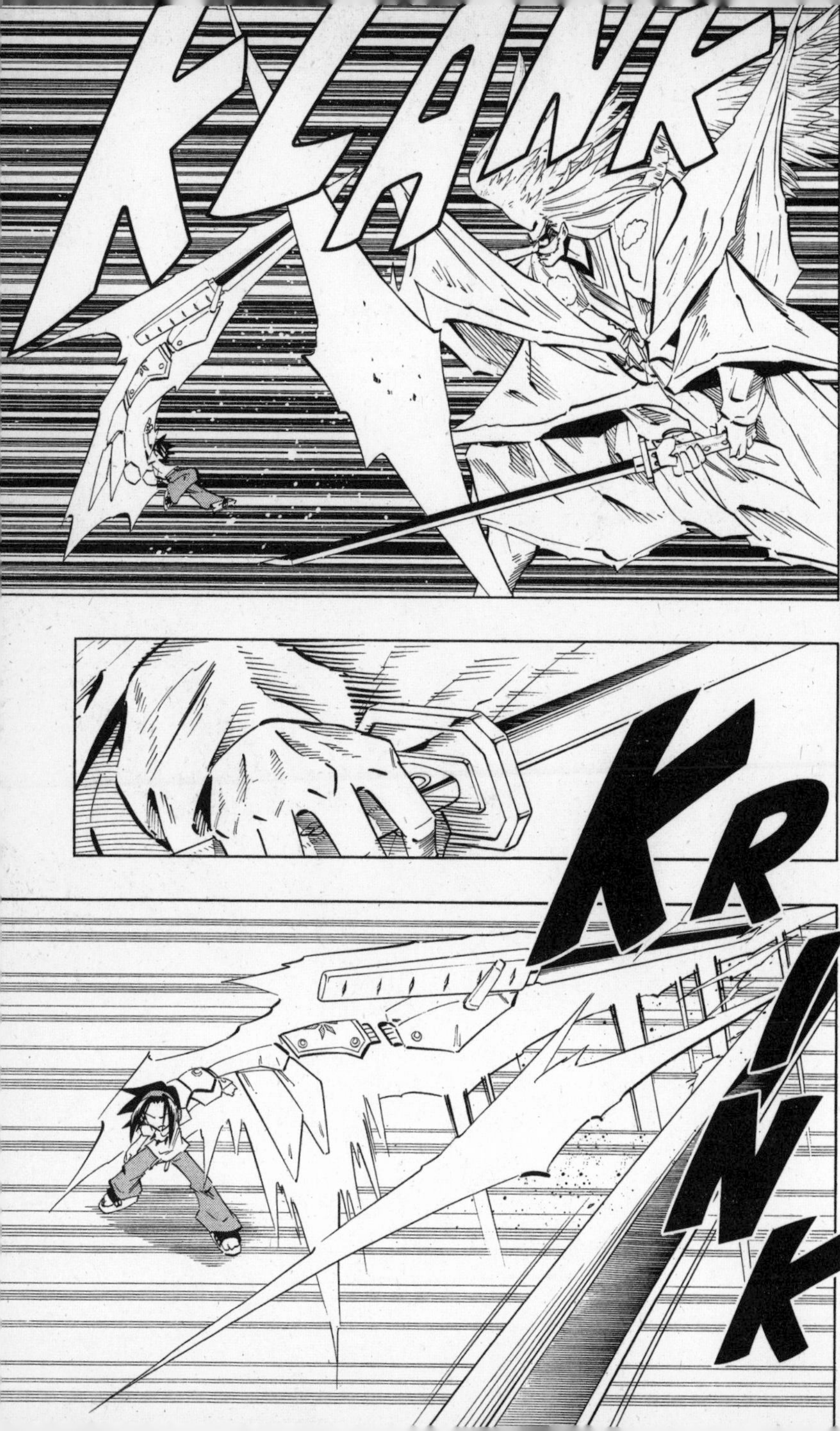
KLANK
KRIINK

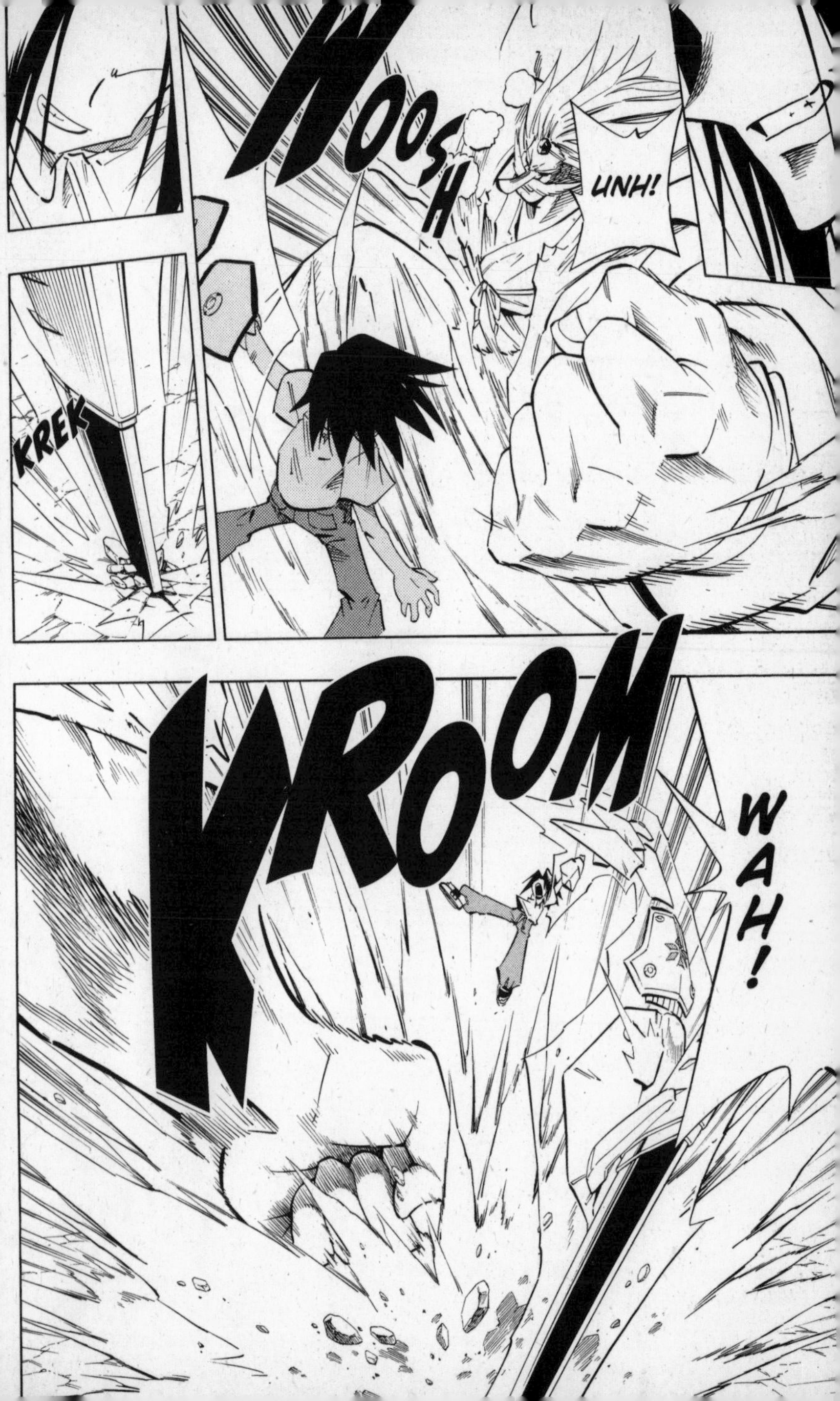
WOOSH
UNH!
KREK
KROOM
WAH!

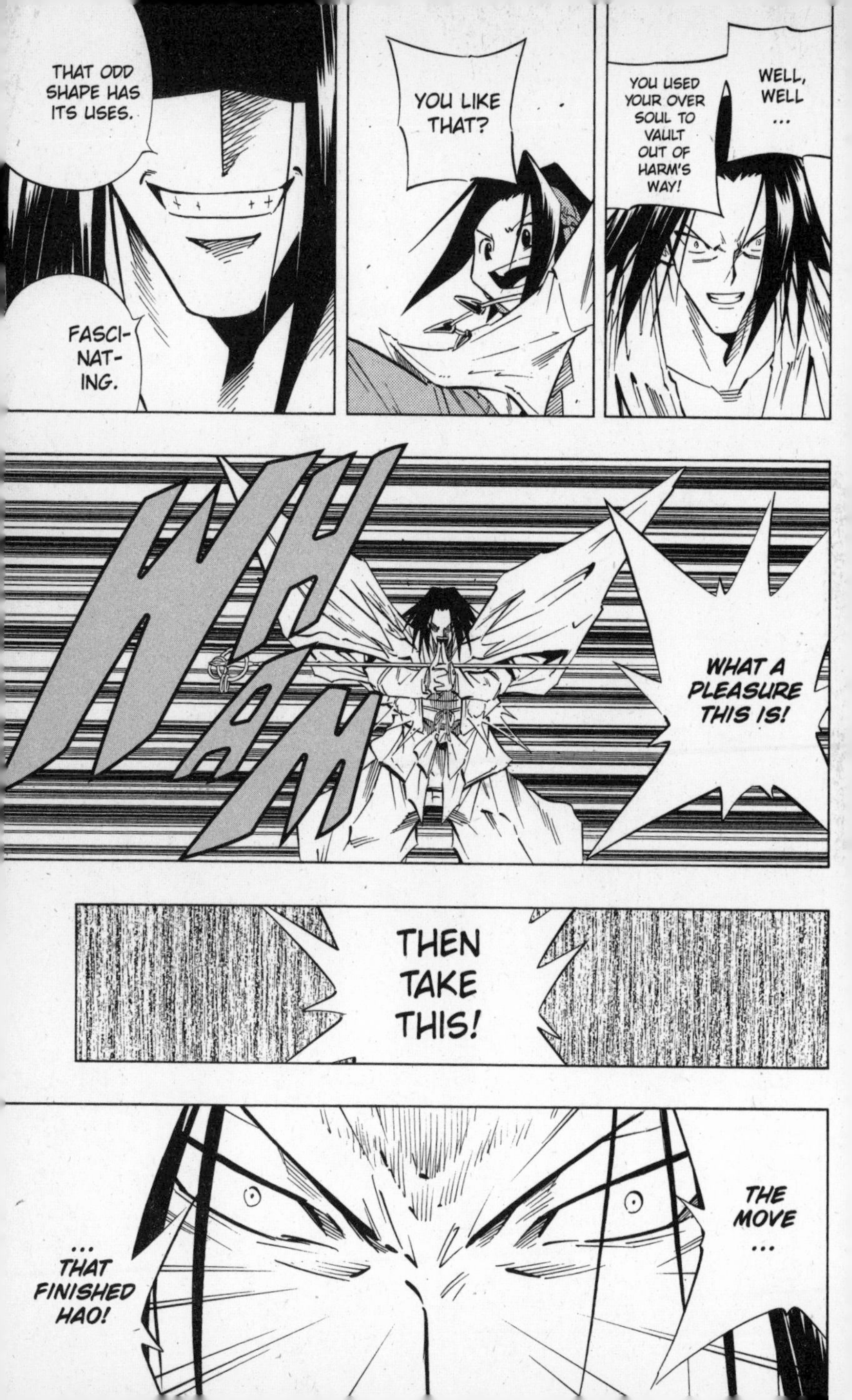
WELL, WELL ...
YOU USED YOUR OVER SOUL TO VAULT OUT OF HARM'S WAY!
YOU LIKE THAT?
THAT ODD SHAPE HAS ITS USES.
FASCI-NAT-ING.
WHAT A PLEASURE THIS IS!
WHAAM
THEN TAKE THIS!
THE MOVE ...
... THAT FINISHED HAO!

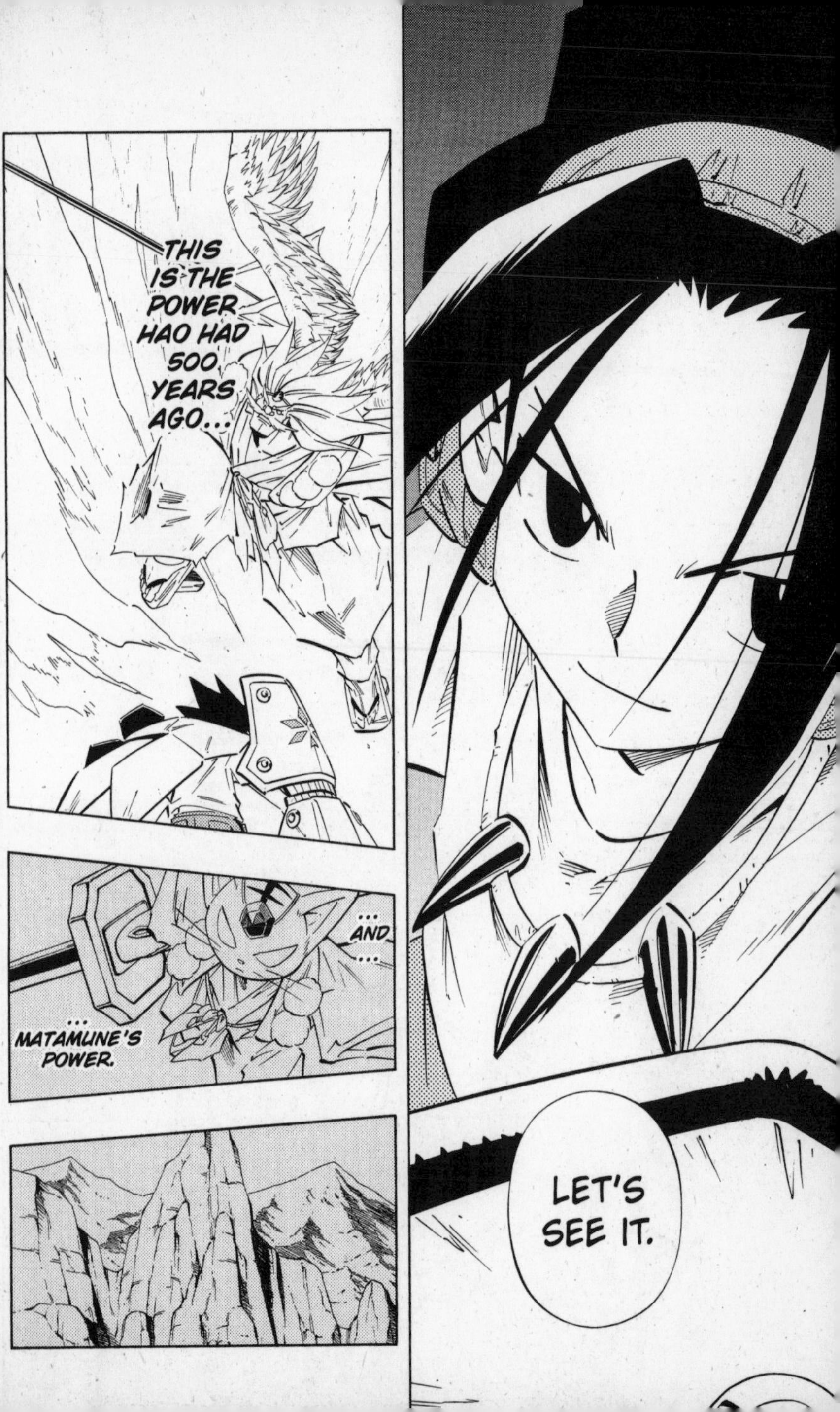
LET'S SEE IT.
THIS IS THE POWER HAO HAD 500 YEARS AGO...
... AND ...
... MATAMUNE'S POWER.

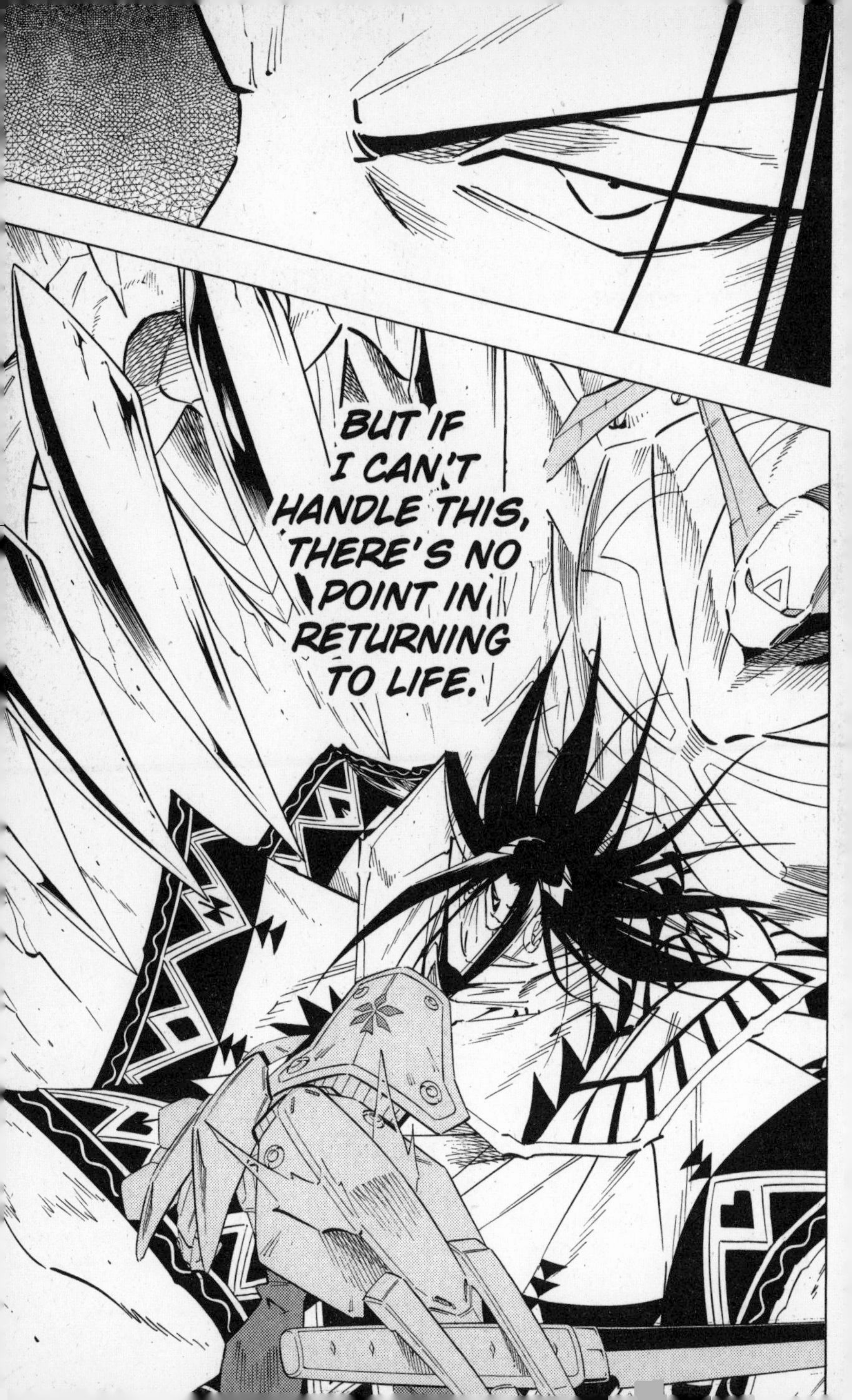
BUT IF I CAN'T HANDLE THIS, THERE'S NO POINT IN RETURNING TO LIFE.

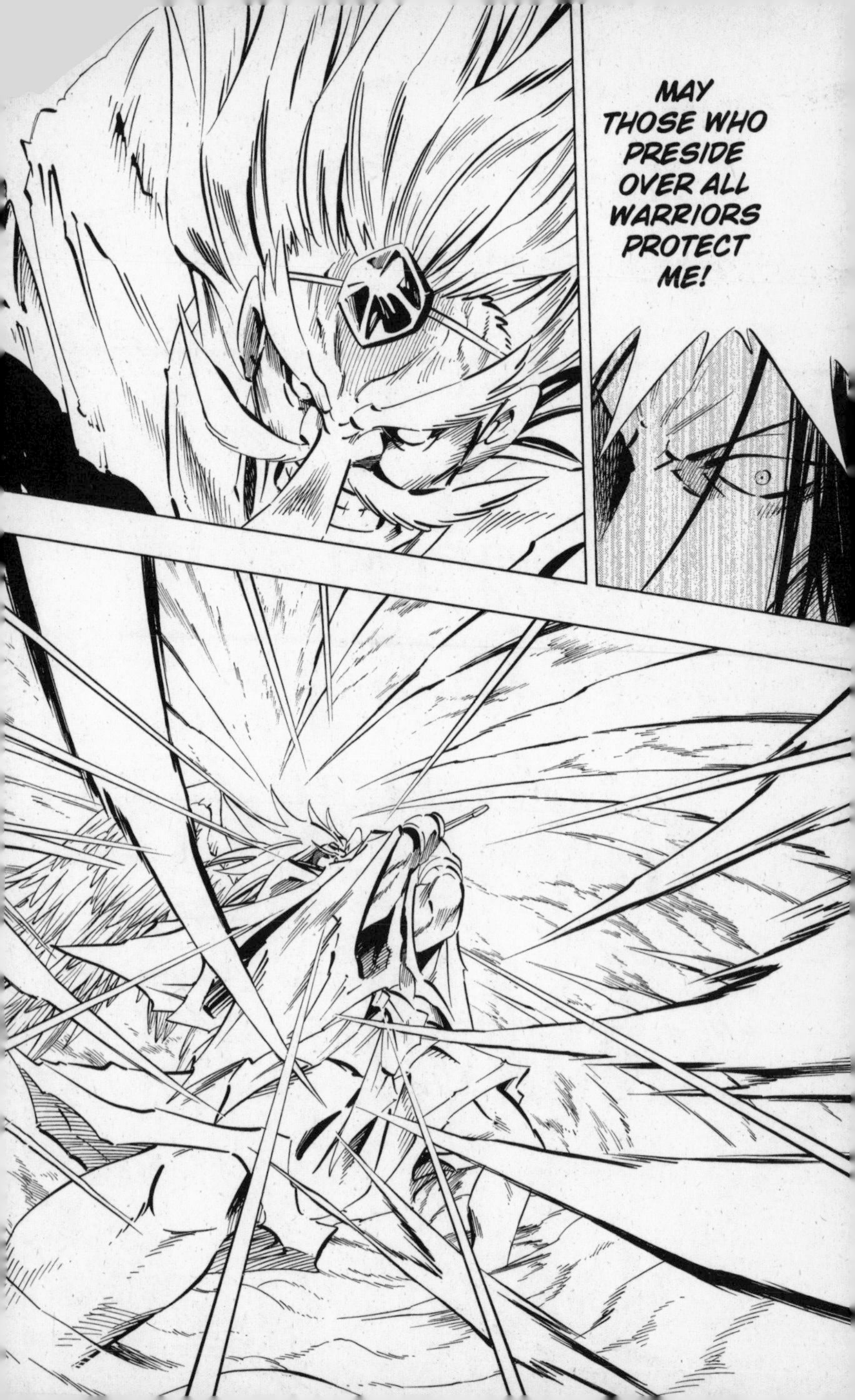
MAY THOSE WHO PRESIDE OVER ALL WARRIORS PROTECT ME!

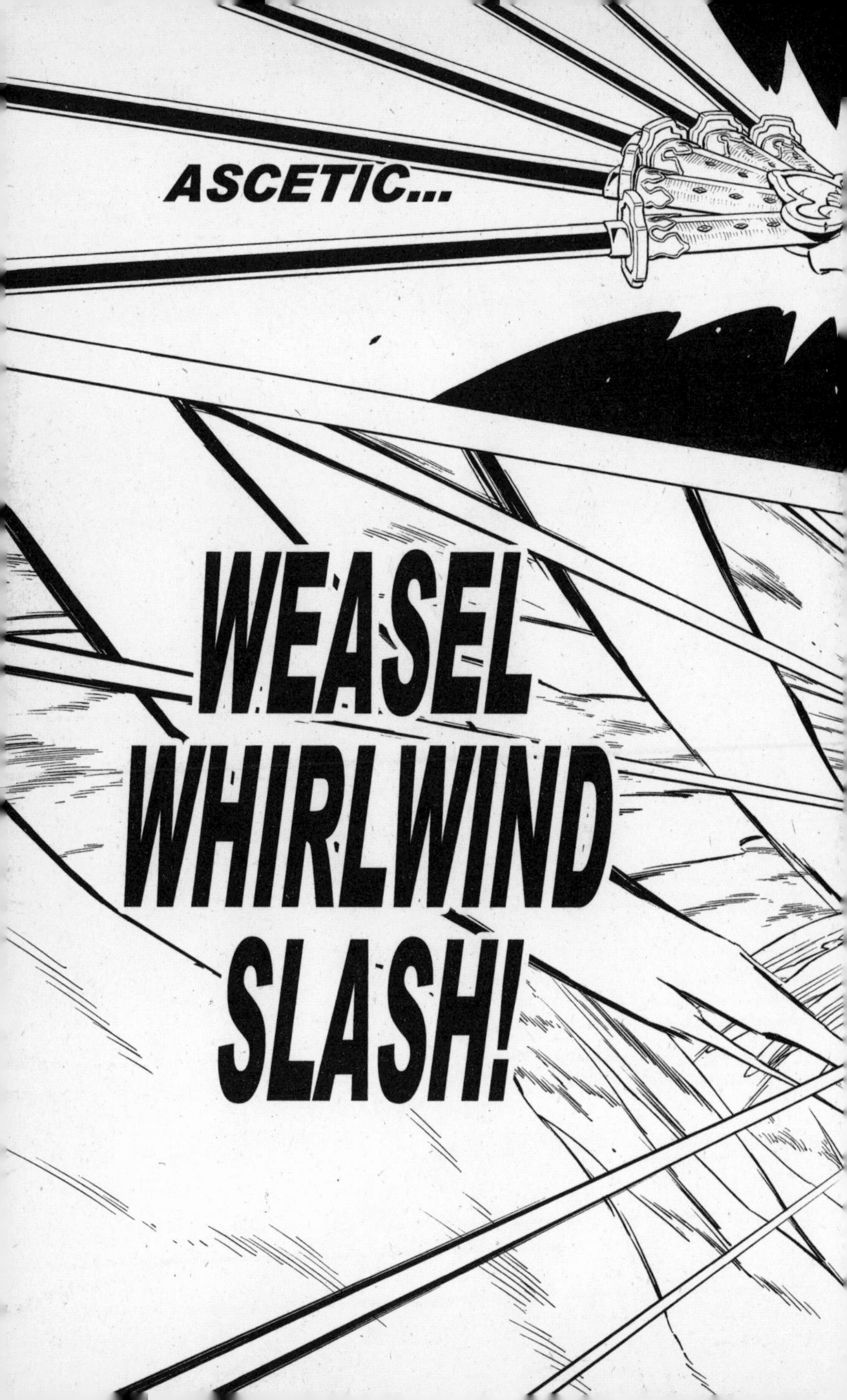
ASCETIC...
WEASEL WHIRLWIND SLASH!

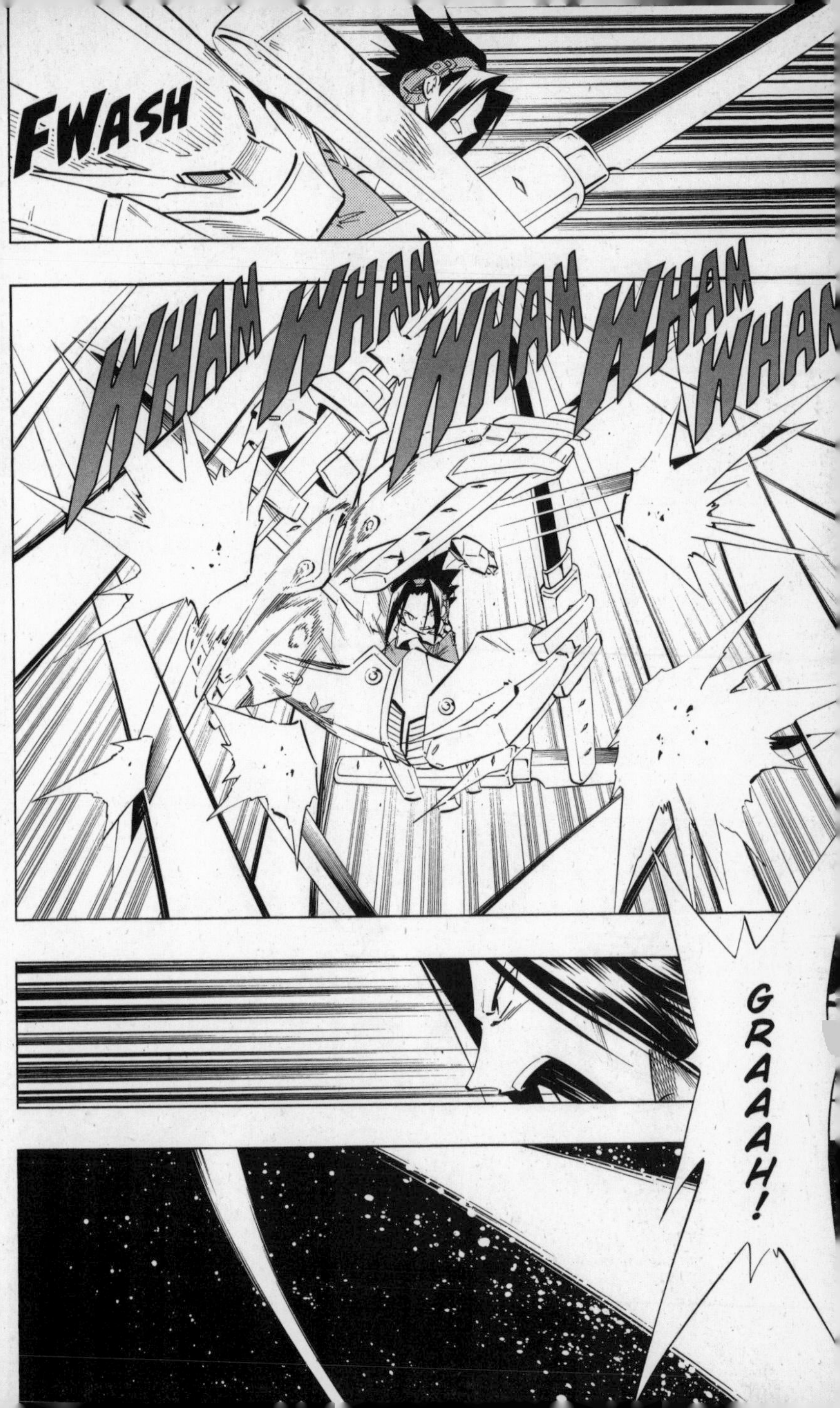
FWASH
WHAM WHAM WHAM WHAM WHAM
GRAAAH!

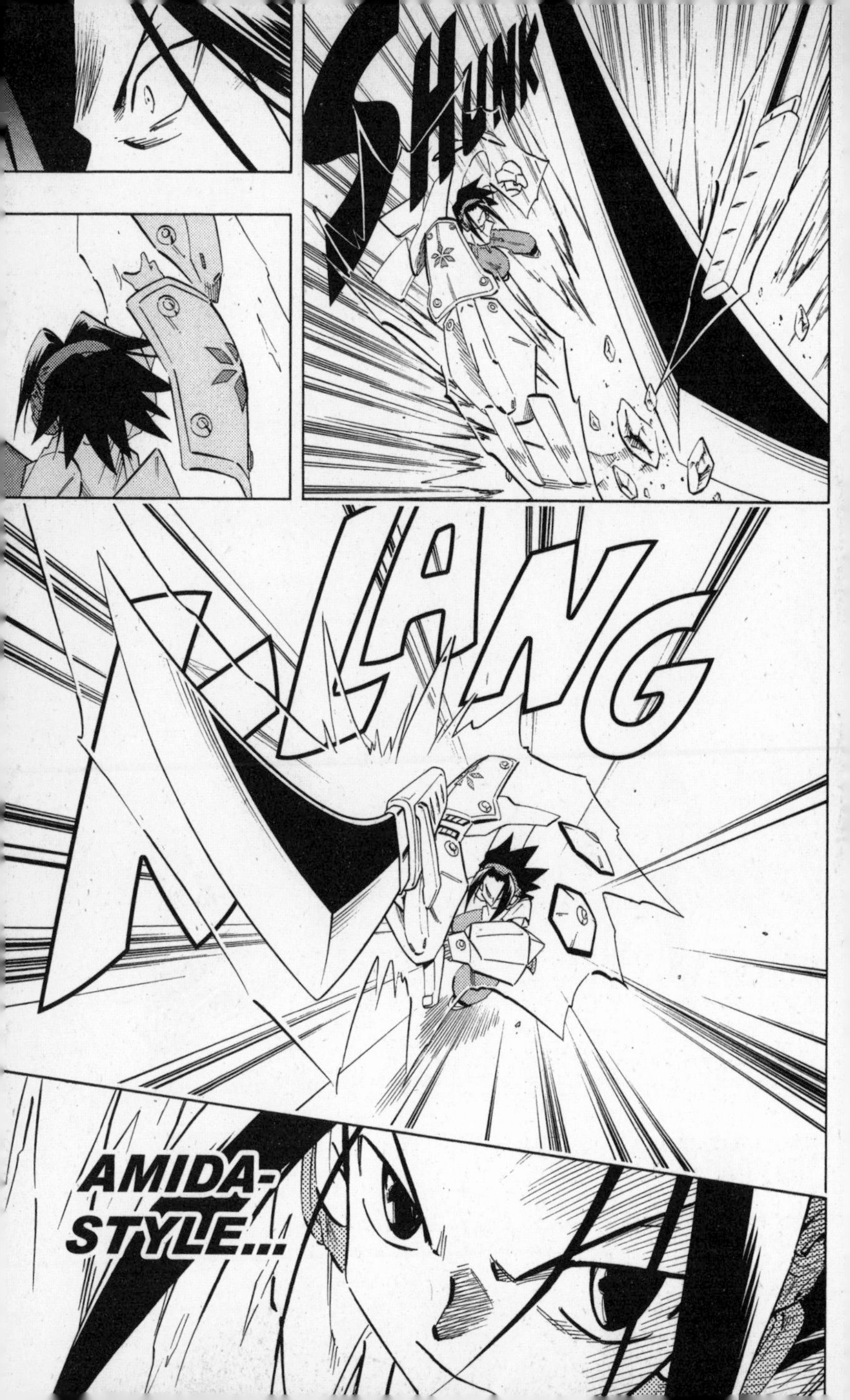
SHUNK
CLANG
AMIDA-
STYLE...

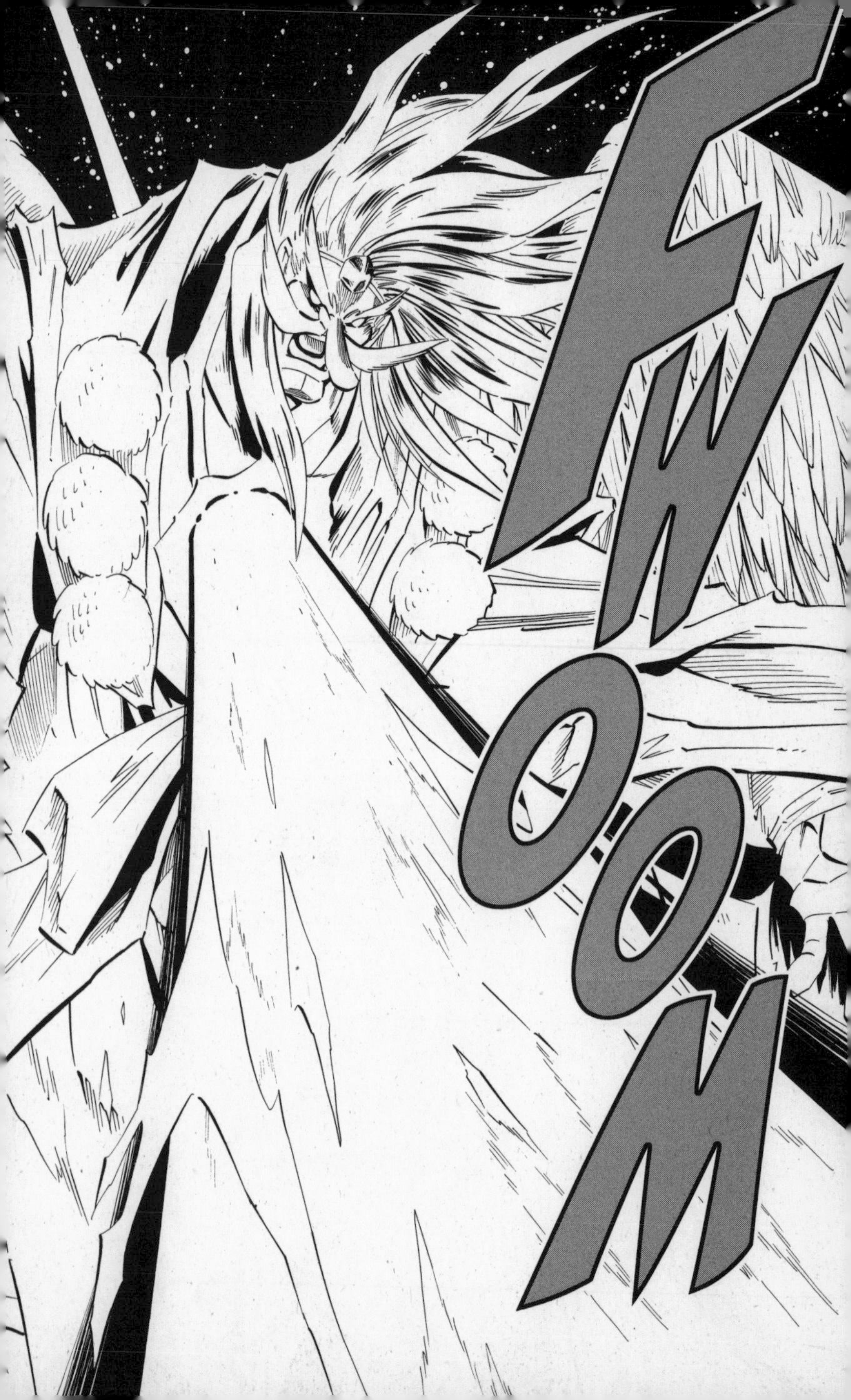
FWOOOM

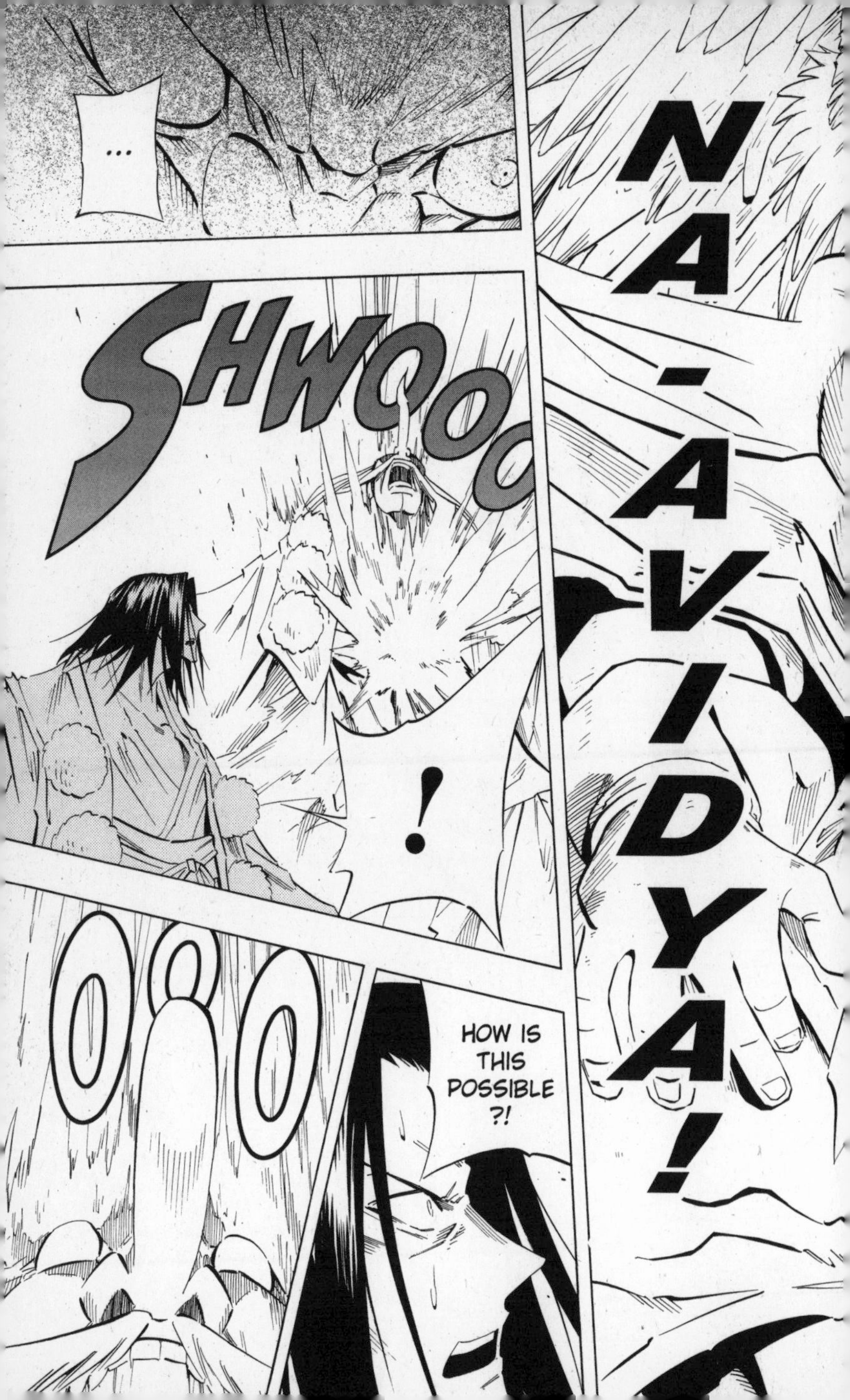
NA-A-VIDYA!
...
SHWOOOO
!
HOW IS THIS POSSIBLE ?!

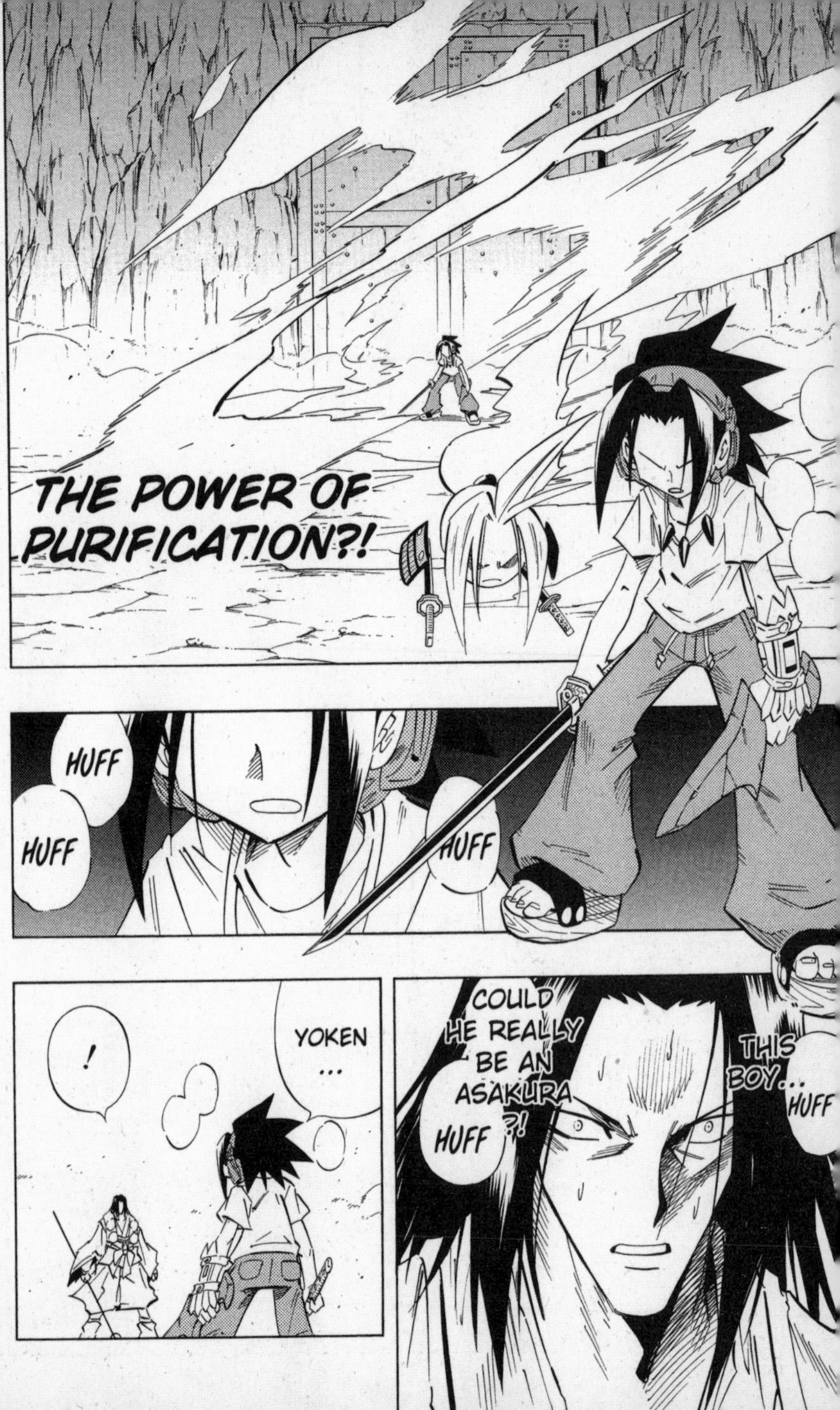
THE POWER OF PURIFICATION?!
HUFF
HUFF
HUFF
THIS BOY...
HUFF
COULD HE REALLY BE AN ASAKURA ?!
HUFF
YOKEN ...
!

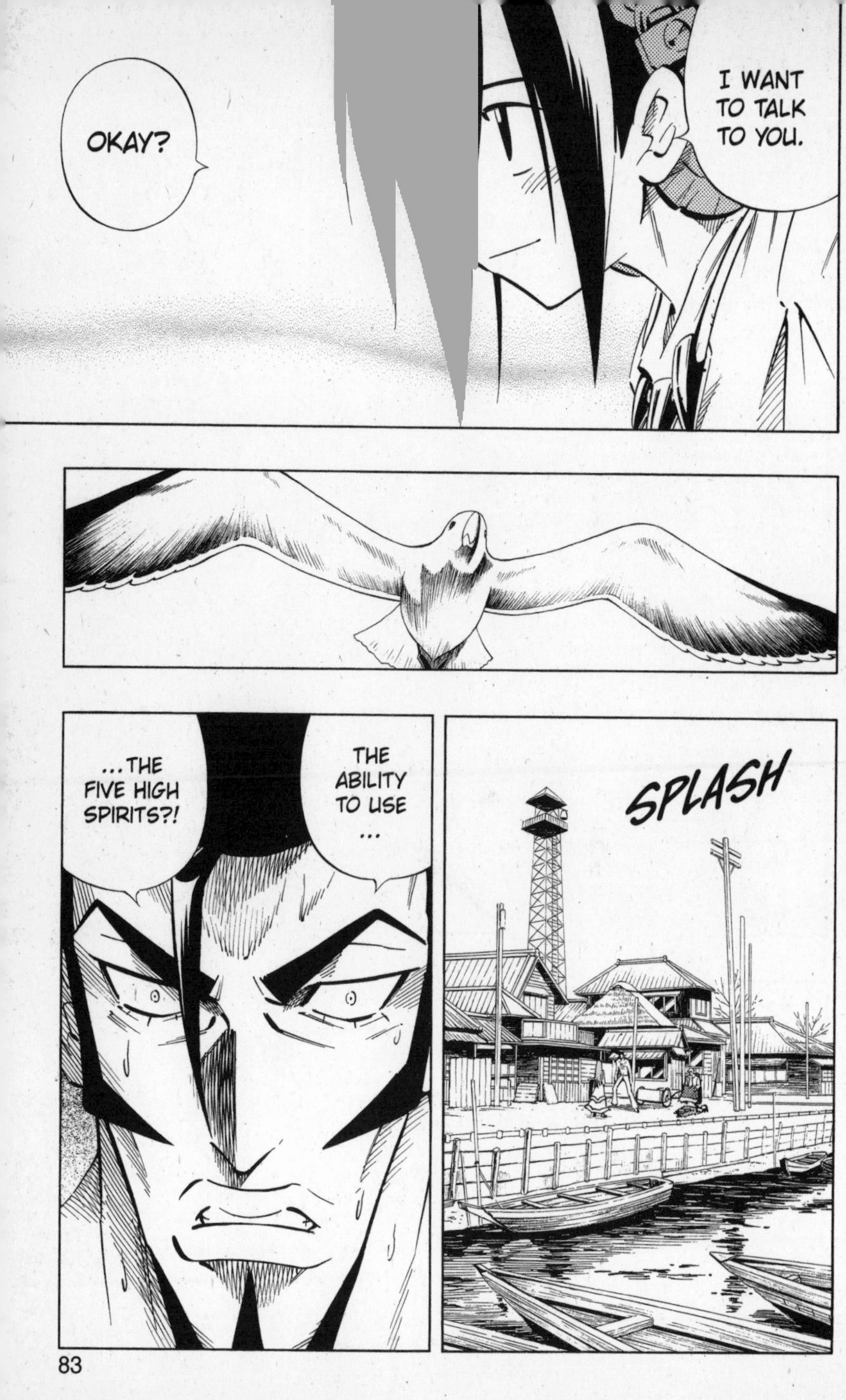
I WANT TO TALK TO YOU.
OKAY?
SPLASH
THE ABILITY TO USE ...
...THE FIVE HIGH SPIRITS?!

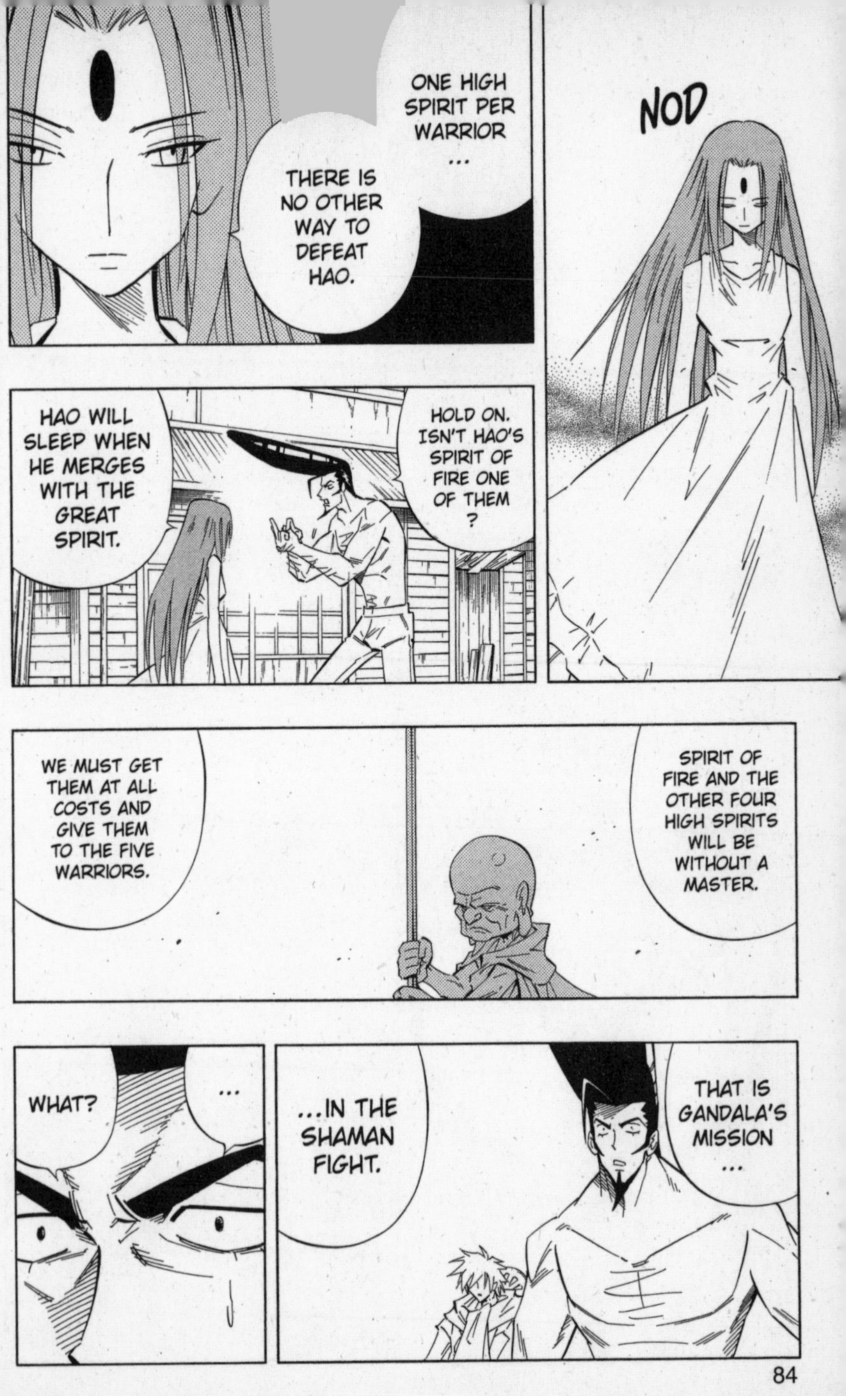
NOD
ONE HIGH SPIRIT PER WARRIOR ...
THERE IS NO OTHER WAY TO DEFEAT HAO.
HOLD ON. ISN'T HAO'S SPIRIT OF FIRE ONE OF THEM ?
HAO WILL SLEEP WHEN HE MERGES WITH THE GREAT SPIRIT.
SPIRIT OF FIRE AND THE OTHER FOUR HIGH SPIRITS WILL BE WITHOUT A MASTER.
WE MUST GET THEM AT ALL COSTS AND GIVE THEM TO THE FIVE WARRIORS.
THAT IS GANDALA'S MISSION ...
...IN THE SHAMAN FIGHT.
...
WHAT?

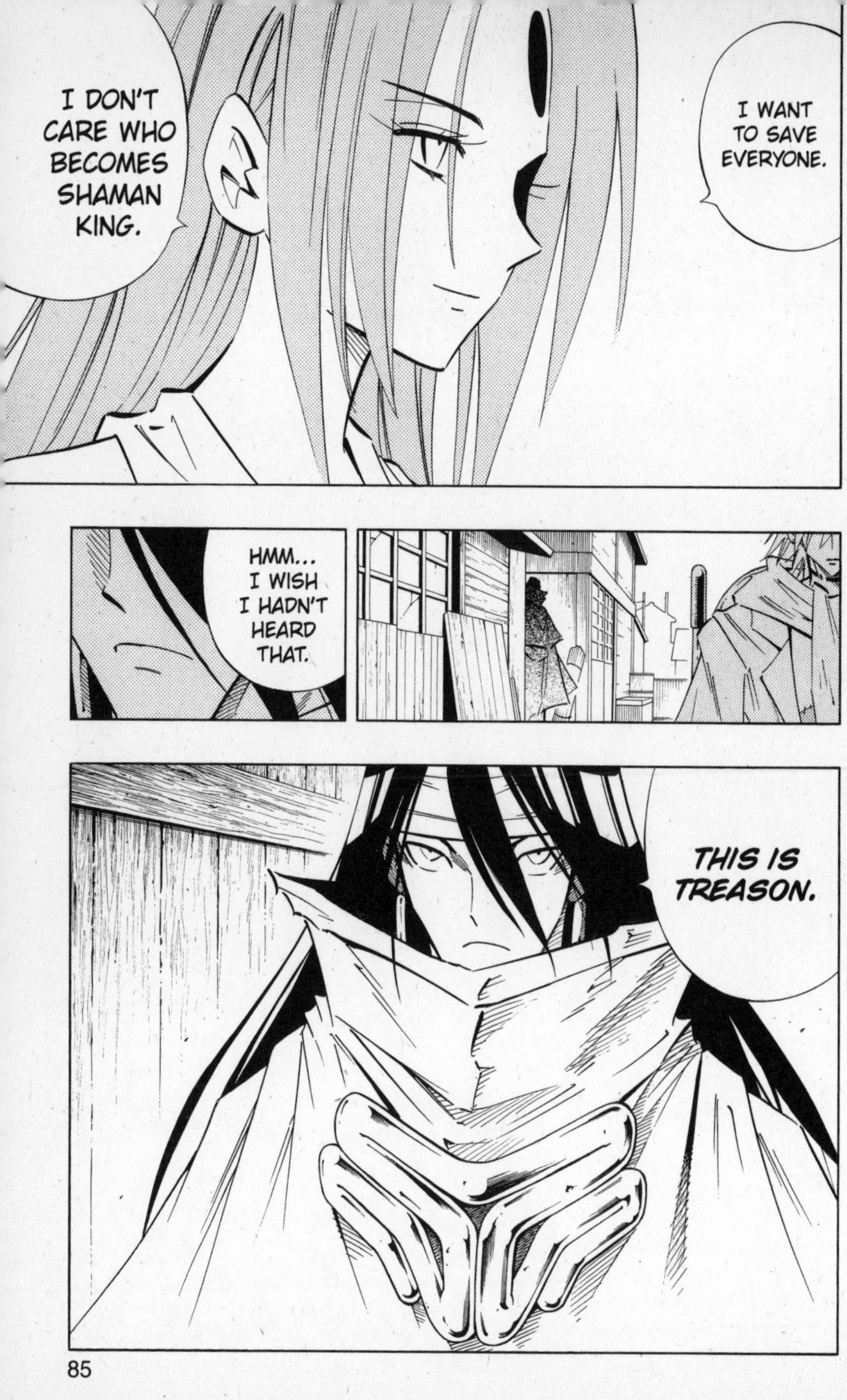
I WANT TO SAVE EVERYONE.
I DON'T CARE WHO BECOMES SHAMAN KING.
HMM... I WISH I HADN'T HEARD THAT.
THIS IS TREASON.

Shaman King

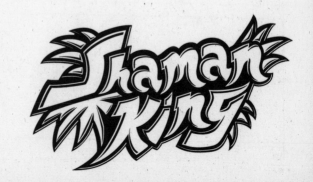

Reincarnation 238: Remain Neutral

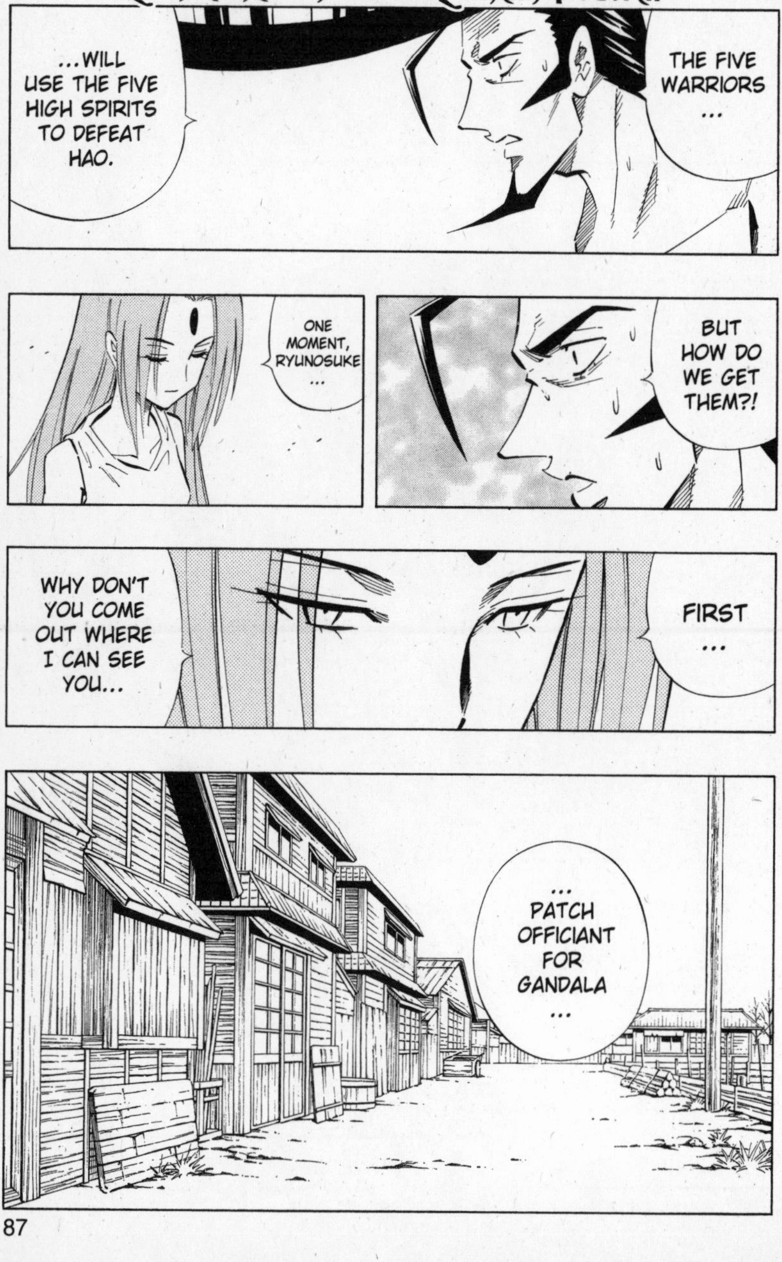
THE FIVE WARRIORS ...
...WILL USE THE FIVE HIGH SPIRITS TO DEFEAT HAO.
BUT HOW DO WE GET THEM?!
ONE MOMENT, RYUNOSUKE ...
FIRST ...
WHY DON'T YOU COME OUT WHERE I CAN SEE YOU...
... PATCH OFFICIANT FOR GANDALA ...

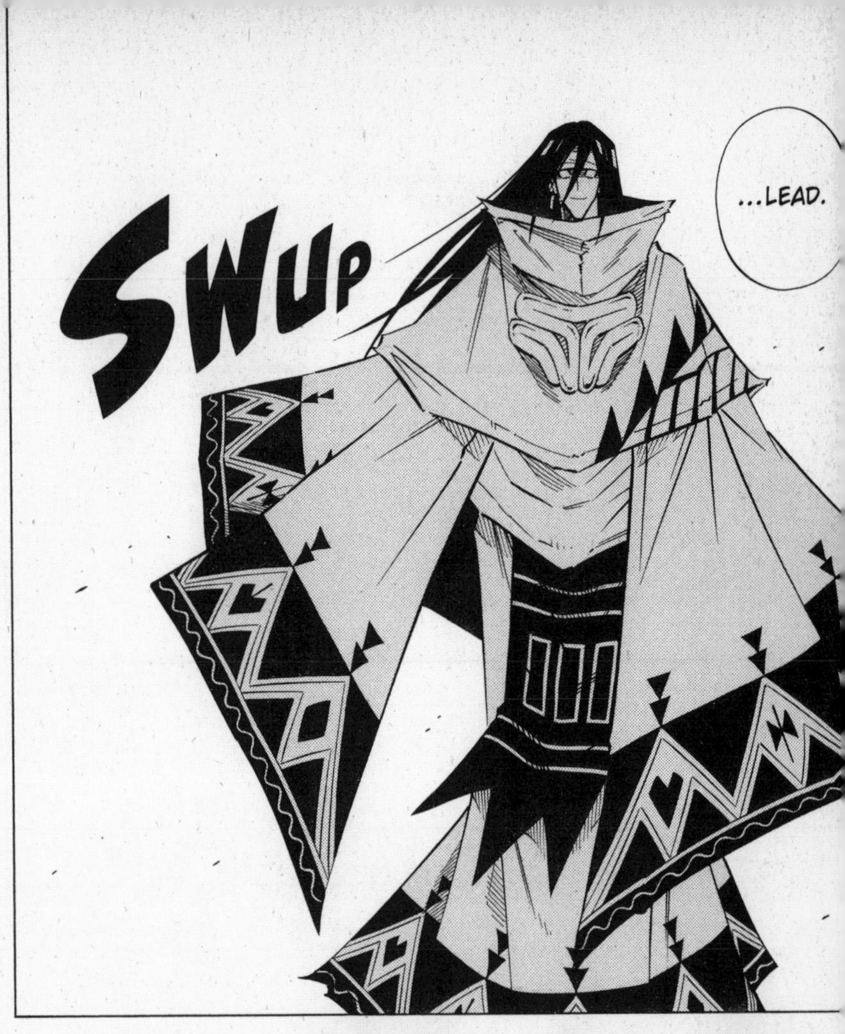
...LEAD.
SWUP
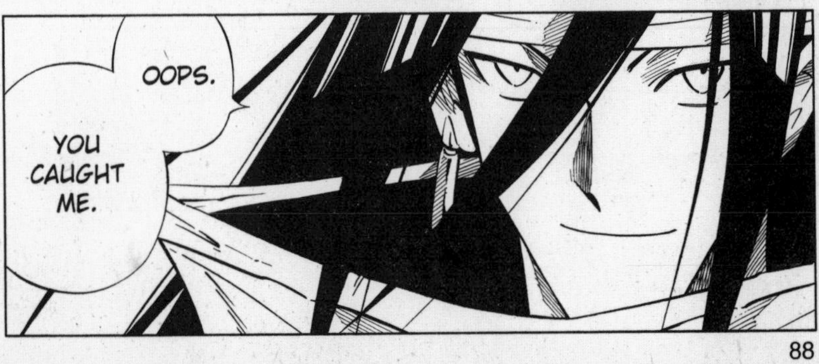
OOPS.
YOU CAUGHT ME.

Reincarnation 238: Remain Neutral

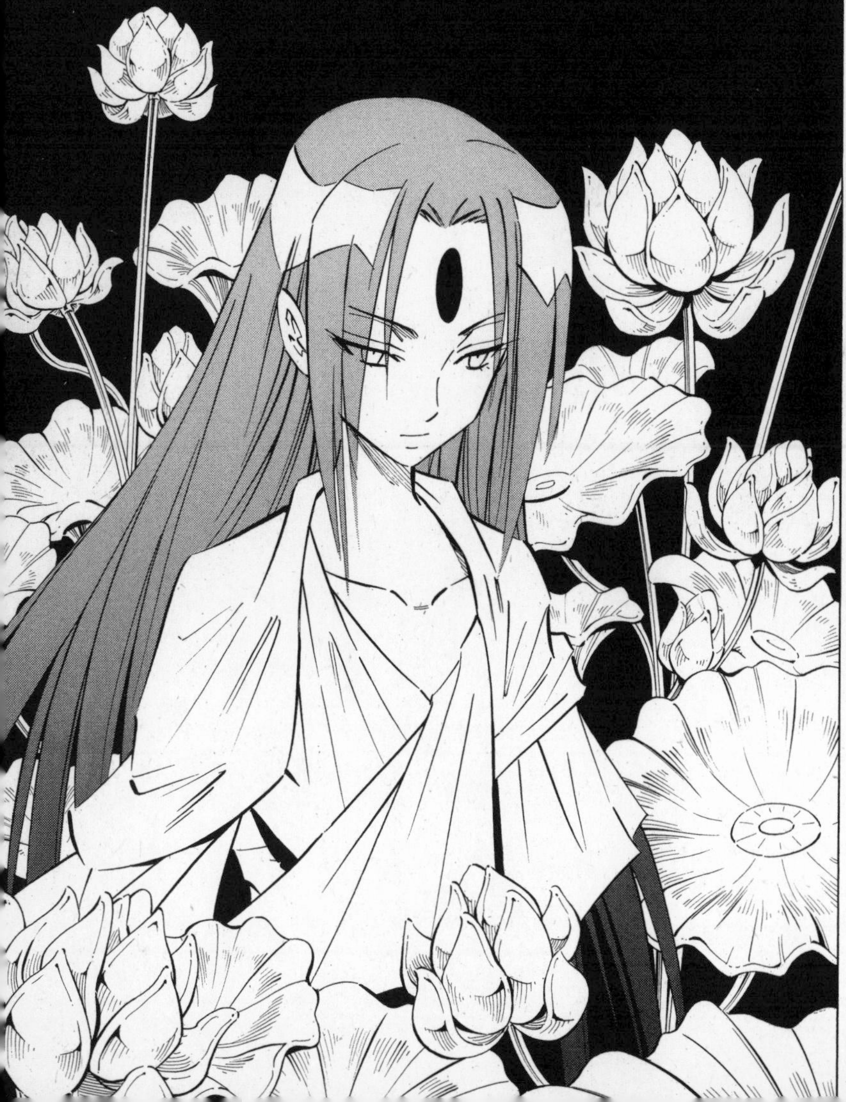

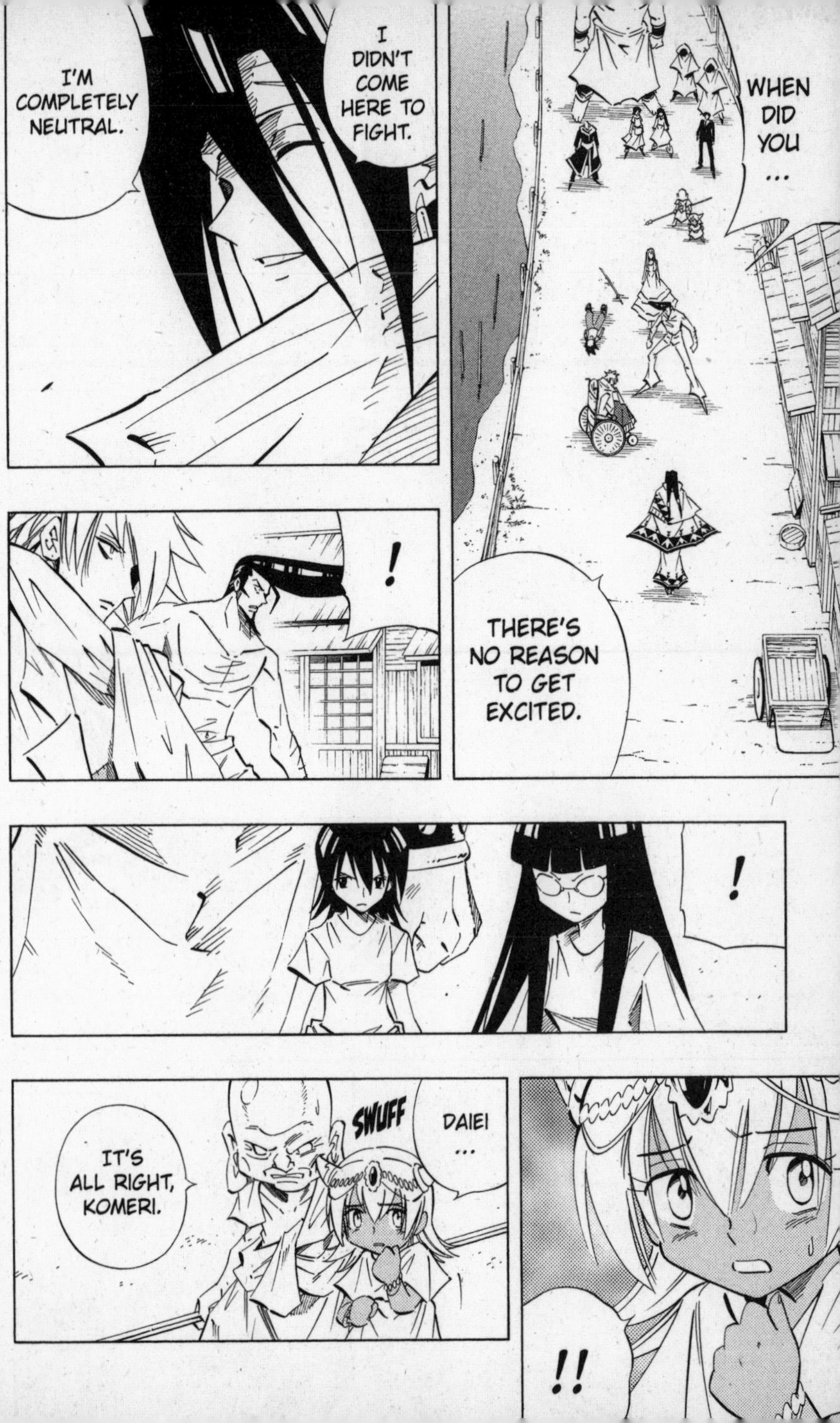
WHEN DID YOU ...
THERE'S NO REASON TO GET EXCITED.
I DIDN'T COME HERE TO FIGHT.
I'M COMPLETELY NEUTRAL.
!
!
!!
DAIEI ...
SWUFF
IT'S ALL RIGHT, KOMERI.

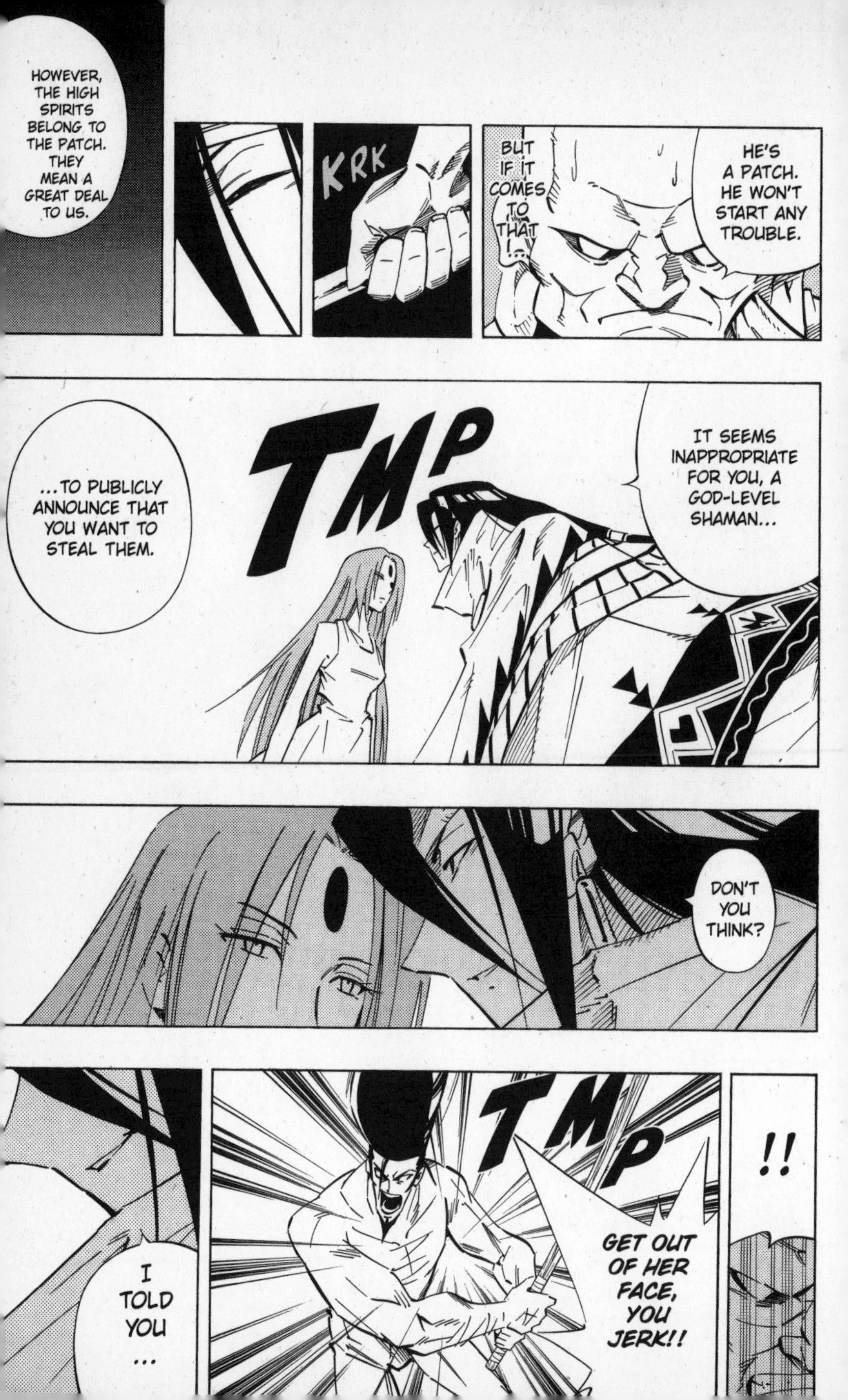

HE'S A PATCH. HE WON'T START ANY TROUBLE.
BUT IF IT COMES TO THAT...
KRK
HOWEVER, THE HIGH SPIRITS BELONG TO THE PATCH. THEY MEAN A GREAT DEAL TO US.
IT SEEMS INAPPROPRIATE FOR YOU, A GOD-LEVEL SHAMAN...
TMP
...TO PUBLICLY ANNOUNCE THAT YOU WANT TO STEAL THEM.
DON'T YOU THINK?
!!
GET OUT OF HER FACE, YOU JERK!!
TMP
I TOLD YOU...

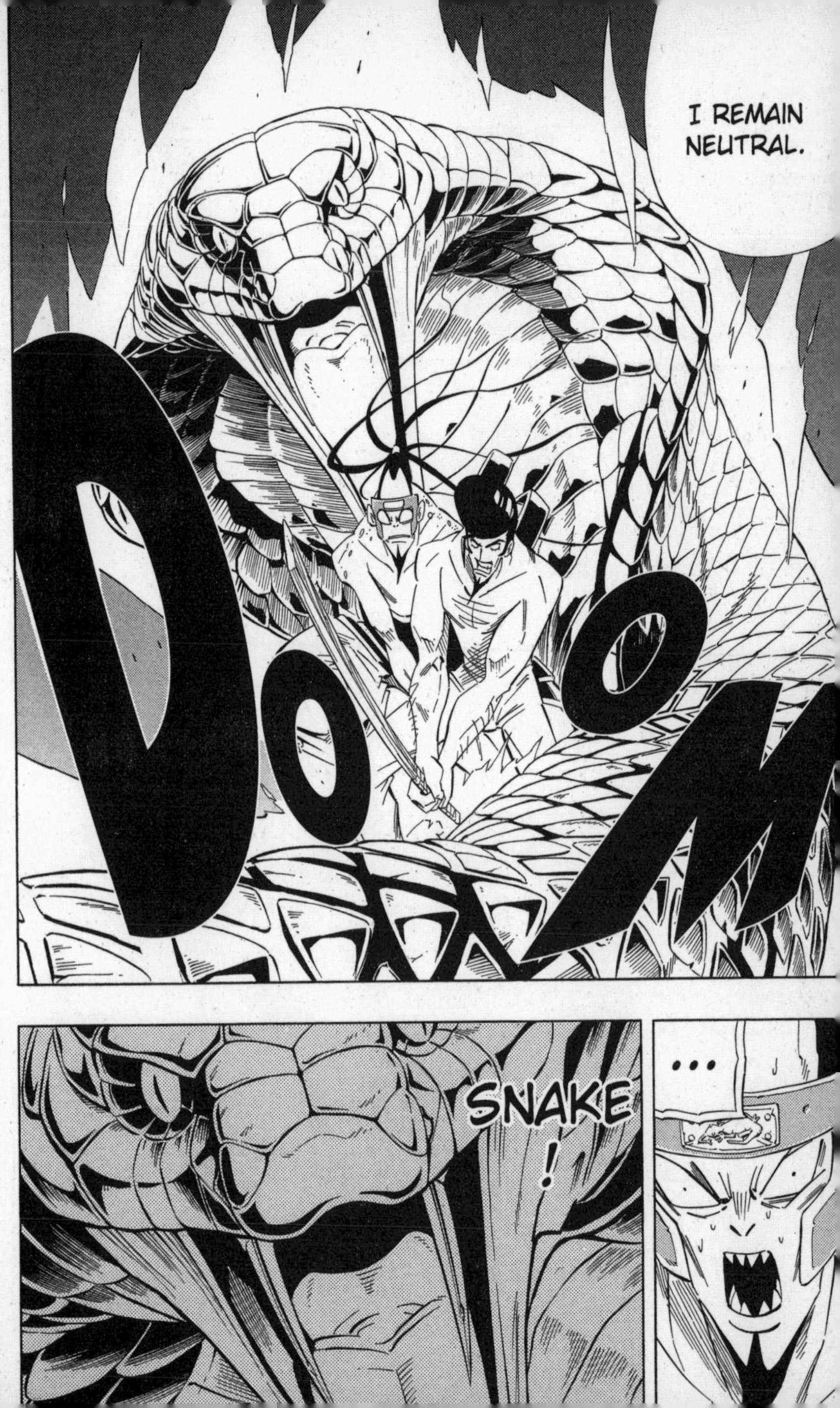
I REMAIN NEUTRAL.
DOOM
...
SNAKE
!

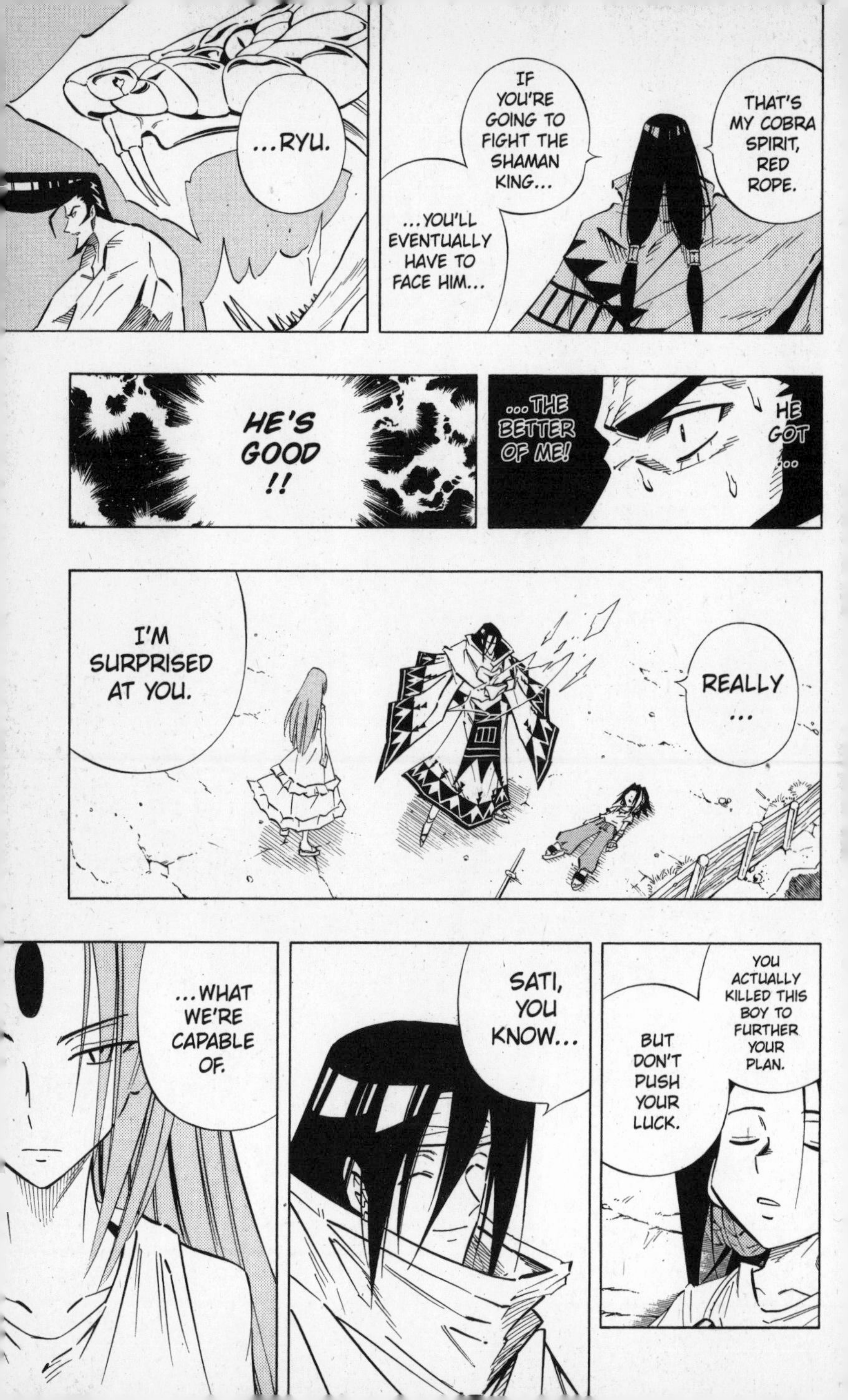
THAT'S MY COBRA SPIRIT, RED ROPE.
IF YOU'RE GOING TO FIGHT THE SHAMAN KING...
...YOU'LL EVENTUALLY HAVE TO FACE HIM...
...RYU.
HE GOT...
...THE BETTER OF ME!
HE'S GOOD !!
REALLY...
I'M SURPRISED AT YOU.
YOU ACTUALLY KILLED THIS BOY TO FURTHER YOUR PLAN.
BUT DON'T PUSH YOUR LUCK.
SATI, YOU KNOW...
...WHAT WE'RE CAPABLE OF.

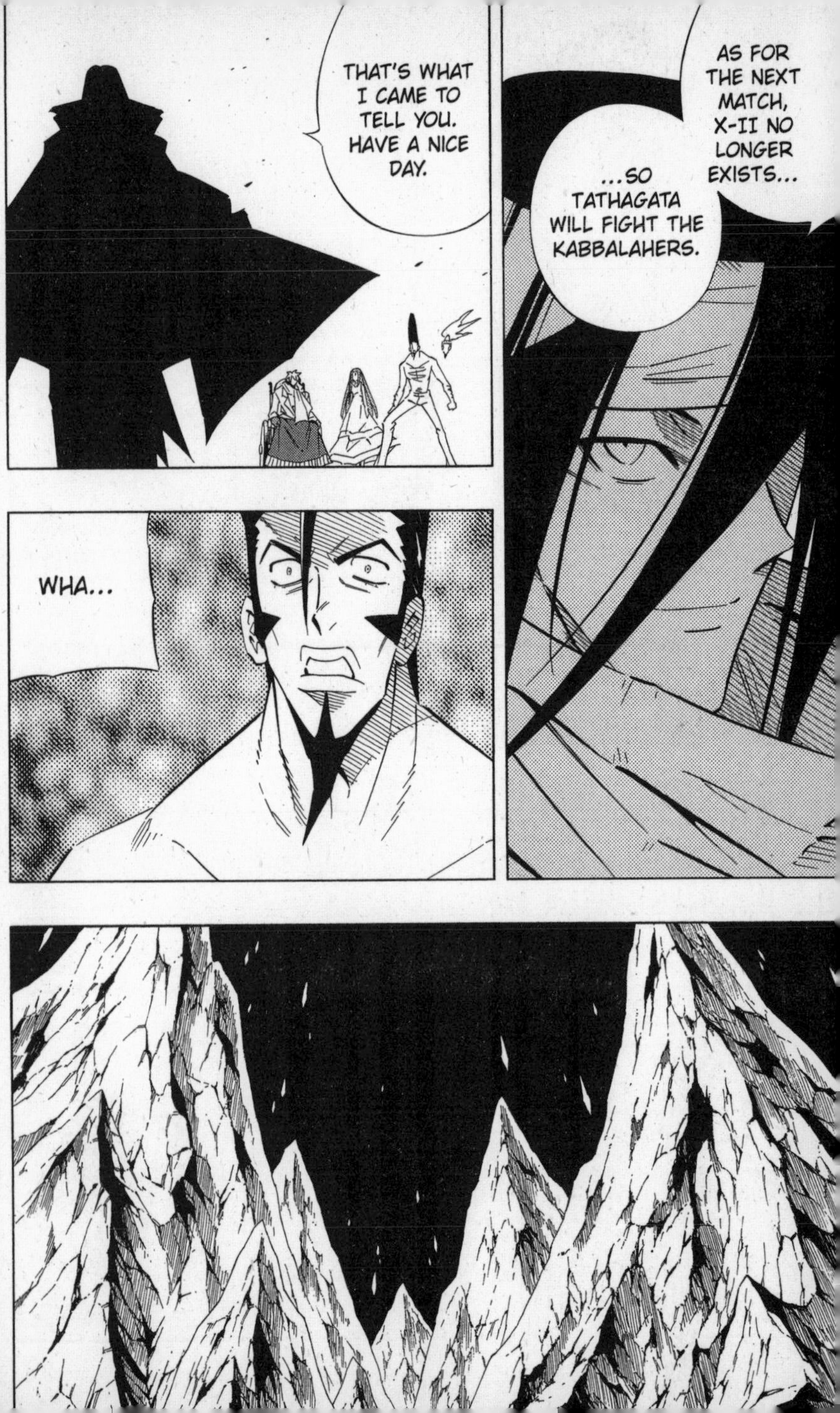
AS FOR THE NEXT MATCH, X-II NO LONGER EXISTS...
...SO TATHAGATA WILL FIGHT THE KABBALAHERS.
THAT'S WHAT I CAME TO TELL YOU. HAVE A NICE DAY.
WHA...

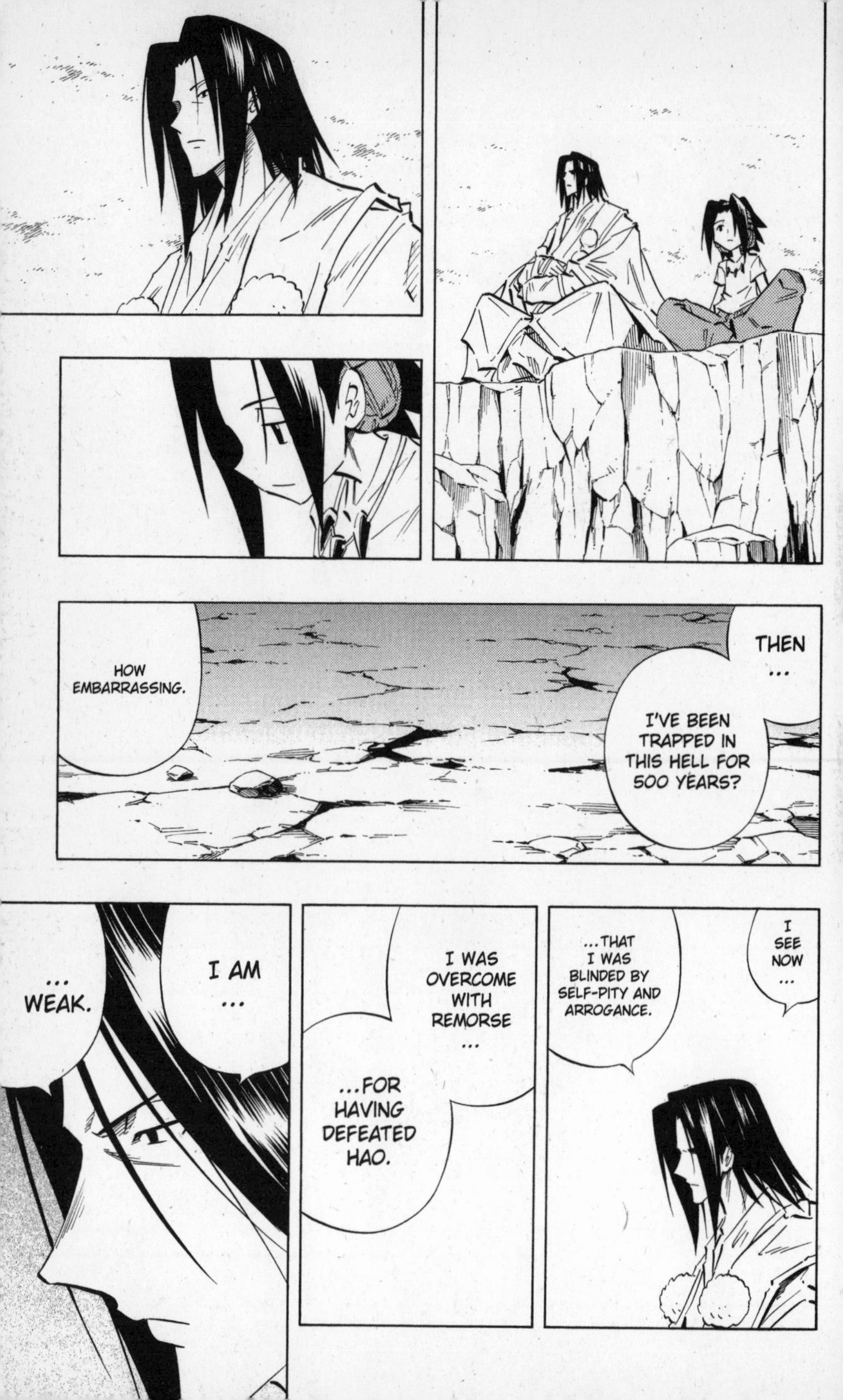
THEN ...
I'VE BEEN TRAPPED IN THIS HELL FOR 500 YEARS?
HOW EMBARRASSING.
I SEE NOW ...
...THAT I WAS BLINDED BY SELF-PITY AND ARROGANCE.
I WAS OVERCOME WITH REMORSE ...
...FOR HAVING DEFEATED HAO.
I AM ...
... WEAK.

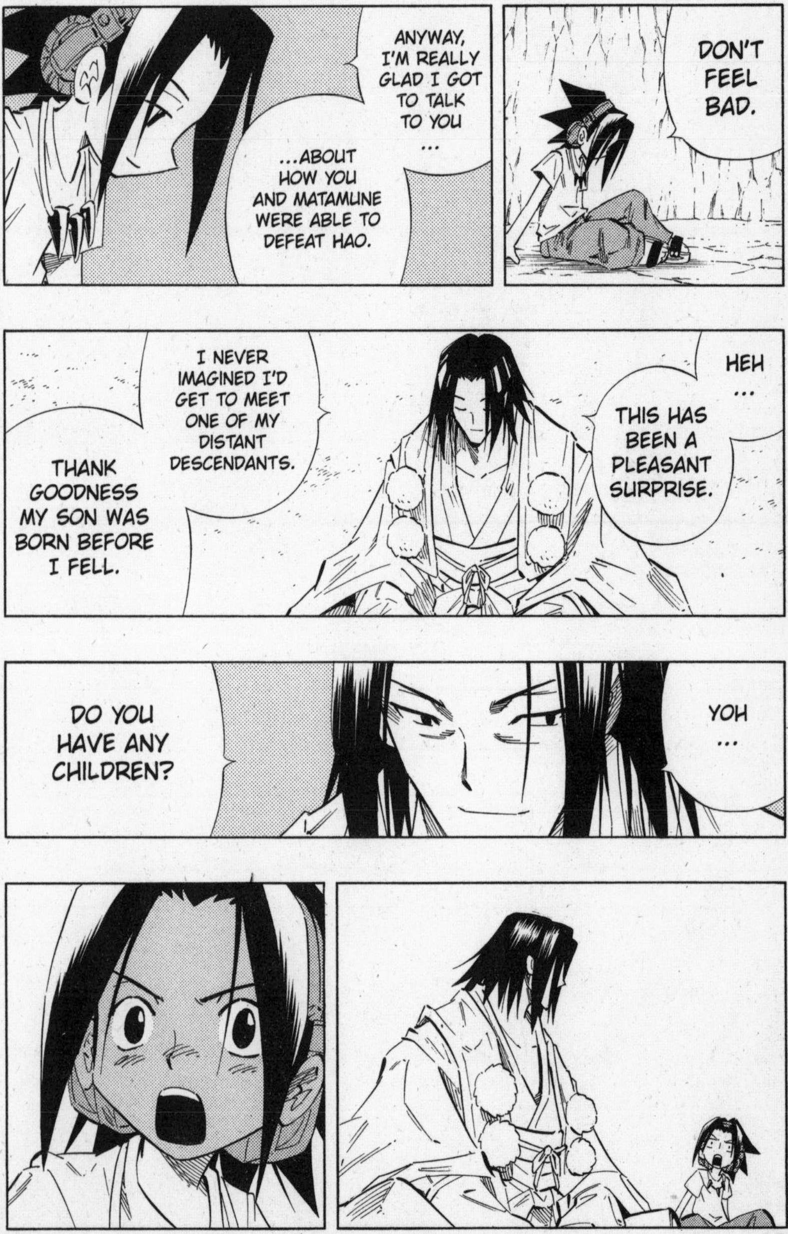
DON'T FEEL BAD.
ANYWAY, I'M REALLY GLAD I GOT TO TALK TO YOU ...
...ABOUT HOW YOU AND MATAMUNE WERE ABLE TO DEFEAT HAO.
HEH ...
THIS HAS BEEN A PLEASANT SURPRISE.
I NEVER IMAGINED I'D GET TO MEET ONE OF MY DISTANT DESCENDANTS.
THANK GOODNESS MY SON WAS BORN BEFORE I FELL.
YOH ...
DO YOU HAVE ANY CHILDREN?

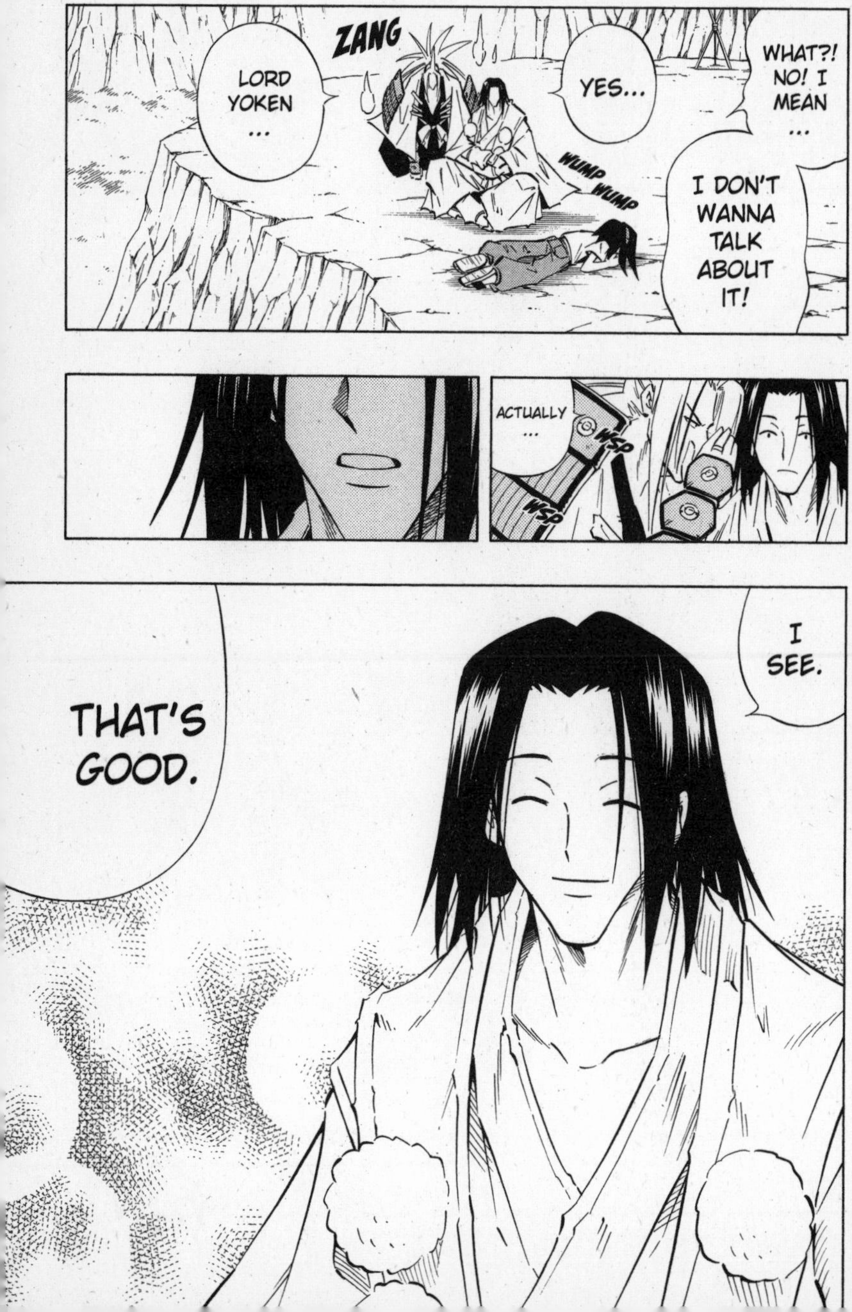
WHAT?! NO! I MEAN ...
I DON'T WANNA TALK ABOUT IT!
YES...
ZANG
LORD YOKEN ...
WUMP WUMP
ACTUALLY ...
WSP
WSP
I SEE.
THAT'S GOOD.

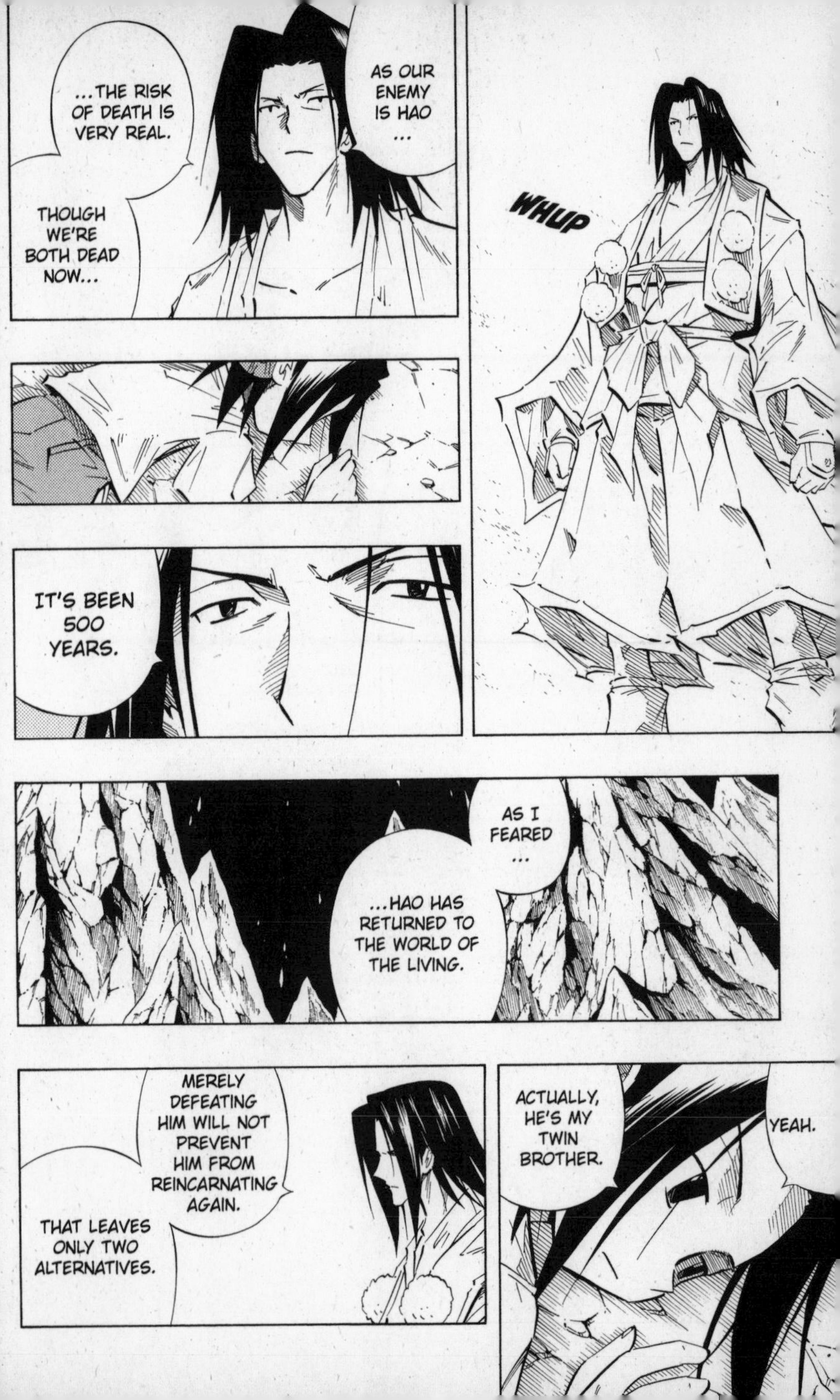
WHUP
AS OUR ENEMY IS HAO ...
...THE RISK OF DEATH IS VERY REAL.
THOUGH WE'RE BOTH DEAD NOW...
IT'S BEEN 500 YEARS.
AS I FEARED ...
...HAO HAS RETURNED TO THE WORLD OF THE LIVING.
YEAH.
ACTUALLY, HE'S MY TWIN BROTHER.
MERELY DEFEATING HIM WILL NOT PREVENT HIM FROM REINCARNATING AGAIN.
THAT LEAVES ONLY TWO ALTERNATIVES.

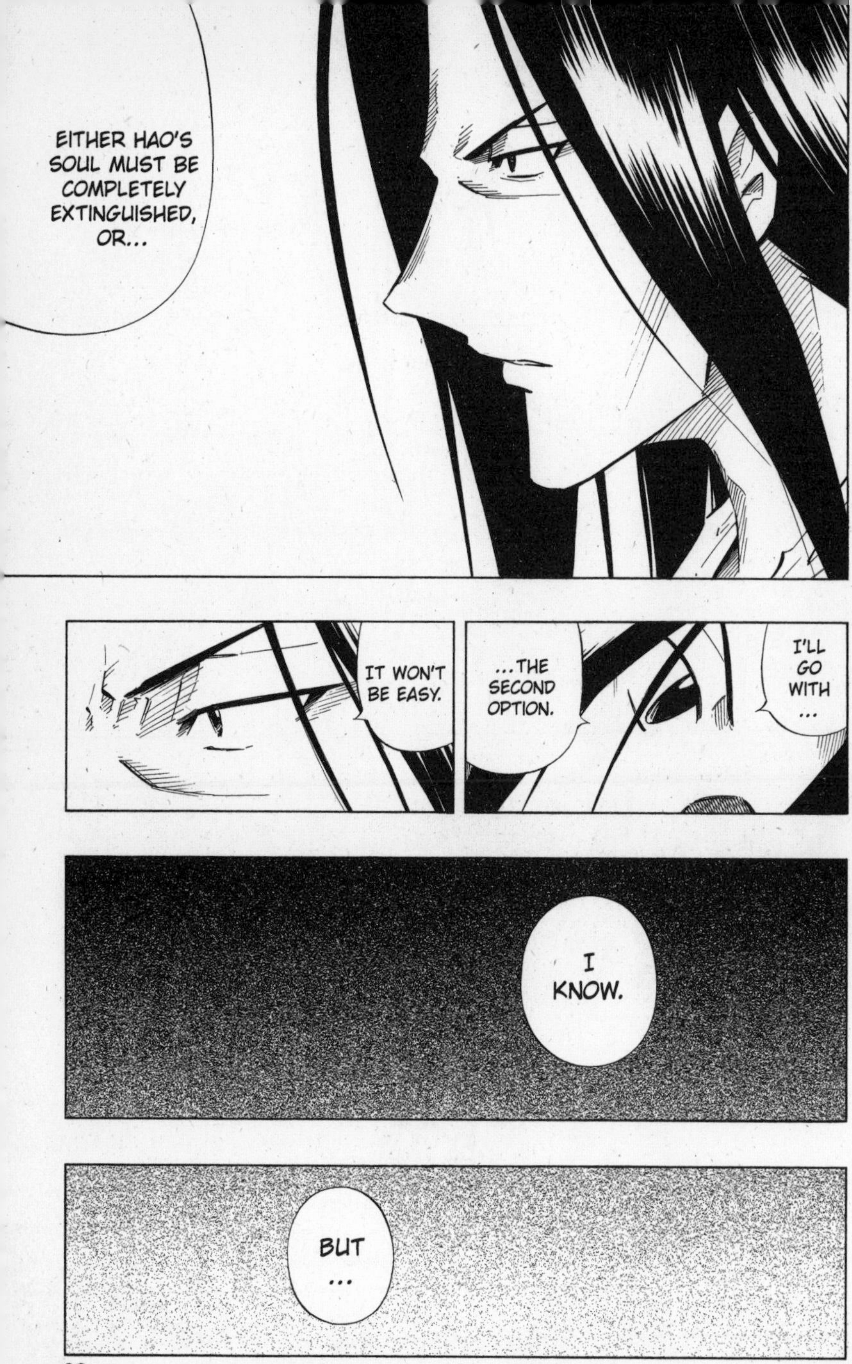
EITHER HAO'S SOUL MUST BE COMPLETELY EXTINGUISHED, OR...
I'LL GO WITH ...
...THE SECOND OPTION.
IT WON'T BE EASY.
I KNOW.
BUT ...

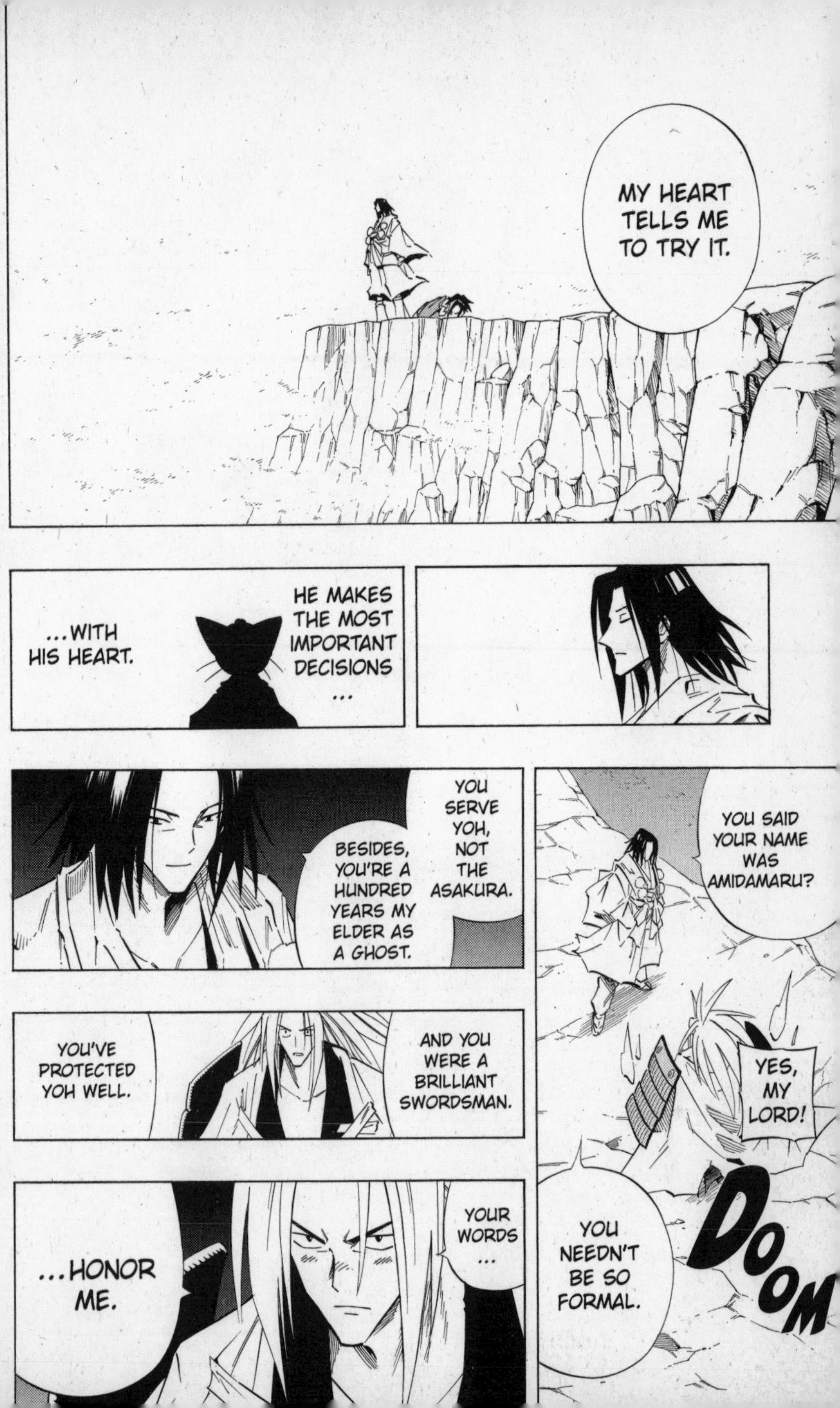
MY HEART TELLS ME TO TRY IT.
HE MAKES THE MOST IMPORTANT DECISIONS ...
...WITH HIS HEART.
YOU SAID YOUR NAME WAS AMIDAMARU?
YES, MY LORD!
DOOM
YOU NEEDN'T BE SO FORMAL.
YOU SERVE YOH, NOT THE ASAKURA.
BESIDES, YOU'RE A HUNDRED YEARS MY ELDER AS A GHOST.
AND YOU WERE A BRILLIANT SWORDSMAN.
YOU'VE PROTECTED YOH WELL.
YOUR WORDS ...
...HONOR ME.

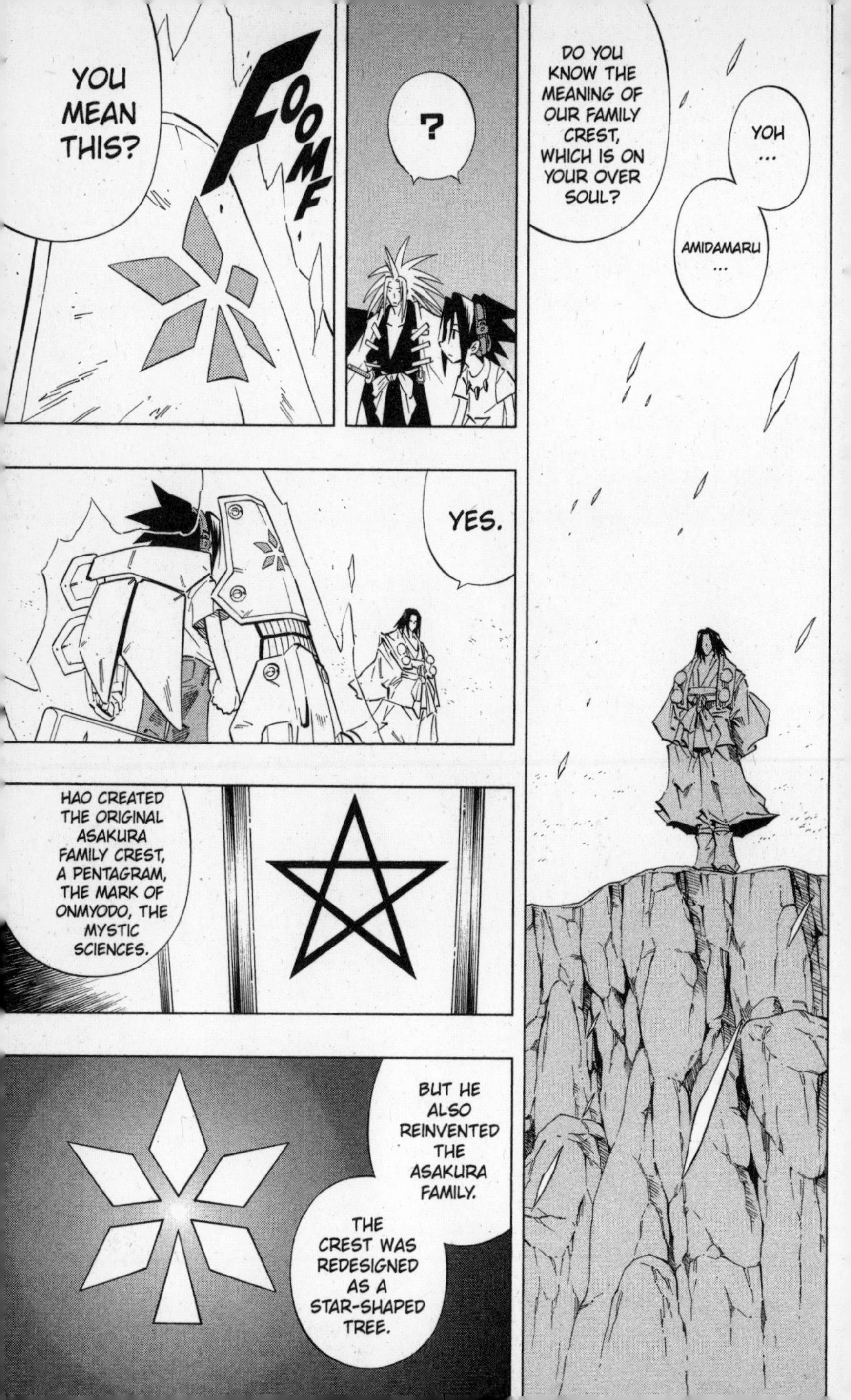
YOH ...
AMIDAMARU ...
DO YOU KNOW THE MEANING OF OUR FAMILY CREST, WHICH IS ON YOUR OVER SOUL?
?
YOU MEAN THIS?
FOOMF
YES.
HAO CREATED THE ORIGINAL ASAKURA FAMILY CREST, A PENTAGRAM, THE MARK OF ONMYODO, THE MYSTIC SCIENCES.
BUT HE ALSO REINVENTED THE ASAKURA FAMILY.
THE CREST WAS REDESIGNED AS A STAR-SHAPED TREE.

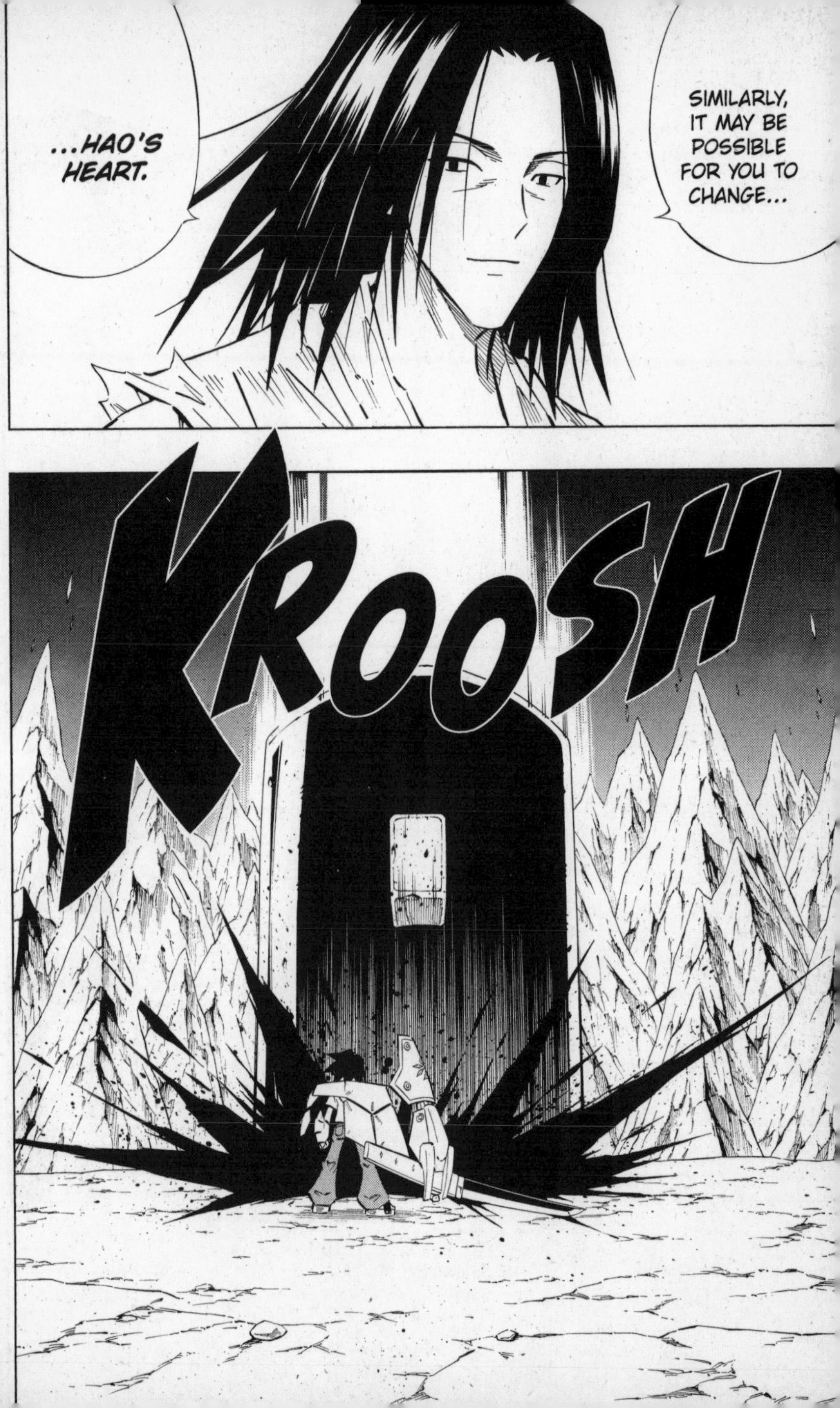
SIMILARLY, IT MAY BE POSSIBLE FOR YOU TO CHANGE...
...HAO'S HEART.
KROOSH

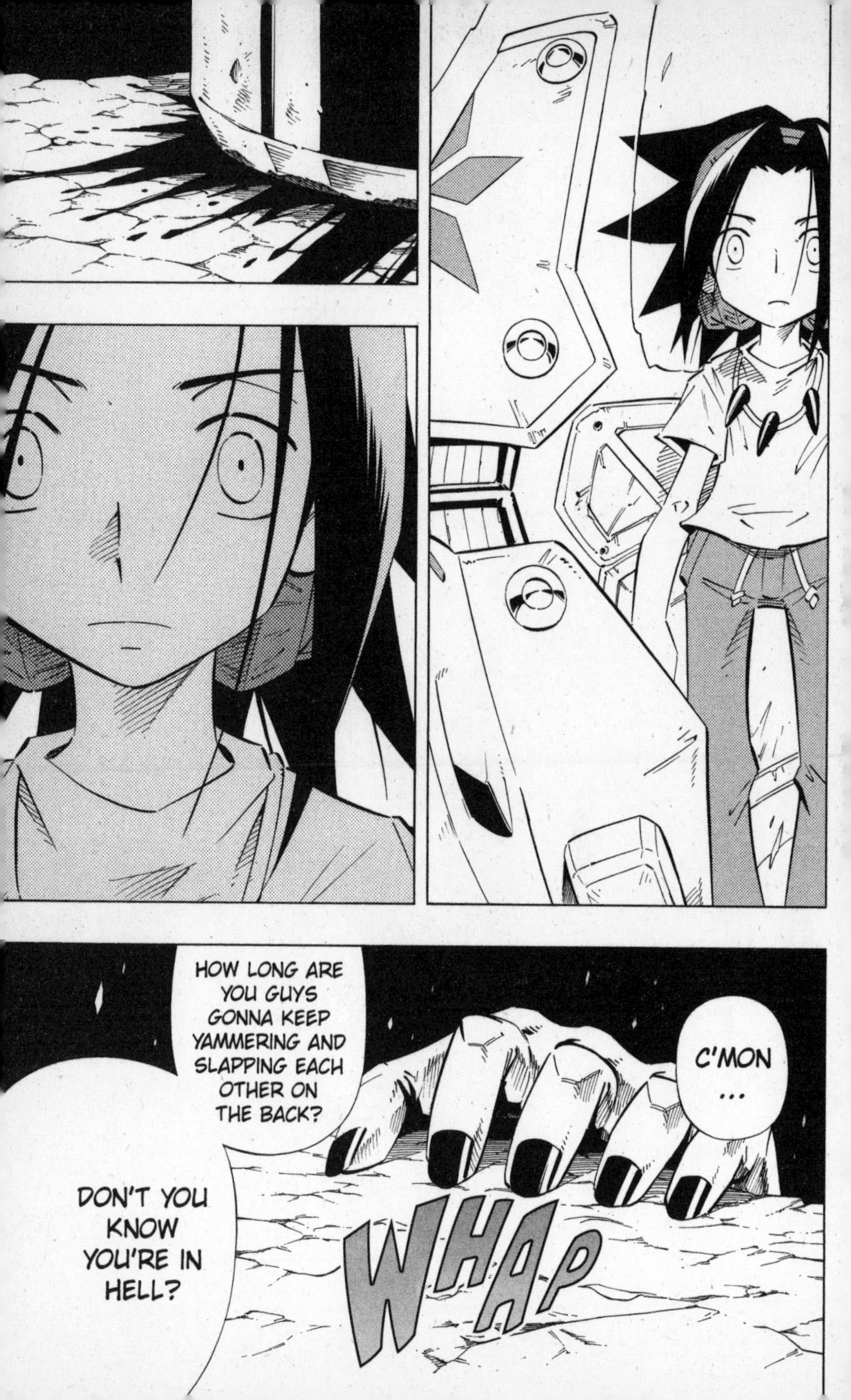
C'MON ...
HOW LONG ARE YOU GUYS GONNA KEEP YAMMERING AND SLAPPING EACH OTHER ON THE BACK?
DON'T YOU KNOW YOU'RE IN HELL?
WHAP

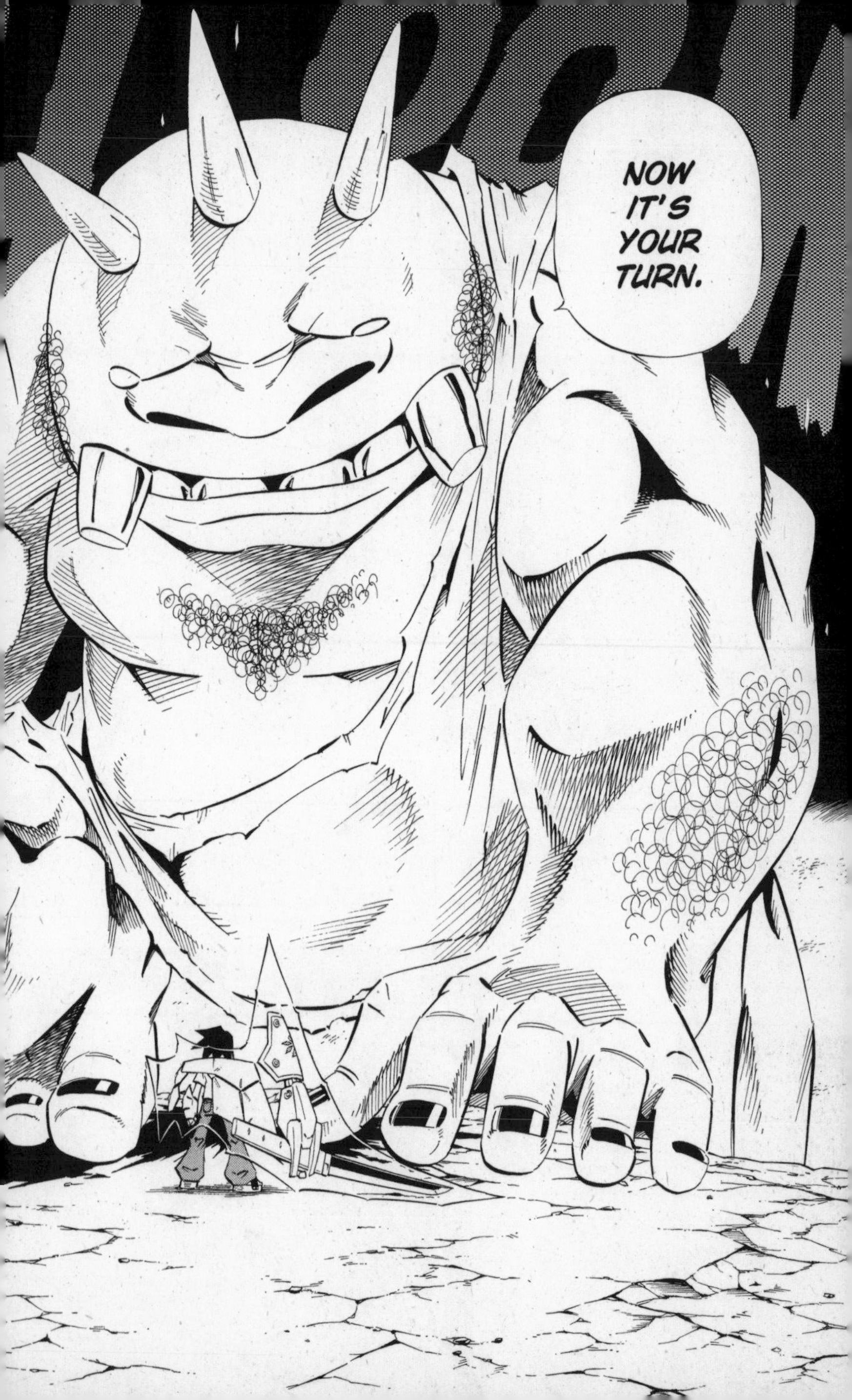
NOW IT'S YOUR TURN.

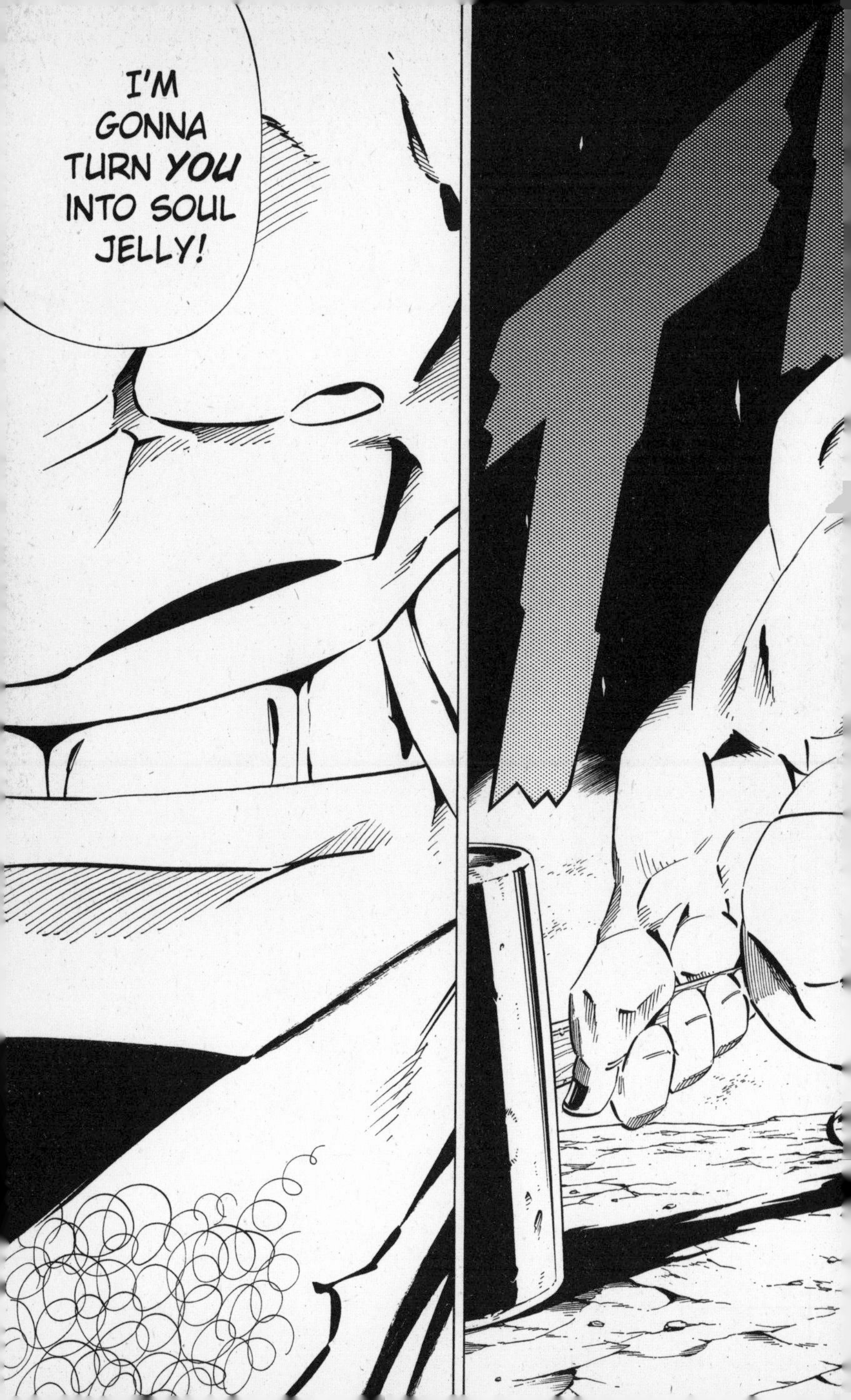
I'M GONNA TURN YOU INTO SOUL JELLY!

SHAMAN KING CHARACTER FILE No.141

2001
(JAN)

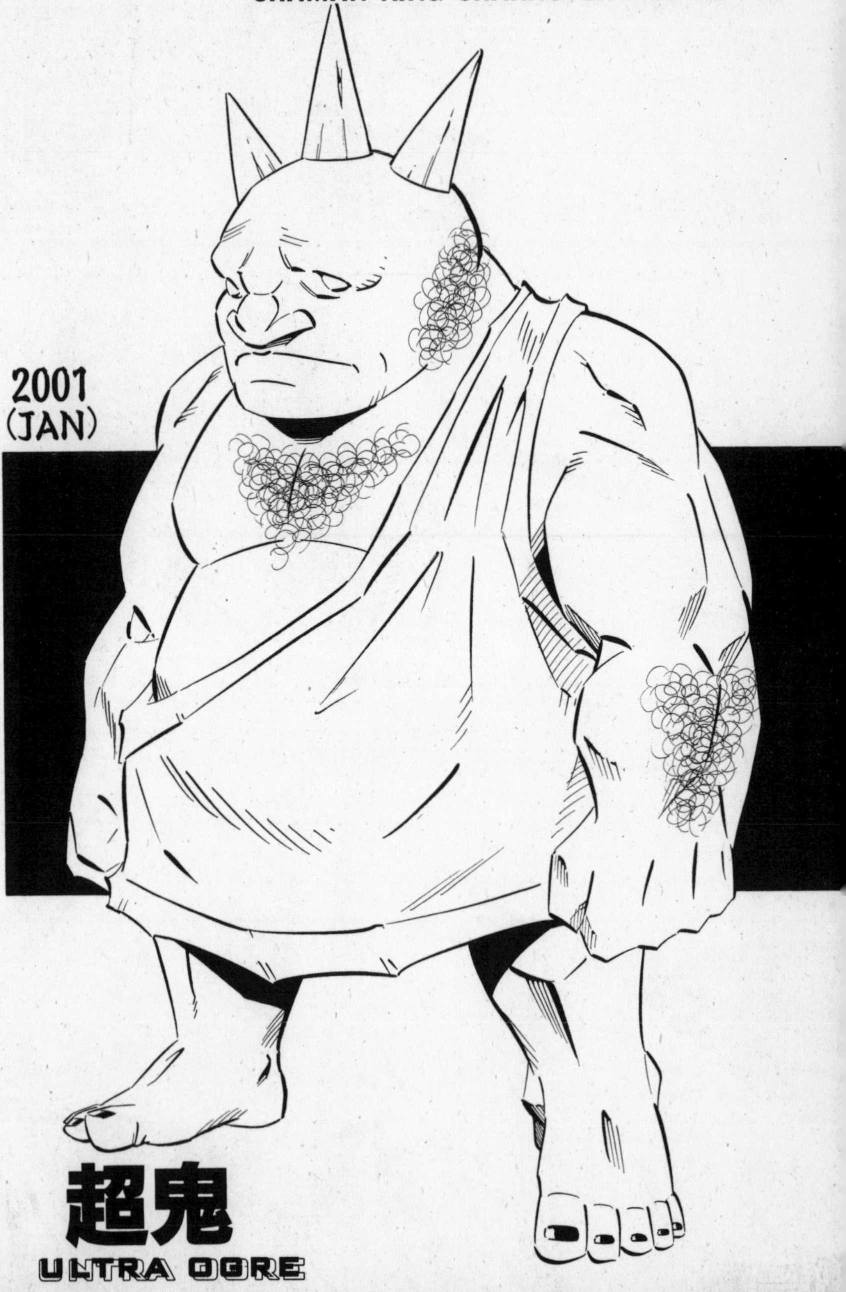

超鬼
ULTRA OGRE

Reincarnation 239: A Great Trial

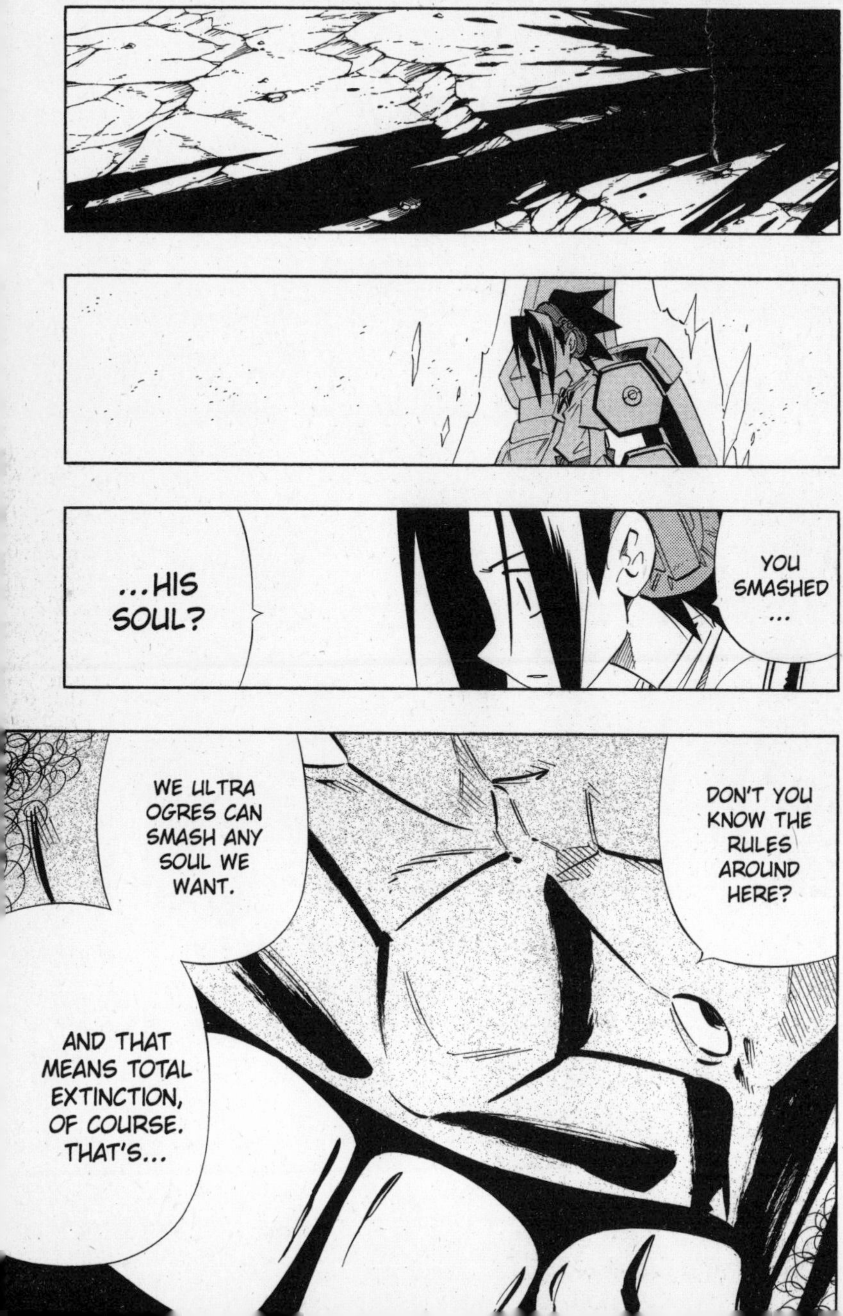
YOU SMASHED ...
...HIS SOUL?
DON'T YOU KNOW THE RULES AROUND HERE?
WE ULTRA OGRES CAN SMASH ANY SOUL WE WANT.
AND THAT MEANS TOTAL EXTINCTION, OF COURSE. THAT'S...

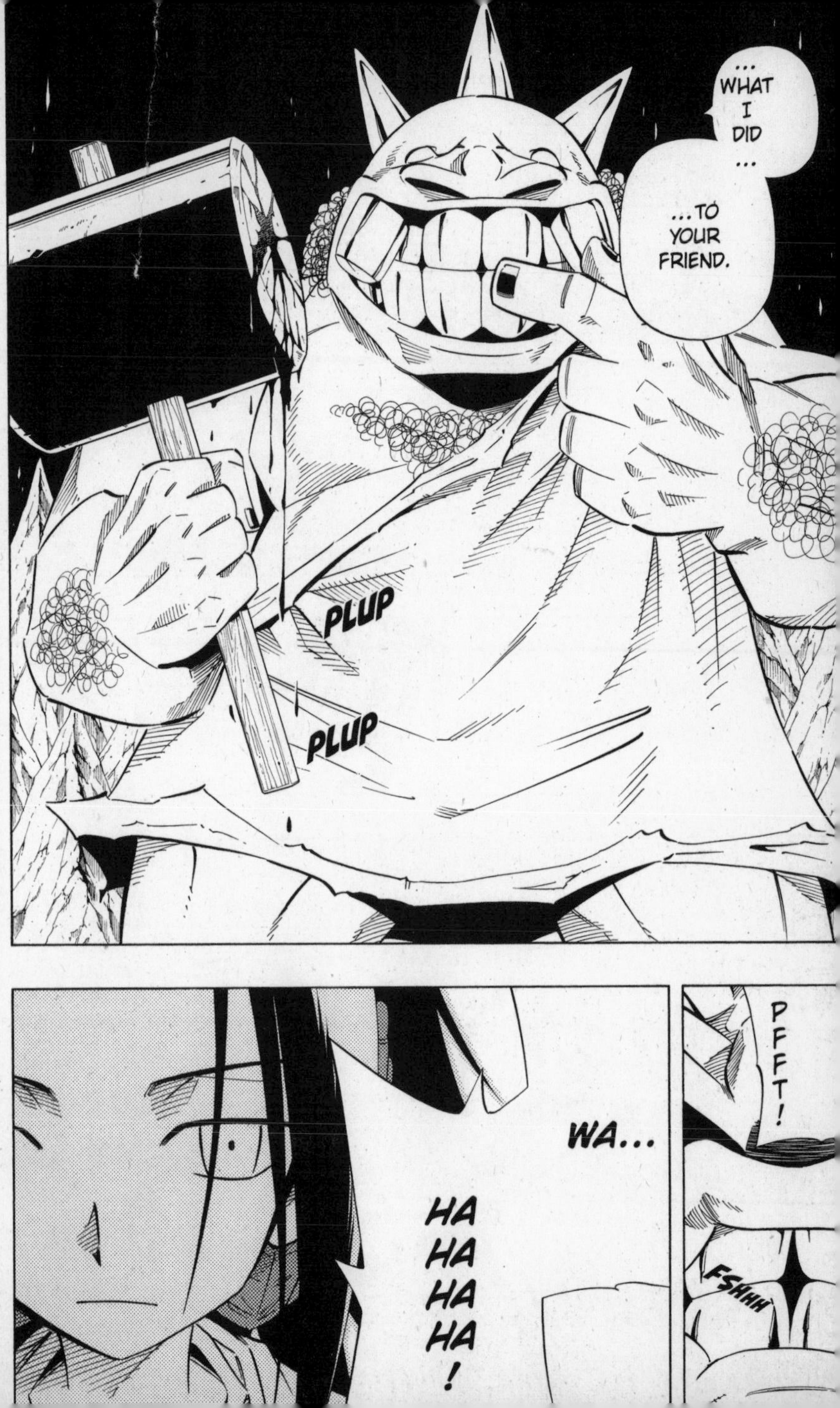
...WHAT I DID...
...TO YOUR FRIEND.
PLUP
PLUP
PFFT!
FSHHH
WA...
HA HA HA HA!

Reincarnation 239: A Great Trial

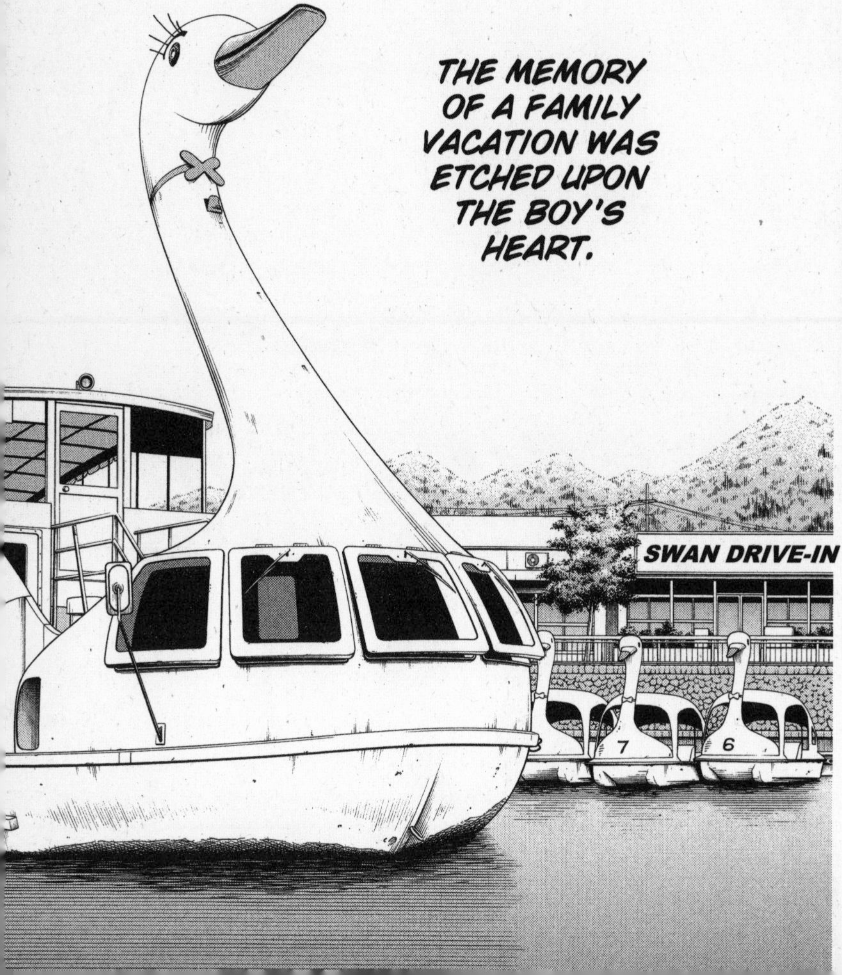
THE MEMORY OF A FAMILY VACATION WAS ETCHED UPON THE BOY'S HEART.
SWAN DRIVE-IN
7
6

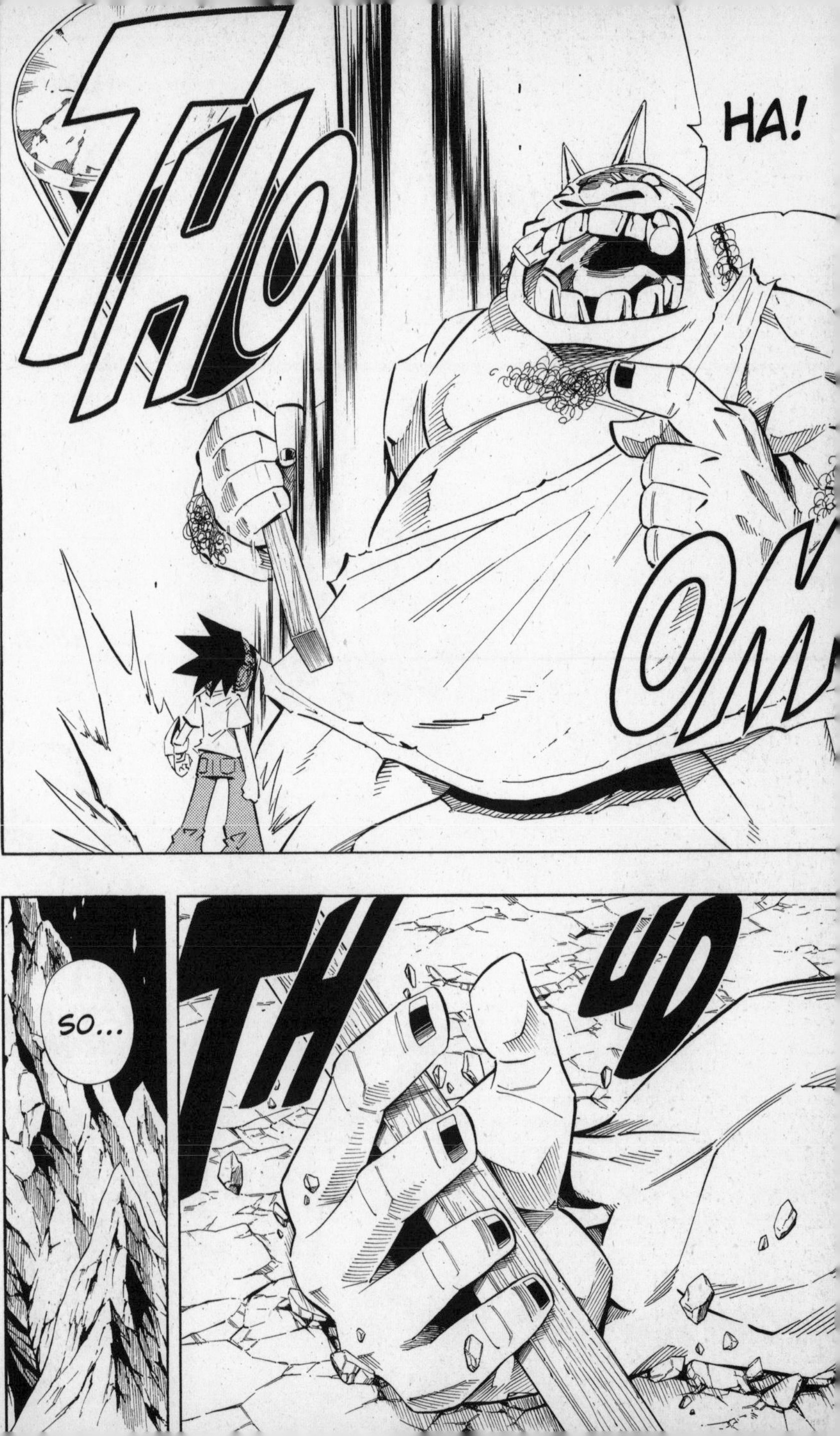
HA!
THOOM
THUD
SO...

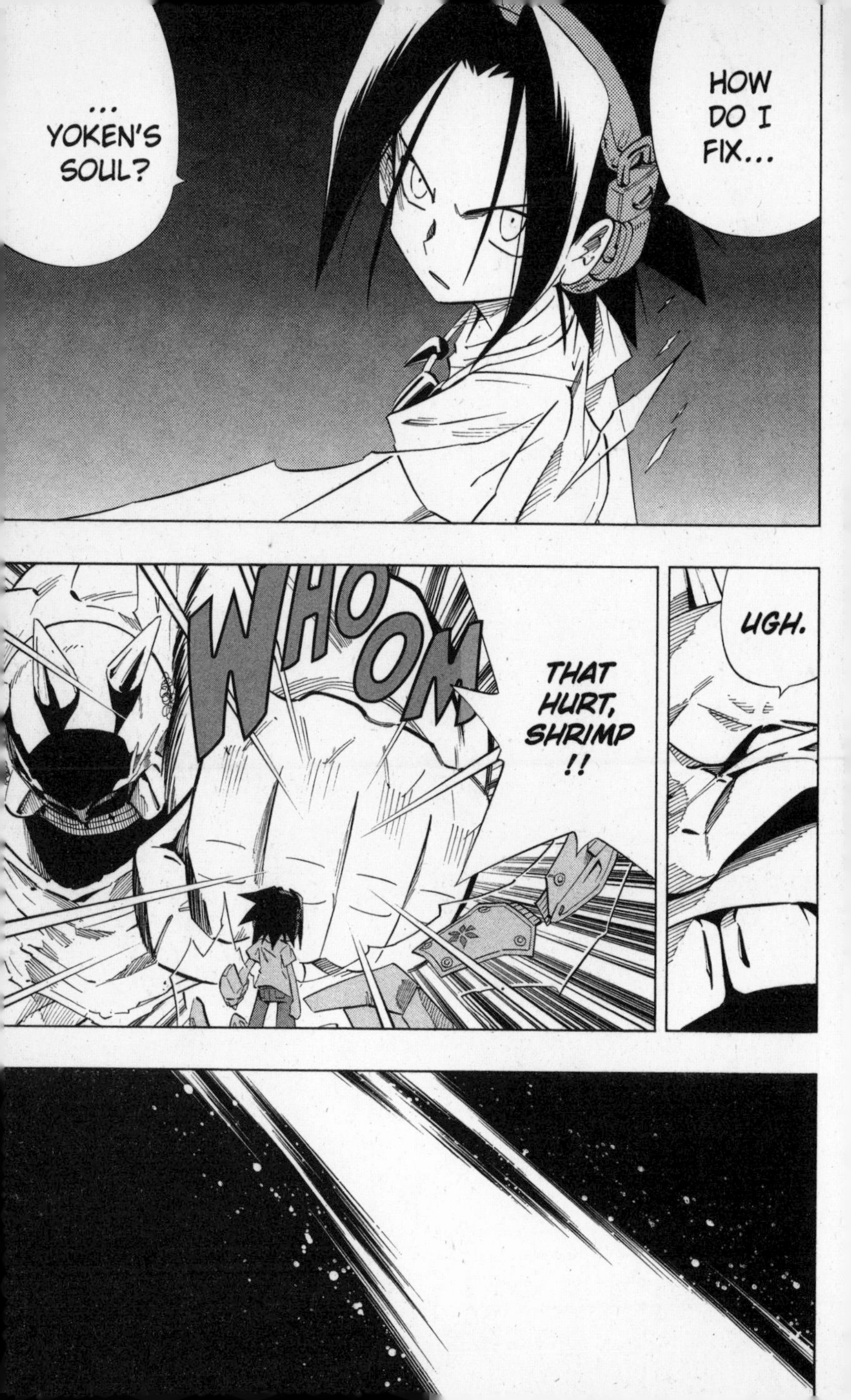
HOW DO I FIX...
... YOKEN'S SOUL?
UGH.
WHOOM
THAT HURT, SHRIMP!!

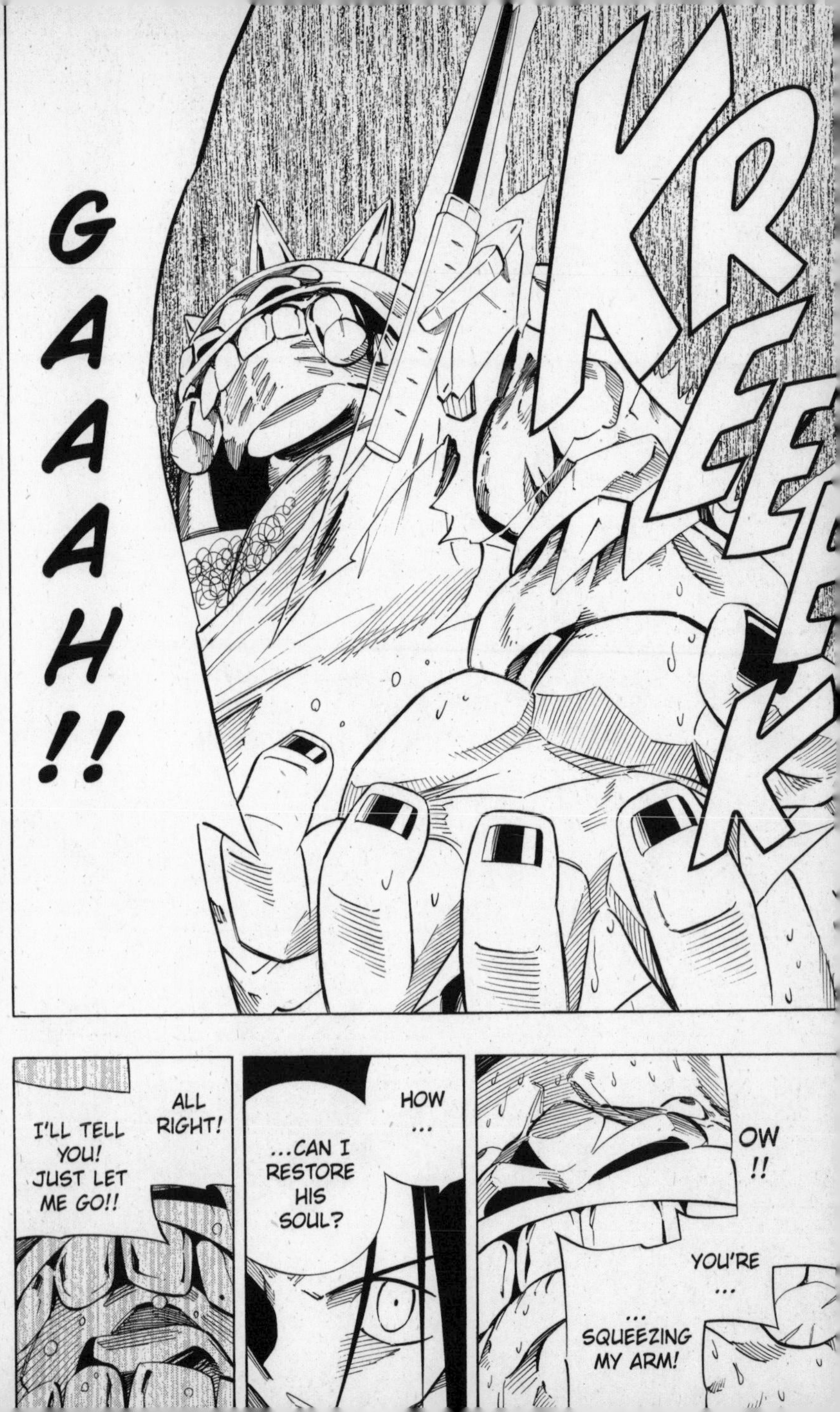
KREEEK
GAAAH!!
OW!!
YOU'RE...
...SQUEEZING MY ARM!
HOW...
...CAN I RESTORE HIS SOUL?
ALL RIGHT!
I'LL TELL YOU! JUST LET ME GO!!

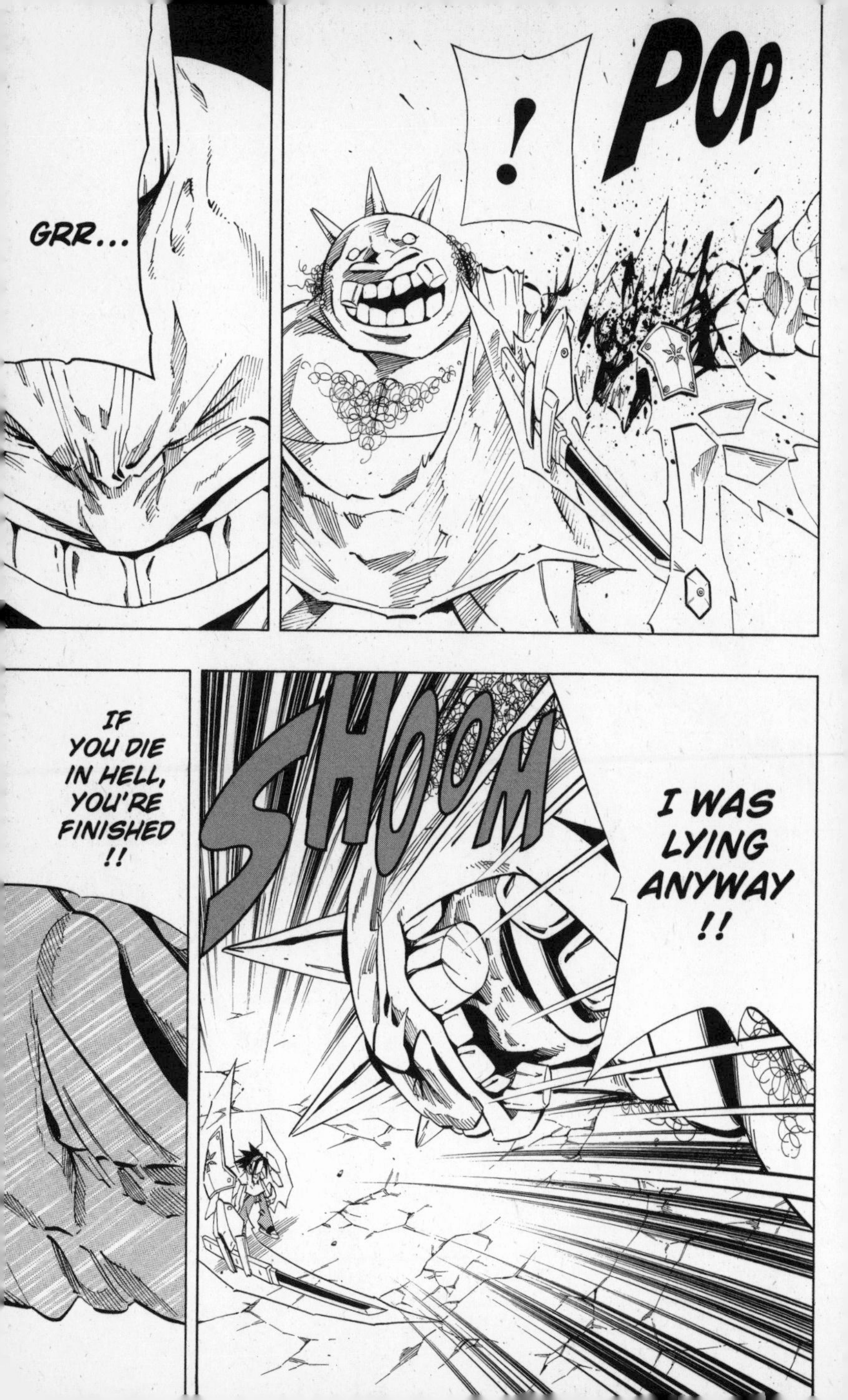
POP
!
GRR...
SHOOM
I WAS LYING ANYWAY !!
IF YOU DIE IN HELL, YOU'RE FINISHED !!

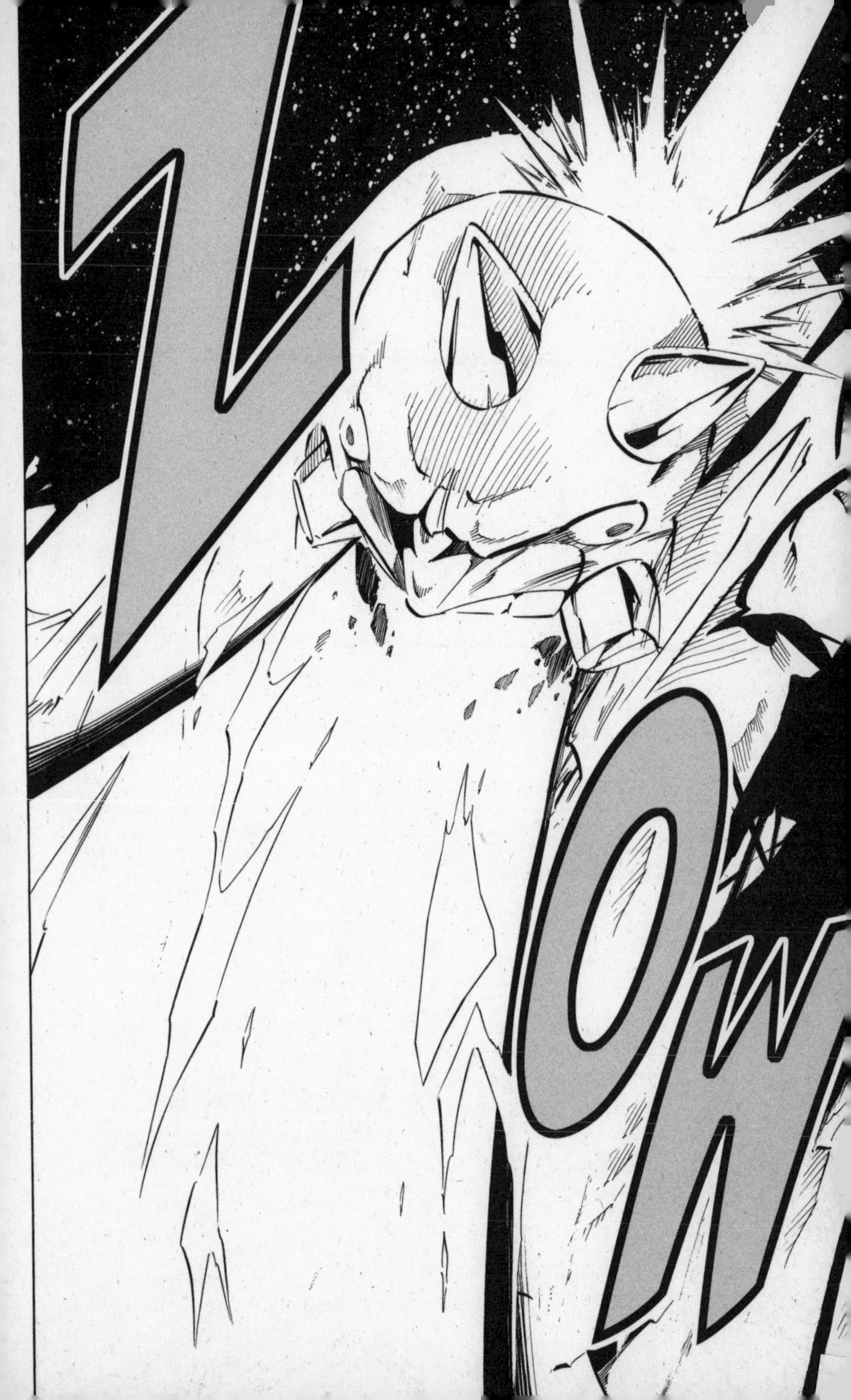
ZOWH

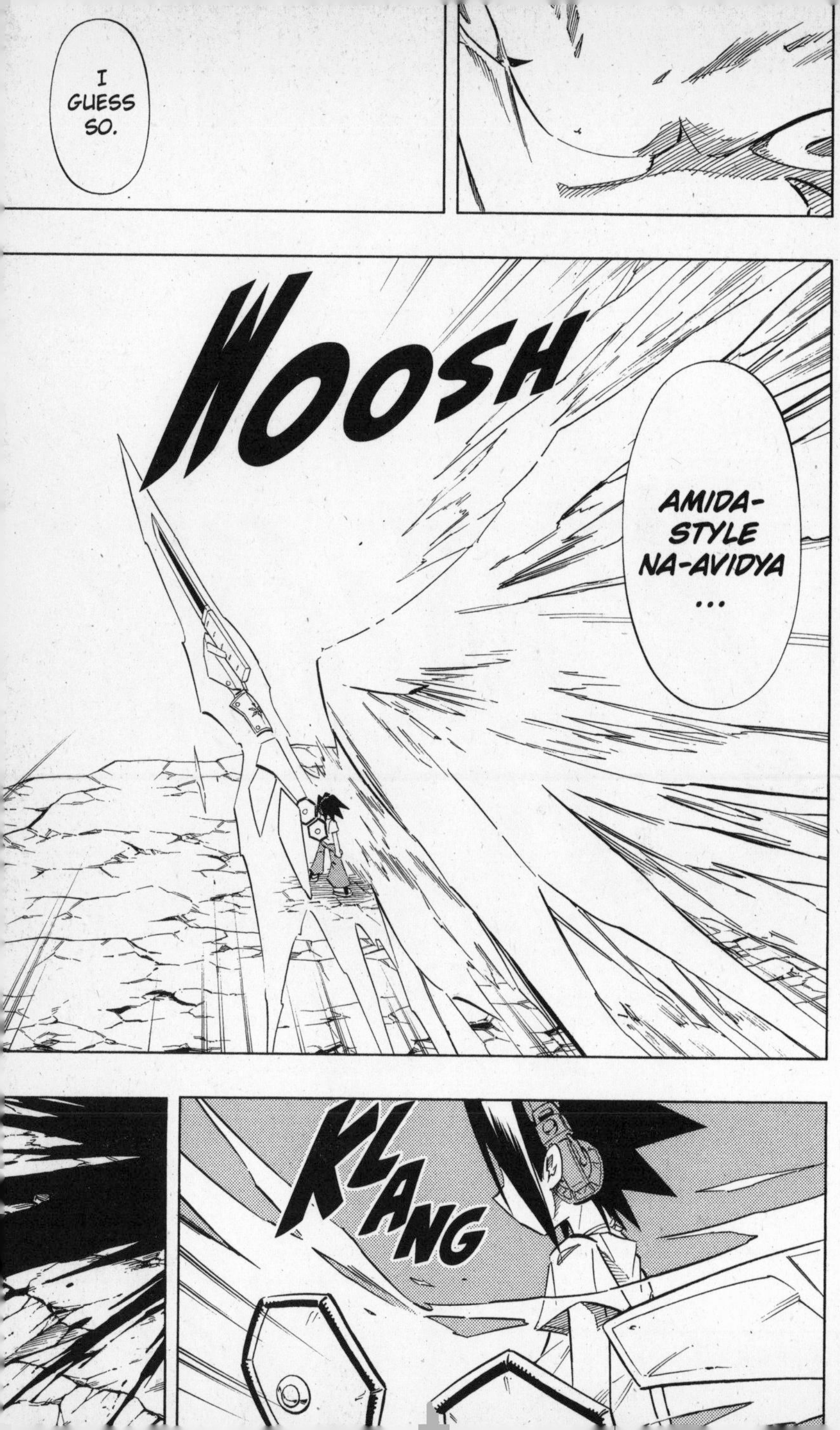
I GUESS SO.
WOOSH
AMIDA-STYLE NA-AVIDYA ...
KLANG

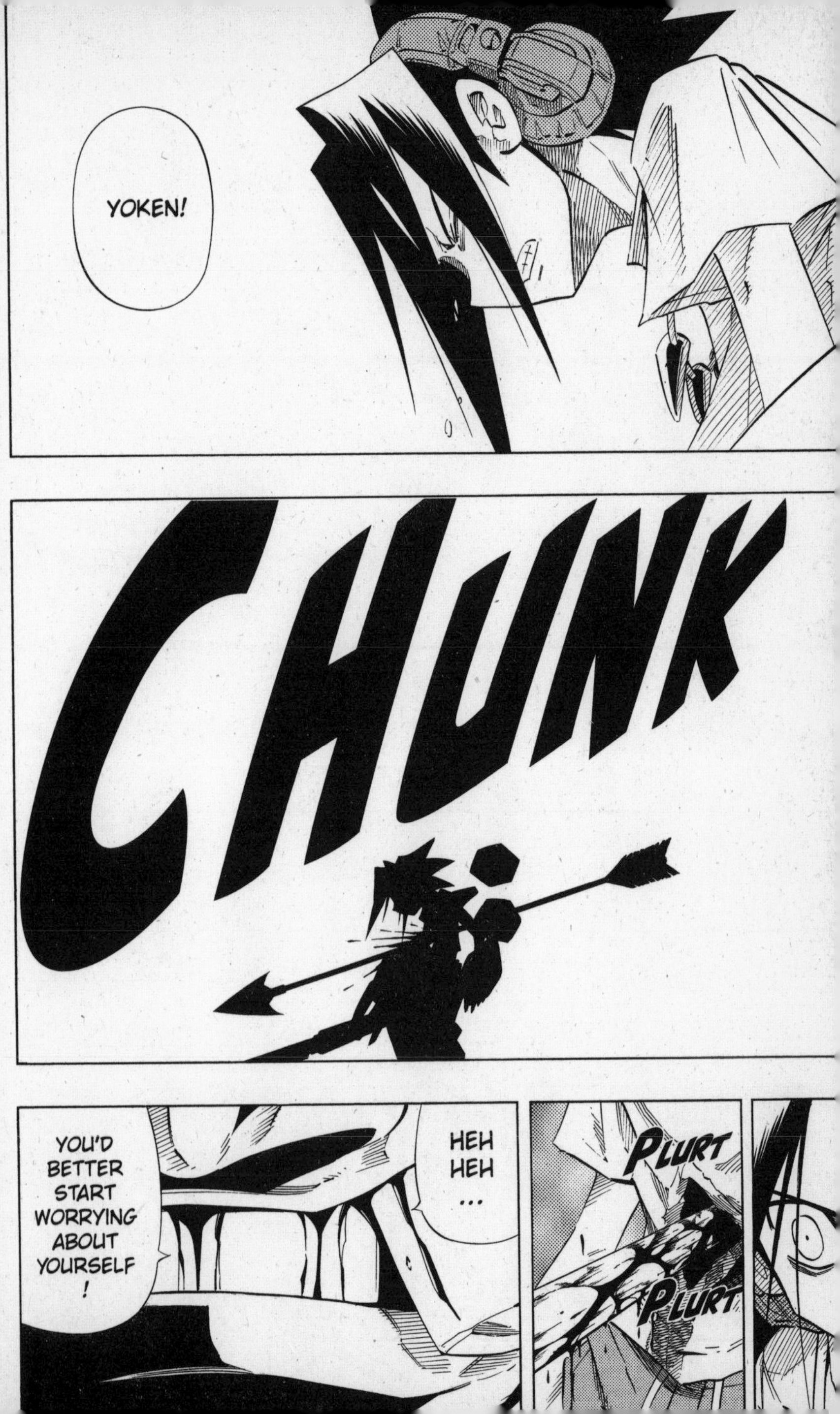
YOKEN!
CHUNK
PLURT
PLURT
HEH HEH ...
YOU'D BETTER START WORRYING ABOUT YOURSELF !

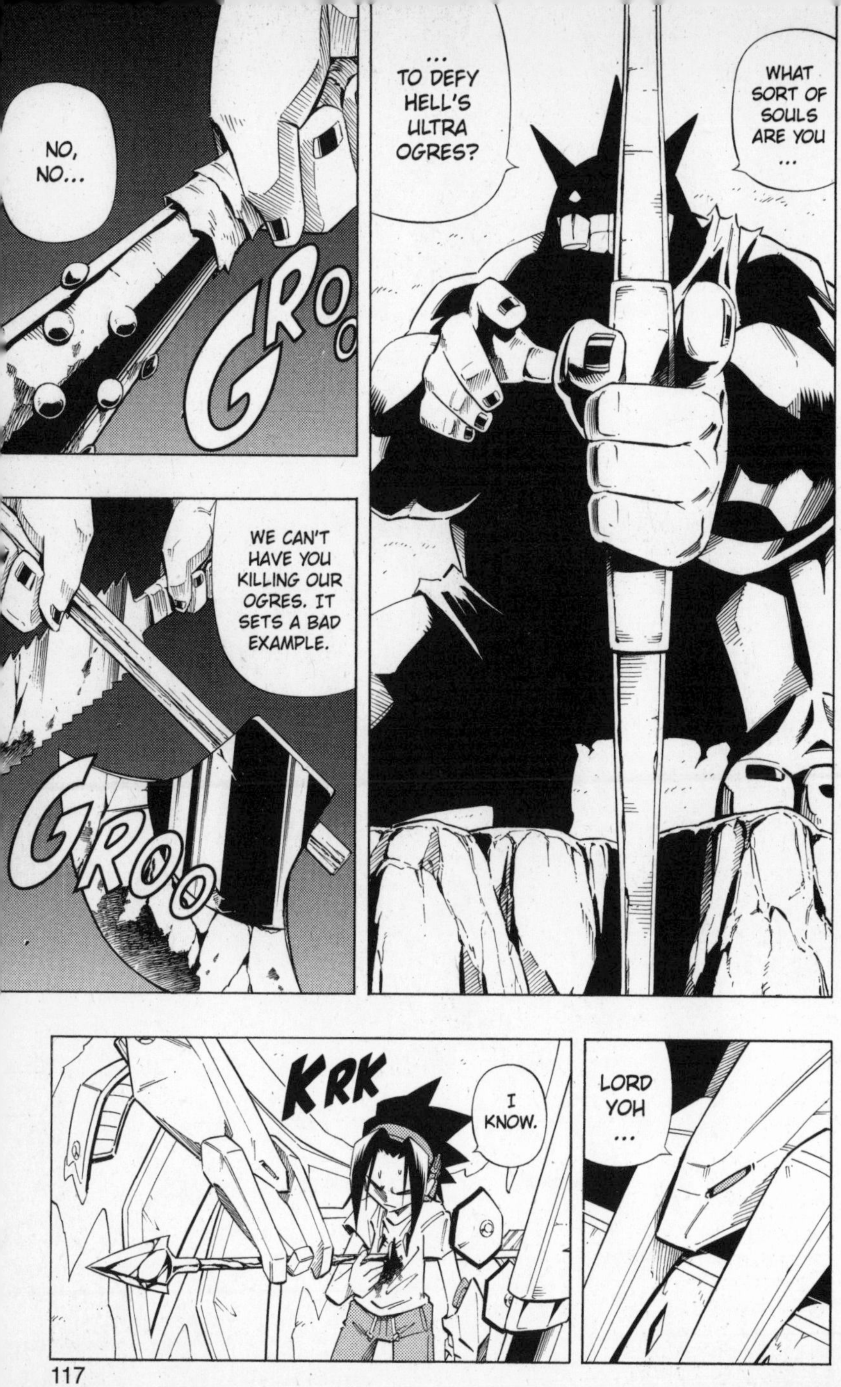
WHAT SORT OF SOULS ARE YOU ...
... TO DEFY HELL'S ULTRA OGRES?
NO, NO...
GROO
WE CAN'T HAVE YOU KILLING OUR OGRES. IT SETS A BAD EXAMPLE.
GROO
LORD YOH ...
KRK
I KNOW.

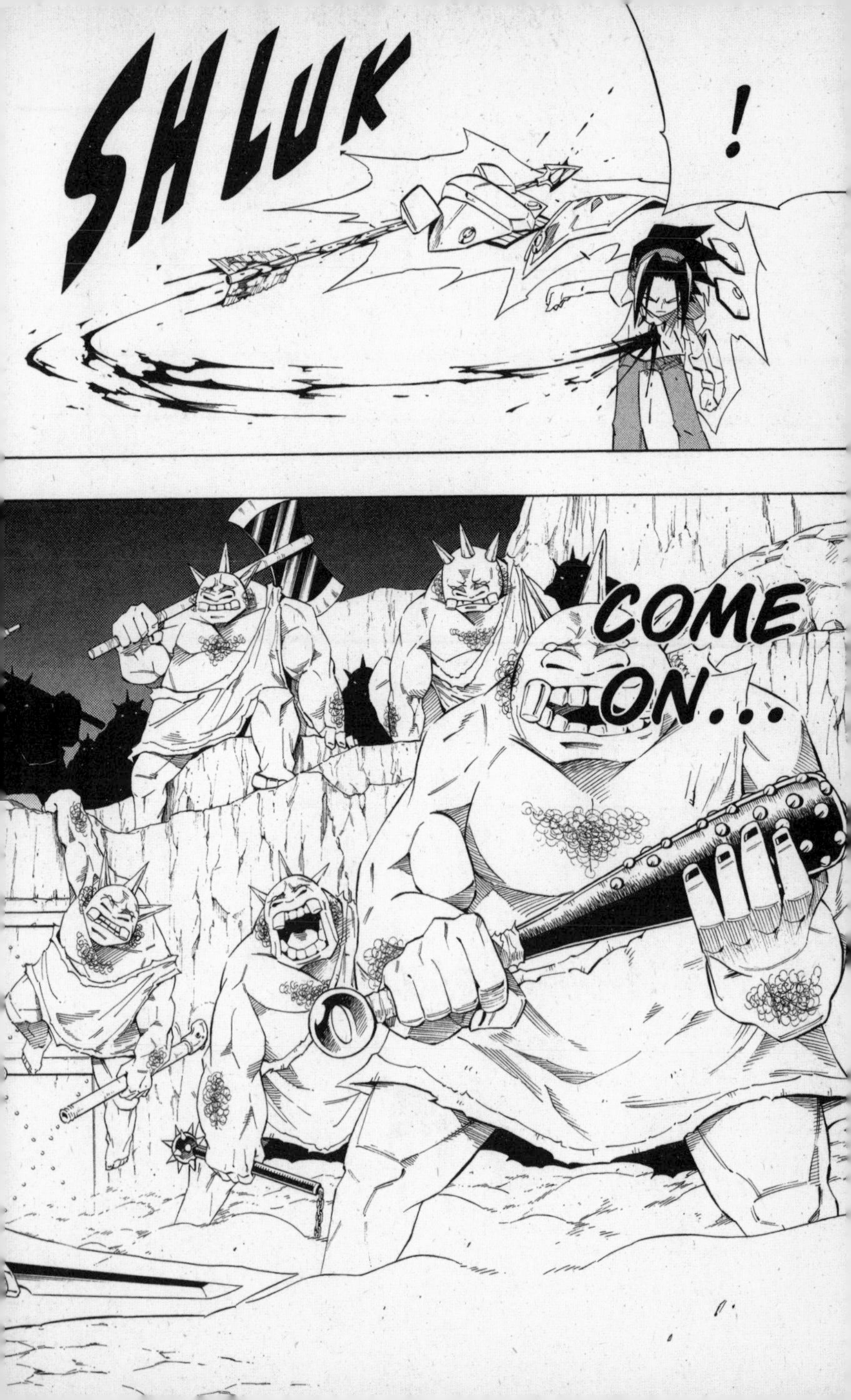
!
SHLUK
COME ON...

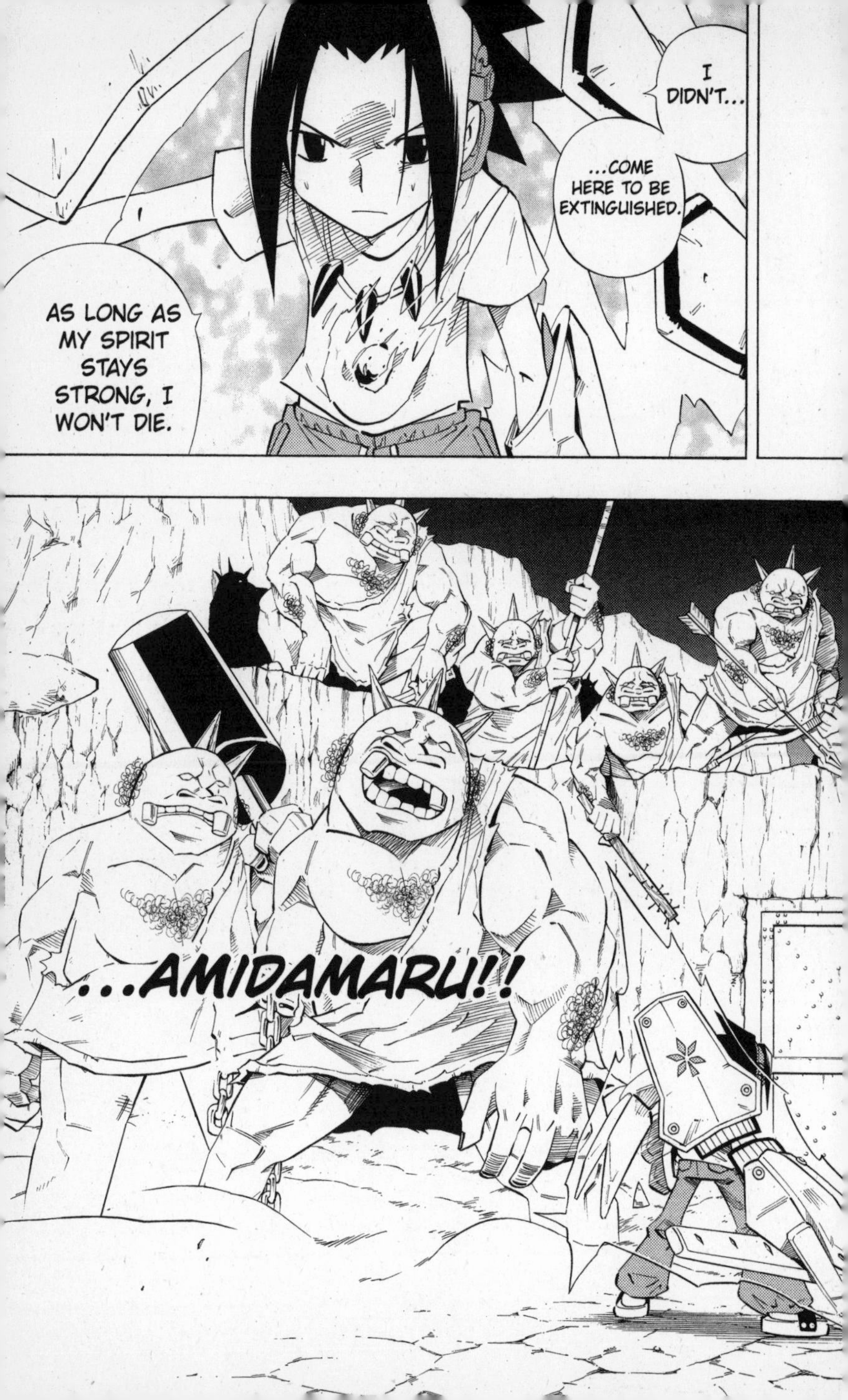
I DIDN'T...
...COME HERE TO BE EXTINGUISHED.
AS LONG AS MY SPIRIT STAYS STRONG, I WON'T DIE.
...AMIDAMARU!!

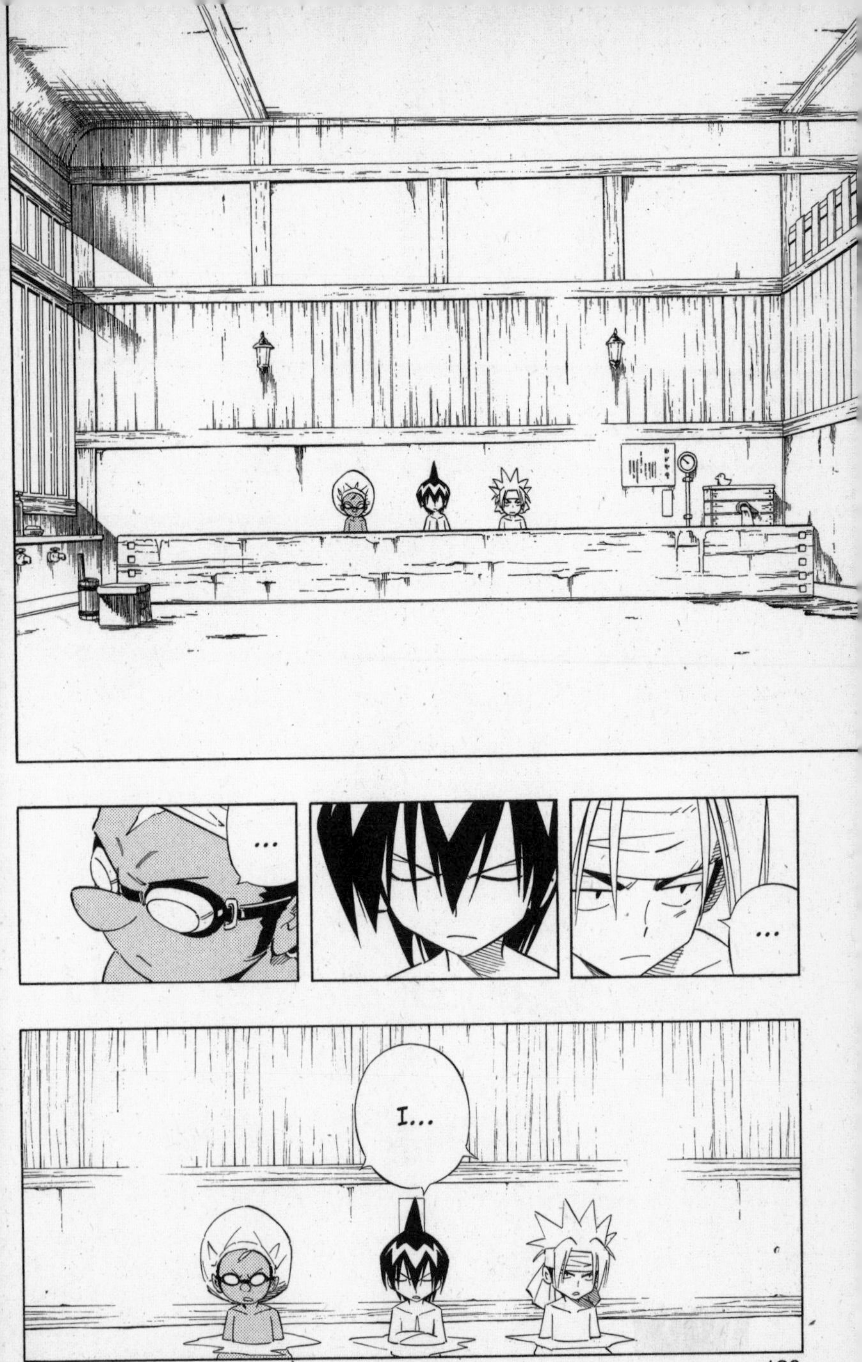
...
...
I...

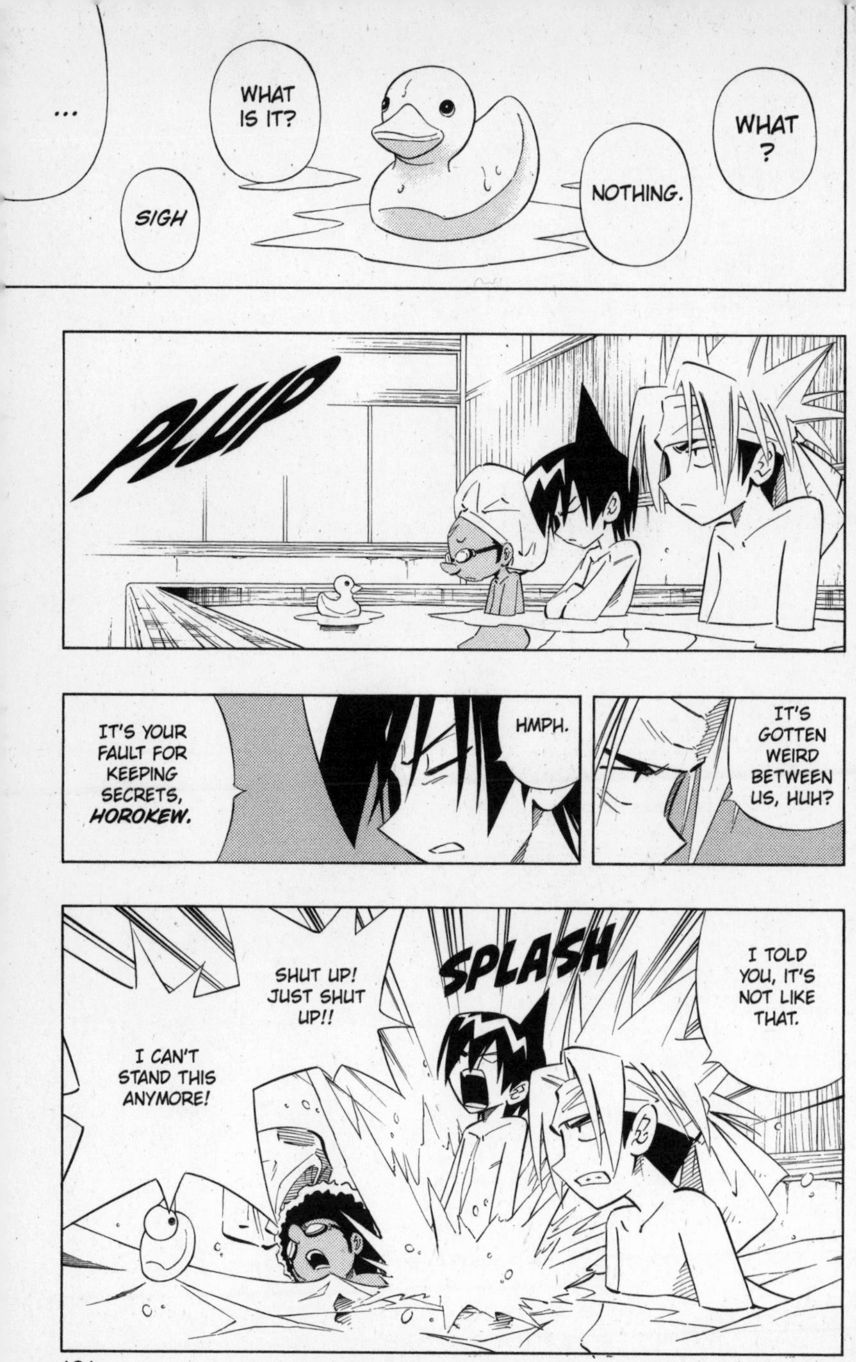
WHAT ?
NOTHING.
WHAT IS IT?
SIGH
...
PLUP
IT'S GOTTEN WEIRD BETWEEN US, HUH?
HMPH.
IT'S YOUR FAULT FOR KEEPING SECRETS, HOROKEW.
I TOLD YOU, IT'S NOT LIKE THAT.
SPLASH
SHUT UP! JUST SHUT UP!!
I CAN'T STAND THIS ANYMORE!

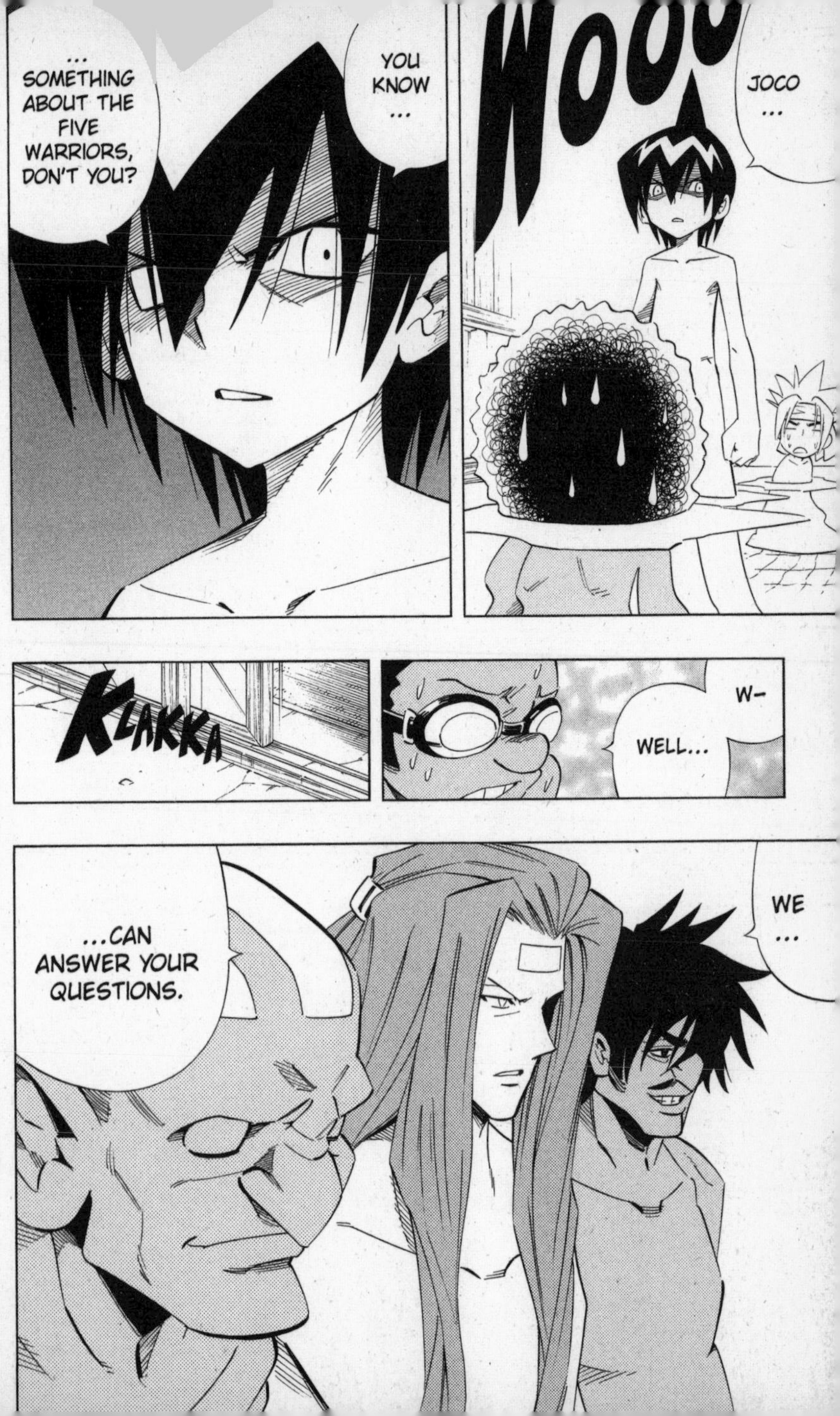
JOCO ...
WOOO
YOU KNOW ...
... SOMETHING ABOUT THE FIVE WARRIORS, DON'T YOU?
W- WELL...
KLAKKA
WE ...
...CAN ANSWER YOUR QUESTIONS.

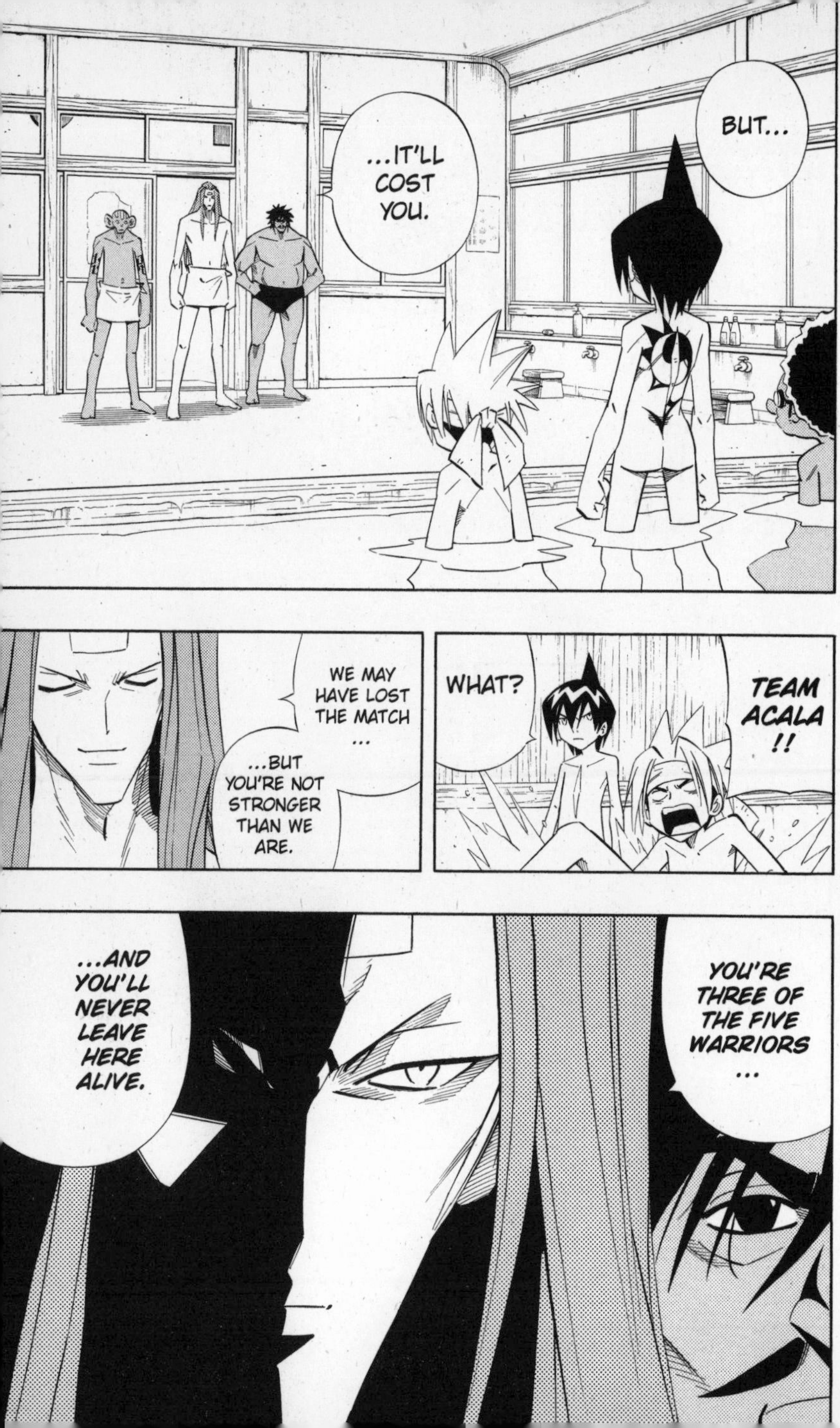
BUT...
...IT'LL COST YOU.
TEAM ACALA!!
WHAT?
WE MAY HAVE LOST THE MATCH...
...BUT YOU'RE NOT STRONGER THAN WE ARE.
YOU'RE THREE OF THE FIVE WARRIORS...
...AND YOU'LL NEVER LEAVE HERE ALIVE.

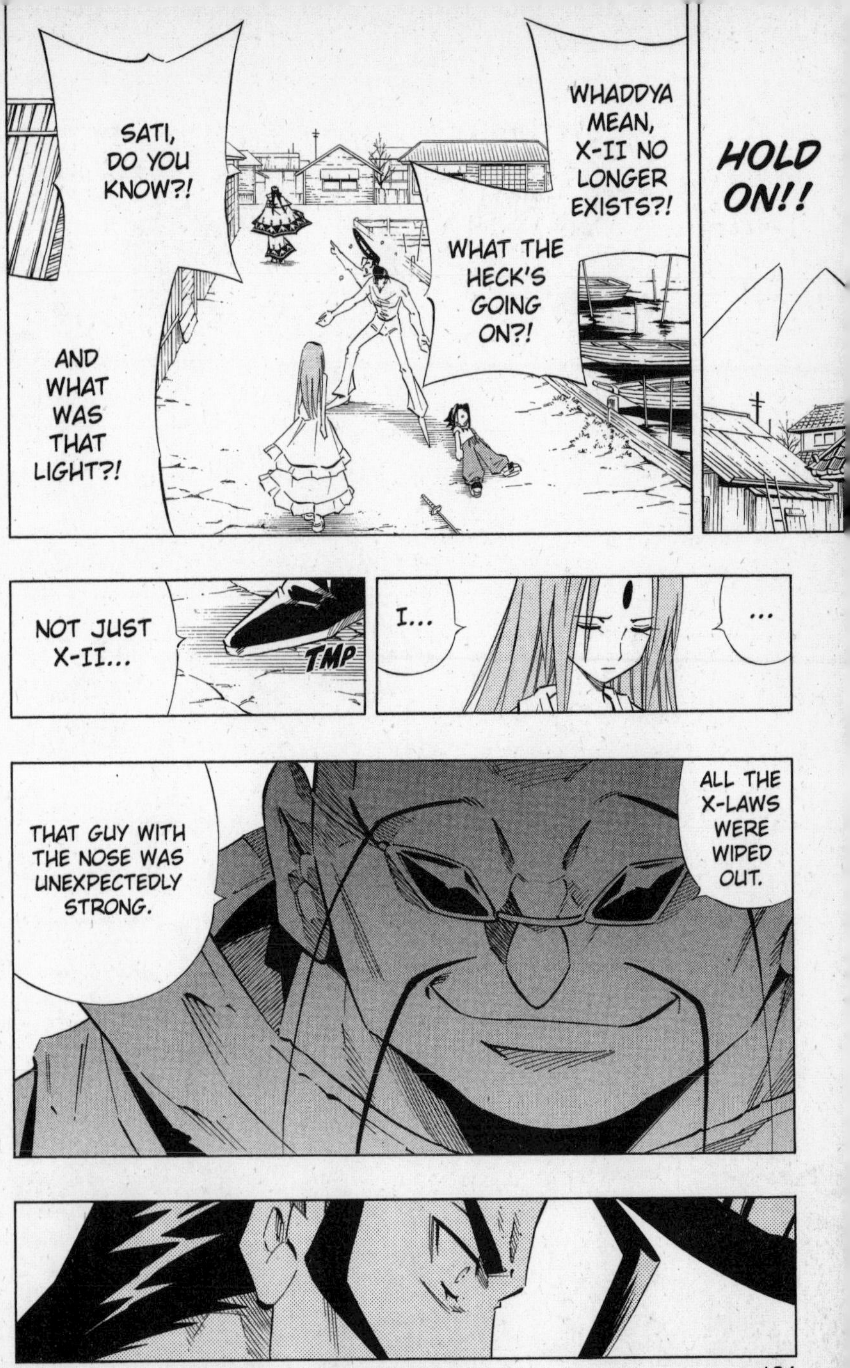
HOLD ON!!
WHADDYA MEAN, X-II NO LONGER EXISTS?!
WHAT THE HECK'S GOING ON?!
SATI, DO YOU KNOW?!
AND WHAT WAS THAT LIGHT?!
...
I...
TMP
NOT JUST X-II...
ALL THE X-LAWS WERE WIPED OUT.
THAT GUY WITH THE NOSE WAS UNEXPECTEDLY STRONG.

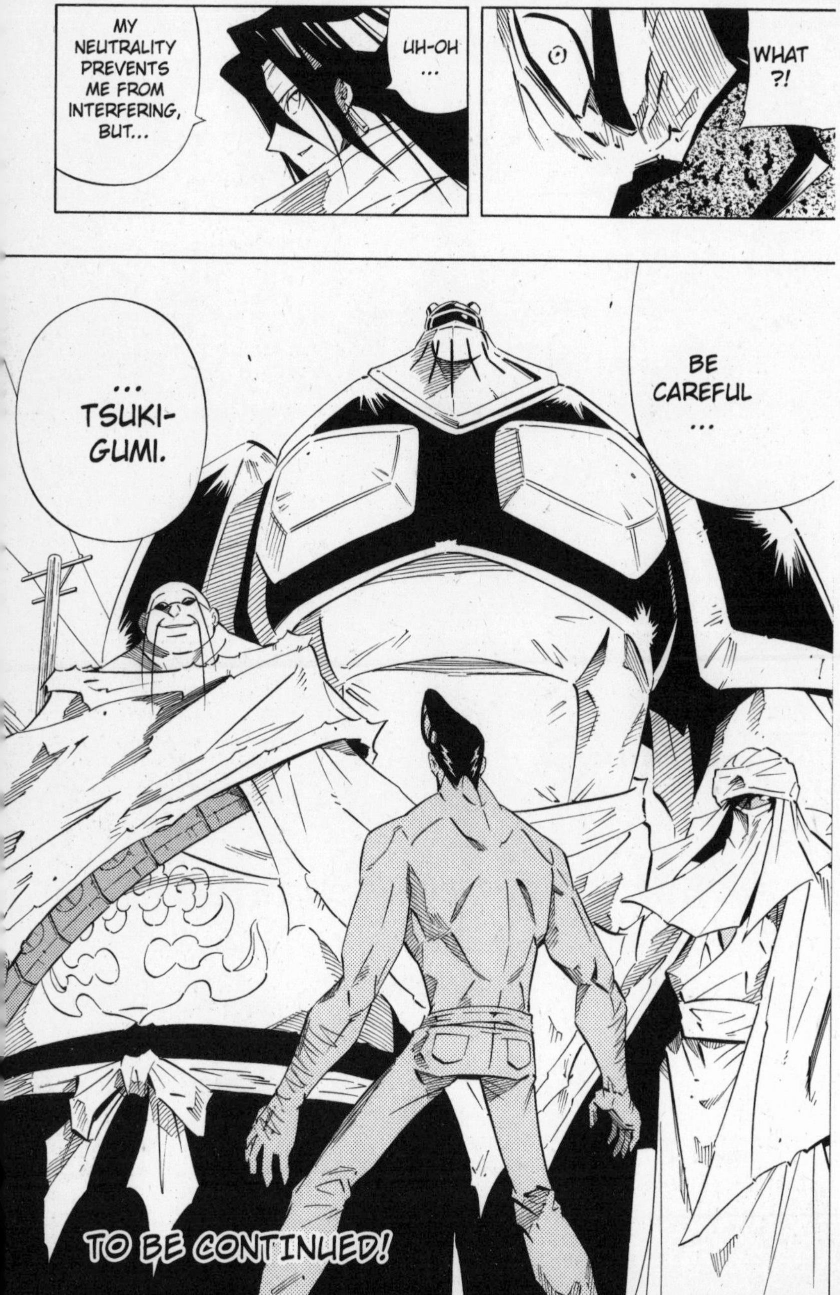
WHAT ?!
UH-OH ...
MY NEUTRALITY PREVENTS ME FROM INTERFERING, BUT...
BE CAREFUL ...
... TSUKI-GUMI.
TO BE CONTINUED!

Shaman King

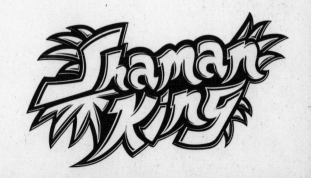

A SPECIAL ONE-SHOT STORY

EXOTICA

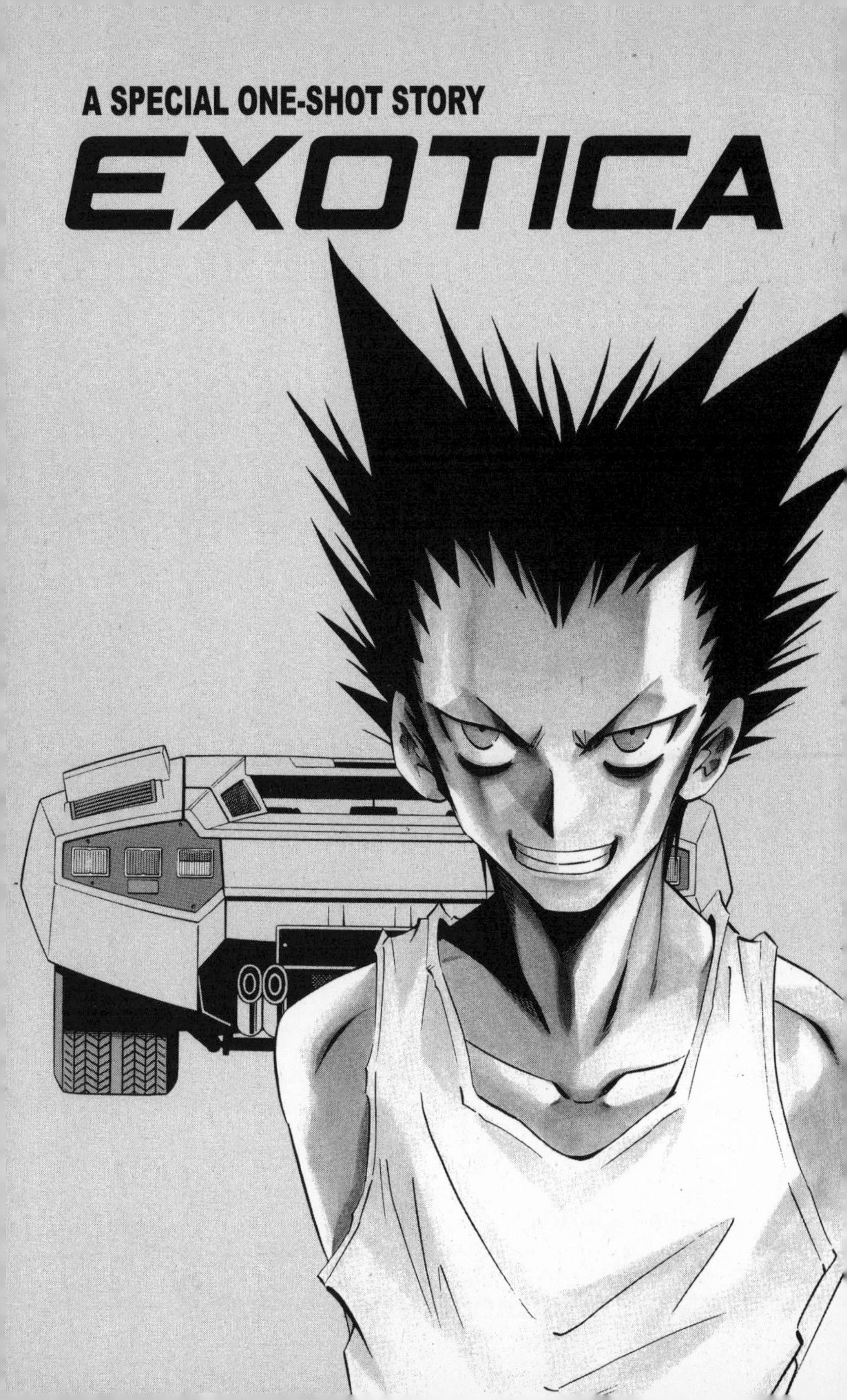

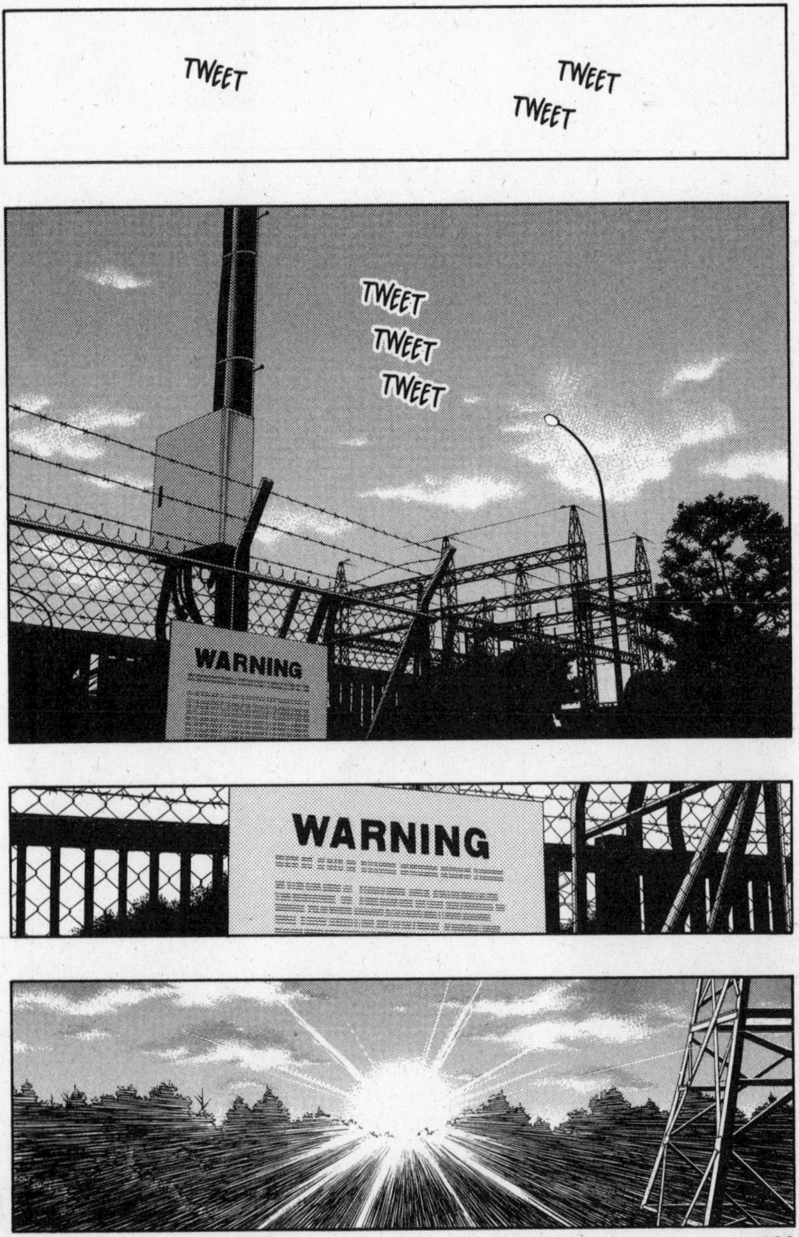
TWEET
TWEET
TWEET
TWEET
TWEET
TWEET
WARNING
WARNING

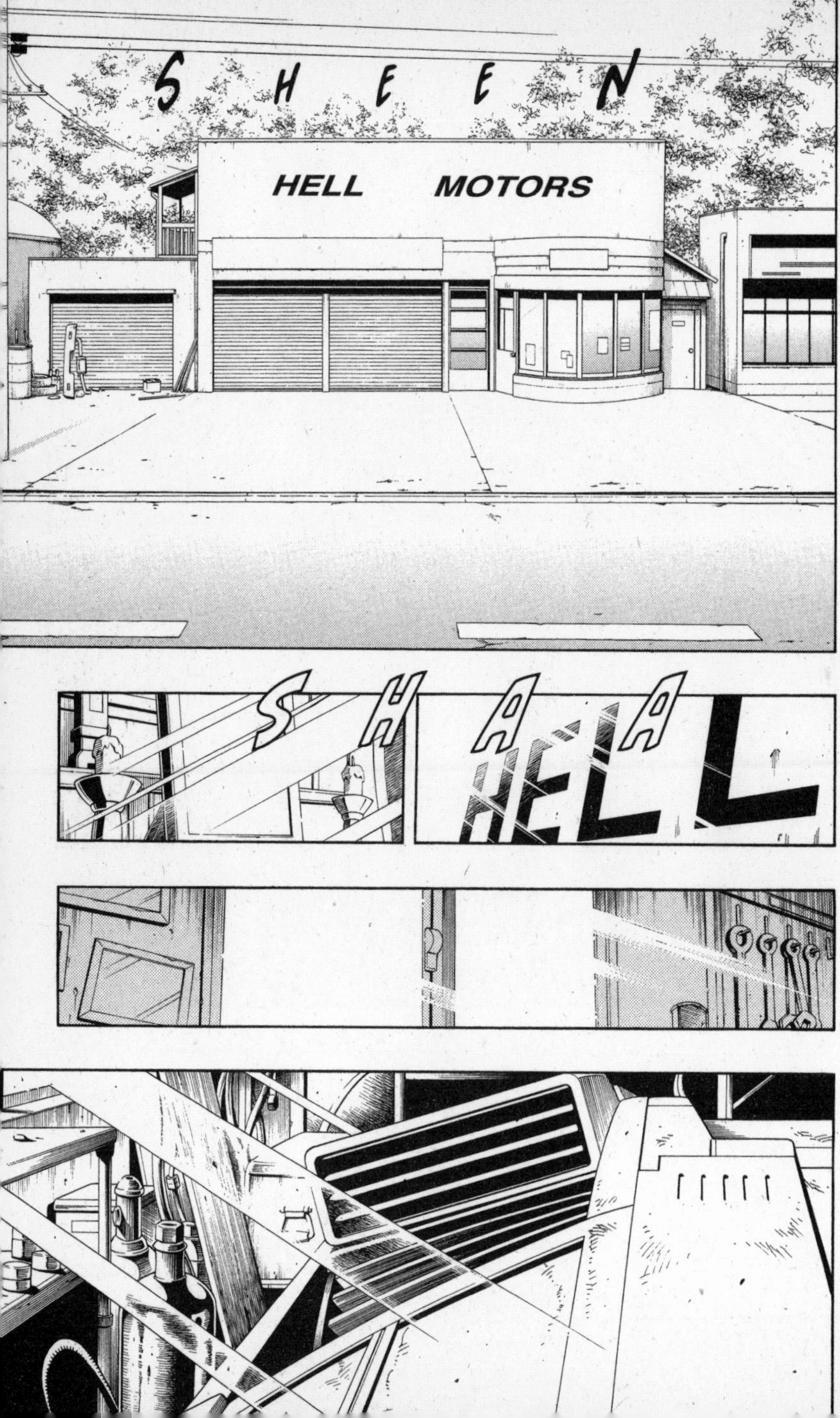
S H E E N
HELL MOTORS
SHAA
HELL

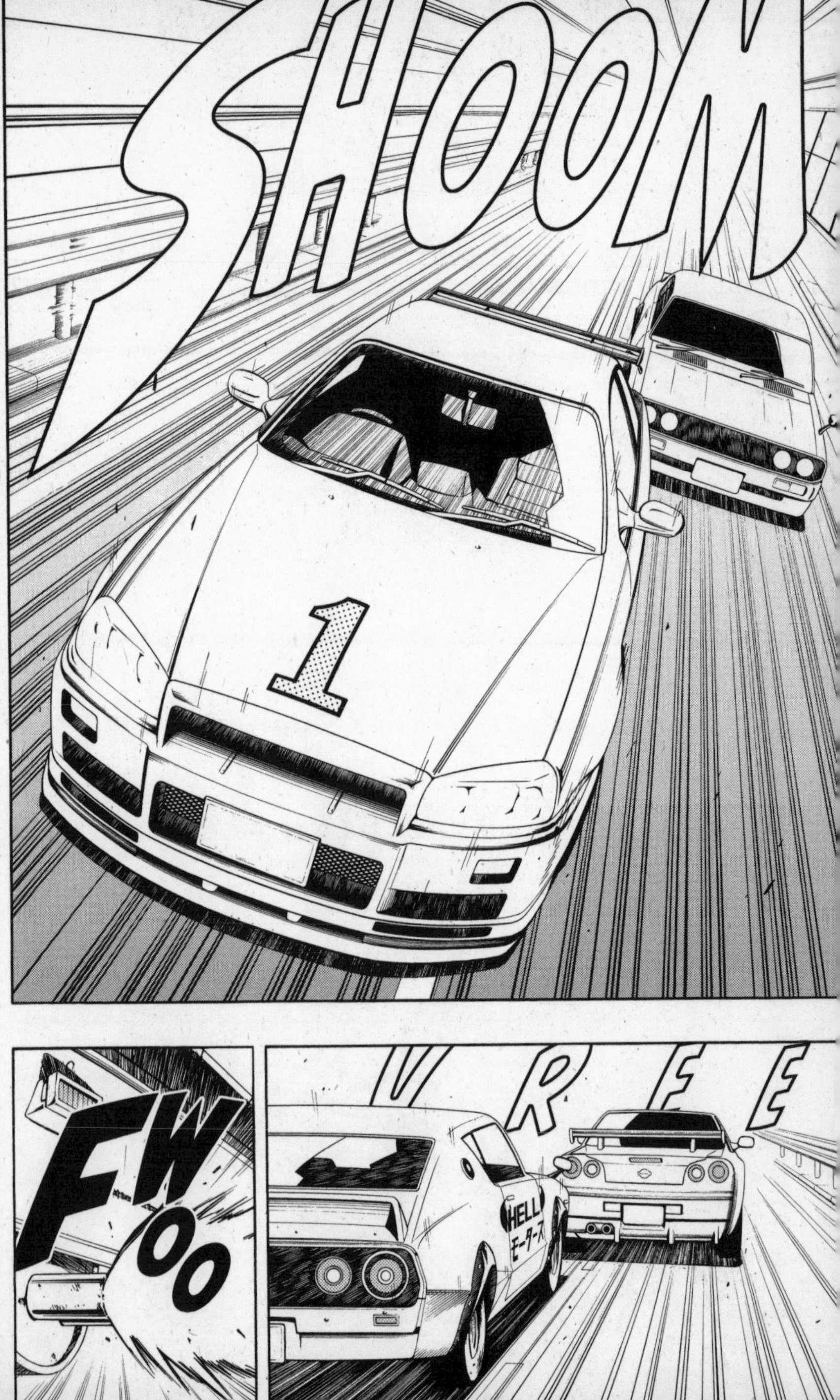
SHOOM
VREEE
HELL
モータース
FWOO

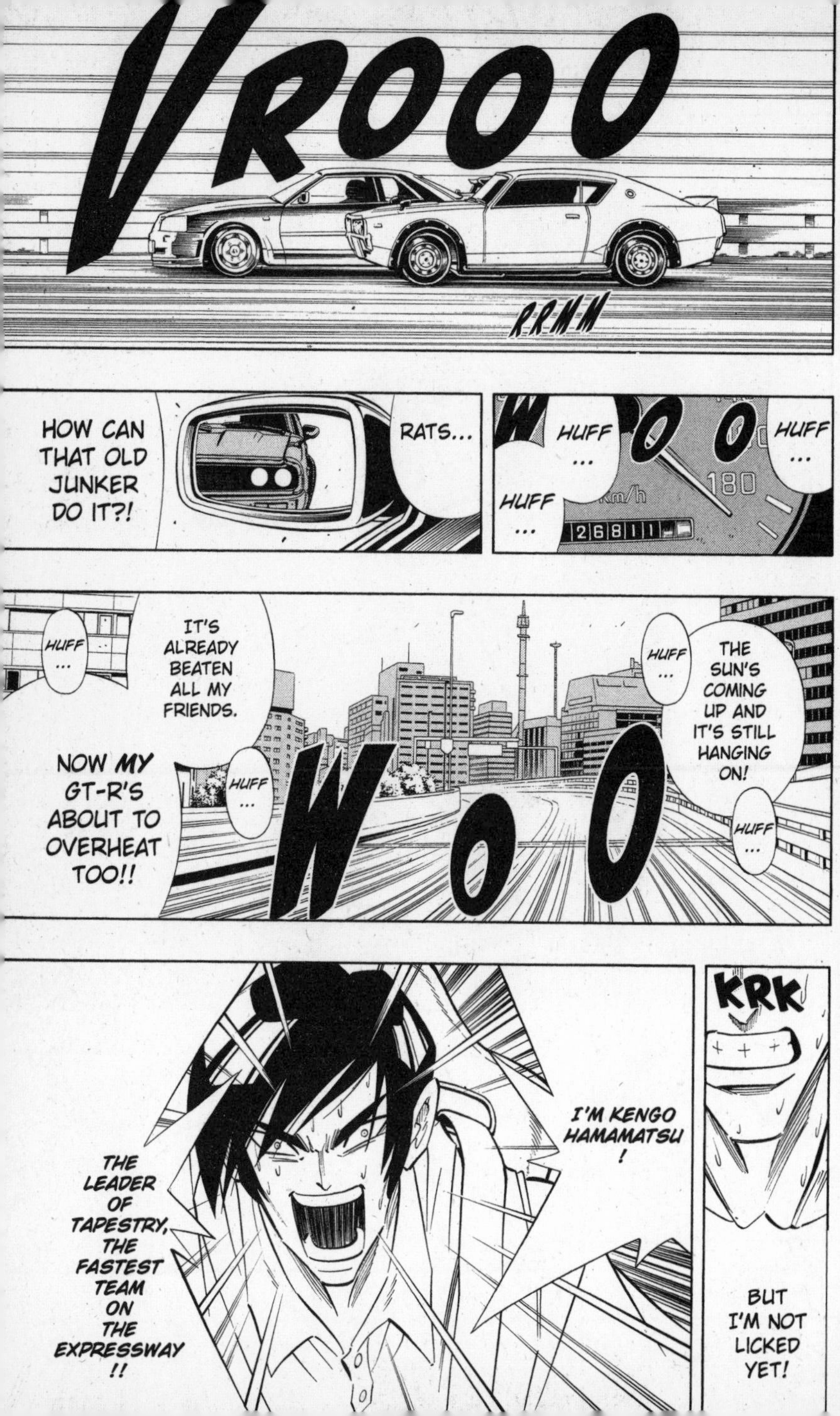
VROOO
RRMM
HUFF...
HUFF...
HUFF...
WOO
RATS...
HOW CAN THAT OLD JUNKER DO IT?!
HUFF...
THE SUN'S COMING UP AND IT'S STILL HANGING ON!
HUFF...
HUFF...
IT'S ALREADY BEATEN ALL MY FRIENDS.
HUFF...
NOW *MY* GT-R'S ABOUT TO OVERHEAT TOO!!
WOO
KRK
BUT I'M NOT LICKED YET!
I'M KENGO HAMAMATSU!
THE LEADER OF TAPESTRY, THE FASTEST TEAM ON THE EXPRESSWAY!!

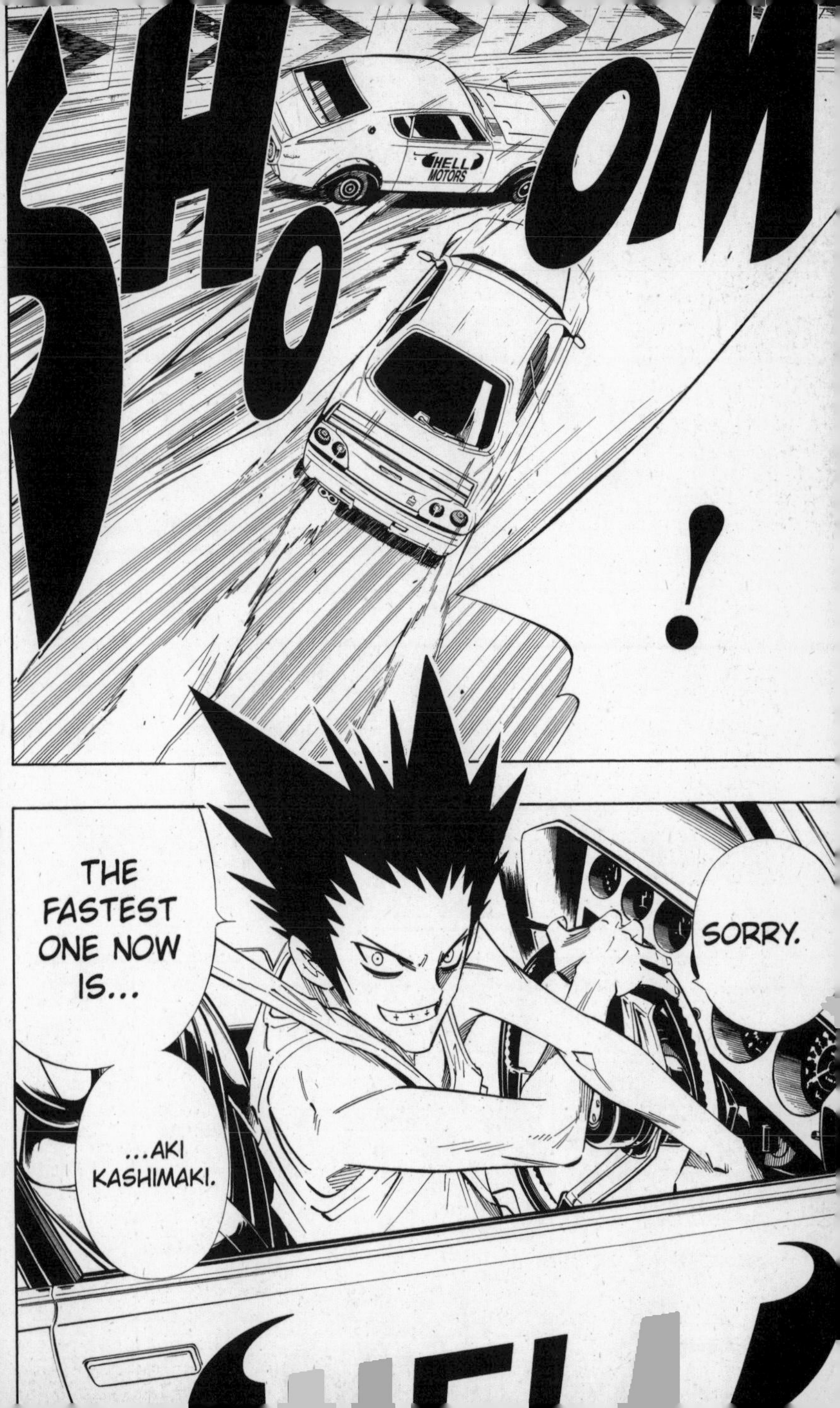
SHOOM
HELL MOTORS
!
SORRY.
THE FASTEST ONE NOW IS...
...AKI KASHIMAKI.

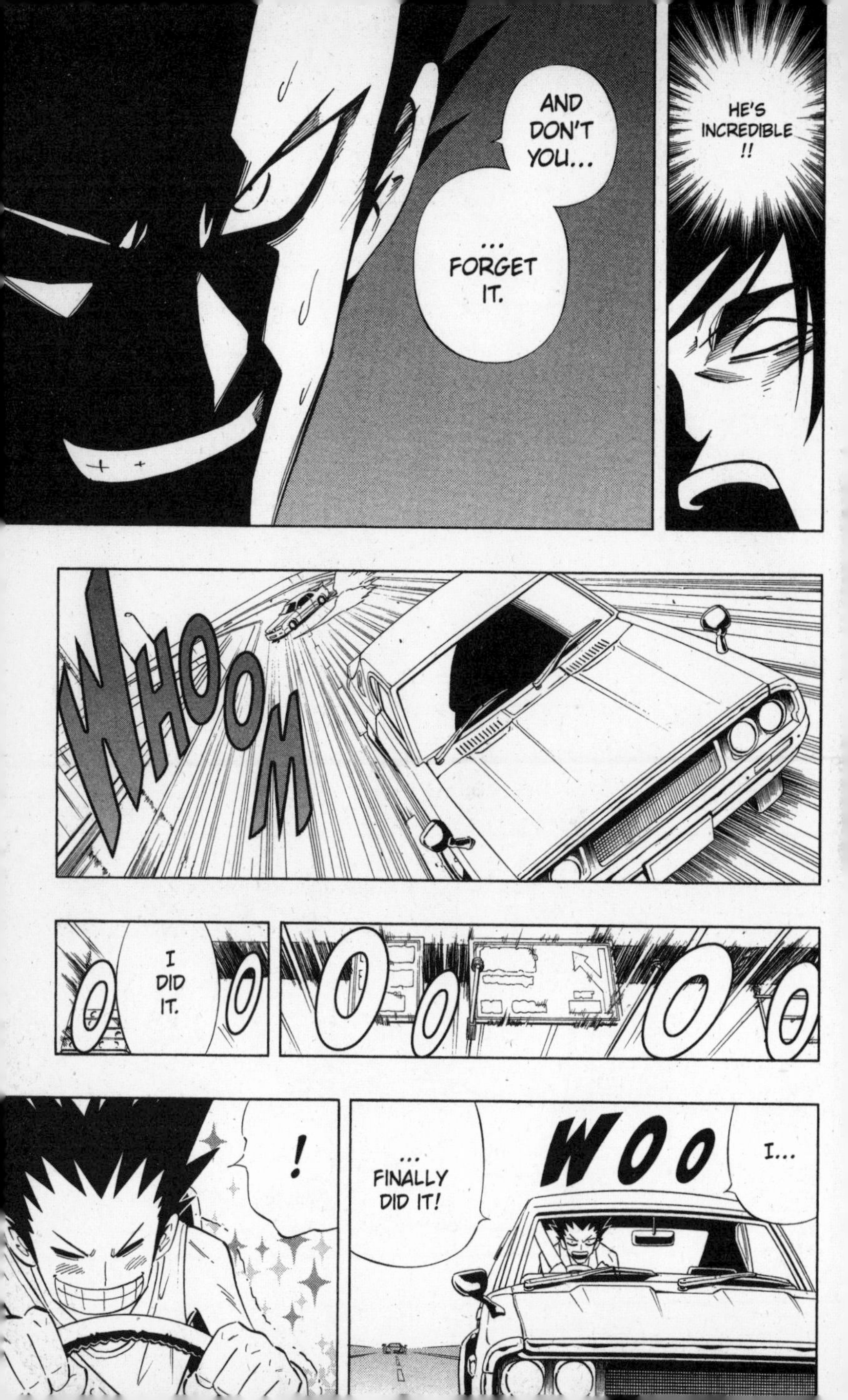
HE'S INCREDIBLE !!
AND DON'T YOU...
...FORGET IT.
WHOOM
OOOO
I DID IT.
OO
I...
WOO
...FINALLY DID IT!
!

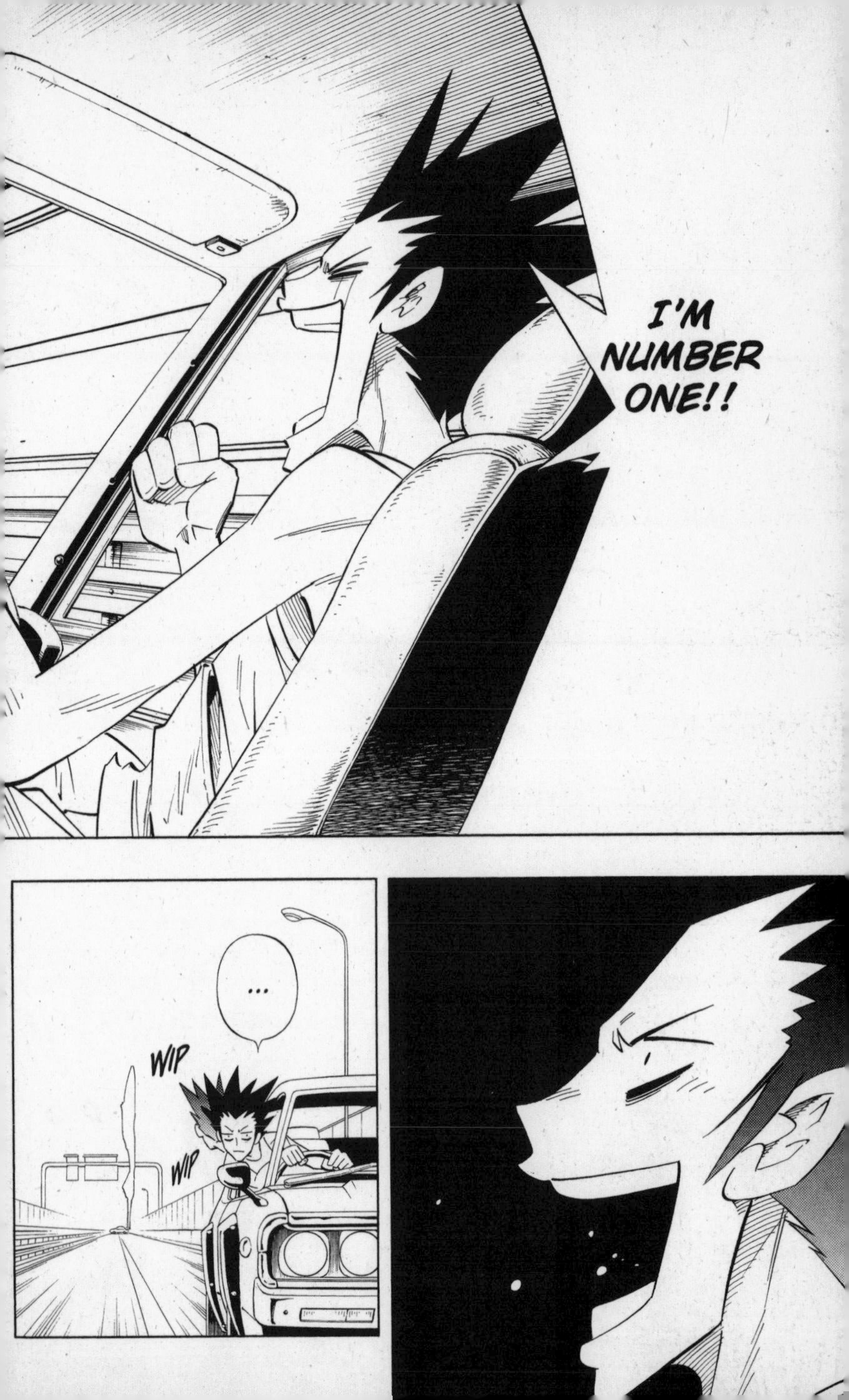
I'M NUMBER ONE!!
...
WIP
WIP

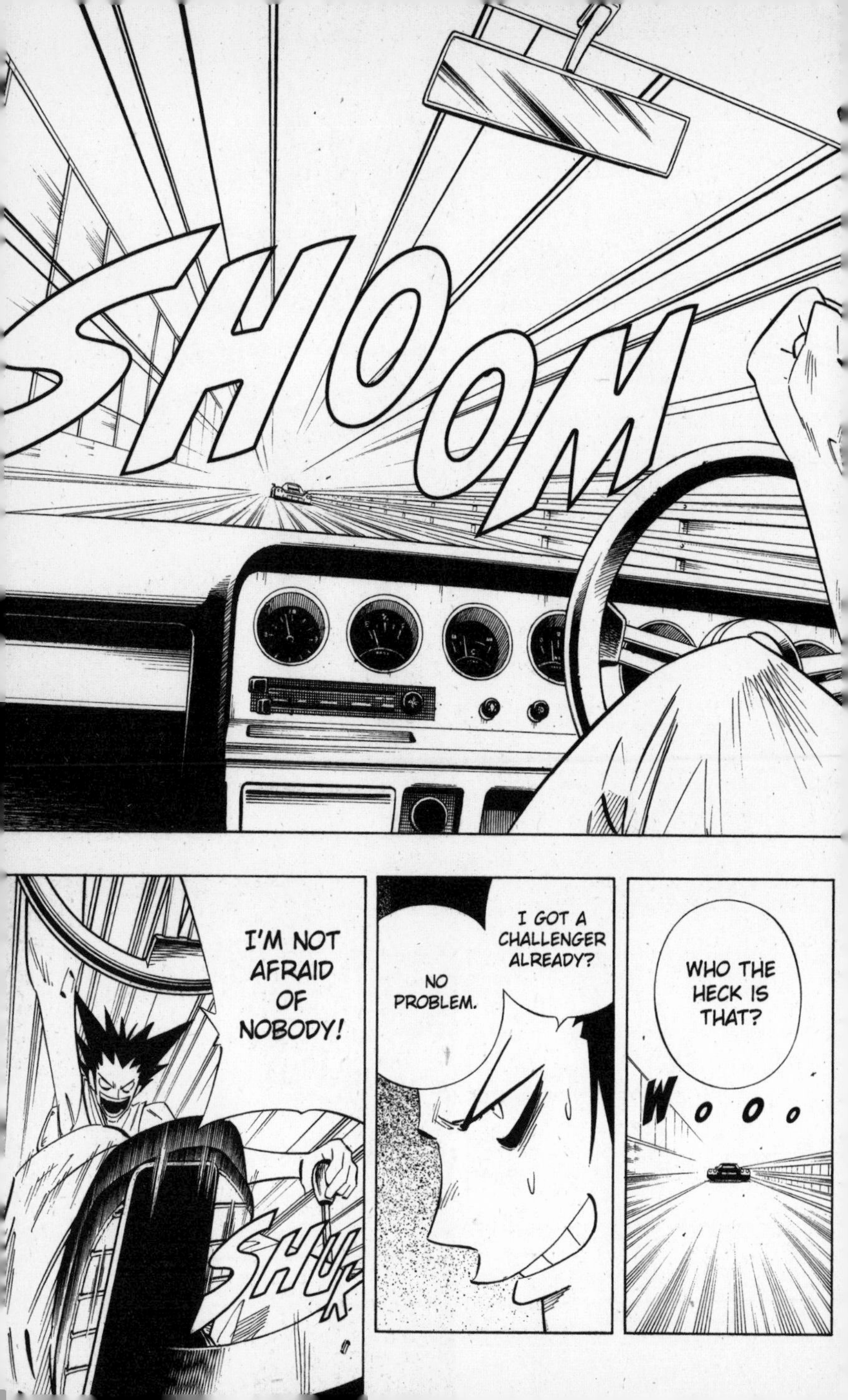
SHOOM
WHO THE HECK IS THAT?
WOOO
I GOT A CHALLENGER ALREADY?
NO PROBLEM.
I'M NOT AFRAID OF NOBODY!
SHUK

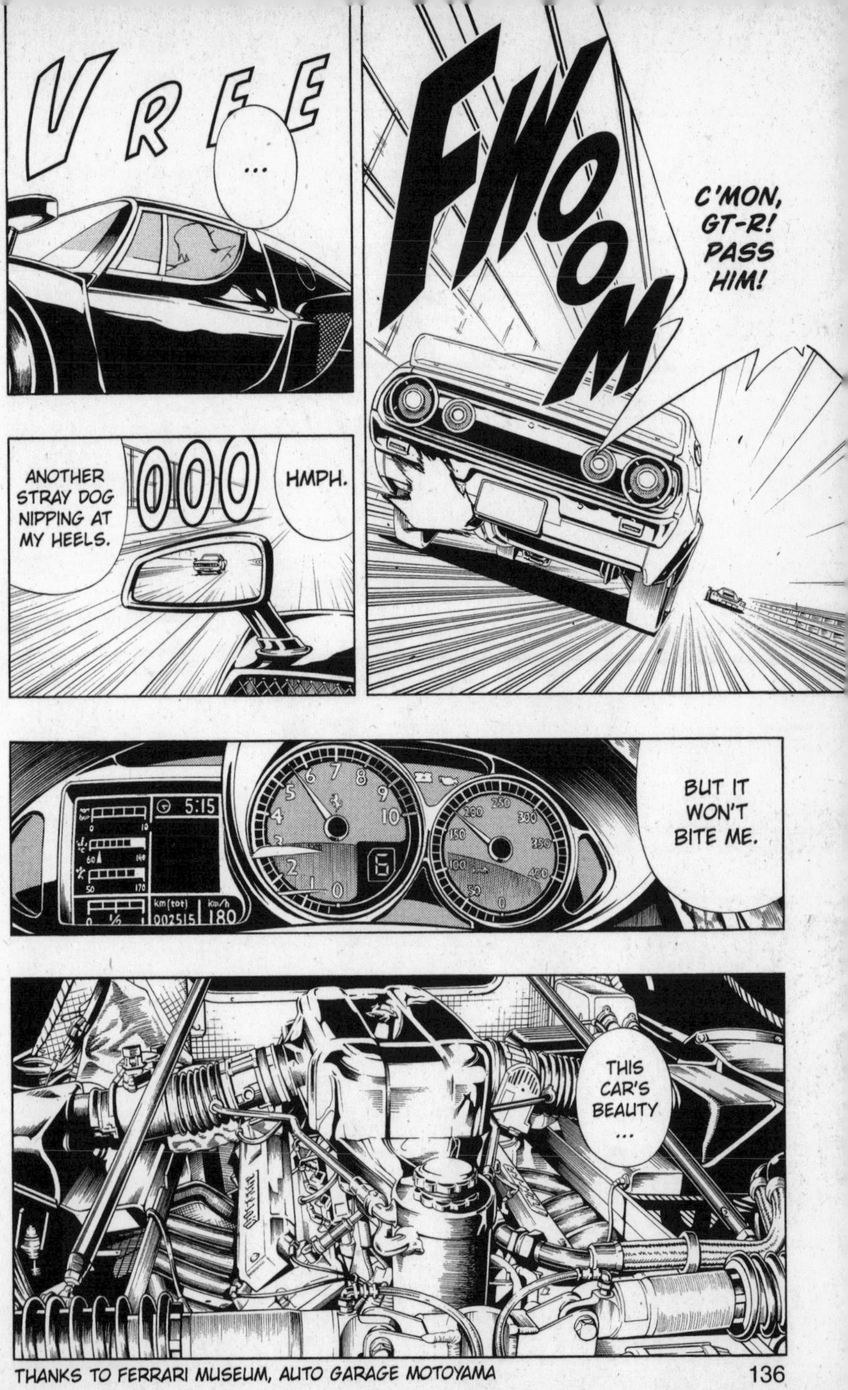
FWOOM
C'MON, GT-R! PASS HIM!
VREE
...
HMPH.
OOO
ANOTHER STRAY DOG NIPPING AT MY HEELS.
BUT IT WON'T BITE ME.
THIS CAR'S BEAUTY ...

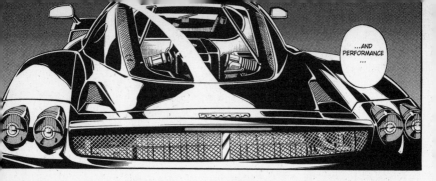

...AND PERFORMANCE...

...REDUCE ORDINARY CARS TO SHABBY INSIGNIFICANCE.

THIS IS THE EXOTIC SUPERCAR OF THE GODS.

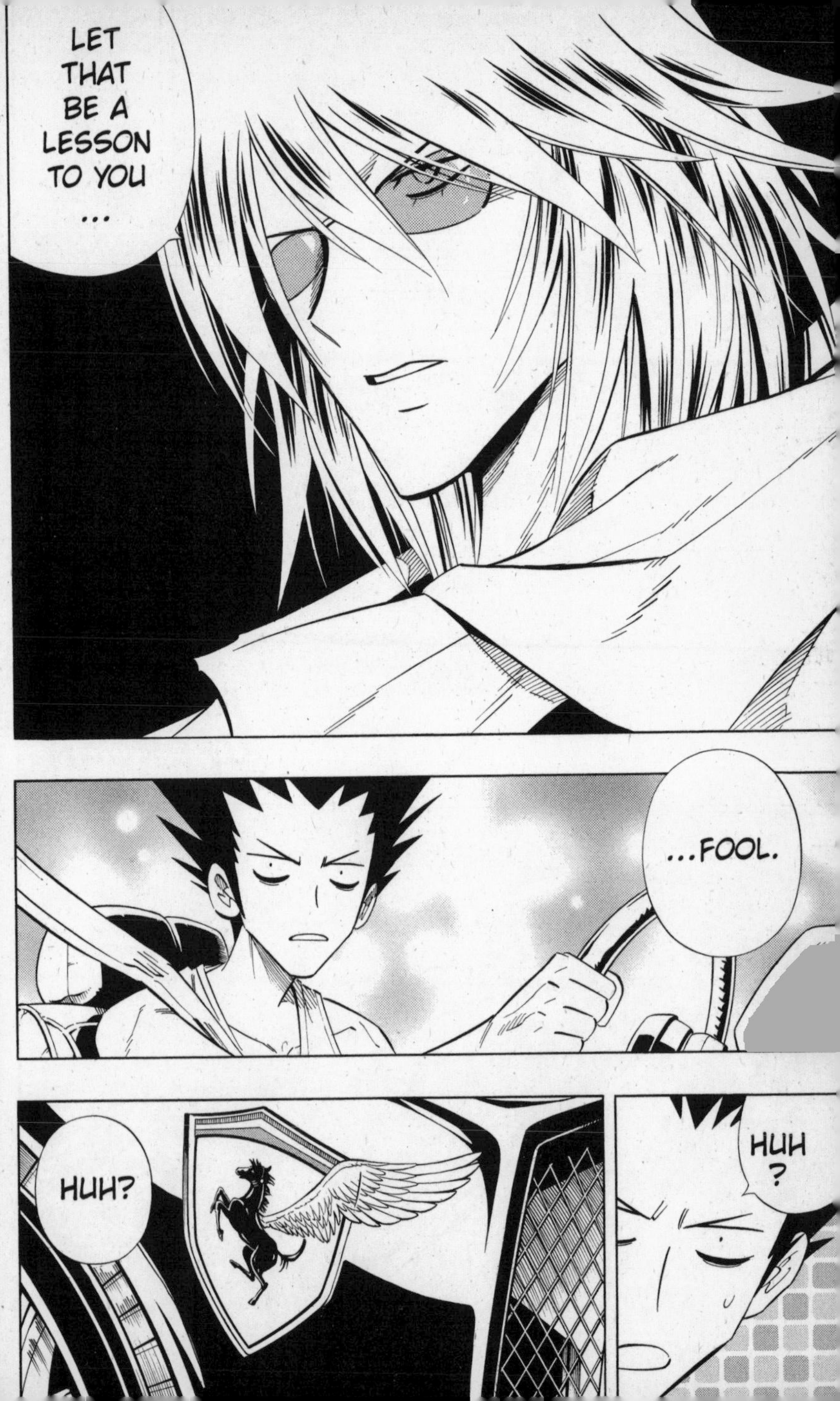
LET THAT BE A LESSON TO YOU ...
...FOOL.
HUH ?
HUH?

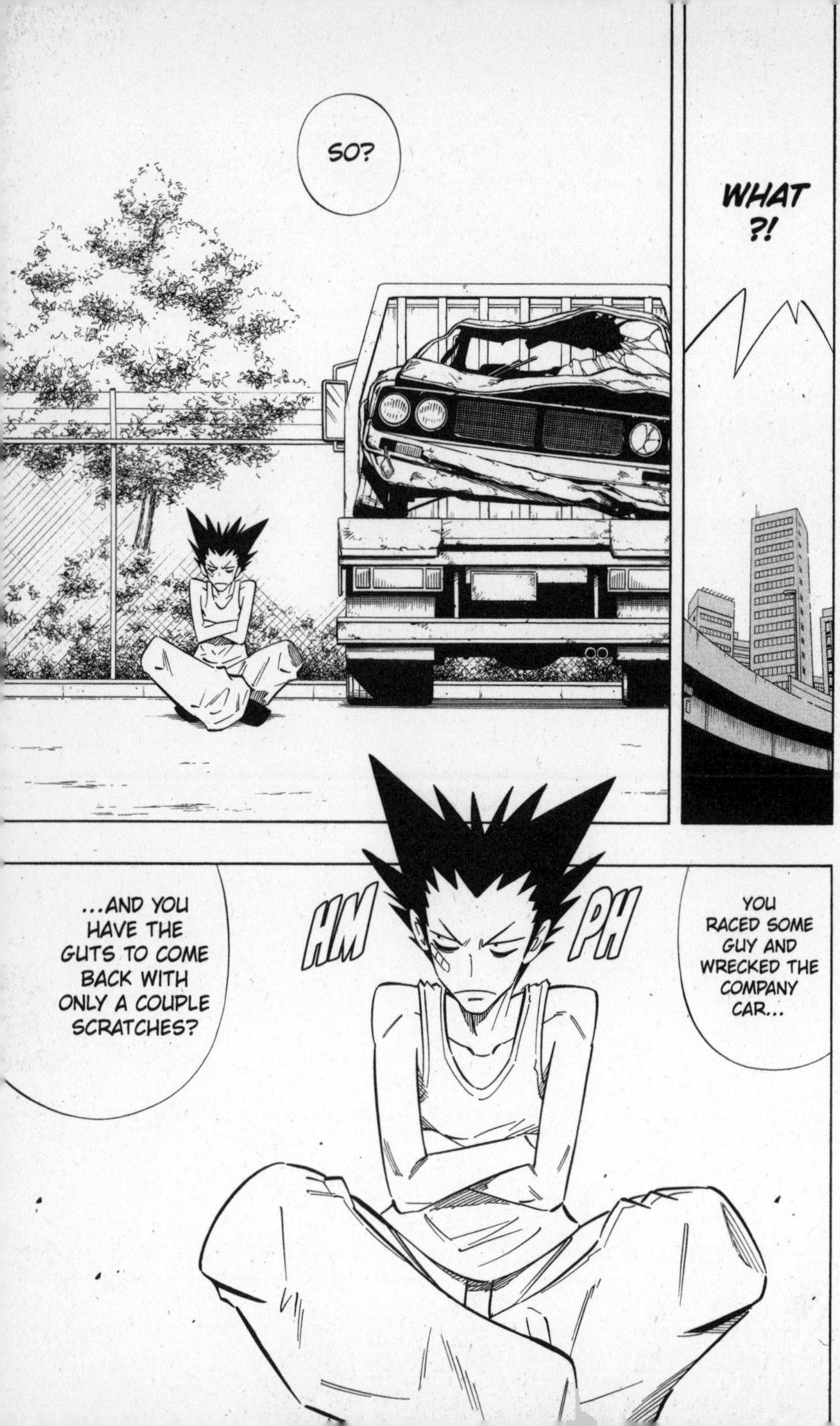
WHAT ?!
SO?
YOU RACED SOME GUY AND WRECKED THE COMPANY CAR...
HM PH
...AND YOU HAVE THE GUTS TO COME BACK WITH ONLY A COUPLE SCRATCHES?

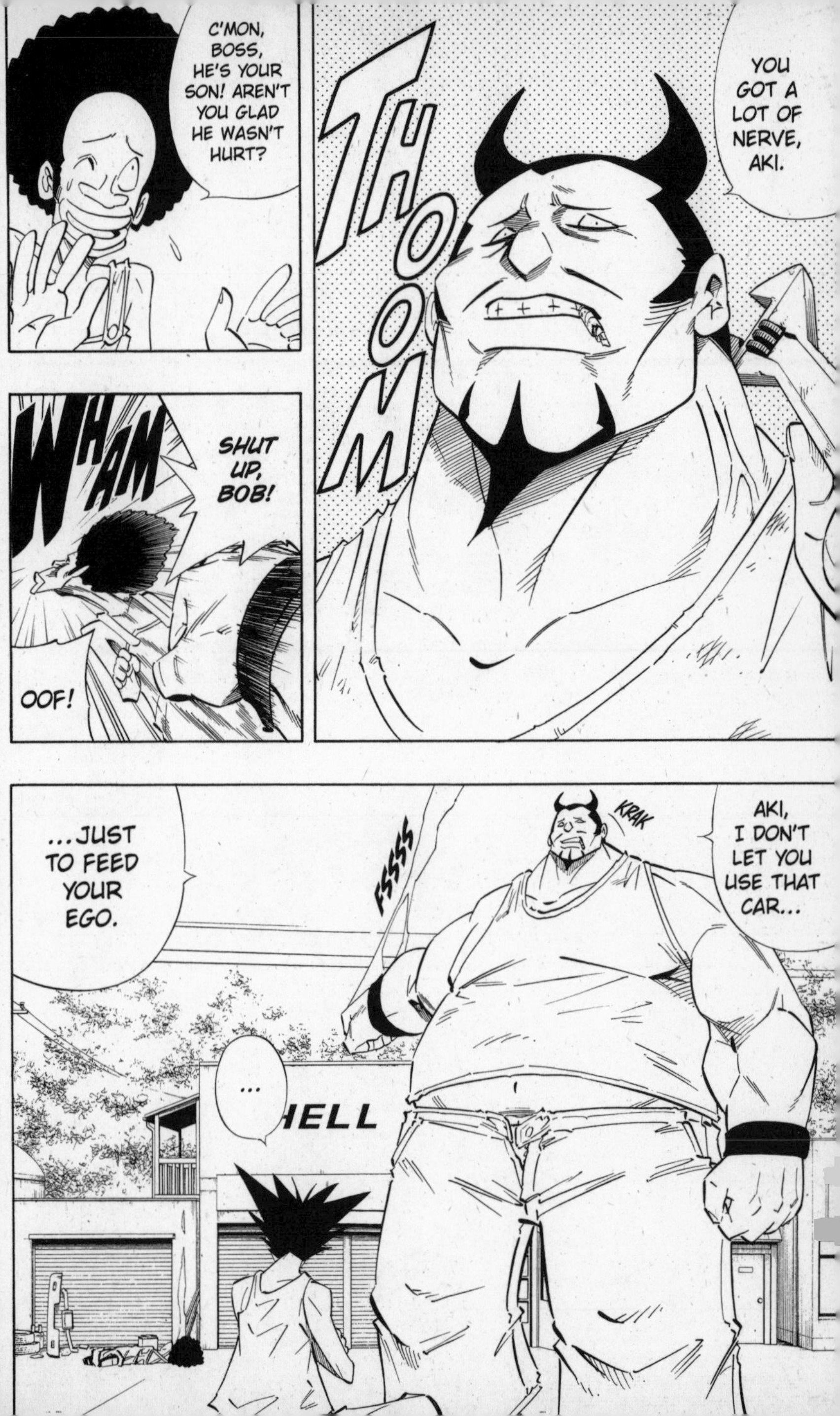
YOU GOT A LOT OF NERVE, AKI.
THOOM
C'MON, BOSS, HE'S YOUR SON! AREN'T YOU GLAD HE WASN'T HURT?
SHUT UP, BOB!
WHAM
OOF!
AKI, I DON'T LET YOU USE THAT CAR...
KRAK
FSSSS
...JUST TO FEED YOUR EGO.
...
HELL

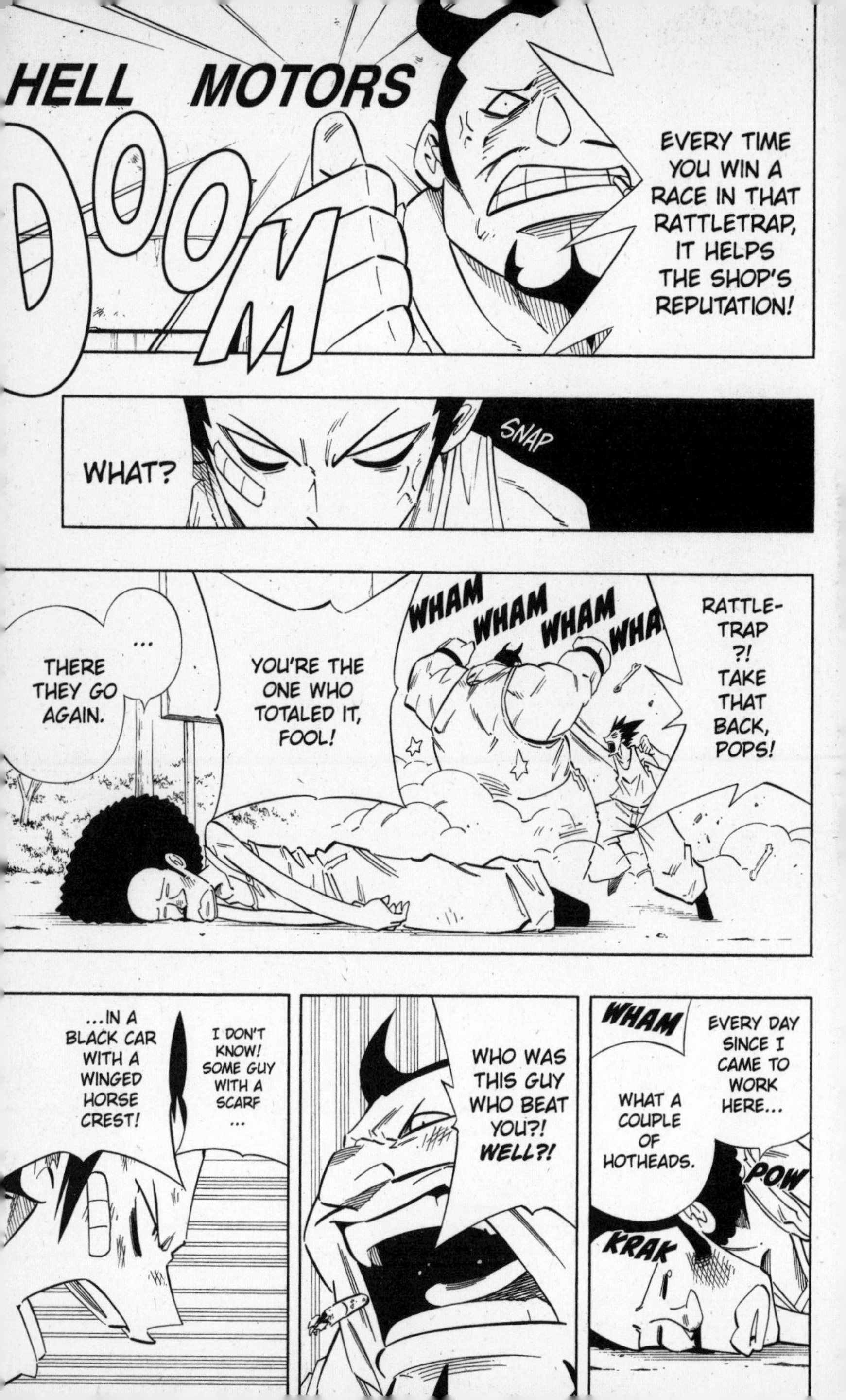
HELL MOTORS
EVERY TIME YOU WIN A RACE IN THAT RATTLETRAP, IT HELPS THE SHOP'S REPUTATION!
DOOOM
SNAP
WHAT?
RATTLE-TRAP?! TAKE THAT BACK, POPS!
WHAM WHAM WHAM WHA
YOU'RE THE ONE WHO TOTALED IT, FOOL!
...
THERE THEY GO AGAIN.
WHAM
EVERY DAY SINCE I CAME TO WORK HERE...
WHAT A COUPLE OF HOTHEADS.
POW
KRAK
WHO WAS THIS GUY WHO BEAT YOU?! WELL?!
I DON'T KNOW! SOME GUY WITH A SCARF...
...IN A BLACK CAR WITH A WINGED HORSE CREST!

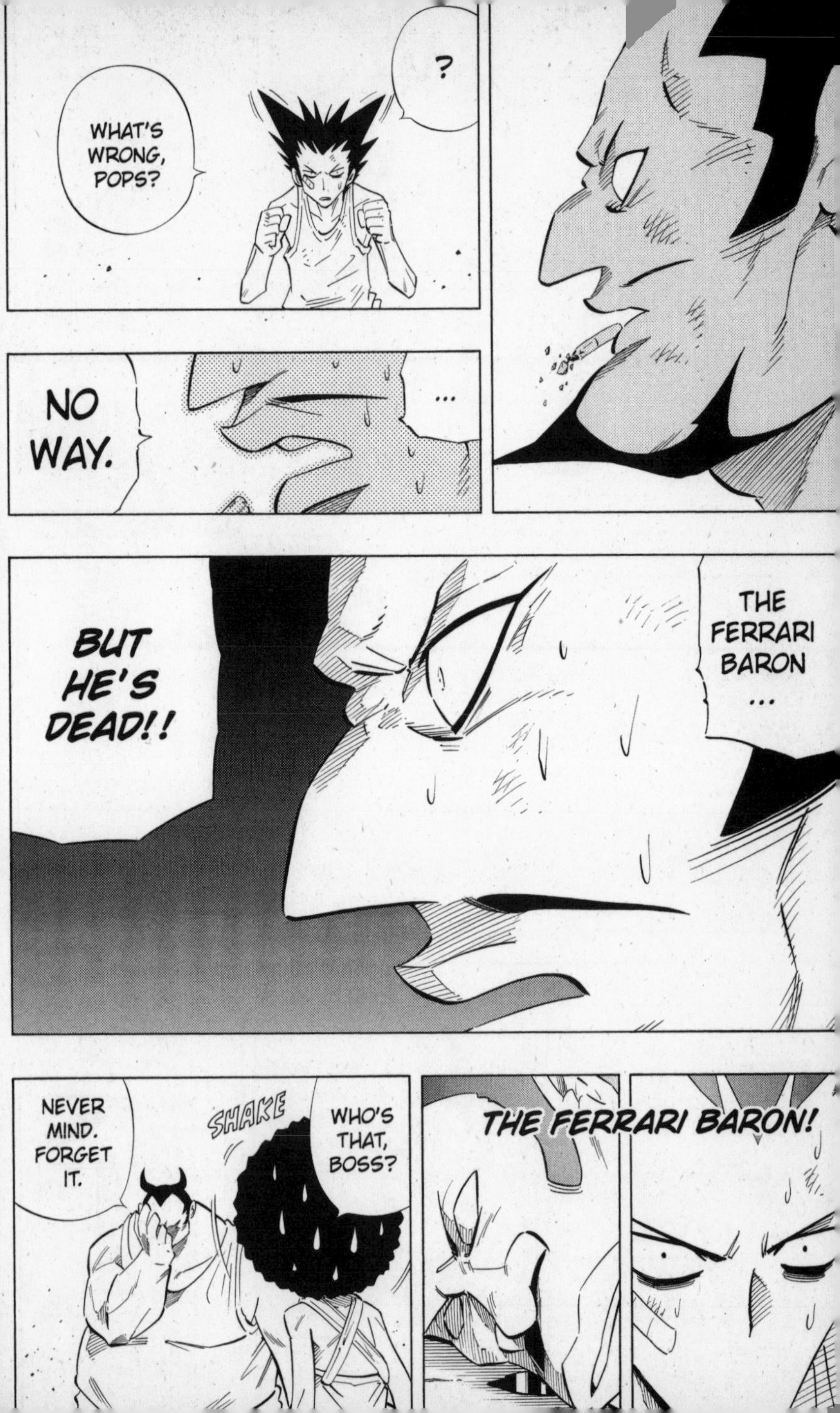
?
WHAT'S WRONG, POPS?
...
NO WAY.
THE FERRARI BARON...
BUT HE'S DEAD!!
THE FERRARI BARON!
WHO'S THAT, BOSS?
SHAKE
NEVER MIND. FORGET IT.

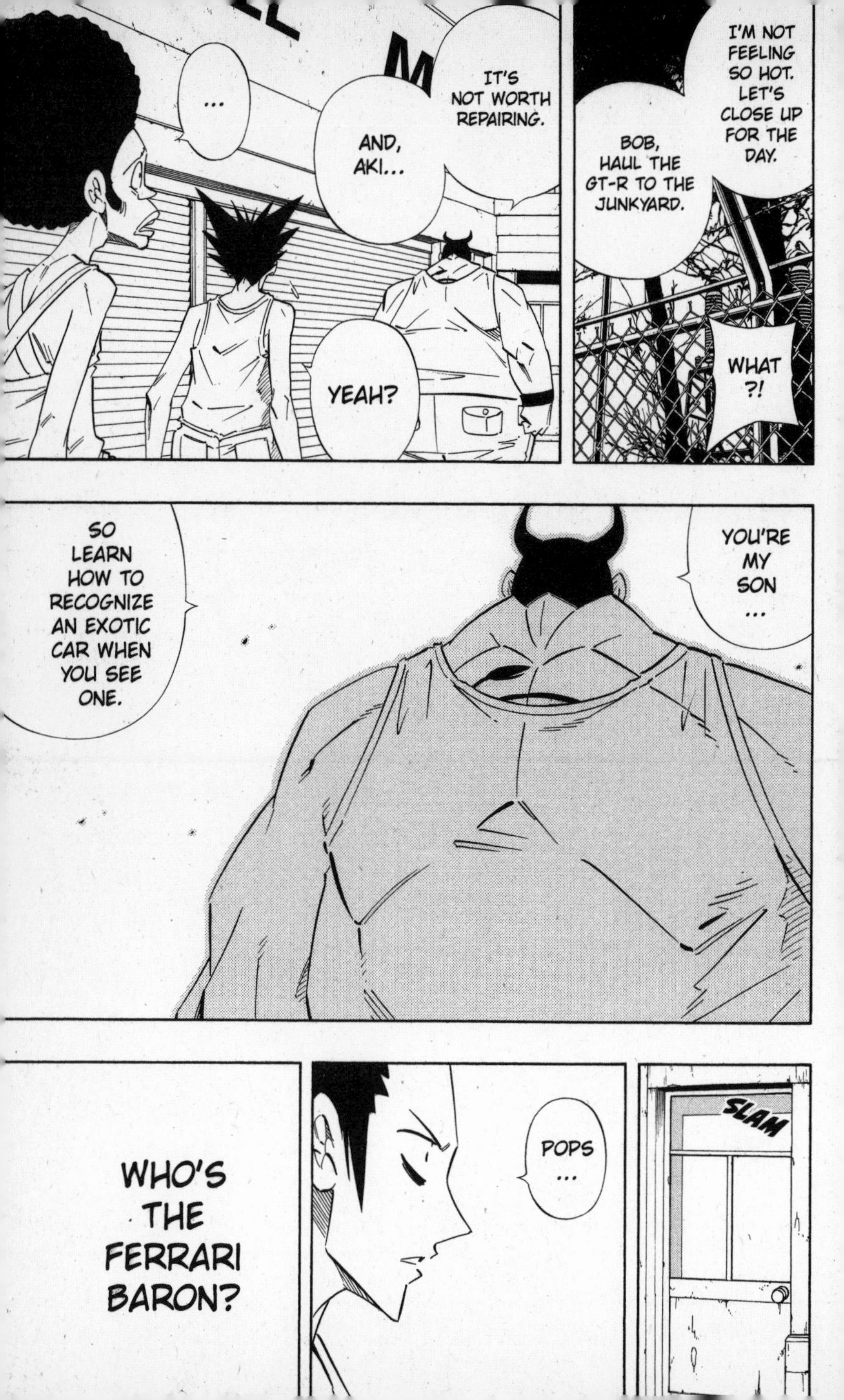
I'M NOT FEELING SO HOT. LET'S CLOSE UP FOR THE DAY.
BOB, HAUL THE GT-R TO THE JUNKYARD.
WHAT ?!
IT'S NOT WORTH REPAIRING.
AND, AKI...
...
YEAH?
YOU'RE MY SON ...
SO LEARN HOW TO RECOGNIZE AN EXOTIC CAR WHEN YOU SEE ONE.
SLAM
POPS ...
WHO'S THE FERRARI BARON?

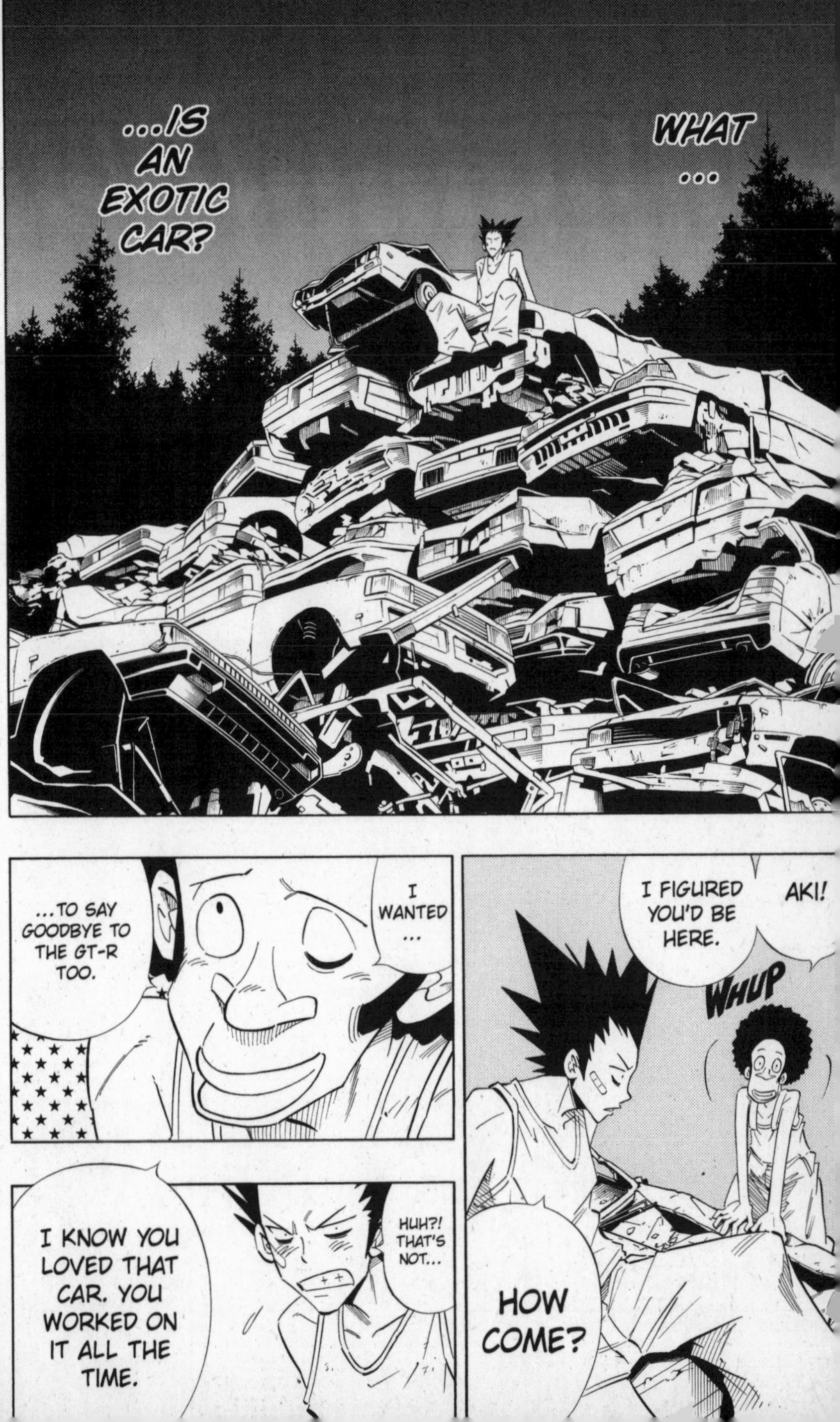
WHAT...
...IS AN EXOTIC CAR?
AKI!
I FIGURED YOU'D BE HERE.
WHUP
HOW COME?
I WANTED...
...TO SAY GOODBYE TO THE GT-R TOO.
HUH?! THAT'S NOT...
I KNOW YOU LOVED THAT CAR. YOU WORKED ON IT ALL THE TIME.

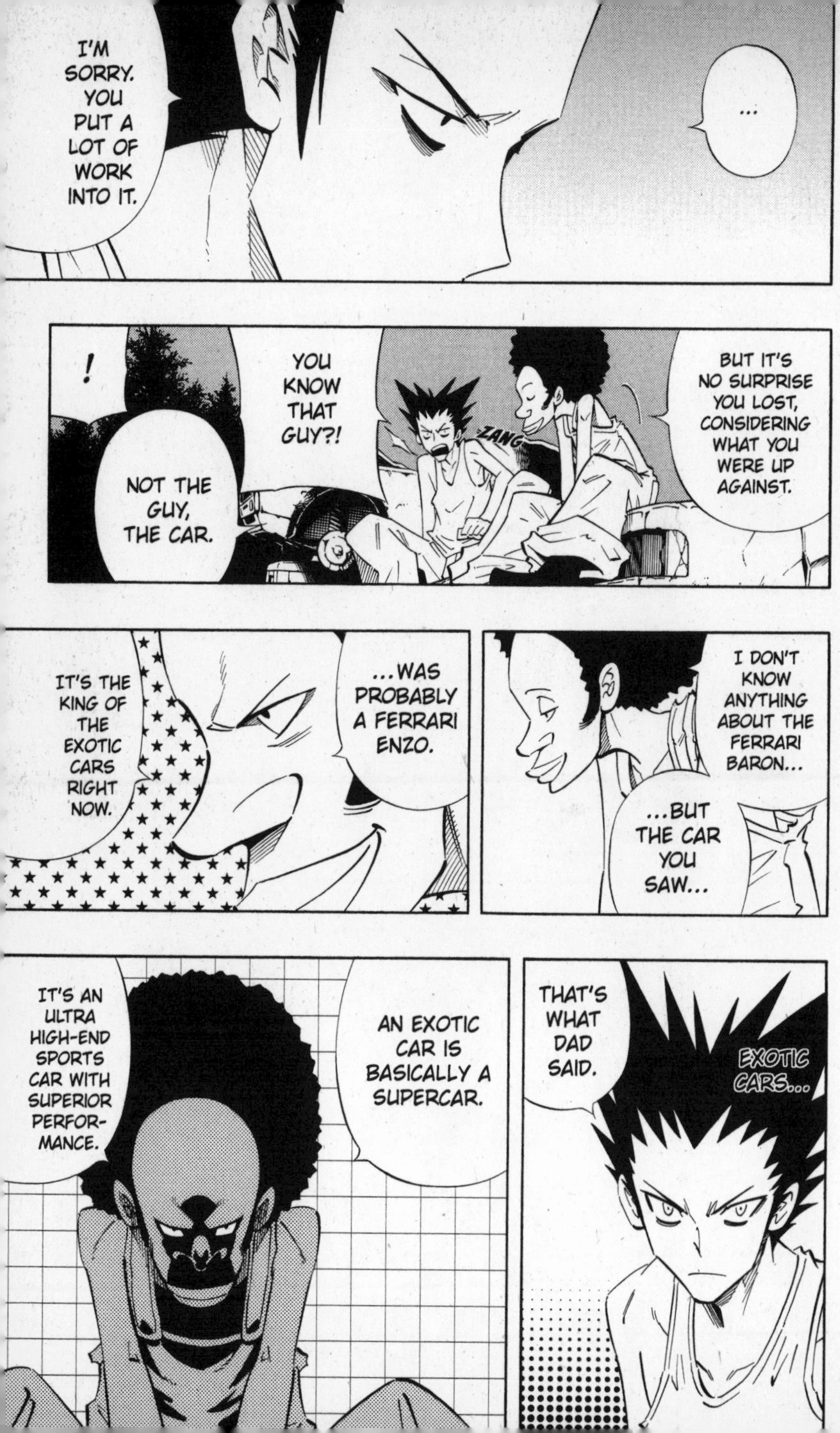
...
I'M SORRY. YOU PUT A LOT OF WORK INTO IT.
BUT IT'S NO SURPRISE YOU LOST, CONSIDERING WHAT YOU WERE UP AGAINST.
ZANG
YOU KNOW THAT GUY?!
!
NOT THE GUY, THE CAR.
I DON'T KNOW ANYTHING ABOUT THE FERRARI BARON...
...BUT THE CAR YOU SAW...
...WAS PROBABLY A FERRARI ENZO.
IT'S THE KING OF THE EXOTIC CARS RIGHT NOW.
EXOTIC CARS...
THAT'S WHAT DAD SAID.
AN EXOTIC CAR IS BASICALLY A SUPERCAR.
IT'S AN ULTRA HIGH-END SPORTS CAR WITH SUPERIOR PERFOR-MANCE.

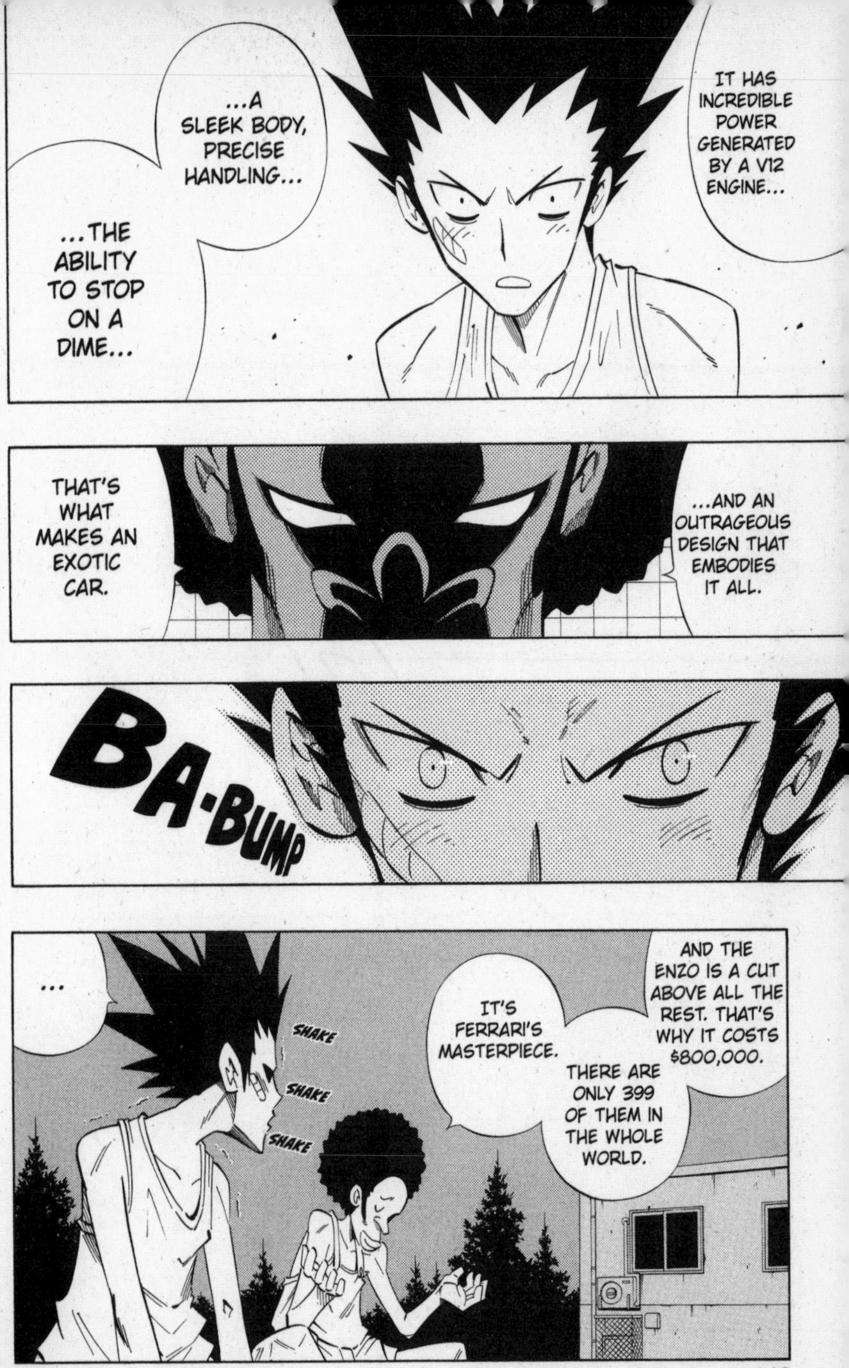
IT HAS INCREDIBLE POWER GENERATED BY A V12 ENGINE...
...A SLEEK BODY, PRECISE HANDLING...
...THE ABILITY TO STOP ON A DIME...
...AND AN OUTRAGEOUS DESIGN THAT EMBODIES IT ALL.
THAT'S WHAT MAKES AN EXOTIC CAR.
BA-BUMP
AND THE ENZO IS A CUT ABOVE ALL THE REST. THAT'S WHY IT COSTS $800,000.
IT'S FERRARI'S MASTERPIECE.
THERE ARE ONLY 399 OF THEM IN THE WHOLE WORLD.
SHAKE
SHAKE
SHAKE
...

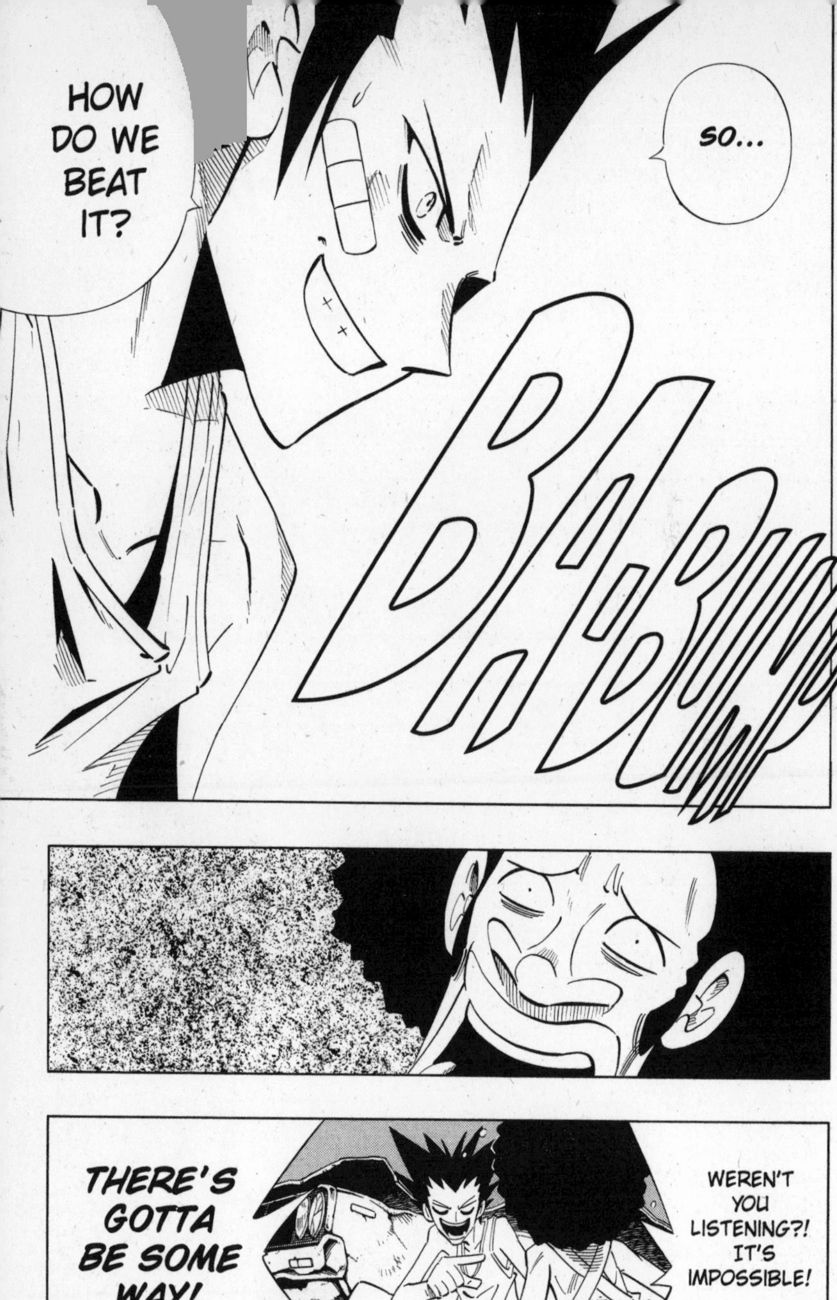
SO...
HOW DO WE BEAT IT?
BABUMP
WEREN'T YOU LISTENING?! IT'S IMPOSSIBLE!
THERE'S GOTTA BE SOME WAY!

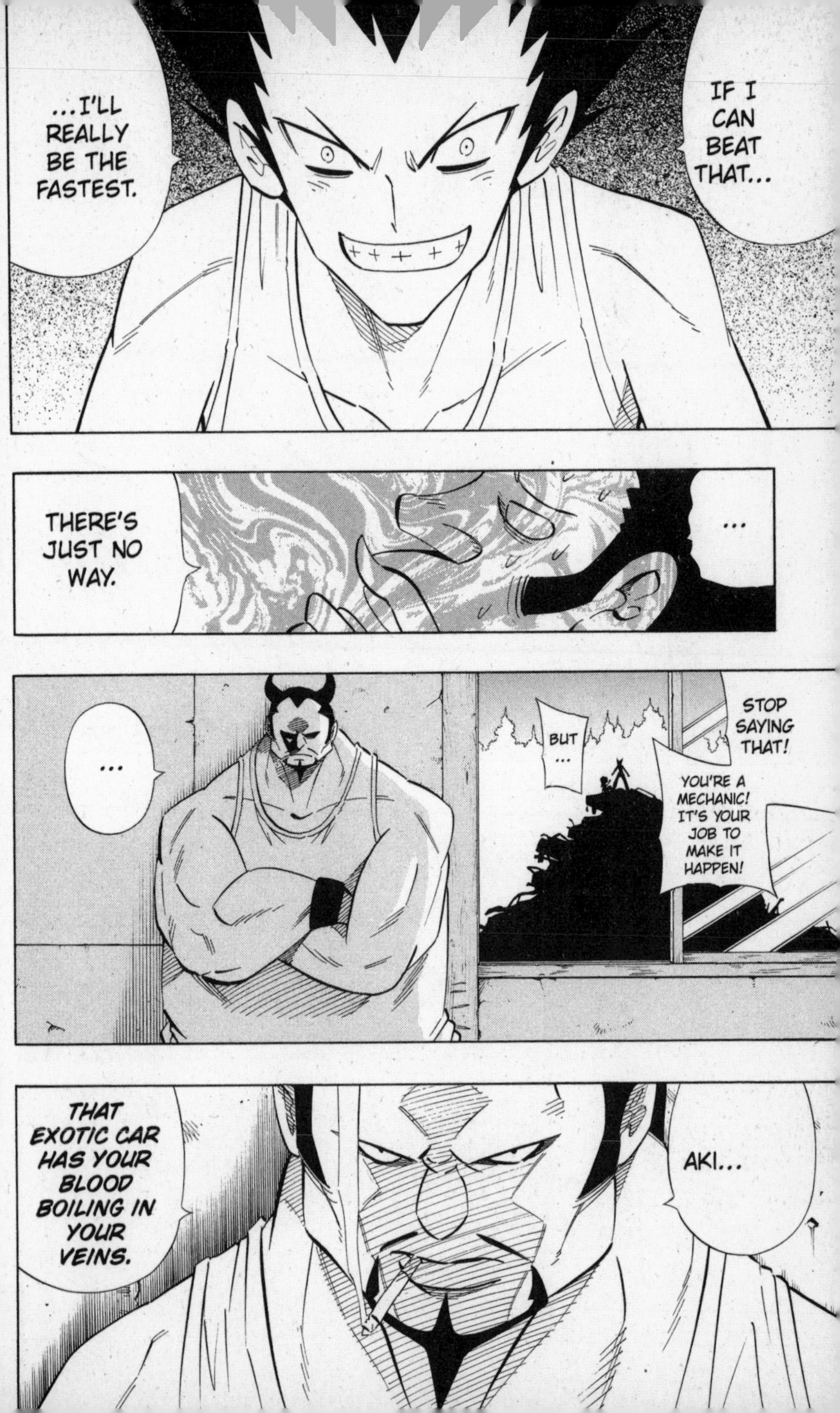
IF I CAN BEAT THAT...
...I'LL REALLY BE THE FASTEST.
...
THERE'S JUST NO WAY.
STOP SAYING THAT!
BUT...
YOU'RE A MECHANIC! IT'S YOUR JOB TO MAKE IT HAPPEN!
...
AKI...
THAT EXOTIC CAR HAS YOUR BLOOD BOILING IN YOUR VEINS.

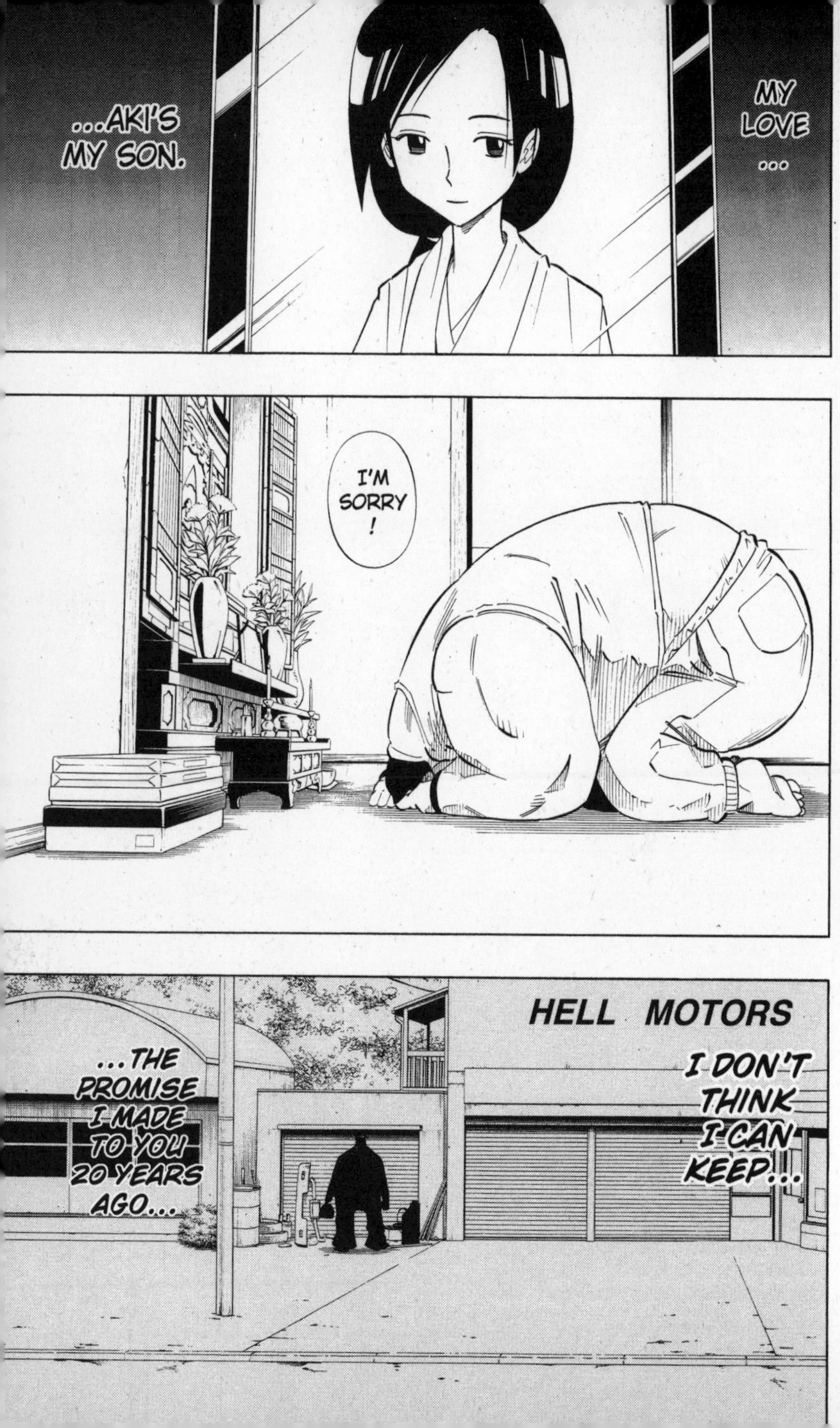
MY LOVE ...
...AKI'S MY SON.
I'M SORRY!
HELL MOTORS
I DON'T THINK I CAN KEEP...
...THE PROMISE I MADE TO YOU 20 YEARS AGO...

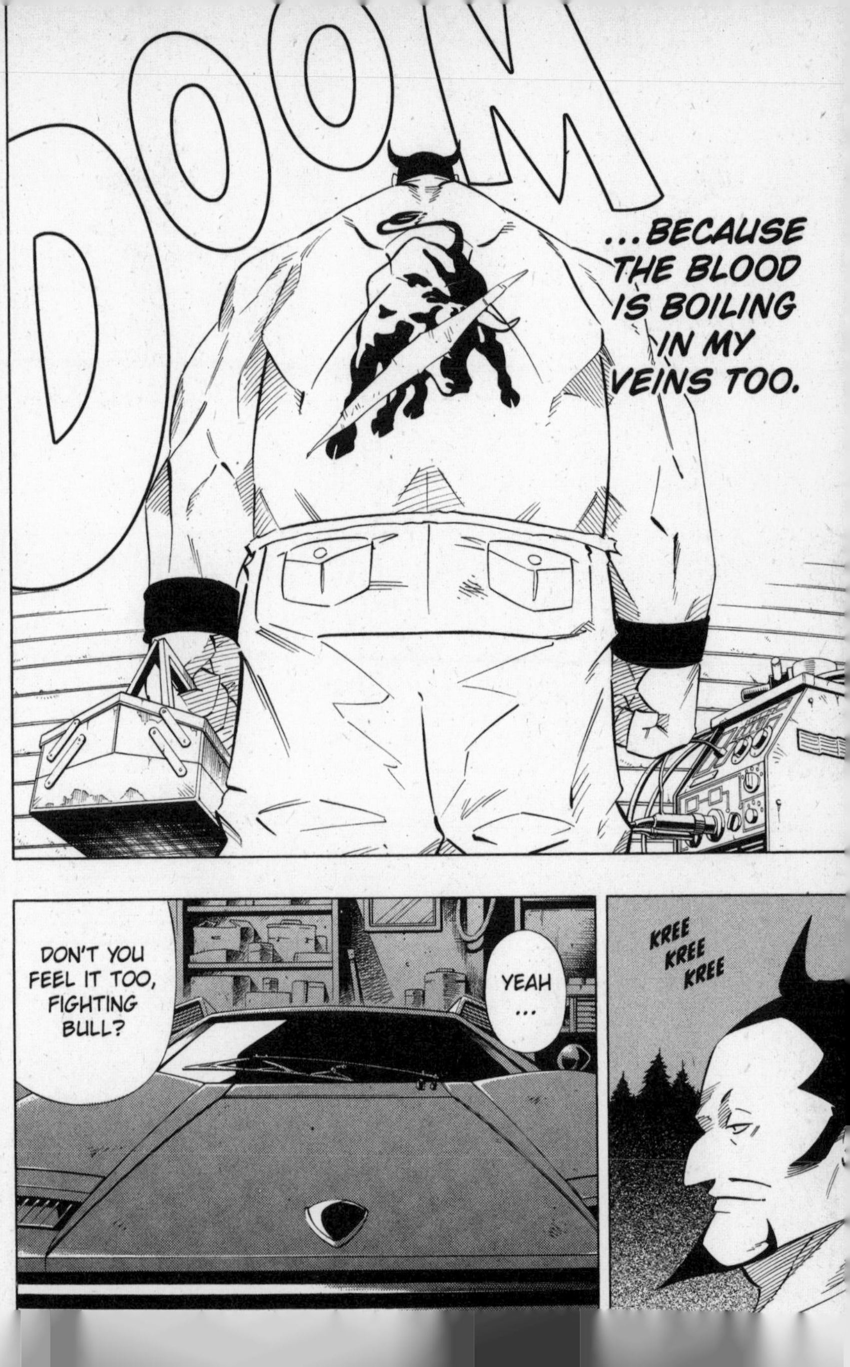
DOOM
...BECAUSE THE BLOOD IS BOILING IN MY VEINS TOO.
KREE KREE KREE
DON'T YOU FEEL IT TOO, FIGHTING BULL?
YEAH ...

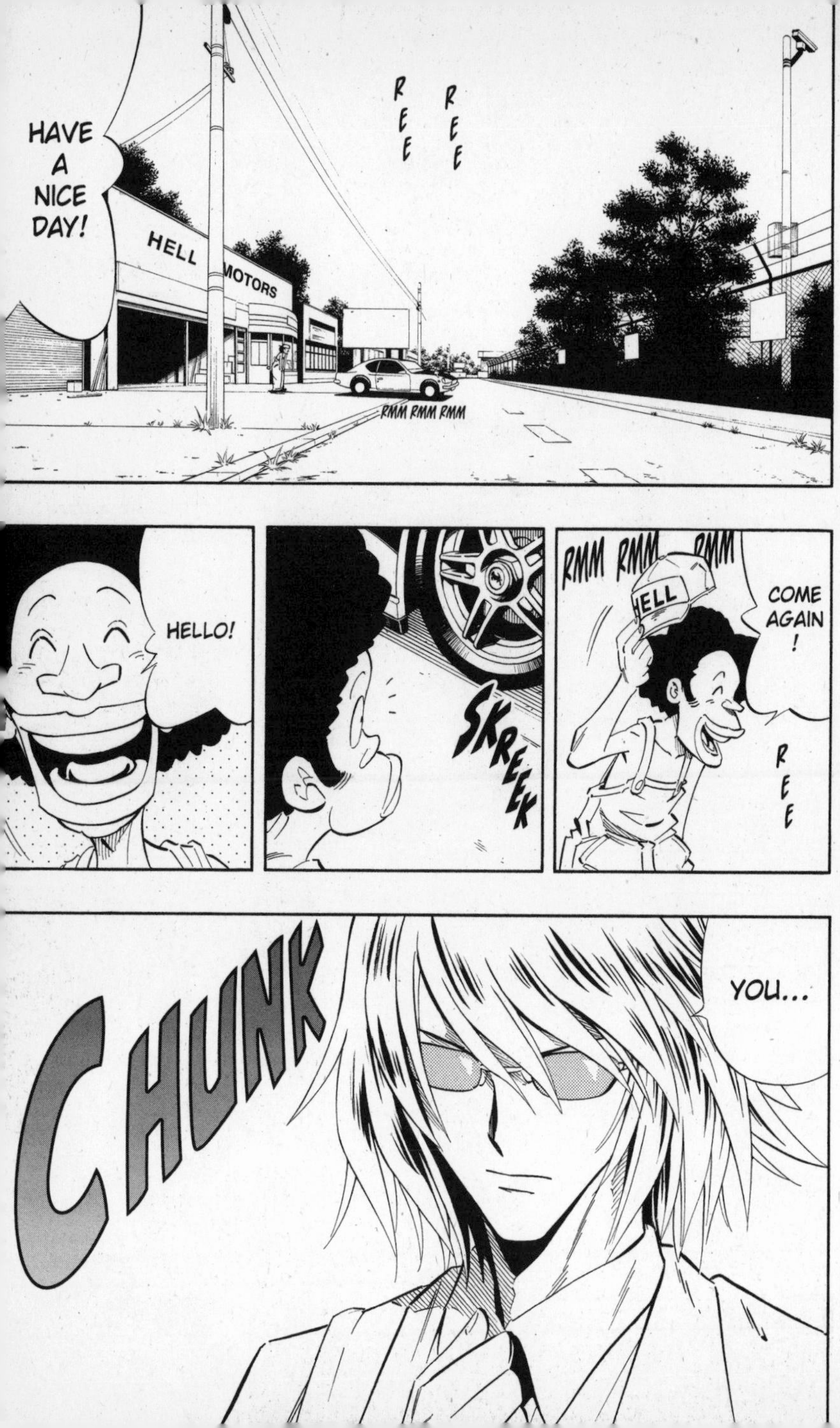
REE REE
HAVE A NICE DAY!
HELL MOTORS
RMM RMM RMM
RMM RMM RMM
COME AGAIN!
REE
SKREEK
HELLO!
YOU...
CHUNK

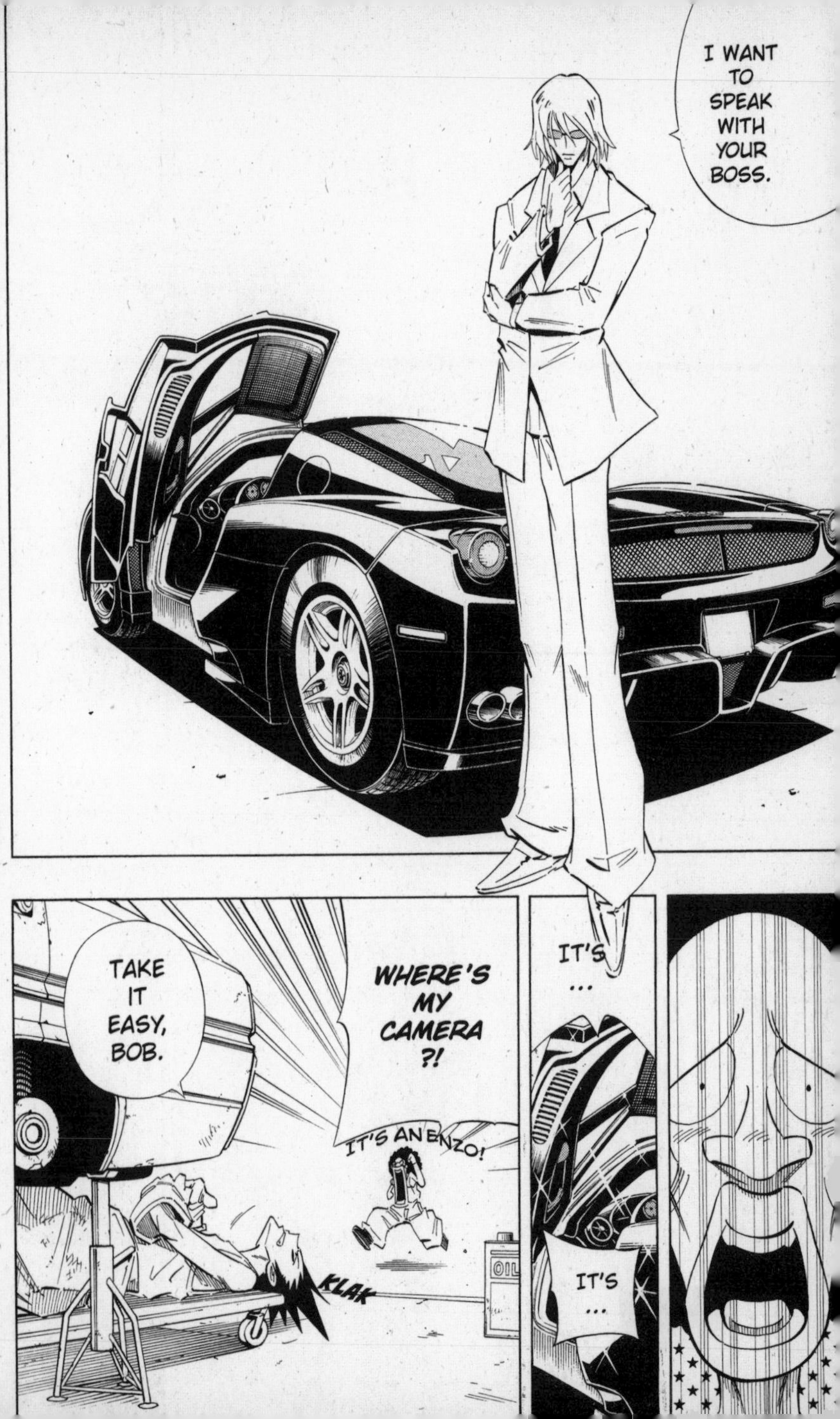
I WANT TO SPEAK WITH YOUR BOSS.
IT'S ...
IT'S ...
WHERE'S MY CAMERA ?!
TAKE IT EASY, BOB.
IT'S AN ENZO!
KLAK
OIL

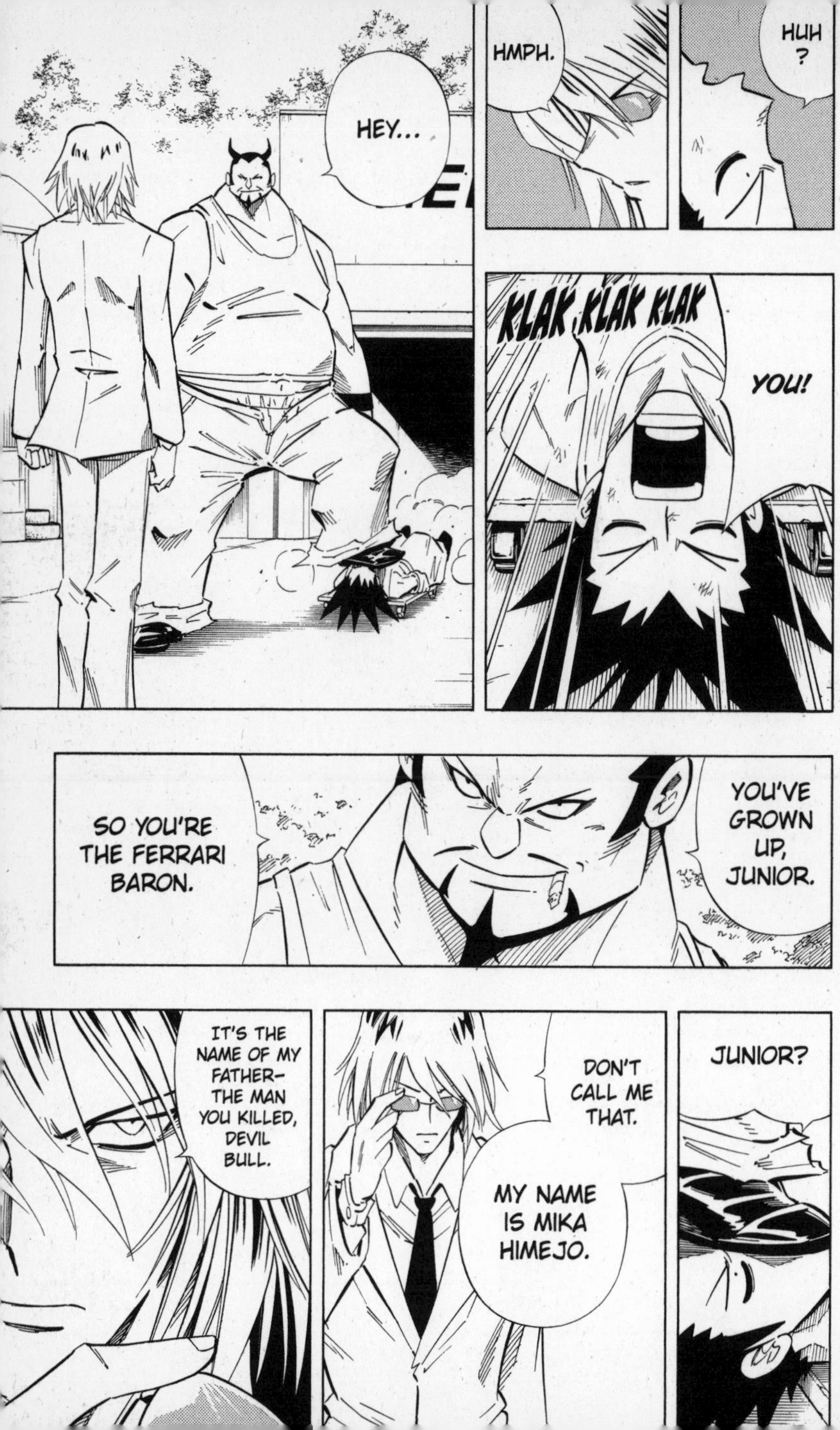
HUH?
HMPH.
KLAK KLAK KLAK
YOU!
HEY...
YOU'VE GROWN UP, JUNIOR.
SO YOU'RE THE FERRARI BARON.
JUNIOR?
DON'T CALL ME THAT.
MY NAME IS MIKA HIMEJO.
IT'S THE NAME OF MY FATHER-THE MAN YOU KILLED, DEVIL BULL.

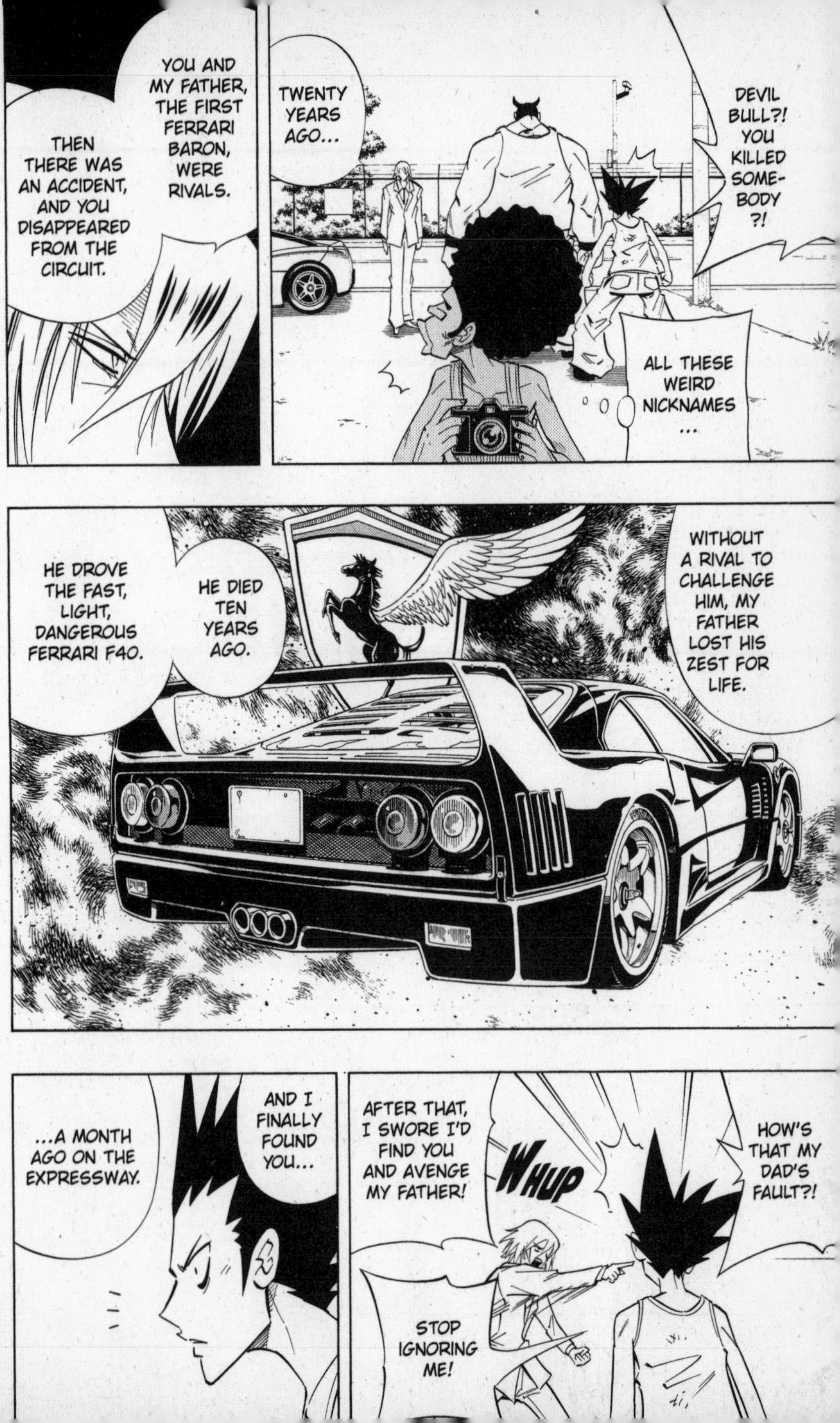
DEVIL BULL?! YOU KILLED SOMEBODY?!
TWENTY YEARS AGO...
ALL THESE WEIRD NICKNAMES...
YOU AND MY FATHER, THE FIRST FERRARI BARON, WERE RIVALS.
THEN THERE WAS AN ACCIDENT, AND YOU DISAPPEARED FROM THE CIRCUIT.
WITHOUT A RIVAL TO CHALLENGE HIM, MY FATHER LOST HIS ZEST FOR LIFE.
HE DIED TEN YEARS AGO.
HE DROVE THE FAST, LIGHT, DANGEROUS FERRARI F40.
HOW'S THAT MY DAD'S FAULT?!
WHUP
AFTER THAT, I SWORE I'D FIND YOU AND AVENGE MY FATHER!
STOP IGNORING ME!
AND I FINALLY FOUND YOU...
...A MONTH AGO ON THE EXPRESSWAY.

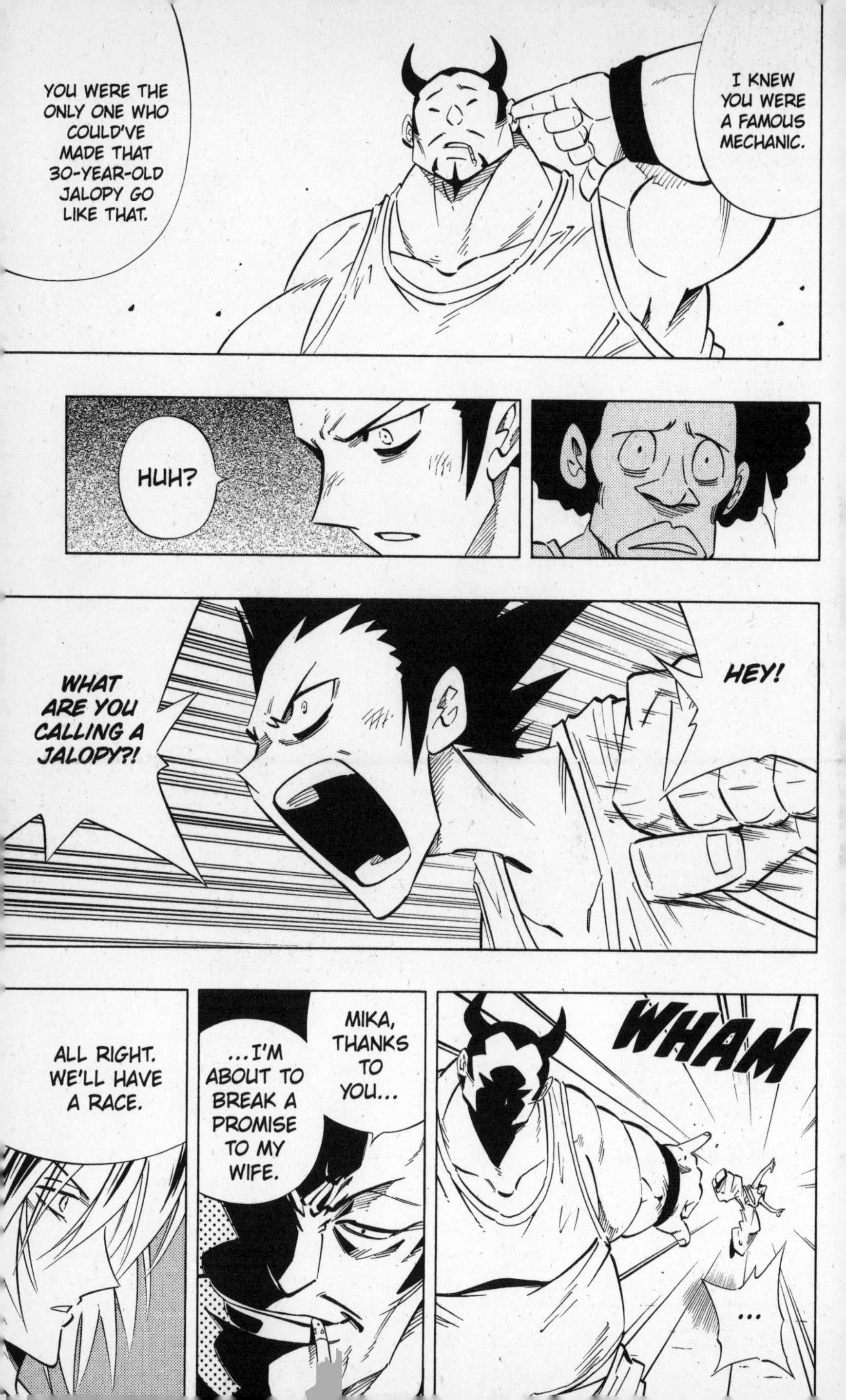
I KNEW YOU WERE A FAMOUS MECHANIC.
YOU WERE THE ONLY ONE WHO COULD'VE MADE THAT 30-YEAR-OLD JALOPY GO LIKE THAT.
HUH?
HEY!
WHAT ARE YOU CALLING A JALOPY?!
WHAM
...
MIKA, THANKS TO YOU...
...I'M ABOUT TO BREAK A PROMISE TO MY WIFE.
ALL RIGHT. WE'LL HAVE A RACE.

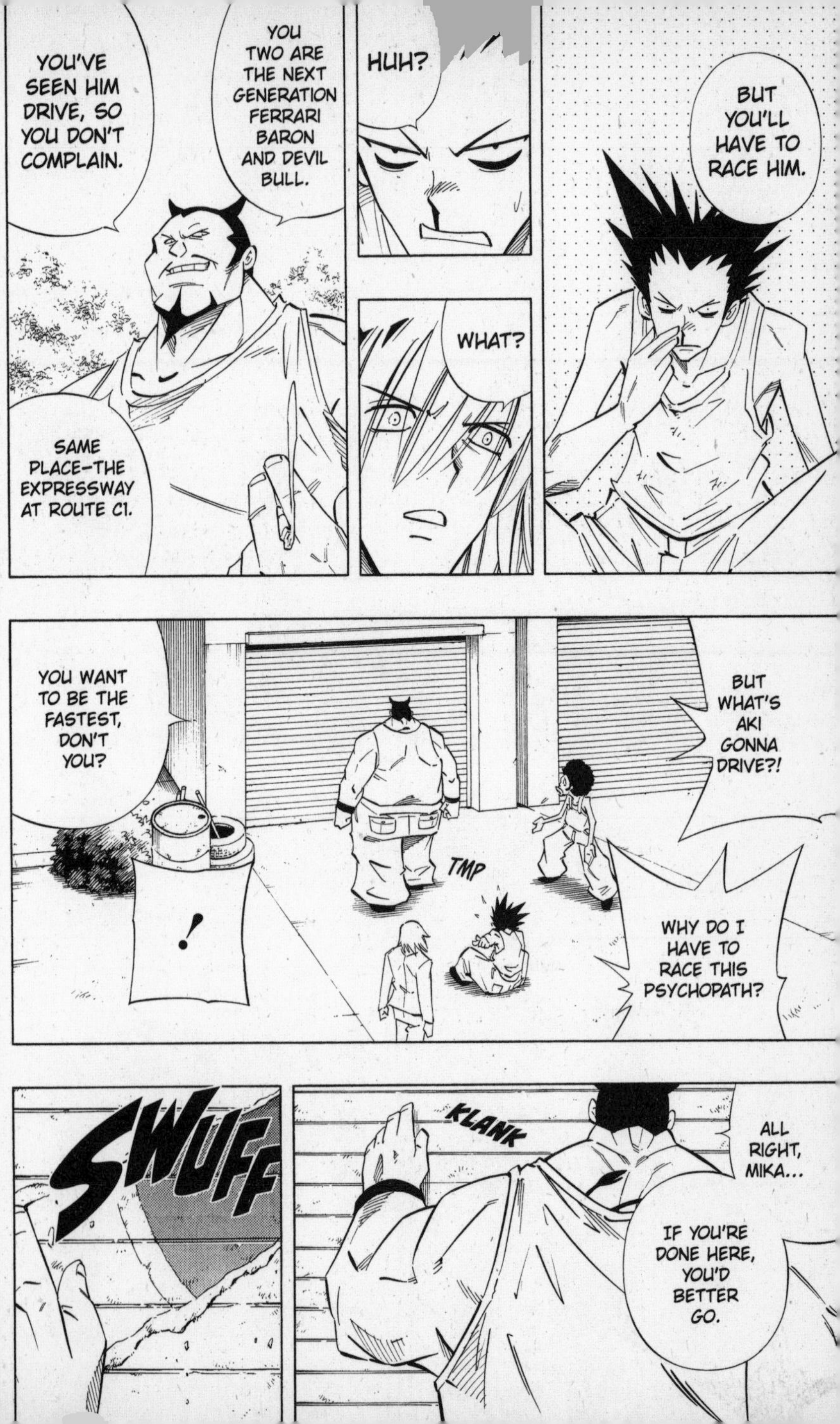
BUT YOU'LL HAVE TO RACE HIM.
HUH?
WHAT?
YOU TWO ARE THE NEXT GENERATION FERRARI BARON AND DEVIL BULL.
YOU'VE SEEN HIM DRIVE, SO YOU DON'T COMPLAIN.
SAME PLACE—THE EXPRESSWAY AT ROUTE C1.
BUT WHAT'S AKI GONNA DRIVE?!
WHY DO I HAVE TO RACE THIS PSYCHOPATH?
TMP
YOU WANT TO BE THE FASTEST, DON'T YOU?
!
KLANK
ALL RIGHT, MIKA...
IF YOU'RE DONE HERE, YOU'D BETTER GO.
SWUFF

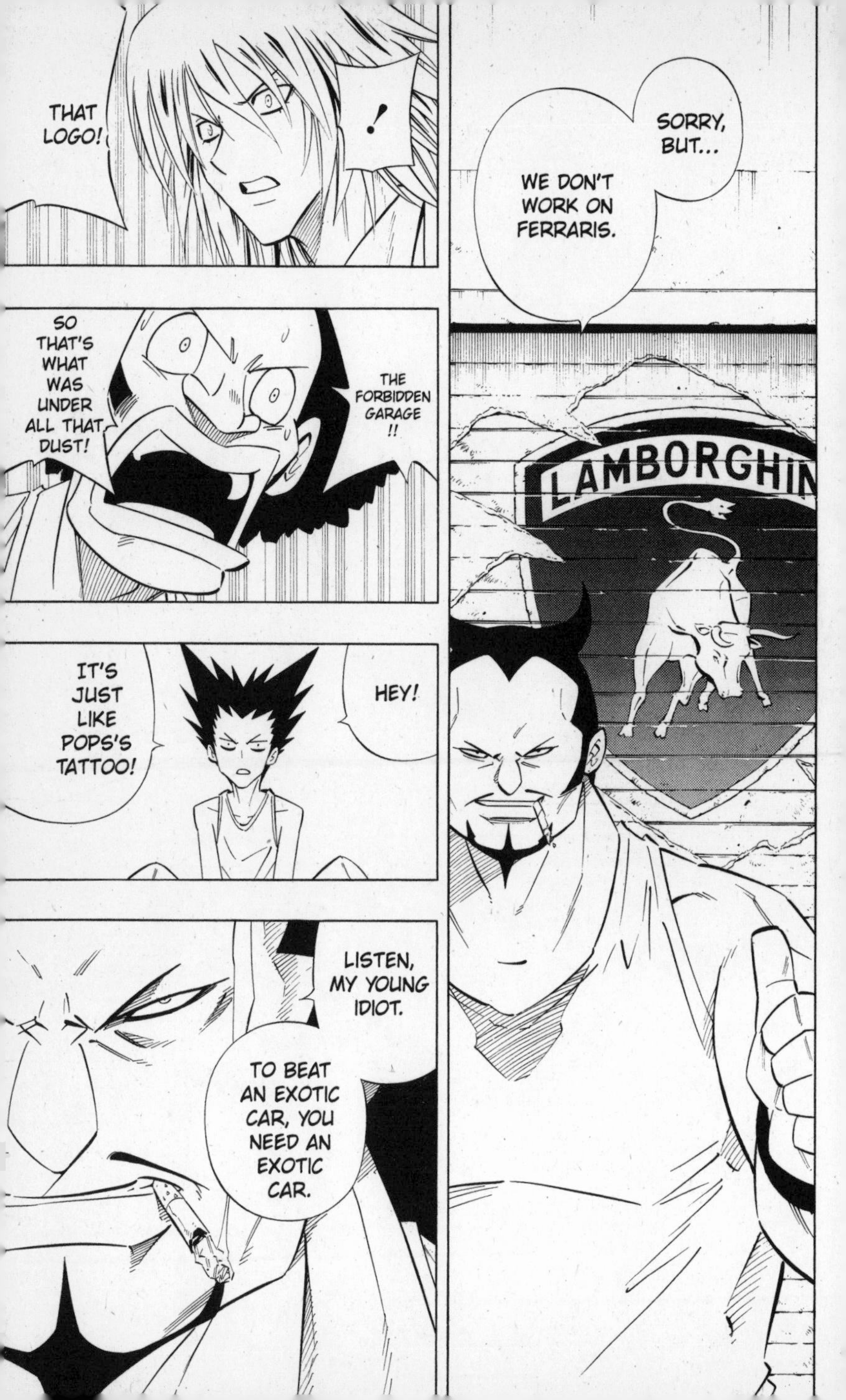
SORRY, BUT...
WE DON'T WORK ON FERRARIS.
LAMBORGHIN
!
THAT LOGO!
THE FORBIDDEN GARAGE !!
SO THAT'S WHAT WAS UNDER ALL THAT DUST!
HEY!
IT'S JUST LIKE POPS'S TATTOO!
LISTEN, MY YOUNG IDIOT.
TO BEAT AN EXOTIC CAR, YOU NEED AN EXOTIC CAR.

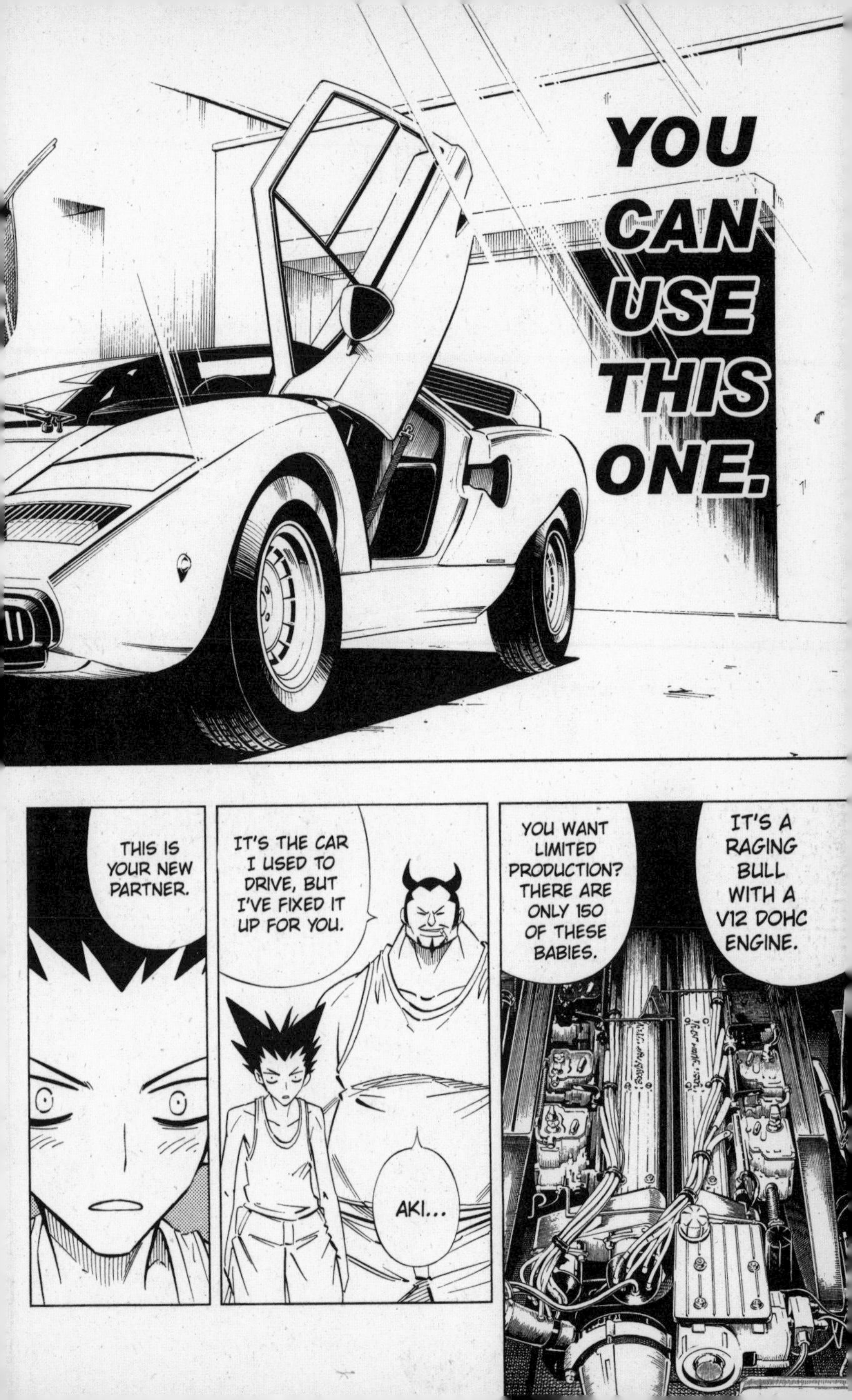
YOU CAN USE THIS ONE.
IT'S A RAGING BULL WITH A V12 DOHC ENGINE.
YOU WANT LIMITED PRODUCTION? THERE ARE ONLY 150 OF THESE BABIES.
IT'S THE CAR I USED TO DRIVE, BUT I'VE FIXED IT UP FOR YOU.
AKI...
THIS IS YOUR NEW PARTNER.

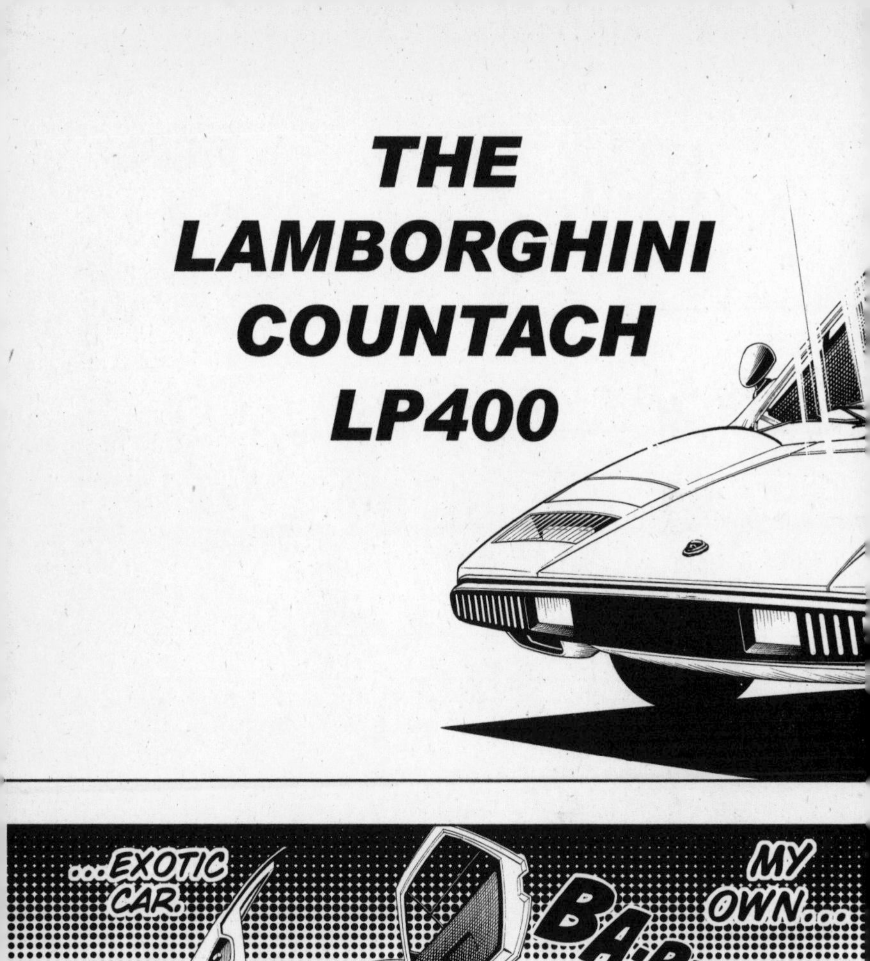
THE LAMBORGHINI COUNTACH LP400

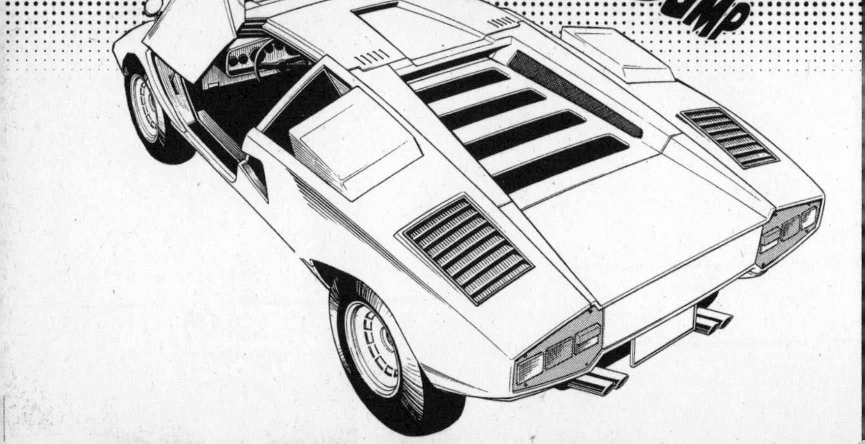
MY OWN...
BA-BUMP
...EXOTIC CAR.

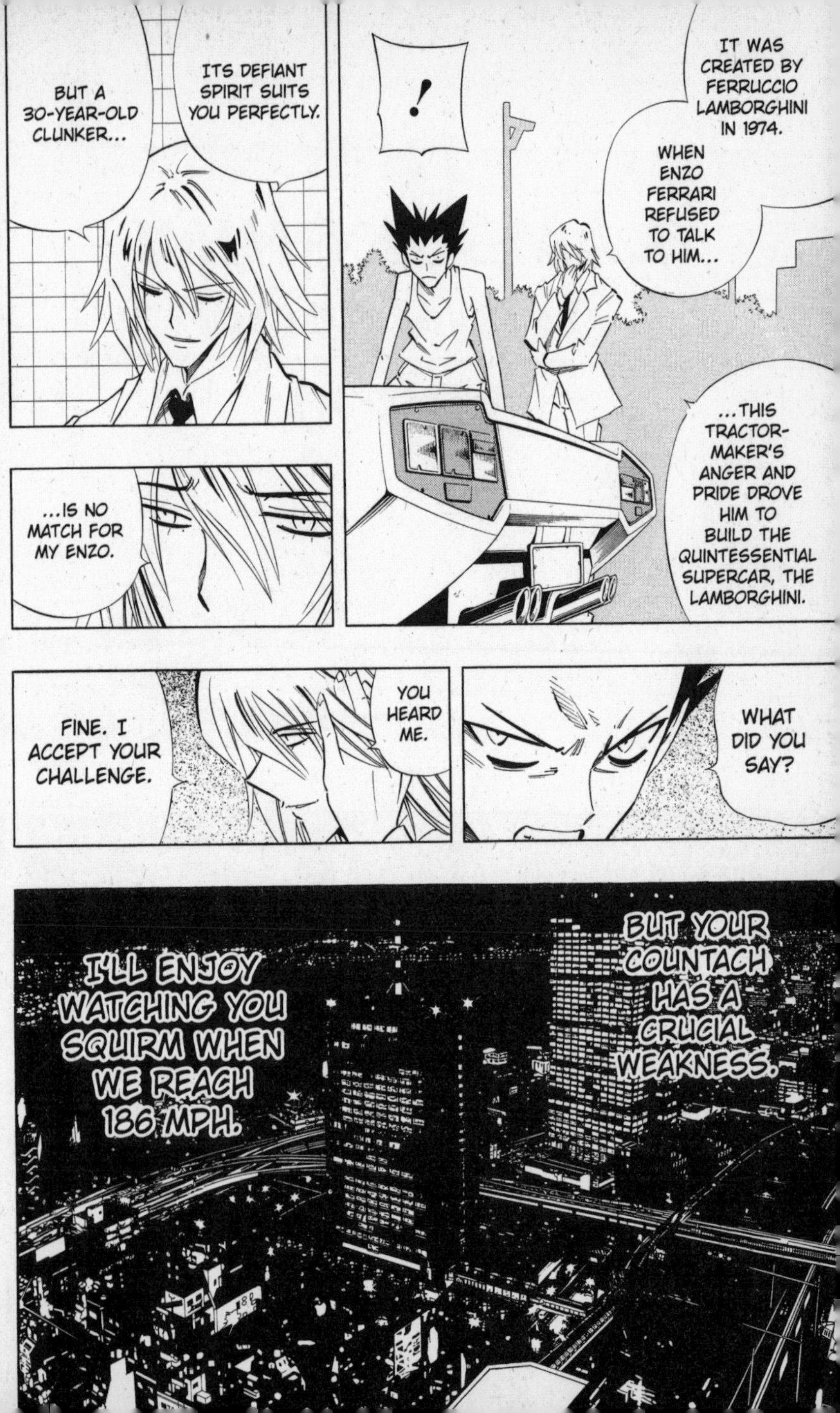
!
IT WAS CREATED BY FERRUCCIO LAMBORGHINI IN 1974.
WHEN ENZO FERRARI REFUSED TO TALK TO HIM...
...THIS TRACTOR-MAKER'S ANGER AND PRIDE DROVE HIM TO BUILD THE QUINTESSENTIAL SUPERCAR, THE LAMBORGHINI.
ITS DEFIANT SPIRIT SUITS YOU PERFECTLY.
BUT A 30-YEAR-OLD CLUNKER...
...IS NO MATCH FOR MY ENZO.
WHAT DID YOU SAY?
YOU HEARD ME.
FINE. I ACCEPT YOUR CHALLENGE.
BUT YOUR COUNTACH HAS A CRUCIAL WEAKNESS.
I'LL ENJOY WATCHING YOU SQUIRM WHEN WE REACH 186 MPH.

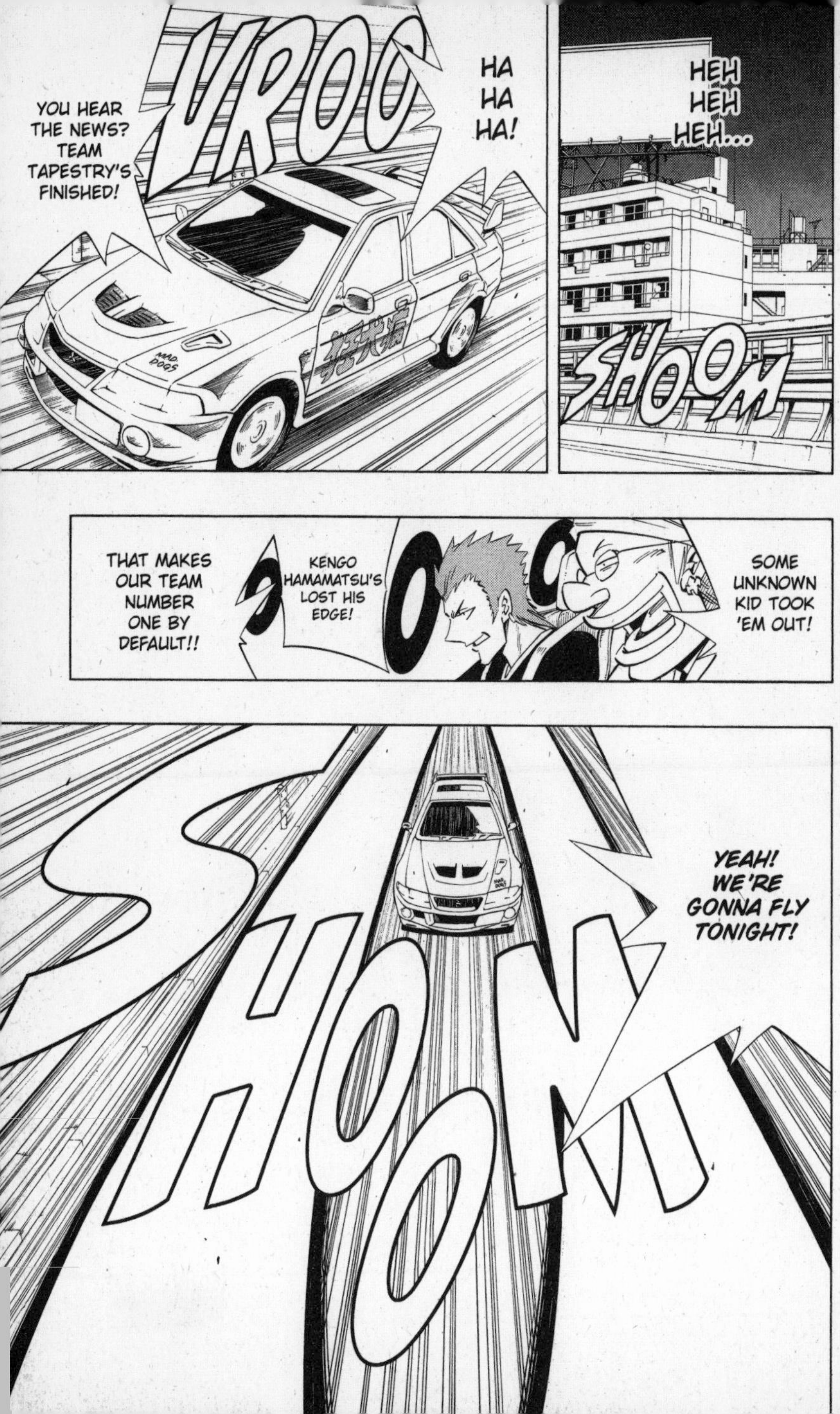
HEH HEH HEH...
SHOOM
HA HA HA!
VROOO
YOU HEAR THE NEWS? TEAM TAPESTRY'S FINISHED!
SOME UNKNOWN KID TOOK 'EM OUT!
KENGO HAMAMATSU'S LOST HIS EDGE!
THAT MAKES OUR TEAM NUMBER ONE BY DEFAULT!!
YEAH! WE'RE GONNA FLY TONIGHT!
SHOOM

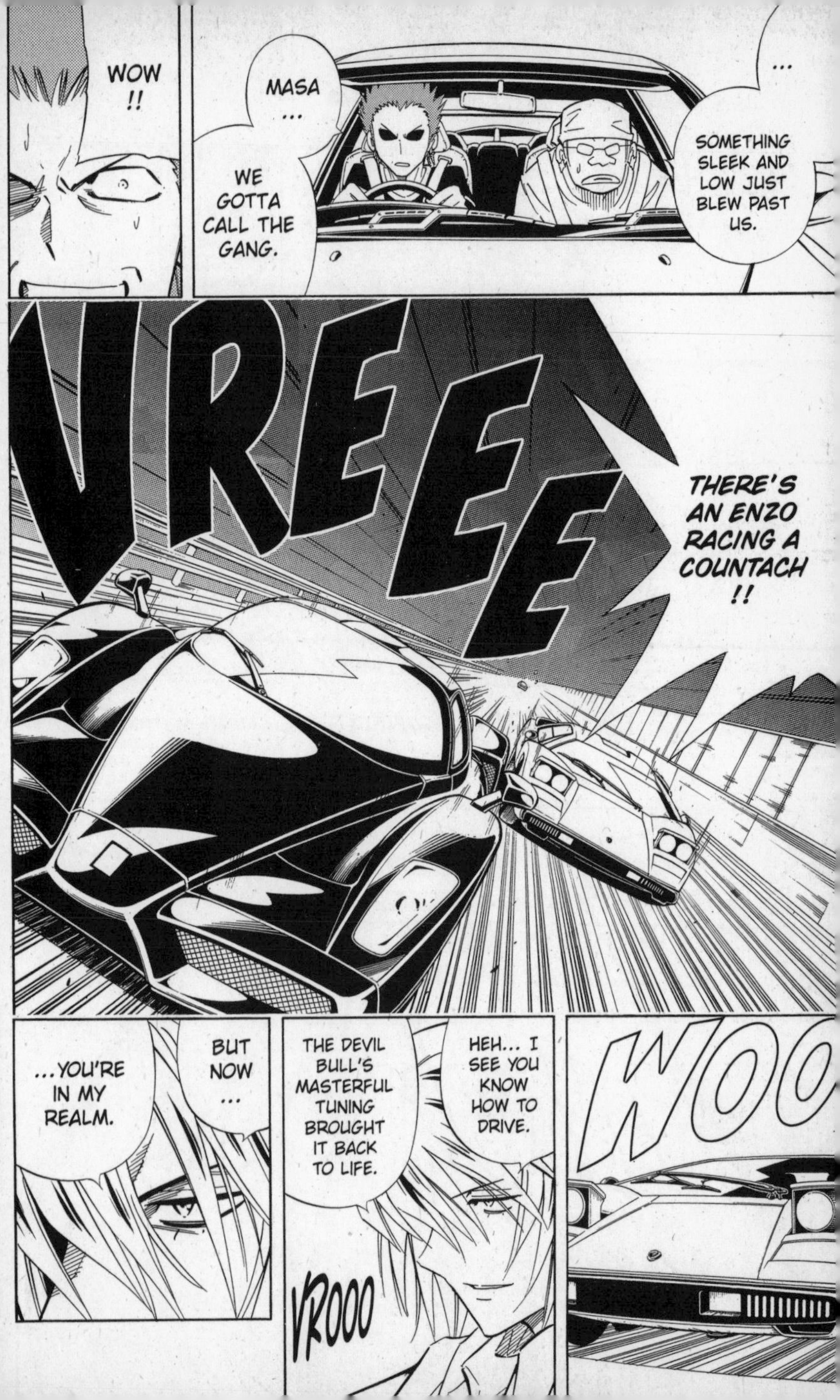
...
SOMETHING SLEEK AND LOW JUST BLEW PAST US.
MASA ...
WE GOTTA CALL THE GANG.
WOW !!
VREEE
THERE'S AN ENZO RACING A COUNTACH !!
WOO
HEH... I SEE YOU KNOW HOW TO DRIVE.
THE DEVIL BULL'S MASTERFUL TUNING BROUGHT IT BACK TO LIFE.
VROOO
BUT NOW ...
...YOU'RE IN MY REALM.

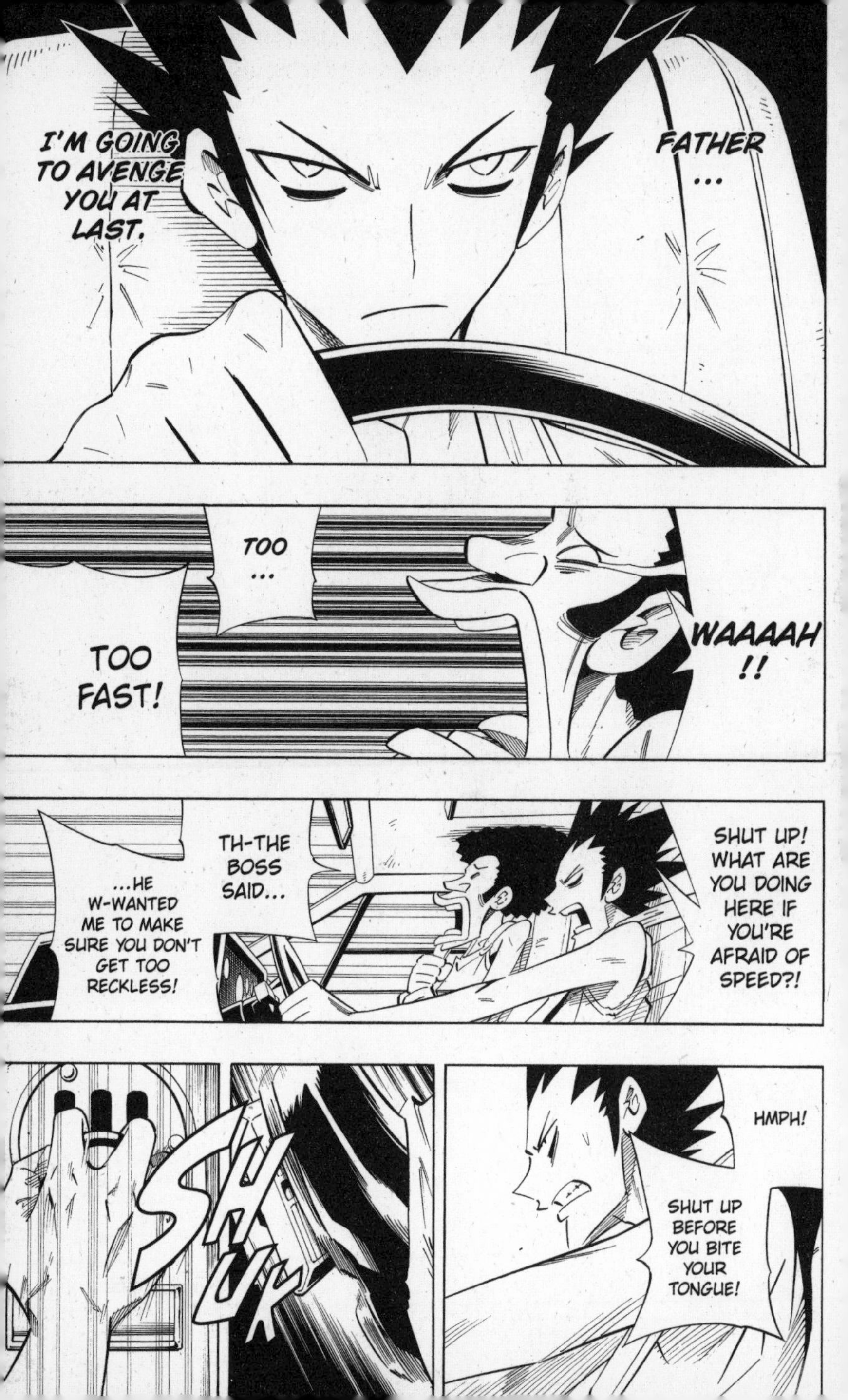

FATHER ...
I'M GOING TO AVENGE YOU AT LAST.
WAAAAH !!
TOO ...
TOO FAST!
SHUT UP! WHAT ARE YOU DOING HERE IF YOU'RE AFRAID OF SPEED?!
TH-THE BOSS SAID...
...HE W-WANTED ME TO MAKE SURE YOU DON'T GET TOO RECKLESS!
HMPH!
SHUT UP BEFORE YOU BITE YOUR TONGUE!
SHUK

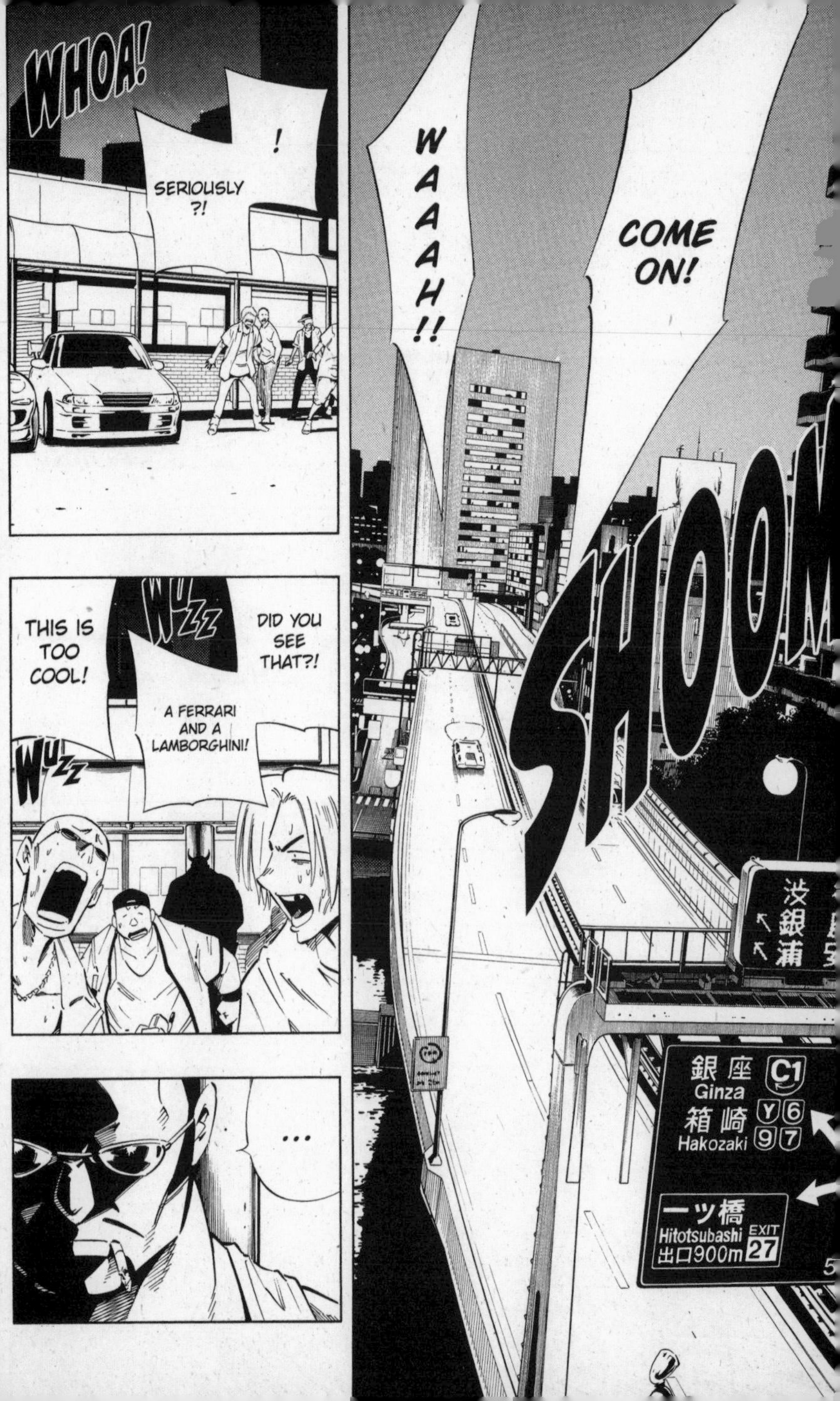
COME ON!
WAAAAH!!
SHOOM
汐
銀
浦
銀座 Ginza C1
箱崎 Hakozaki Y 6 9 7
一ツ橋 Hitotsubashi 出口900m EXIT 27
!
SERIOUSLY?!
WHOA!
DID YOU SEE THAT?!
WUZZ
A FERRARI AND A LAMBORGHINI!
THIS IS TOO COOL!
WUZZ
...

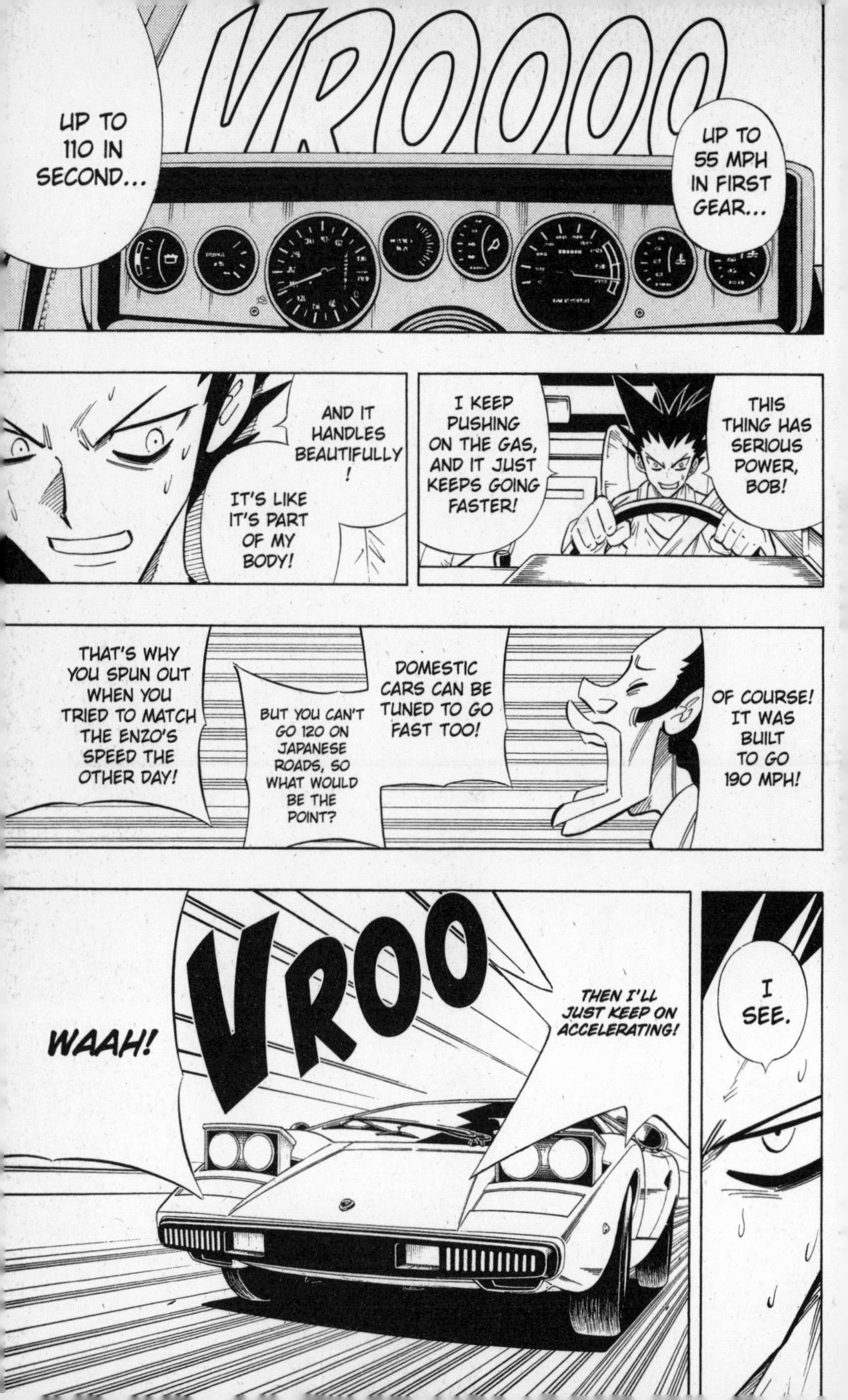
VROOOO
UP TO 55 MPH IN FIRST GEAR...
UP TO 110 IN SECOND...
THIS THING HAS SERIOUS POWER, BOB!
I KEEP PUSHING ON THE GAS, AND IT JUST KEEPS GOING FASTER!
AND IT HANDLES BEAUTIFULLY!
IT'S LIKE IT'S PART OF MY BODY!
OF COURSE! IT WAS BUILT TO GO 190 MPH!
DOMESTIC CARS CAN BE TUNED TO GO FAST TOO!
BUT YOU CAN'T GO 120 ON JAPANESE ROADS, SO WHAT WOULD BE THE POINT?
THAT'S WHY YOU SPUN OUT WHEN YOU TRIED TO MATCH THE ENZO'S SPEED THE OTHER DAY!
I SEE.
THEN I'LL JUST KEEP ON ACCELERATING!
VROO
WAAH!

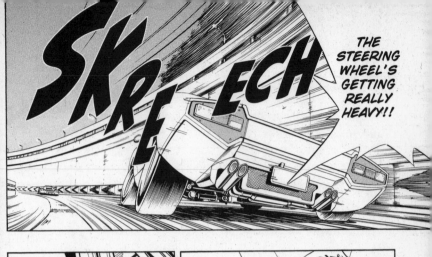

THE STEERING WHEEL'S GETTING REALLY HEAVY!!

THIS IS WHERE THE BATTLE REALLY BEGINS.

GOOD.

STILL COMING.

KLIK NOW YOU'LL SEE!...

...THE POWER OF THE GODS!

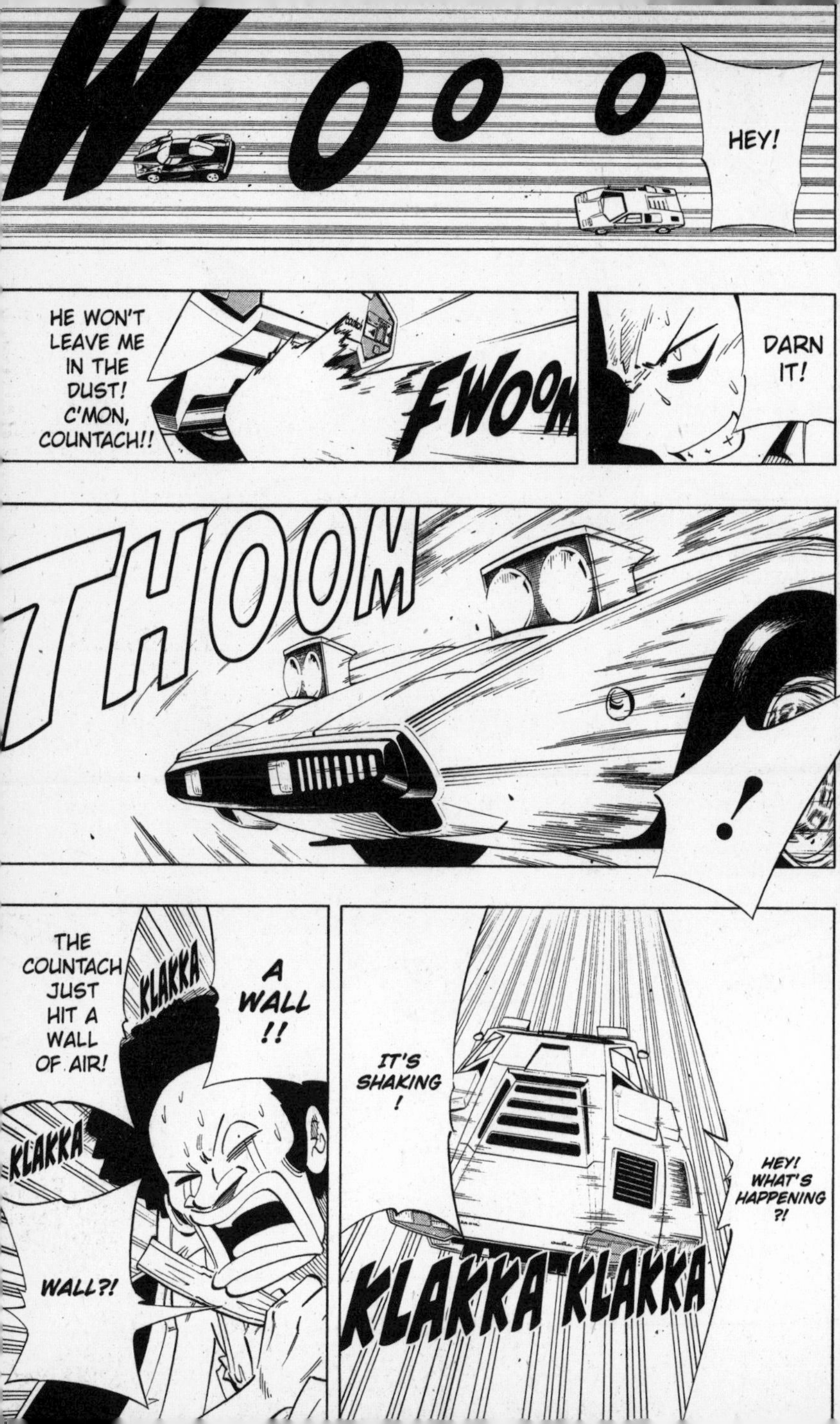
WOOOO
HEY!
DARN IT!
HE WON'T LEAVE ME IN THE DUST! C'MON, COUNTACH!!
FWOOM
THOOM
!
HEY! WHAT'S HAPPENING?!
IT'S SHAKING!
KLAKKA KLAKKA
A WALL!!
THE COUNTACH JUST HIT A WALL OF AIR!
KLAKKA
KLAKKA
WALL?!

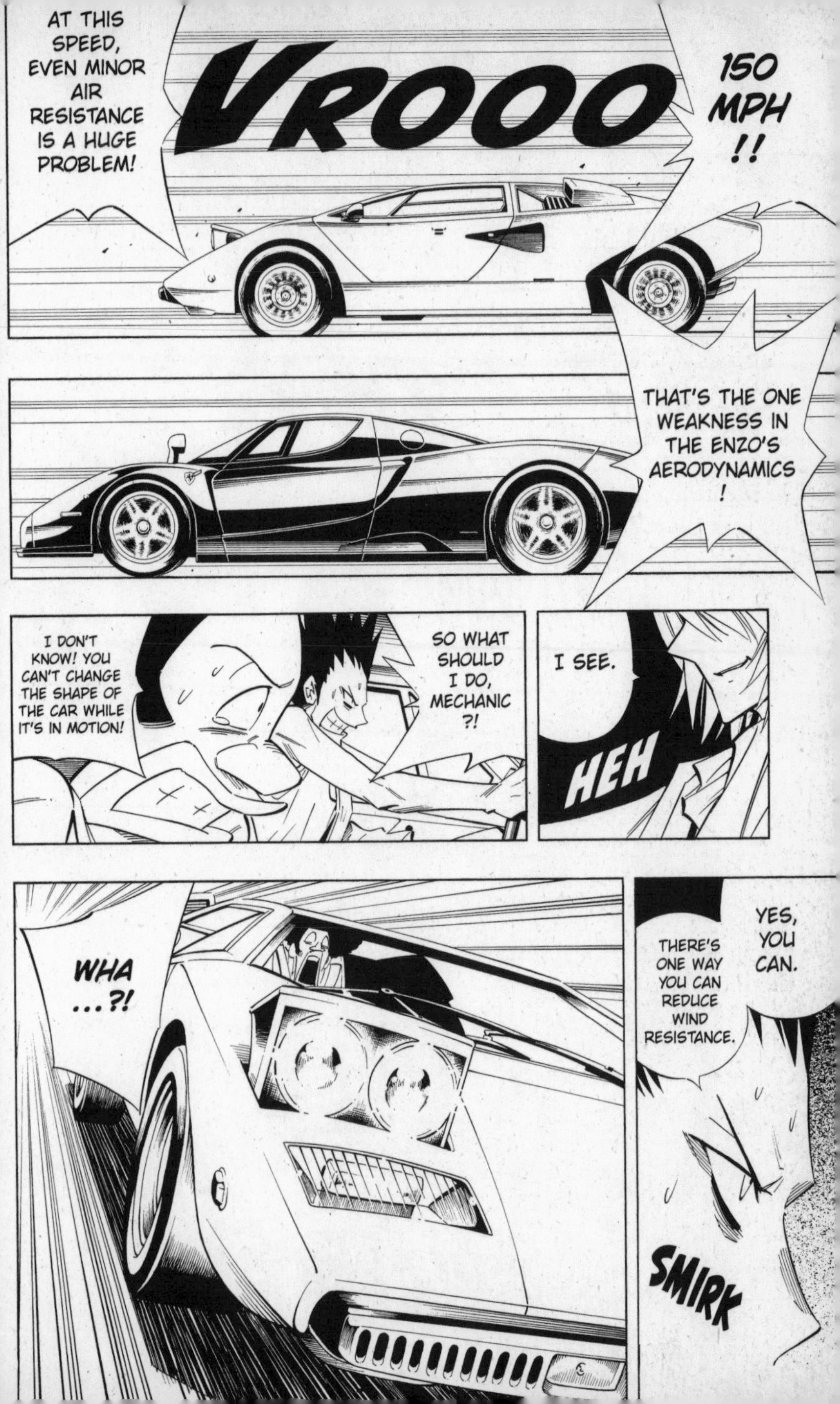
150 MPH !!
VROOO
AT THIS SPEED, EVEN MINOR AIR RESISTANCE IS A HUGE PROBLEM!
THAT'S THE ONE WEAKNESS IN THE ENZO'S AERODYNAMICS!
I SEE.
HEH
SO WHAT SHOULD I DO, MECHANIC?!
I DON'T KNOW! YOU CAN'T CHANGE THE SHAPE OF THE CAR WHILE IT'S IN MOTION!
YES, YOU CAN.
THERE'S ONE WAY YOU CAN REDUCE WIND RESISTANCE.
SMIRK
WHA...?!

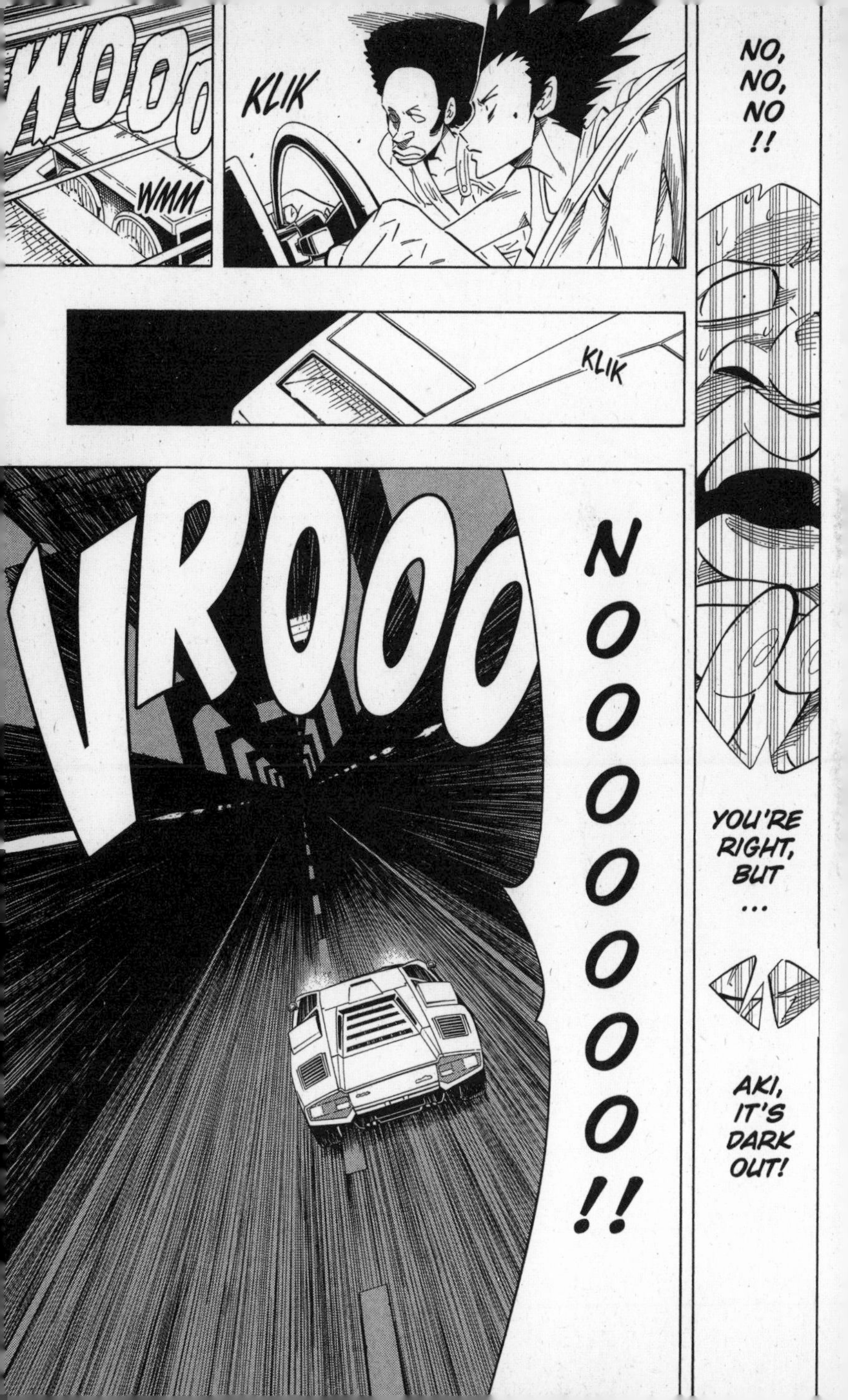
NO, NO, NO!!
YOU'RE RIGHT, BUT...
AKI, IT'S DARK OUT!
KLIK
WOOO
WMM
KLIK
VROOO
NOOOOOOO!!

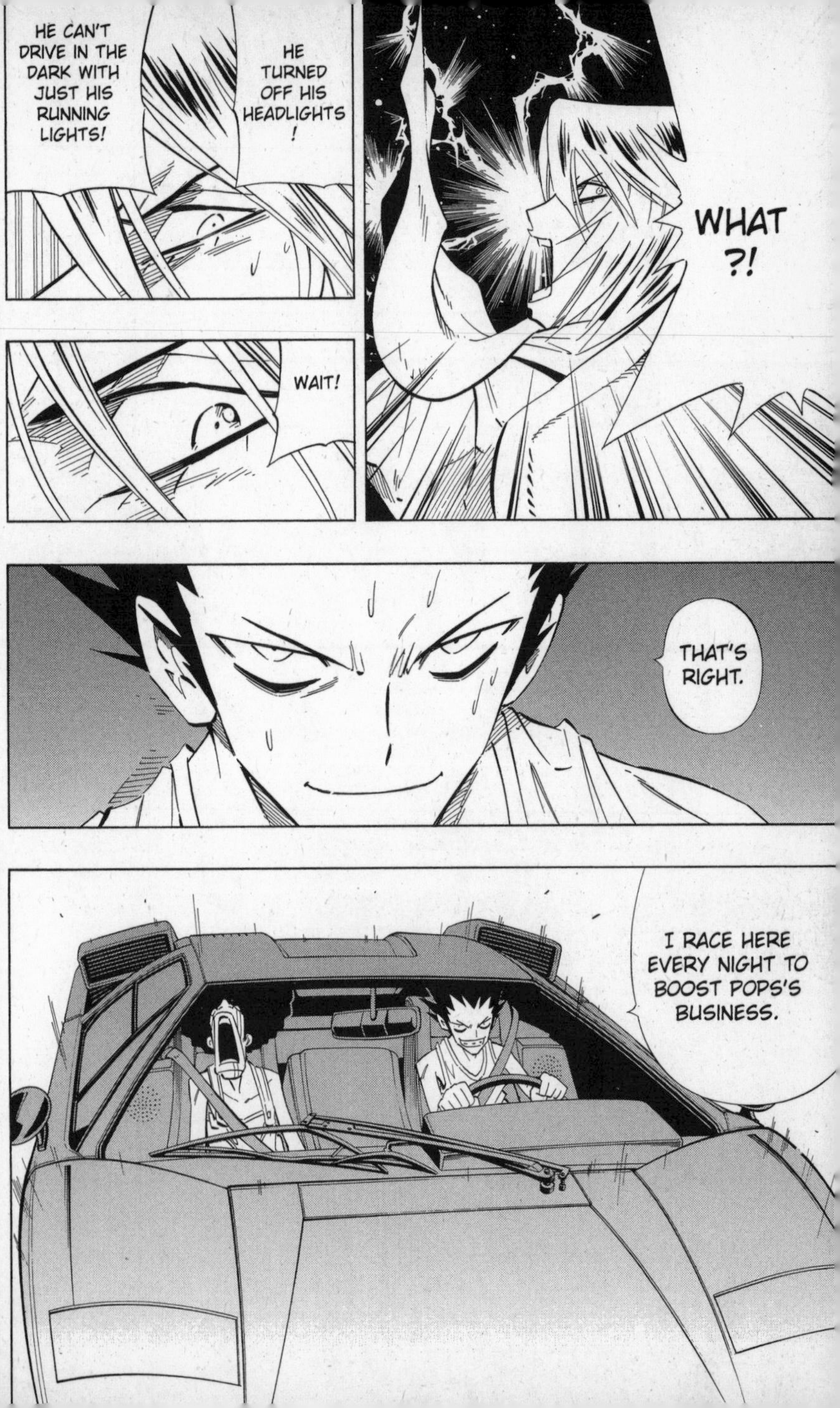
WHAT ?!
HE TURNED OFF HIS HEADLIGHTS!
HE CAN'T DRIVE IN THE DARK WITH JUST HIS RUNNING LIGHTS!
WAIT!
THAT'S RIGHT.
I RACE HERE EVERY NIGHT TO BOOST POPS'S BUSINESS.

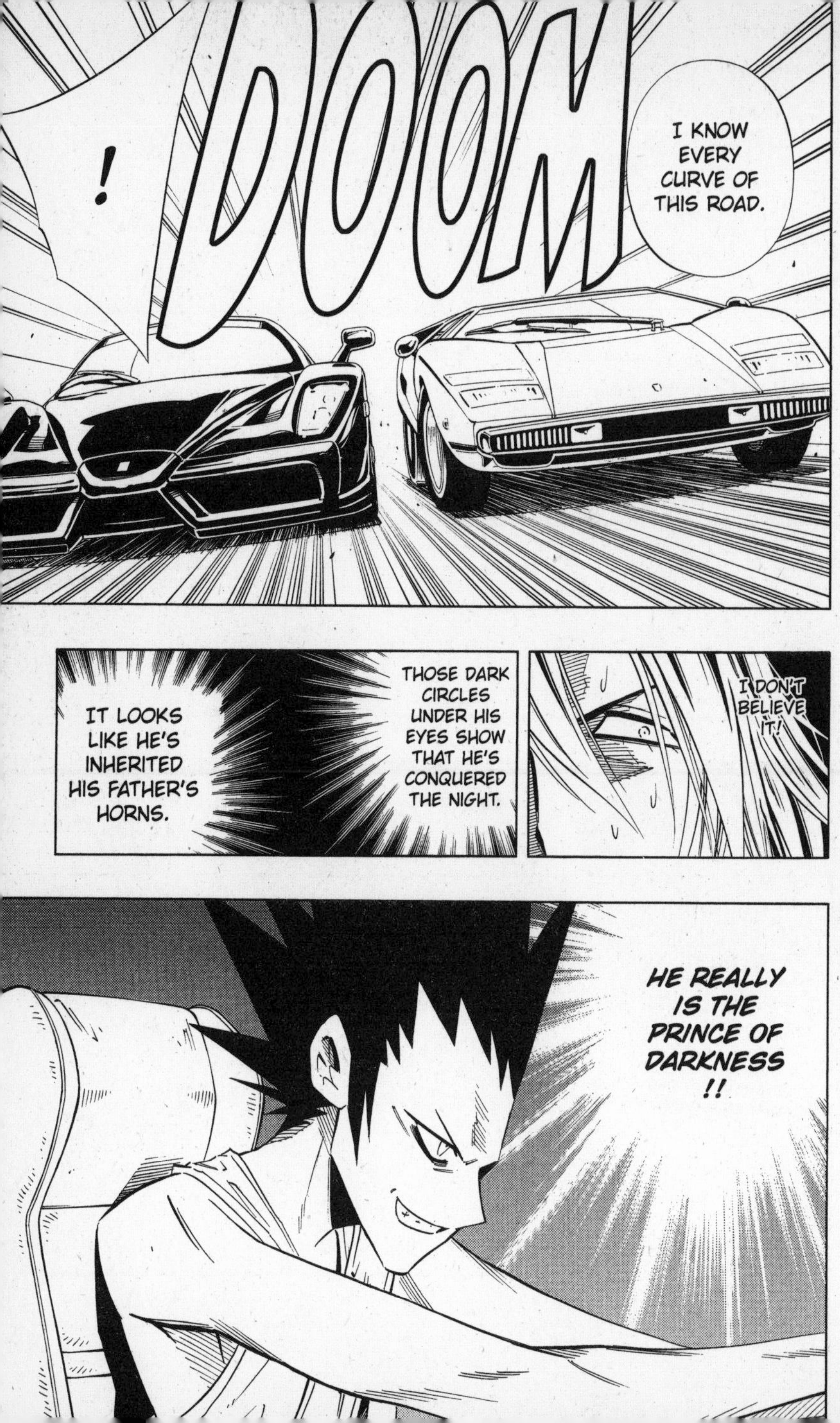
I KNOW EVERY CURVE OF THIS ROAD.
DOOM
!
I DON'T BELIEVE IT!
THOSE DARK CIRCLES UNDER HIS EYES SHOW THAT HE'S CONQUERED THE NIGHT.
IT LOOKS LIKE HE'S INHERITED HIS FATHER'S HORNS.
HE REALLY IS THE PRINCE OF DARKNESS !!

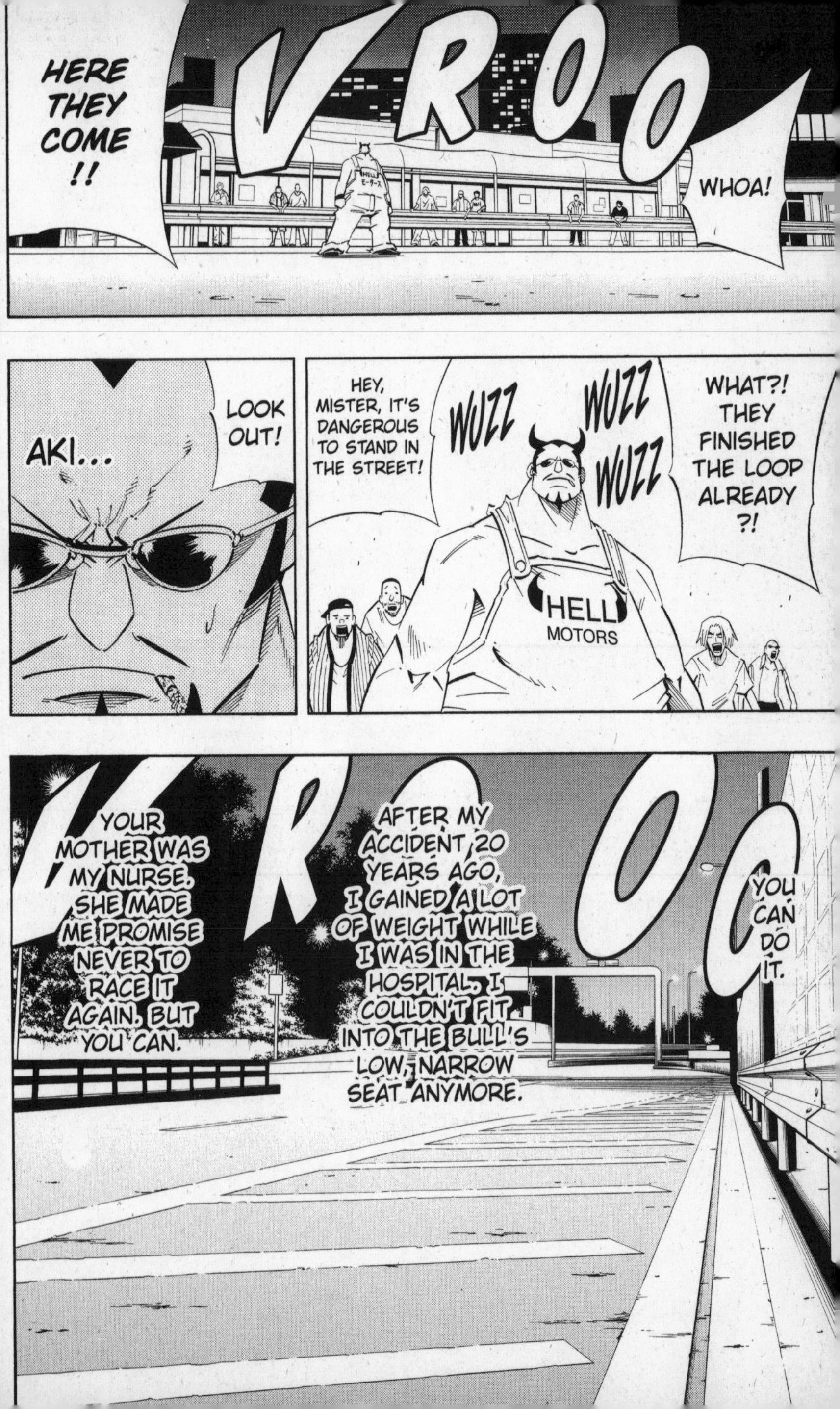
VROO
WHOA!
HERE THEY COME!!
WHAT?! THEY FINISHED THE LOOP ALREADY?!
WUZZ WUZZ WUZZ
HEY, MISTER, IT'S DANGEROUS TO STAND IN THE STREET!
HELL MOTORS
LOOK OUT!
AKI...
VROOO
YOU CAN DO IT.
AFTER MY ACCIDENT 20 YEARS AGO, I GAINED A LOT OF WEIGHT WHILE I WAS IN THE HOSPITAL. I COULDN'T FIT INTO THE BULL'S LOW, NARROW SEAT ANYMORE.
YOUR MOTHER WAS MY NURSE. SHE MADE ME PROMISE NEVER TO RACE IT AGAIN. BUT YOU CAN.

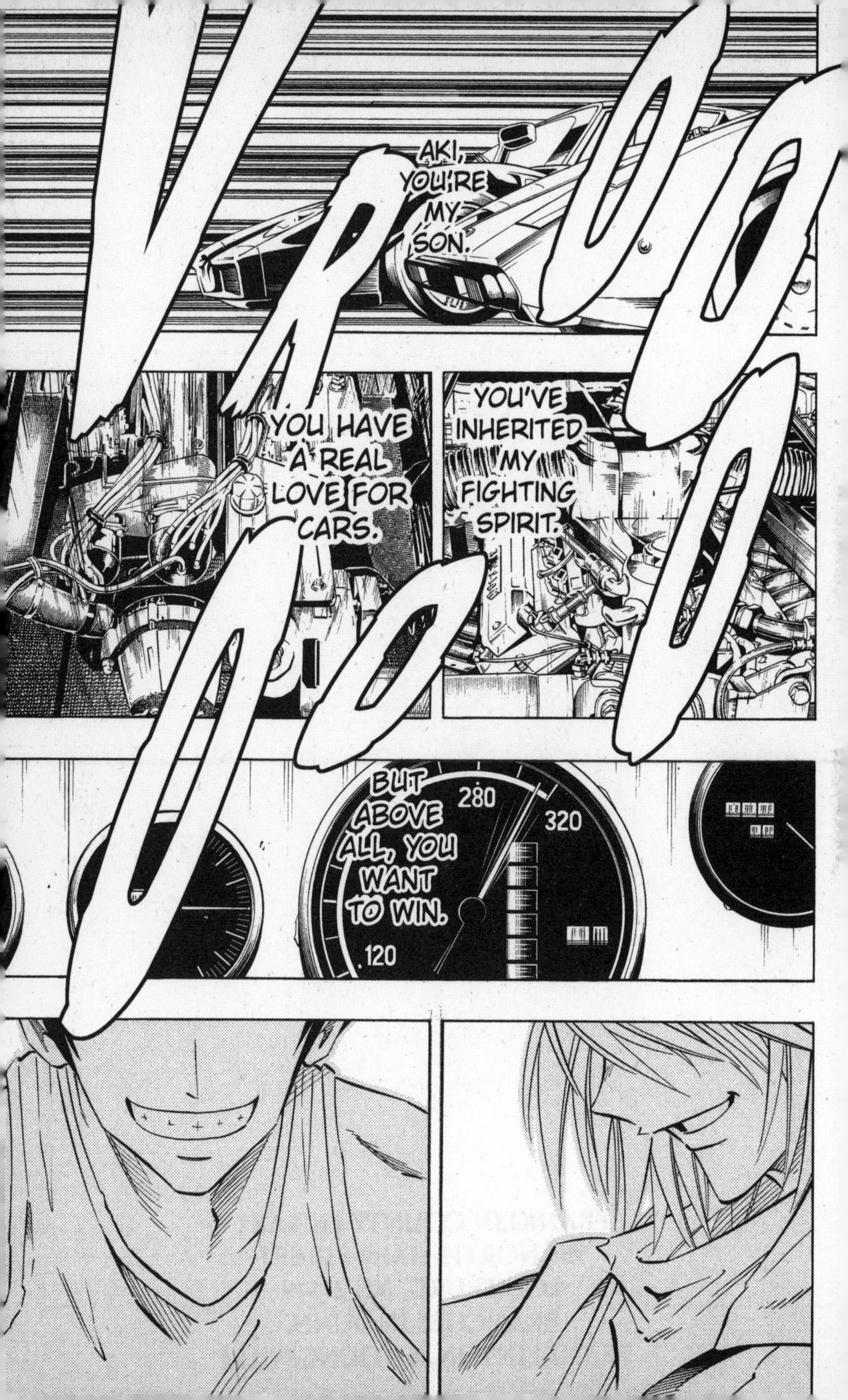
AKI, YOU'RE MY SON.
YOU'VE INHERITED MY FIGHTING SPIRIT.
YOU HAVE A REAL LOVE FOR CARS.
BUT ABOVE ALL, YOU WANT TO WIN.
280
320
120

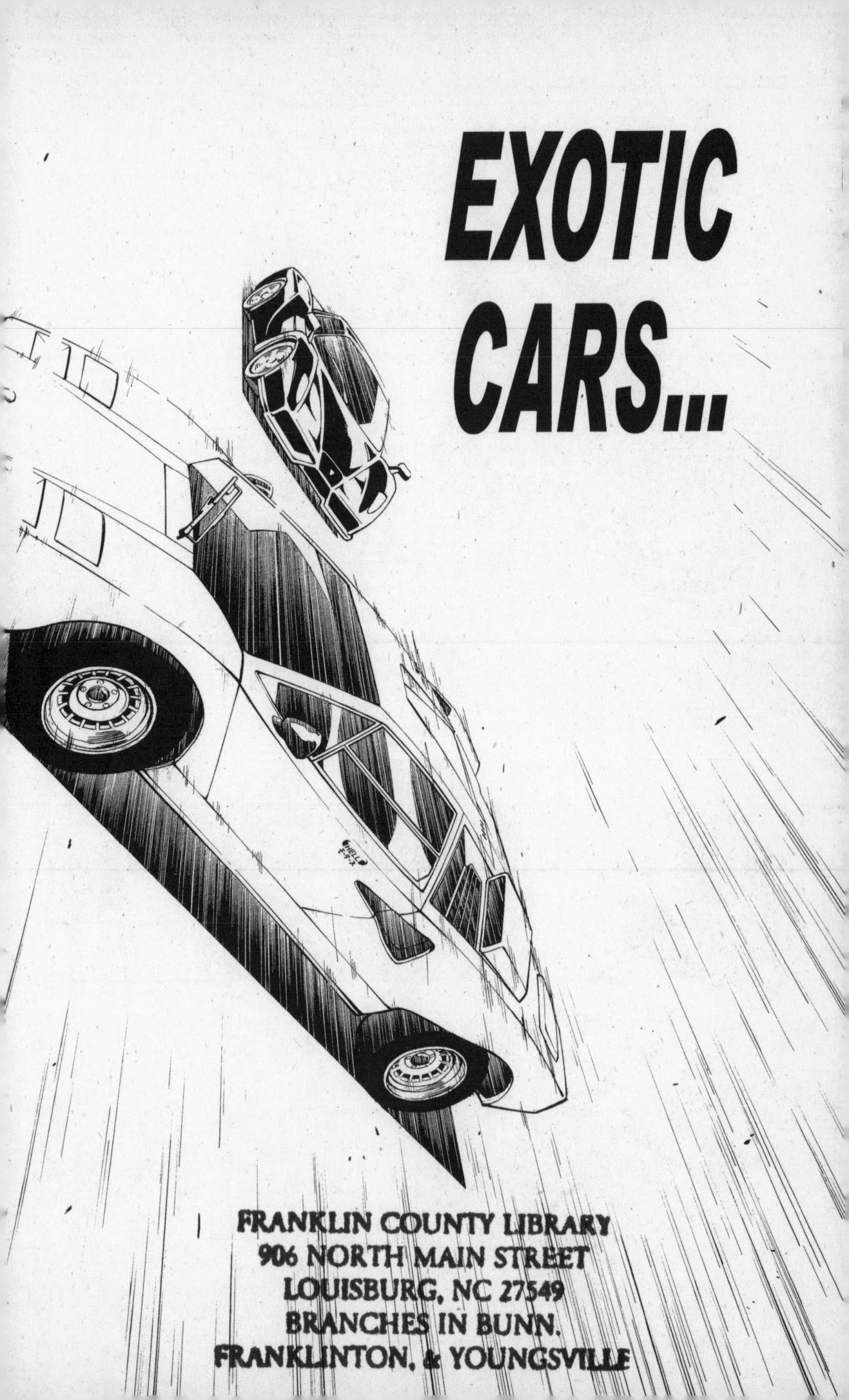

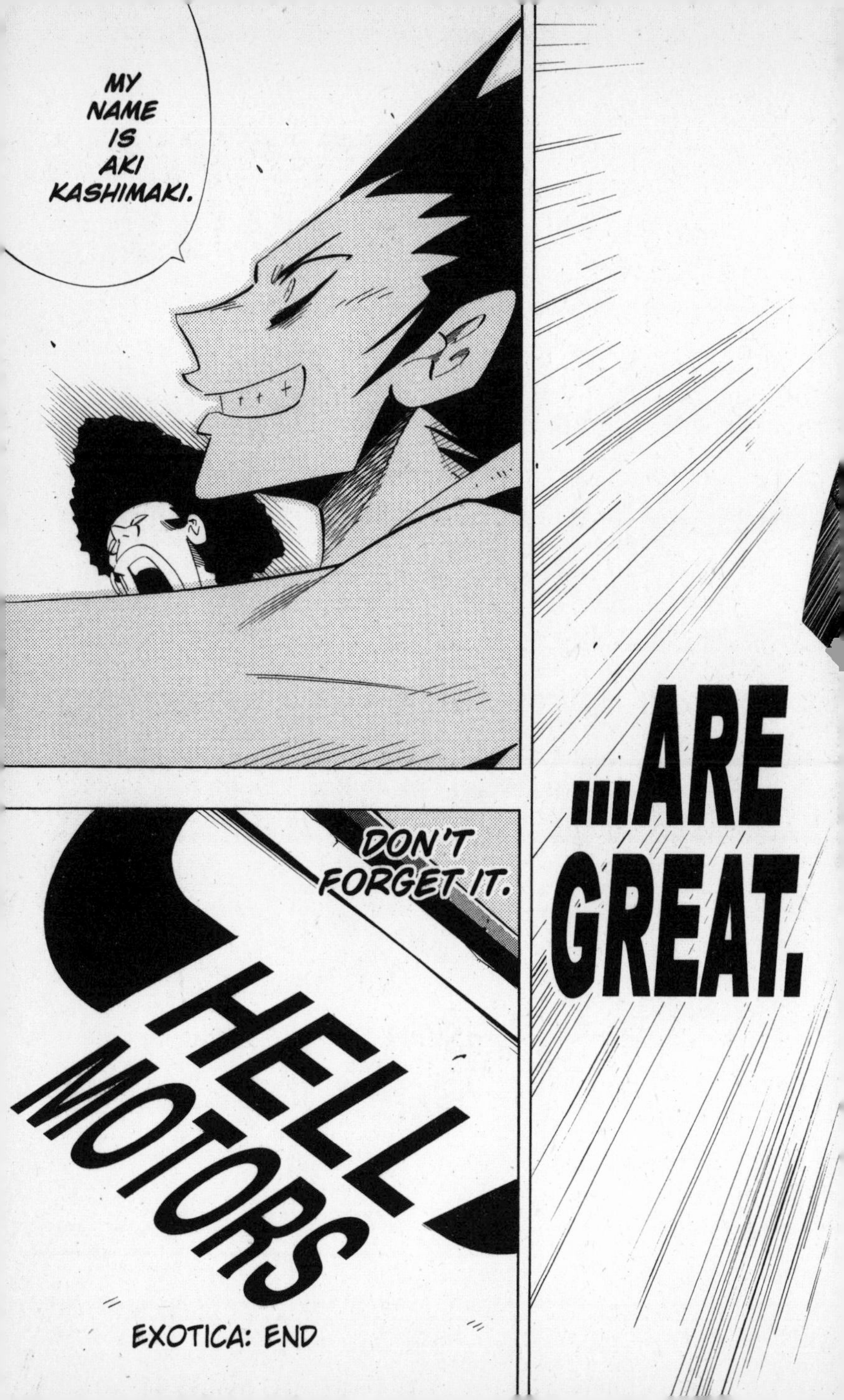
MY NAME IS AKI KASHIMAKI.
DON'T FORGET IT.
HELL MOTORS
...ARE GREAT.
EXOTICA: END

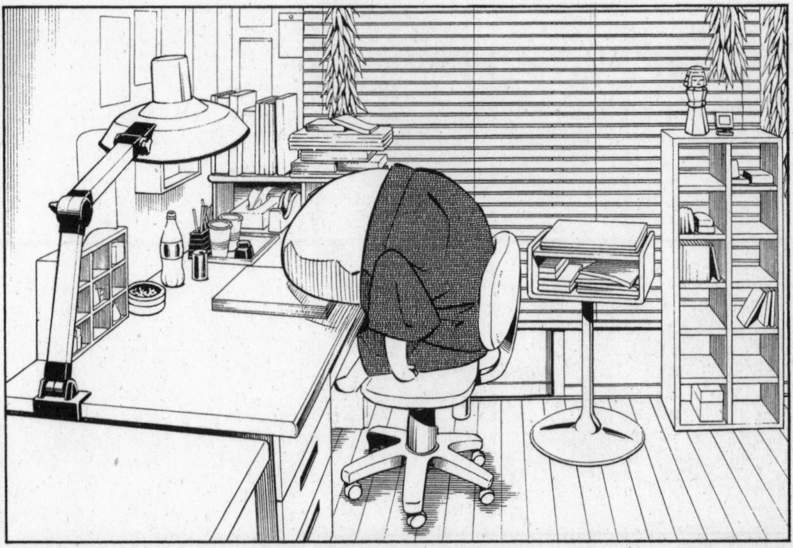

THREE WEEKS IN PRODUCTION.

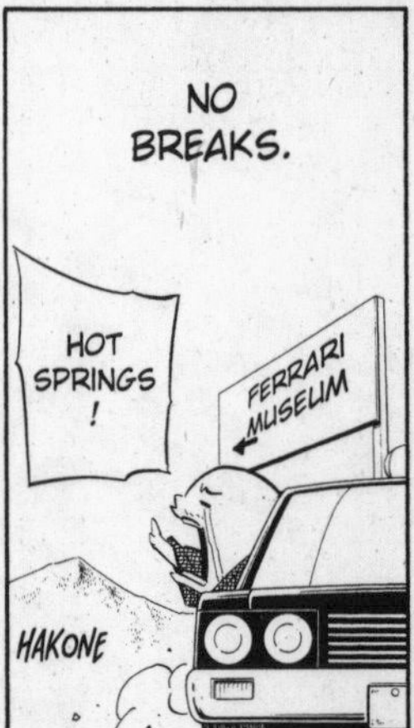
NO BREAKS.
HOT SPRINGS !
FERRARI MUSEUM
HAKONE

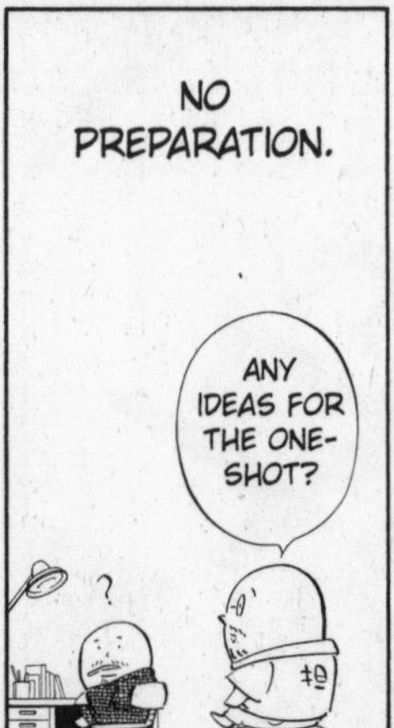
NO PREPARATION.
ANY IDEAS FOR THE ONE-SHOT?
?

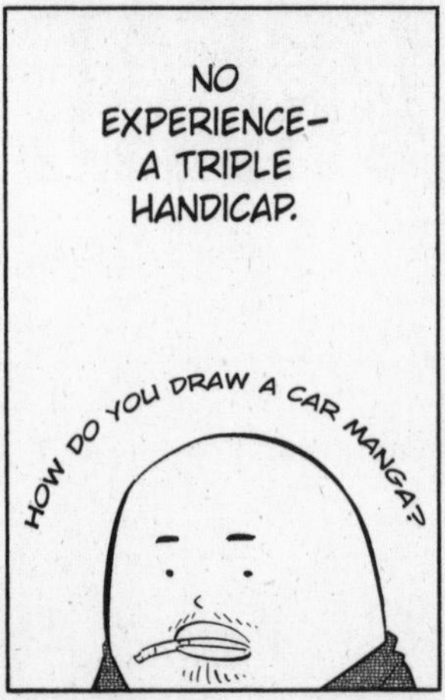
NO EXPERIENCE— A TRIPLE HANDICAP.
HOW DO YOU DRAW A CAR MANGA?

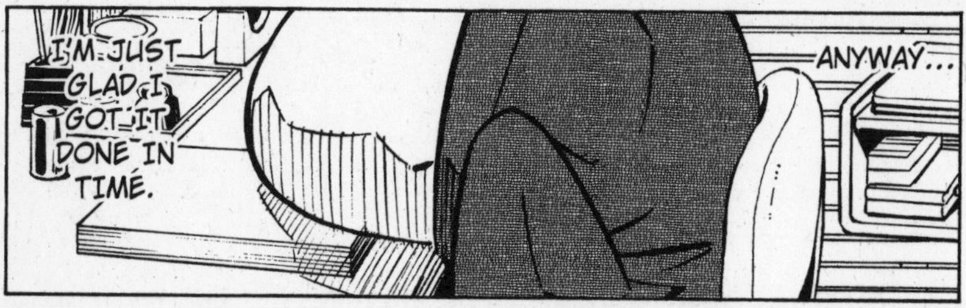
ANYWAY...
I'M JUST GLAD I GOT IT DONE IN TIME.

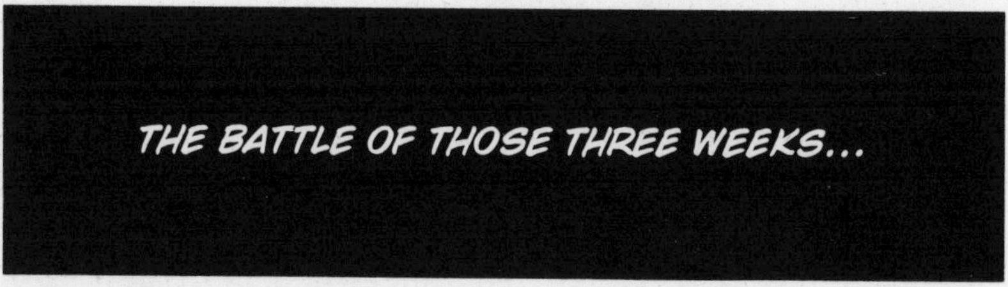
THE BATTLE OF THOSE THREE WEEKS...

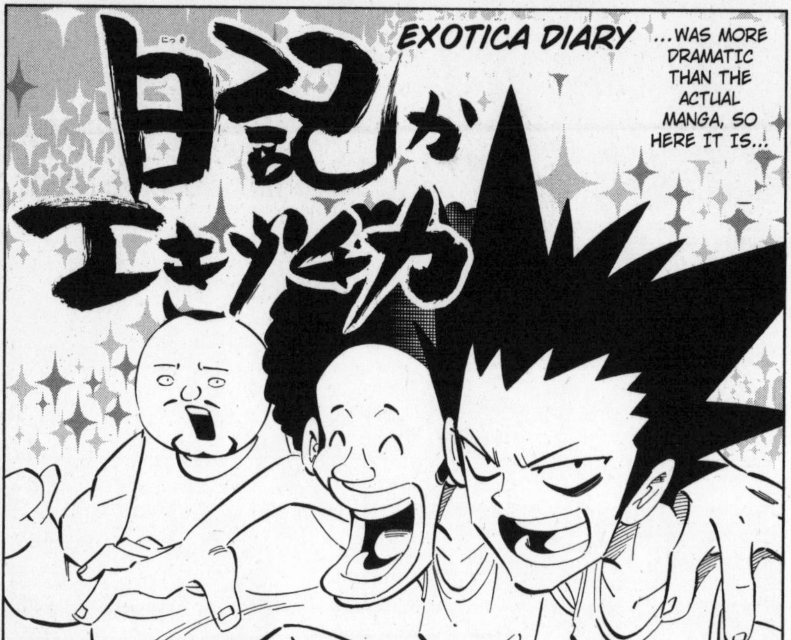
日記がエキゾチカ
EXOTICA DIARY
...WAS MORE DRAMATIC THAN THE ACTUAL MANGA, SO HERE IT IS...

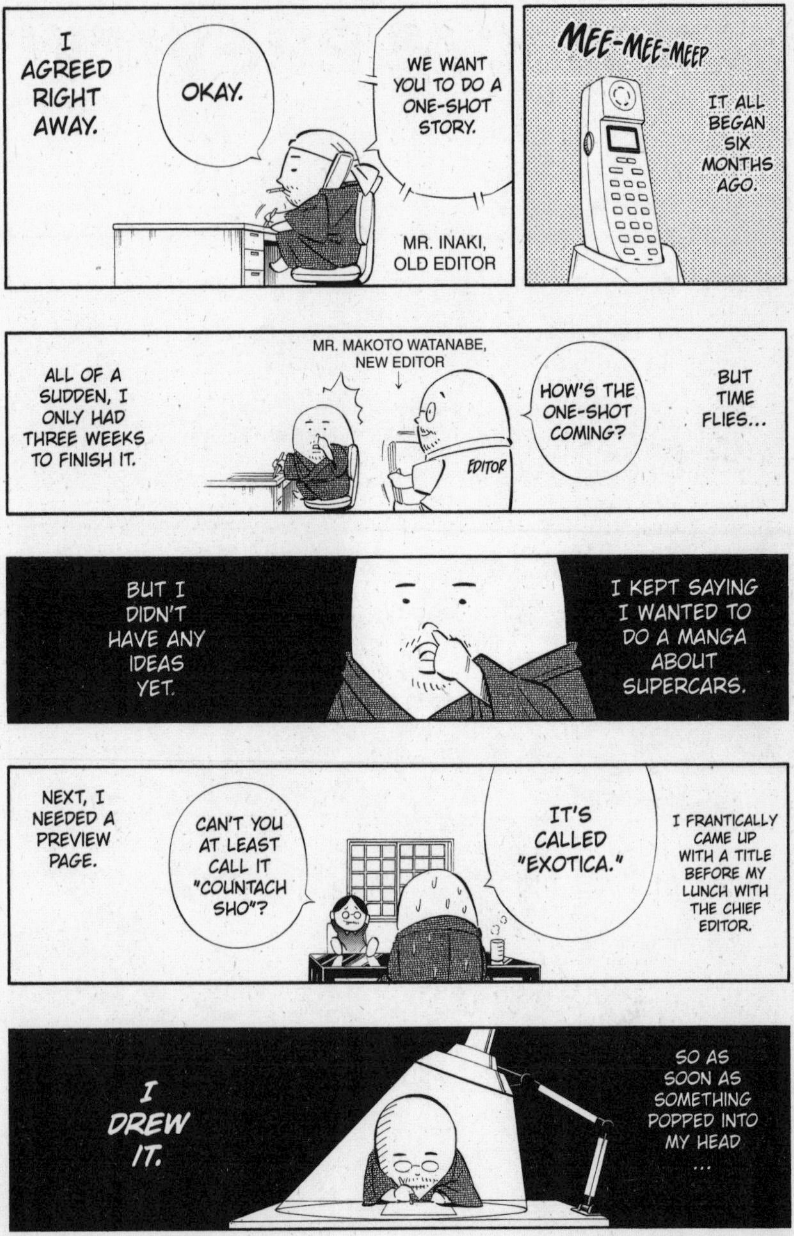
MEE-MEE-MEEP
IT ALL BEGAN SIX MONTHS AGO.
WE WANT YOU TO DO A ONE-SHOT STORY.
MR. INAKI, OLD EDITOR
OKAY.
I AGREED RIGHT AWAY.
BUT TIME FLIES...
HOW'S THE ONE-SHOT COMING?
MR. MAKOTO WATANABE, NEW EDITOR
EDITOR
ALL OF A SUDDEN, I ONLY HAD THREE WEEKS TO FINISH IT.
I KEPT SAYING I WANTED TO DO A MANGA ABOUT SUPERCARS.
BUT I DIDN'T HAVE ANY IDEAS YET.
I FRANTICALLY CAME UP WITH A TITLE BEFORE MY LUNCH WITH THE CHIEF EDITOR.
IT'S CALLED "EXOTICA."
CAN'T YOU AT LEAST CALL IT "COUNTACH SHO"?
NEXT, I NEEDED A PREVIEW PAGE.
SO AS SOON AS SOMETHING POPPED INTO MY HEAD ...
I DREW IT.

"EXOTICA" PREVIEW

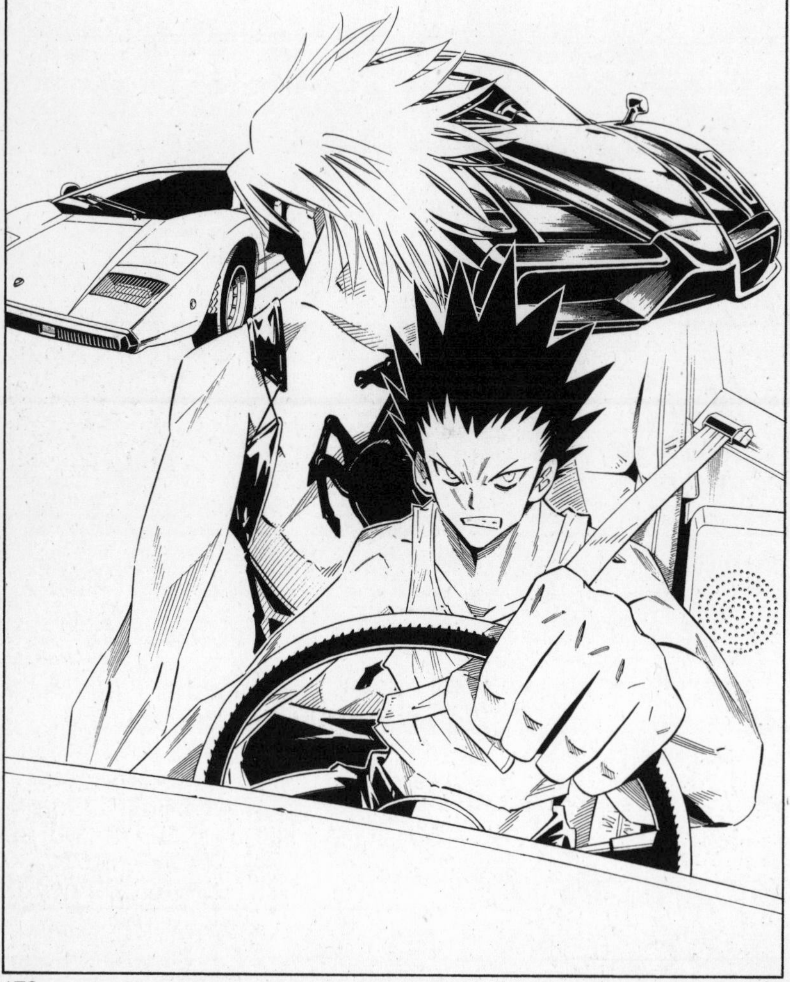

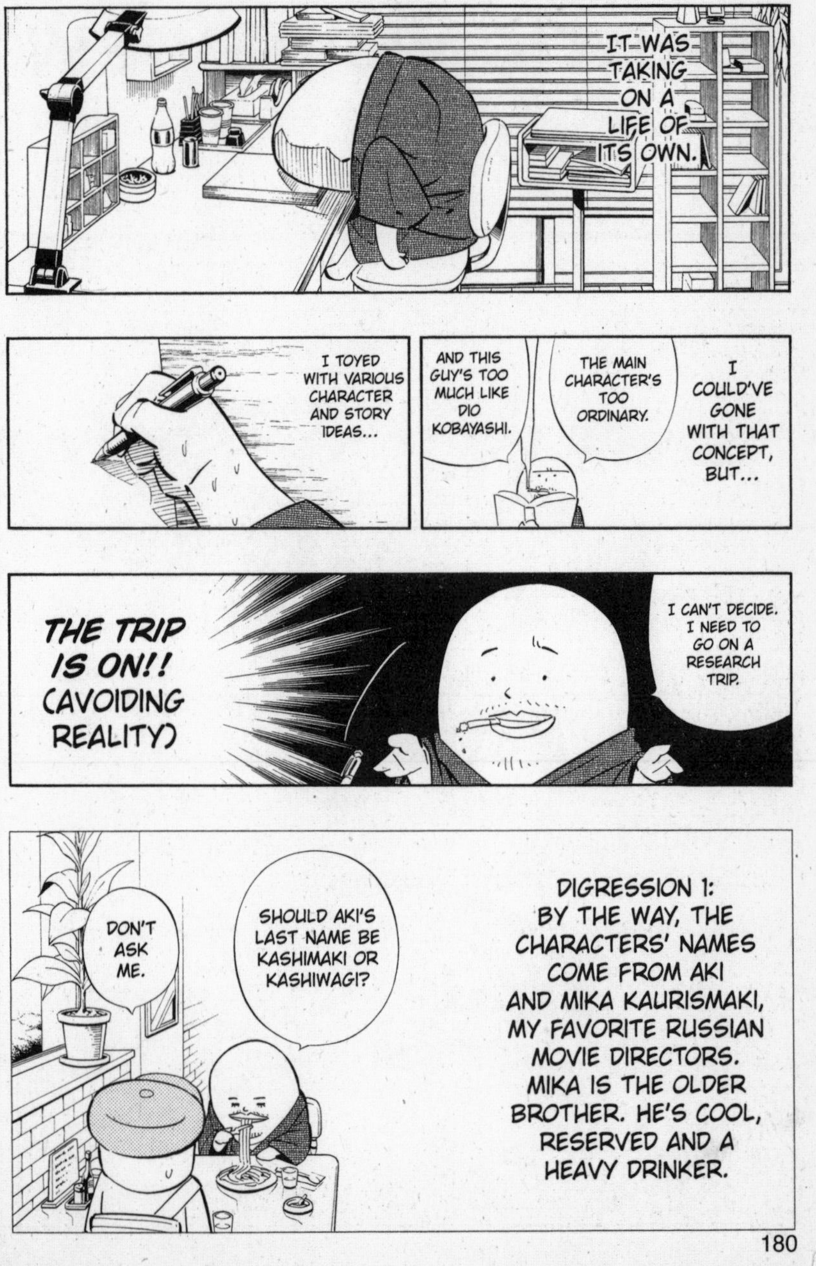
IT WAS TAKING ON A LIFE OF ITS OWN.
I COULD'VE GONE WITH THAT CONCEPT, BUT...
THE MAIN CHARACTER'S TOO ORDINARY.
AND THIS GUY'S TOO MUCH LIKE DIO KOBAYASHI.
I TOYED WITH VARIOUS CHARACTER AND STORY IDEAS...
I CAN'T DECIDE. I NEED TO GO ON A RESEARCH TRIP.
THE TRIP IS ON!! (AVOIDING REALITY)
DIGRESSION 1: BY THE WAY, THE CHARACTERS' NAMES COME FROM AKI AND MIKA KAURISMAKI, MY FAVORITE RUSSIAN MOVIE DIRECTORS. MIKA IS THE OLDER BROTHER. HE'S COOL, RESERVED AND A HEAVY DRINKER.
SHOULD AKI'S LAST NAME BE KASHIMAKI OR KASHIWAGI?
DON'T ASK ME.

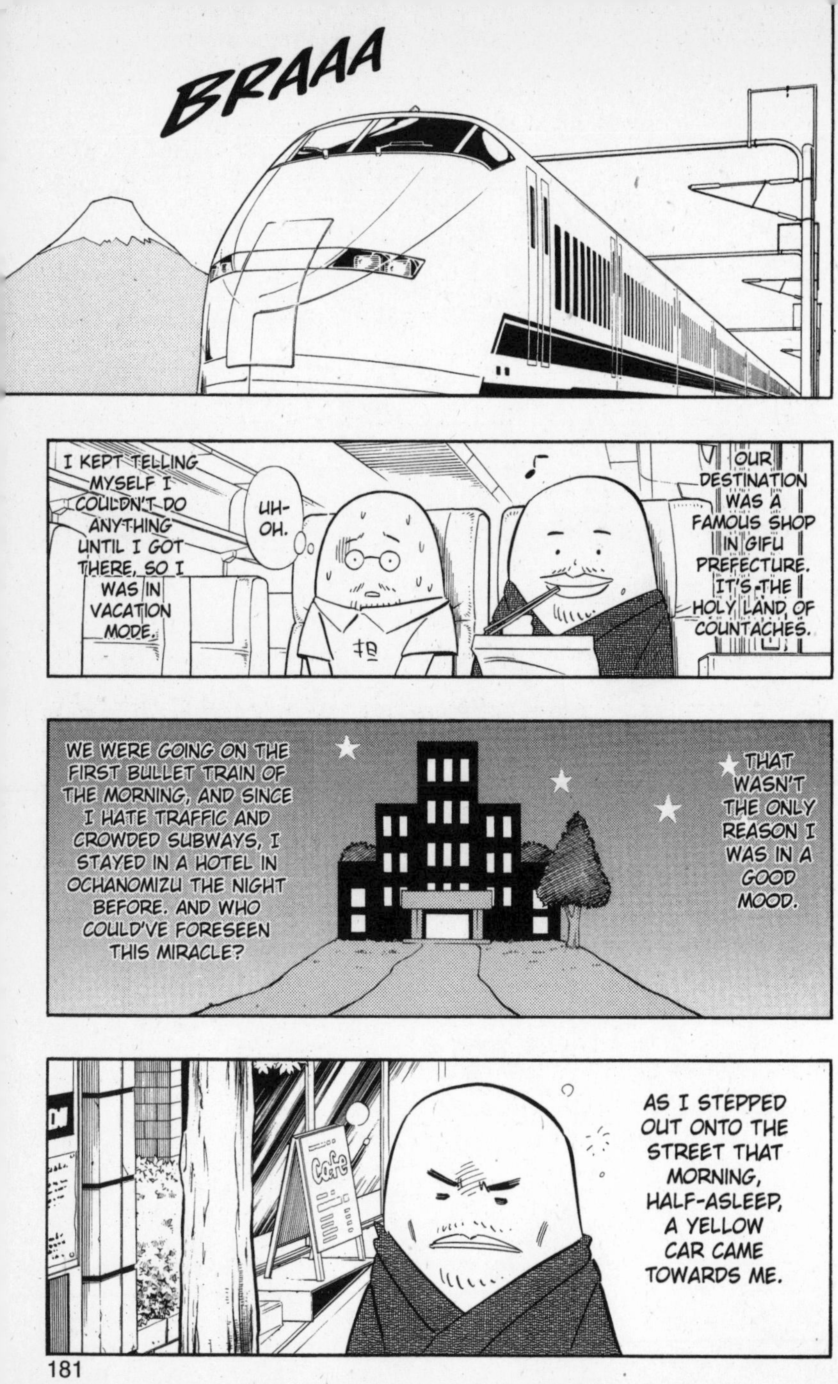
BRAAA
OUR DESTINATION WAS A FAMOUS SHOP IN GIFU PREFECTURE. IT'S THE HOLY LAND OF COUNTACHES.
UH-OH.
I KEPT TELLING MYSELF I COULDN'T DO ANYTHING UNTIL I GOT THERE, SO I WAS IN VACATION MODE.
THAT WASN'T THE ONLY REASON I WAS IN A GOOD MOOD.
WE WERE GOING ON THE FIRST BULLET TRAIN OF THE MORNING, AND SINCE I HATE TRAFFIC AND CROWDED SUBWAYS, I STAYED IN A HOTEL IN OCHANOMIZU THE NIGHT BEFORE. AND WHO COULD'VE FORESEEN THIS MIRACLE?
AS I STEPPED OUT ONTO THE STREET THAT MORNING, HALF-ASLEEP, A YELLOW CAR CAME TOWARDS ME.
Cafe

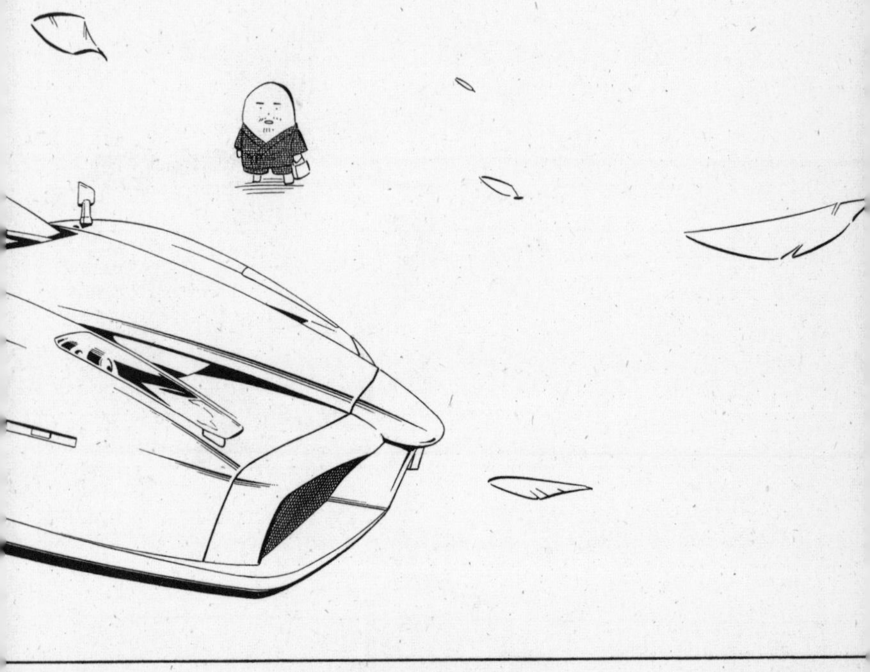
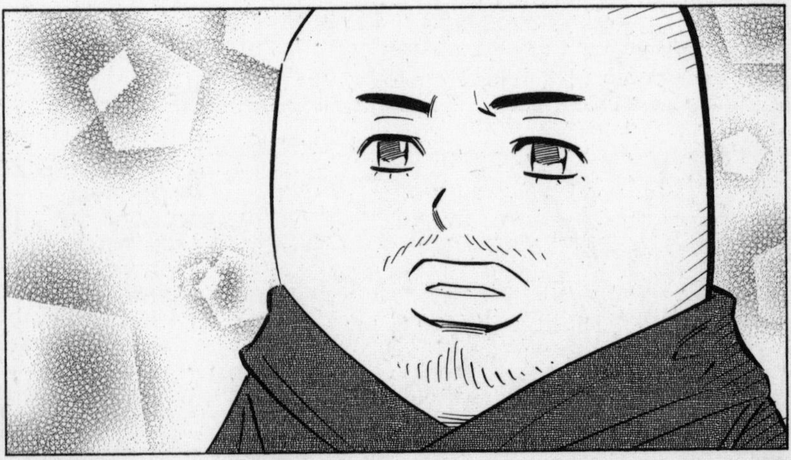

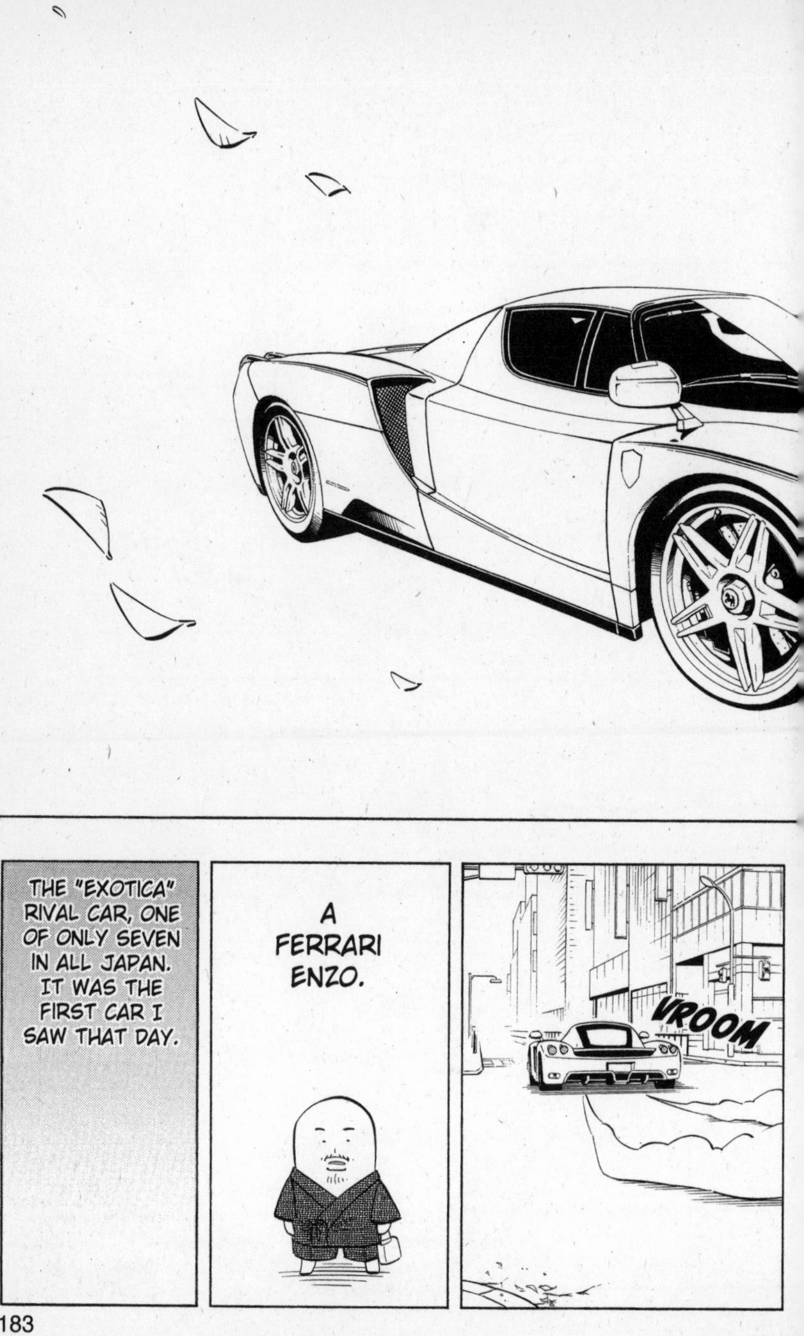
VROOM
A FERRARI ENZO.
THE "EXOTICA" RIVAL CAR, ONE OF ONLY SEVEN IN ALL JAPAN. IT WAS THE FIRST CAR I SAW THAT DAY.

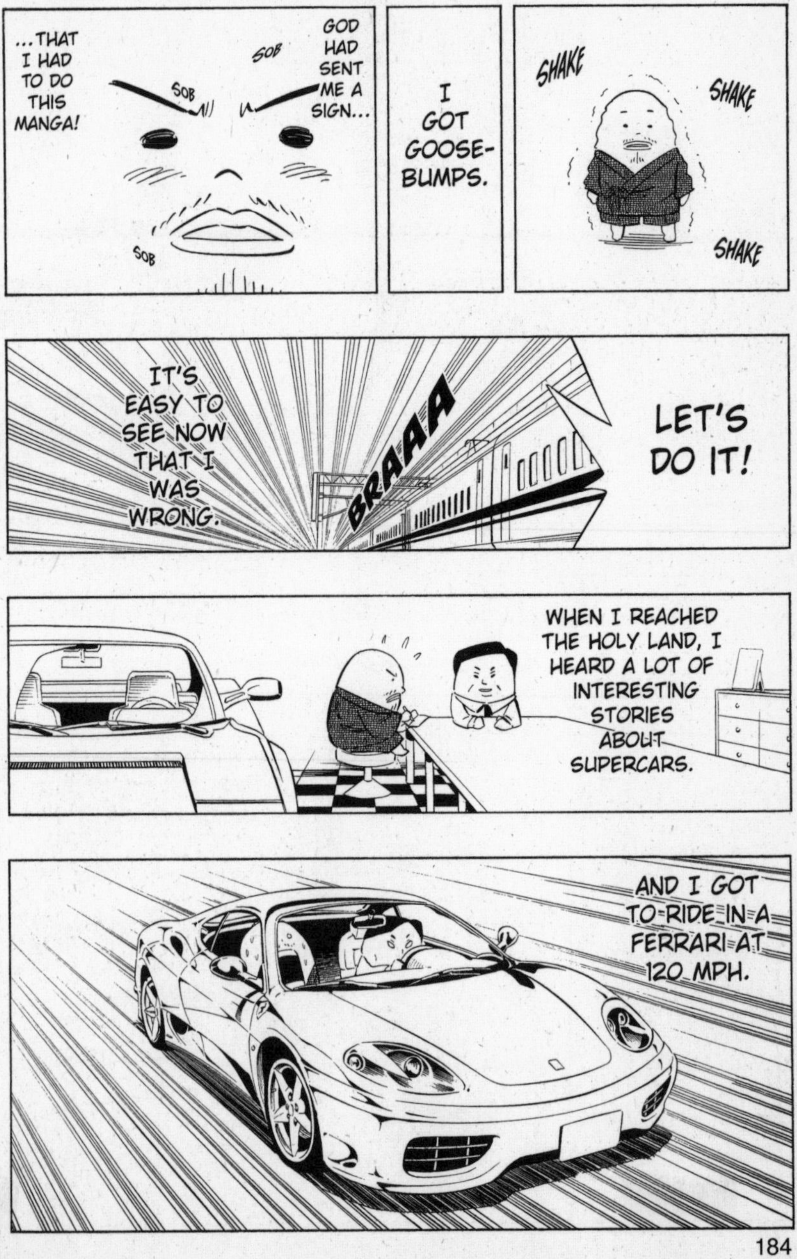
SHAKE
SHAKE
SHAKE
I GOT GOOSE-BUMPS.
GOD HAD SENT ME A SIGN...
SOB
...THAT I HAD TO DO THIS MANGA!
SOB
SOB
LET'S DO IT!
BRAAA
IT'S EASY TO SEE NOW THAT I WAS WRONG.
WHEN I REACHED THE HOLY LAND, I HEARD A LOT OF INTERESTING STORIES ABOUT SUPERCARS.
AND I GOT TO RIDE IN A FERRARI AT 120 MPH.

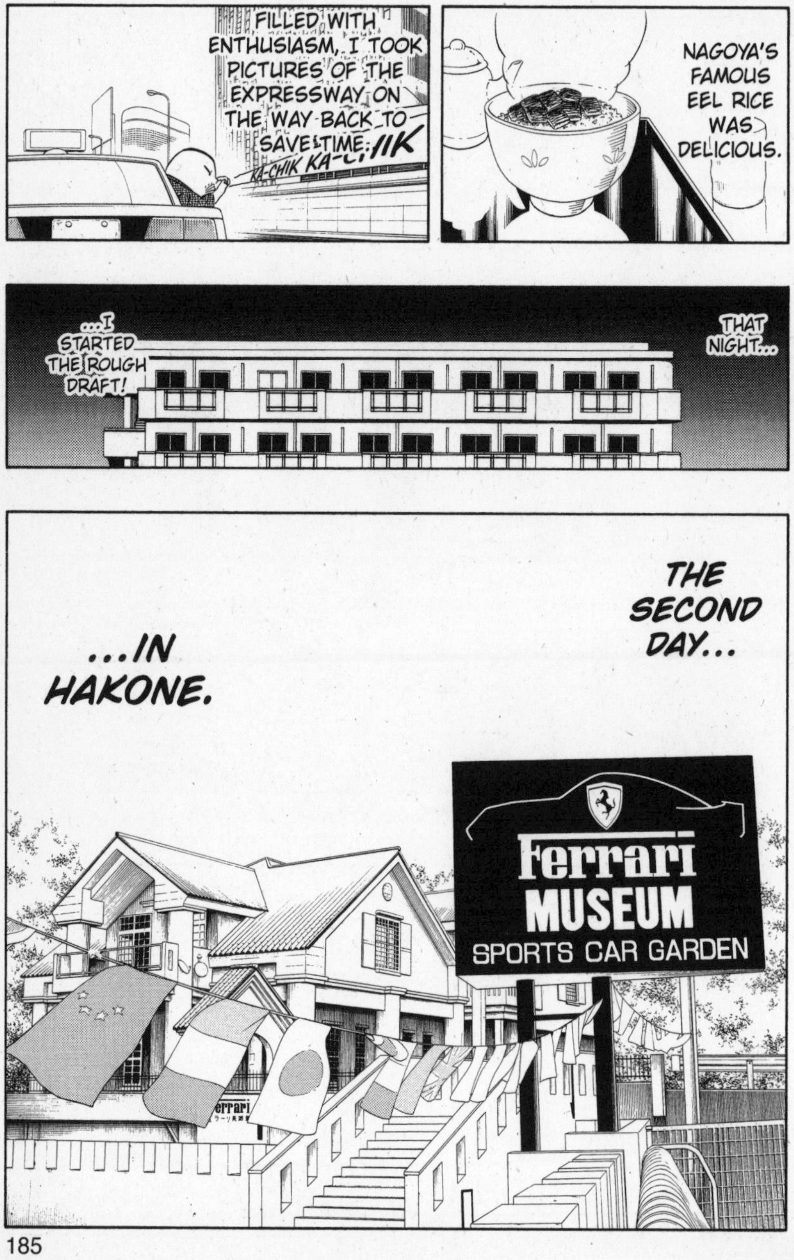
NAGOYA'S FAMOUS EEL RICE WAS DELICIOUS.
FILLED WITH ENTHUSIASM, I TOOK PICTURES OF THE EXPRESSWAY ON THE WAY BACK TO SAVE TIME.
KA-CHIK
THAT NIGHT...
...I STARTED THE ROUGH DRAFT!
THE SECOND DAY...
...IN HAKONE.
Ferrari
MUSEUM
SPORTS CAR GARDEN

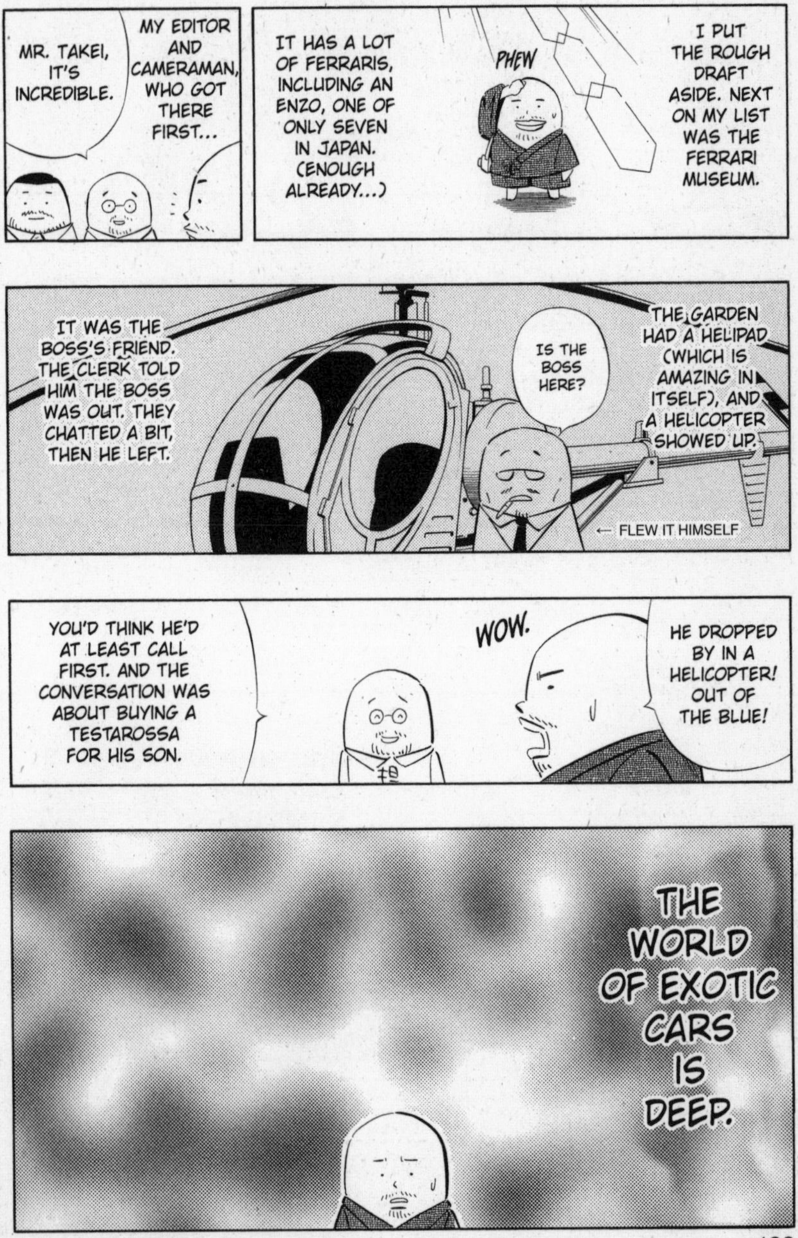
I PUT THE ROUGH DRAFT ASIDE. NEXT ON MY LIST WAS THE FERRARI MUSEUM.
PHEW
IT HAS A LOT OF FERRARIS, INCLUDING AN ENZO, ONE OF ONLY SEVEN IN JAPAN. (ENOUGH ALREADY...)
MY EDITOR AND CAMERAMAN, WHO GOT THERE FIRST...
MR. TAKEI, IT'S INCREDIBLE.
THE GARDEN HAD A HELIPAD (WHICH IS AMAZING IN ITSELF), AND A HELICOPTER SHOWED UP.
IS THE BOSS HERE?
IT WAS THE BOSS'S FRIEND. THE CLERK TOLD HIM THE BOSS WAS OUT. THEY CHATTED A BIT, THEN HE LEFT.
← FLEW IT HIMSELF
HE DROPPED BY IN A HELICOPTER! OUT OF THE BLUE!
WOW.
YOU'D THINK HE'D AT LEAST CALL FIRST. AND THE CONVERSATION WAS ABOUT BUYING A TESTAROSSA FOR HIS SON.
THE WORLD OF EXOTIC CARS IS DEEP.

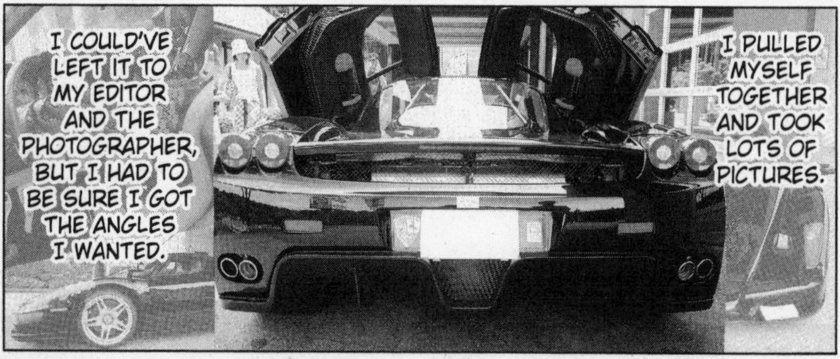
I PULLED MYSELF TOGETHER AND TOOK LOTS OF PICTURES.
I COULD'VE LEFT IT TO MY EDITOR AND THE PHOTOGRAPHER, BUT I HAD TO BE SURE I GOT THE ANGLES I WANTED.

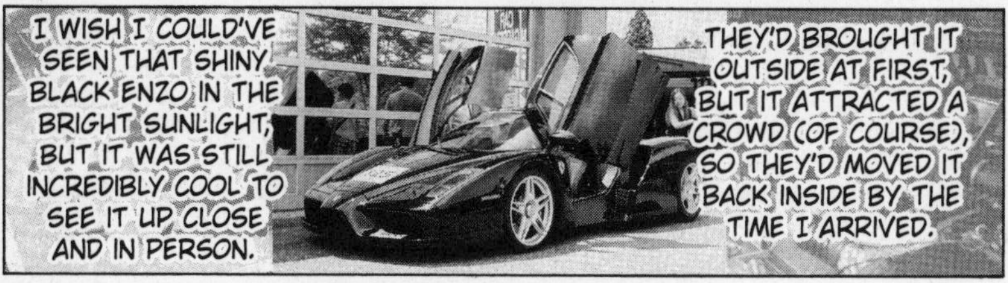
THEY'D BROUGHT IT OUTSIDE AT FIRST, BUT IT ATTRACTED A CROWD (OF COURSE), SO THEY'D MOVED IT BACK INSIDE BY THE TIME I ARRIVED.
I WISH I COULD'VE SEEN THAT SHINY BLACK ENZO IN THE BRIGHT SUNLIGHT, BUT IT WAS STILL INCREDIBLY COOL TO SEE IT UP CLOSE AND IN PERSON.

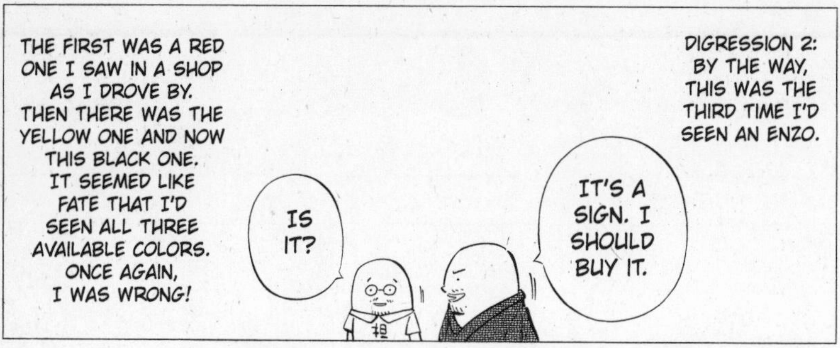
DIGRESSION 2: BY THE WAY, THIS WAS THE THIRD TIME I'D SEEN AN ENZO.
IT'S A SIGN. I SHOULD BUY IT.
IS IT?
THE FIRST WAS A RED ONE I SAW IN A SHOP AS I DROVE BY. THEN THERE WAS THE YELLOW ONE AND NOW THIS BLACK ONE. IT SEEMED LIKE FATE THAT I'D SEEN ALL THREE AVAILABLE COLORS. ONCE AGAIN, I WAS WRONG!

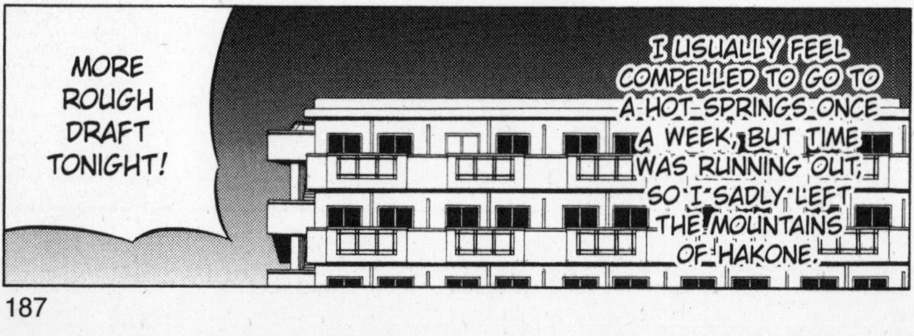
I USUALLY FEEL COMPELLED TO GO TO A HOT SPRINGS ONCE A WEEK, BUT TIME WAS RUNNING OUT, SO I SADLY LEFT THE MOUNTAINS OF HAKONE.
MORE ROUGH DRAFT TONIGHT!

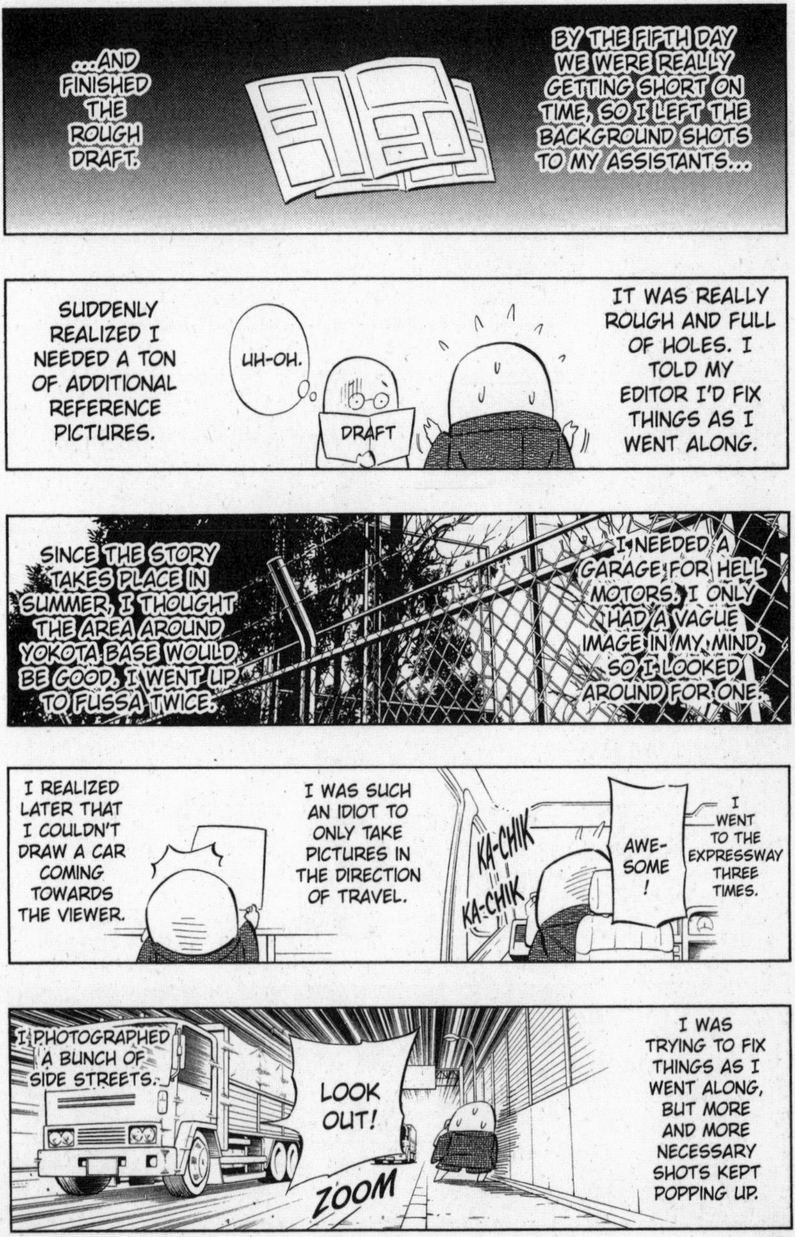
BY THE FIFTH DAY WE WERE REALLY GETTING SHORT ON TIME, SO I LEFT THE BACKGROUND SHOTS TO MY ASSISTANTS...
...AND FINISHED THE ROUGH DRAFT.
IT WAS REALLY ROUGH AND FULL OF HOLES. I TOLD MY EDITOR I'D FIX THINGS AS I WENT ALONG.
UH-OH.
DRAFT
SUDDENLY REALIZED I NEEDED A TON OF ADDITIONAL REFERENCE PICTURES.
I NEEDED A GARAGE FOR HELL MOTORS. I ONLY HAD A VAGUE IMAGE IN MY MIND, SO I LOOKED AROUND FOR ONE.
SINCE THE STORY TAKES PLACE IN SUMMER, I THOUGHT THE AREA AROUND YOKOTA BASE WOULD BE GOOD. I WENT UP TO FUSSA TWICE.
I WENT TO THE EXPRESSWAY THREE TIMES.
AWE-SOME!
KA-CHIK
KA-CHIK
I WAS SUCH AN IDIOT TO ONLY TAKE PICTURES IN THE DIRECTION OF TRAVEL.
I REALIZED LATER THAT I COULDN'T DRAW A CAR COMING TOWARDS THE VIEWER.
I WAS TRYING TO FIX THINGS AS I WENT ALONG, BUT MORE AND MORE NECESSARY SHOTS KEPT POPPING UP.
LOOK OUT!
ZOOM
I PHOTOGRAPHED A BUNCH OF SIDE STREETS.

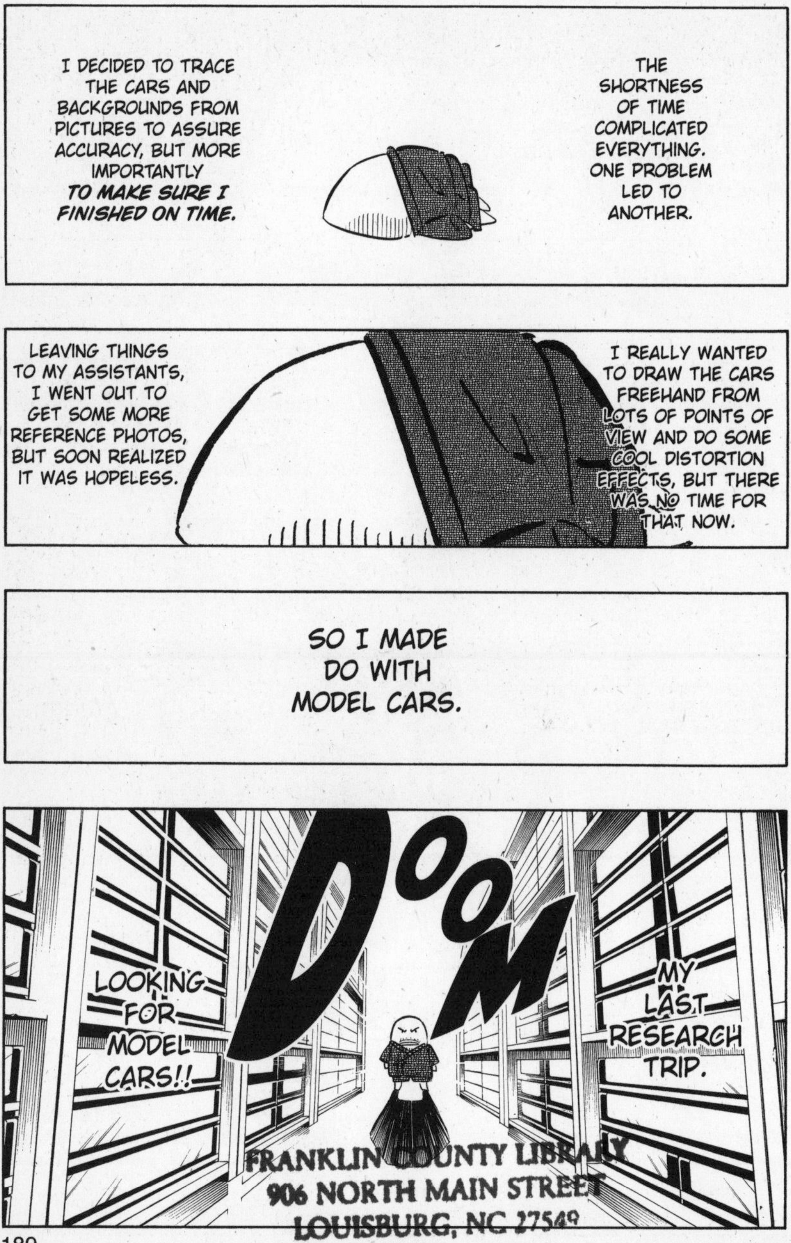
THE SHORTNESS OF TIME COMPLICATED EVERYTHING. ONE PROBLEM LED TO ANOTHER.
I DECIDED TO TRACE THE CARS AND BACKGROUNDS FROM PICTURES TO ASSURE ACCURACY, BUT MORE IMPORTANTLY *TO MAKE SURE I FINISHED ON TIME.*
I REALLY WANTED TO DRAW THE CARS FREEHAND FROM LOTS OF POINTS OF VIEW AND DO SOME COOL DISTORTION EFFECTS, BUT THERE WAS NO TIME FOR THAT NOW.
LEAVING THINGS TO MY ASSISTANTS, I WENT OUT TO GET SOME MORE REFERENCE PHOTOS, BUT SOON REALIZED IT WAS HOPELESS.
SO I MADE DO WITH MODEL CARS.
DOOM
MY LAST RESEARCH TRIP.
LOOKING FOR MODEL CARS!!

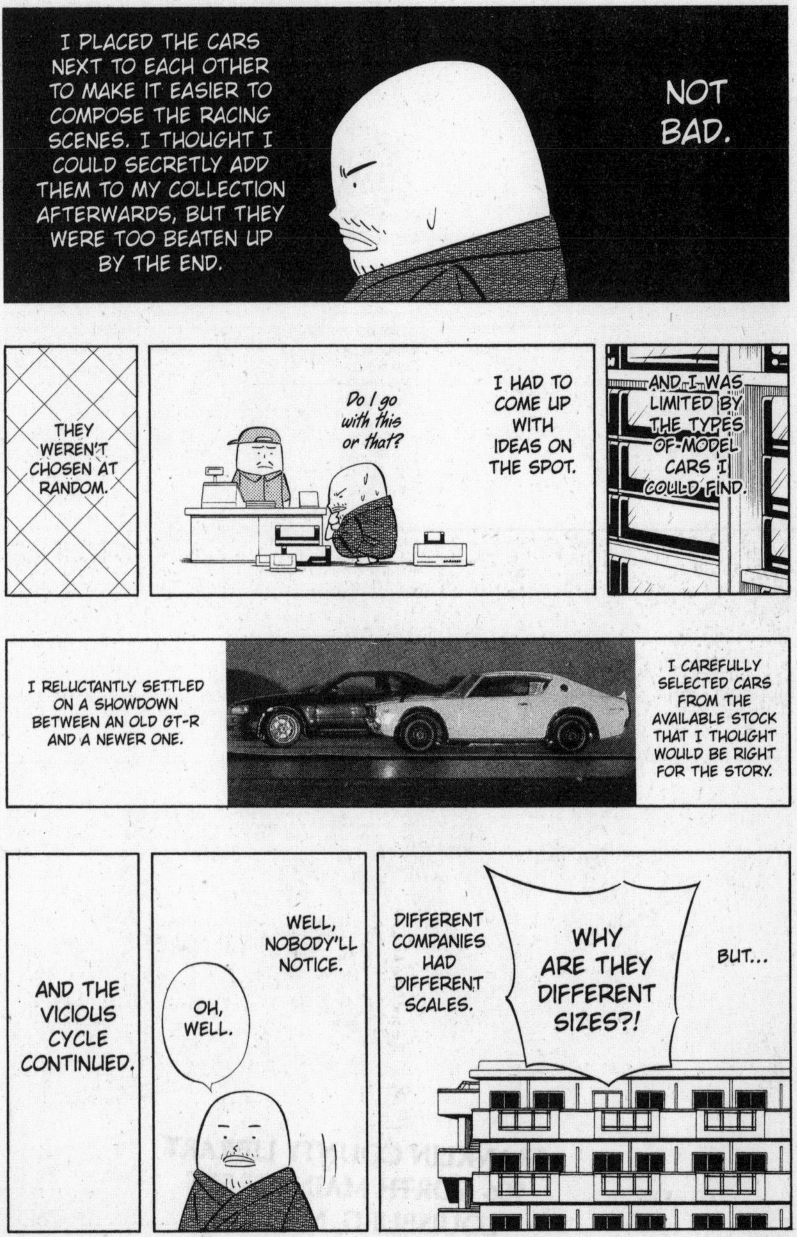
NOT BAD.
I PLACED THE CARS NEXT TO EACH OTHER TO MAKE IT EASIER TO COMPOSE THE RACING SCENES. I THOUGHT I COULD SECRETLY ADD THEM TO MY COLLECTION AFTERWARDS, BUT THEY WERE TOO BEATEN UP BY THE END.
AND I WAS LIMITED BY THE TYPES OF MODEL CARS I COULD FIND.
I HAD TO COME UP WITH IDEAS ON THE SPOT.
Do I go with this or that?
THEY WEREN'T CHOSEN AT RANDOM.
I CAREFULLY SELECTED CARS FROM THE AVAILABLE STOCK THAT I THOUGHT WOULD BE RIGHT FOR THE STORY.
I RELUCTANTLY SETTLED ON A SHOWDOWN BETWEEN AN OLD GT-R AND A NEWER ONE.
BUT...
WHY ARE THEY DIFFERENT SIZES?!
DIFFERENT COMPANIES HAD DIFFERENT SCALES.
WELL, NOBODY'LL NOTICE.
OH, WELL.
AND THE VICIOUS CYCLE CONTINUED.

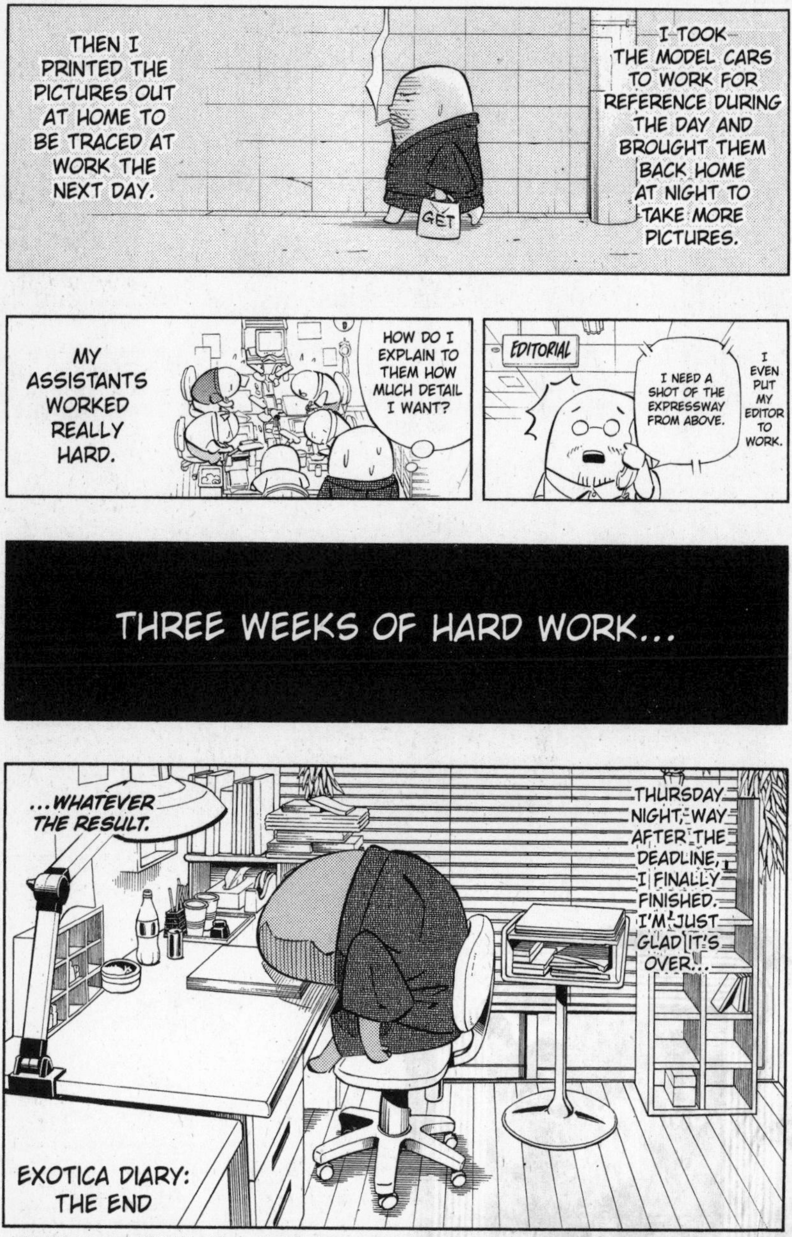
I TOOK THE MODEL CARS TO WORK FOR REFERENCE DURING THE DAY AND BROUGHT THEM BACK HOME AT NIGHT TO TAKE MORE PICTURES.
THEN I PRINTED THE PICTURES OUT AT HOME TO BE TRACED AT WORK THE NEXT DAY.
GET
I EVEN PUT MY EDITOR TO WORK.
EDITORIAL
I NEED A SHOT OF THE EXPRESSWAY FROM ABOVE.
HOW DO I EXPLAIN TO THEM HOW MUCH DETAIL I WANT?
MY ASSISTANTS WORKED REALLY HARD.
THREE WEEKS OF HARD WORK...
THURSDAY NIGHT, WAY AFTER THE DEADLINE, I FINALLY FINISHED. I'M JUST GLAD IT'S OVER...
...WHATEVER THE RESULT.
EXOTICA DIARY: THE END

THANKS SO MUCH TO EVERYBODY WHO HELPED, AND TO MY READERS.

IN THE NEXT VOLUME...

Yoh, Ren, Horohoro, Joco and Lyserg find themselves trapped in their own version of Hell. Each of them must defeat their personal demons to be powerful enough to become the Five Warriors. Only then can they possess the awesome strength of the Five High Spirits and escape their infernal torment.

AVAILABLE MAY 2010!